Home is Where You're Going

Crossing Borders and Risking Solidarity through Women's Studies

Cherith Lundin *Untitled (Suitcase)* 1999
Courtesy Cherith Lundin

Home is Where You're Going

*Crossing Borders and Risking
Solidarity through Women's Studies*

Nancy Linton and
Elizabeth Morgan

HEART *&* LUNGS PRESS
SAINT PAUL, MINNESOTA

Front and back cover art:
Allen Wexler *Gardening Sukkah* 2000
Courtesy Ronald Feldman Gallery, New York
Design: Thomas Gokey
Set in Minino Pro 10/12

Printed in the United States of America
05 06 07 08 09 10 11   1 2 3 4

Library of Congress Control Number: 2005930198

Home Is Where You're Going: Crossing Boarders and Risking Solidarity
through Women's Studies / Linton, Nancy and Elizabeth Morgan ... [et. al.].
  p. cm.
  ISBN 0-9771185-0-9
  1. Women's Studies. 2. Religion. I. Linton, Nancy and Elizabeth Morgan.
  II. Title.

Contents

I. Setting Out

The Questions Asked

HOME IS WHERE YOU'RE GOING is designed to introduce women's studies to persons in faith-based contexts, or persons interested in the integration of thought and spirit, both in academic contexts and otherwise. It arises out of a Women's Studies May Term in Ashland, Oregon, where faculty, undergraduate and graduate students gather every other year to explore literary, theological and psychological ramifications of gender, race and class in Western culture and abroad.

If you have opened these pages, you probably have some idea of what women's studies is about and why it is important. But if you are totally new to the subject, or decidedly skeptical about its efficacy, skip ahead to Martha Nussbaum's essay "Women's Studies" where she traces the history of the discipline and the need it fills in the academy. Or treat yourself to Karen Bloomquist's "Let God be God" and Leila Ahmed's "Harem" where each writer illustrates not only what happens when only the male half of the population determines who God/Allah is and what *he* wants, but also how women are moving to reclaim their rightful place at the table of faith. Or skip ahead to Toinette Eugene's "Moral Values and Black Womanists" where she describes the history of black women's oppression and exemplary resistance during slavery and beyond. If, then, after sampling these pages, you can assent to the idea that *all* human beings have been made in the image of God and are therefore worthy to be heard and studied and encouraged to resist violence, you are part of the journey this book advocates.

But, even if you are already an ardent feminist, you may well be asking, along with others, why the world needs yet another anthology of writings by and about women. Obviously, many anthologies already on the market focus on various aspects of women's and gender studies. While they are wonderful resources for teaching and thinking, they often present a limited focus (both in terms of content and of style) that may be misleading for persons beginning the journey. They are often collections of theoretical academic pieces, or personal narrative pieces; they may focus on theological issues or post-colonial issues, etc. This anthology, however, invites *many* voices to the table, helping the reader to understand right from the beginning that women's studies is about multiple issues, and comes in a variety of styles.

So, for instance, "faith-based" is defined in a broad sense, including the participation of evangelicals, liberals, mainline Christians, mystics and downright skeptics. In addition, the anthology embraces several Jewish contributors, one Sufi convert and a Muslim feminist. There are pieces by young women who were students in the May Term and who continue to pursue careers in varied disciplines, including writing. You will encounter the work of resident and associate faculty of the Women's Studies May Term. And, of course, you will hear from well-known theologians, psychologists, literary theorists, and cultural critics. The writers are white, African-American, Asian, Latina, and African. Many of the writers represent marginalized communities: several are lesbian, one is severely disabled, one freely calls herself "white trash." They include womanists and *mujeristas*. They don't always agree with one another. They often deal with topics pertaining to men as well as women. Their works can be used to call one another into question. Most of all, they represent the vast diversity of writers interested in defining and redefining what it means to be female (or male), therefore human, therefore children of God.

The book is entitled *Home is where You're Going* because the journey of coming into selfhood, female or otherwise, is continuous; the final goal is always waiting for us, calling to us from further down the road. Thus, at any given moment, we can feel "at home" with ourselves—with our bodies, our voices, our abilities to resist unjust coercion—and still seek a fuller sense of what home means. One might talk here of the infinite passion of expectations, for that is what it is—a passionate attachment to what is yet to be revealed as we reflect on the past, talk across borders, build solidarities with those different from ourselves, and keep walking. To receive gifts of knowledge and kinship along the way, we must speak many languages. That is why the table of contents includes essays, poetry, stories, personal narratives, letters, biblical meditations and historical reflections—all the ways we have of speaking and writing what we know.

And so we begin, not with theory, as important as that is for shaping and explaining reality, but with a story, for the simple reason that stories, seeking to embody the richness of lived experience, invite both writer and reader to embrace the complexity that any compelling set of ideas or cultural values posits. This story, written by an alumnus of the Women's Studies May Term who spent part of her childhood in Kenya and now works with young women in Cambodia, explores the painful complexities of gender socialization in an African context. Well, not purely an African context—the paradoxes start already—because most of the story takes place in a boarding school designed by Western missionaries. So in addition to gender differences, we are drawn into differences within genders and between cultures, all of them exacerbating the sense of alienation experienced not only by the female protagonist but by the male protagonist as well.

Blood

Lisa Arensen

IT IS TWILIGHT ON THE MISSION STATION, the last half hour before the nightly curfew. A boy and a girl have come secretly to an old cistern in the forest to cut themselves with a razor. Around the cistern stand great cedar trees swathed in skeins of moss. Colobus monkeys watch silently from the tops of these trees. When the children are finished they staunch each other's wounds with the moss and then trudge up the side of the Great Rift Valley to their dormitories. The faint shouts of children on the playing fields rise in the distance.

It is not the blood that is strange. All the children in this boarding school in Kenya bleed. They shed blood in the gardens and in the woodsheds, tumbling on the playing fields and scrapping in the school halls. They shed blood rising and falling, sleeping and waking. They know the taste of it, the shine of it. They are accustomed to the way it wells up in grazes, beads along scrapes and drips from gashes. They have blood to spare, like all children who are young and well and fiercely alive.

It is not even the razor that is strange. Such things have been heard of before. Such things can be purchased from the Kenyan men who cook the food and guard the school's perimeters and wash the laundry of the young boarders. If a boy with his pocket full of shillings slipped behind the dining hall where the men take their breaks around great vats of warm milky tea, a boy could purchase such a thing.

What is strange is that a boy and a girl are together in the forest. There are rules for girls. They seldom stray far from the elementary school grounds. They ascend and descend the hill to the dining hall in packs. They sense the necessity of this, although it is not written in the rulebooks. Safety, such as it is, is most likely to be found in numbers. Nights, lying on their thin mattresses after the lights are turned out in their dormitories, the stories begin of girls vanished, ruined, and gone forever. Any step off a known path could be fatal. They like this fear; they nurture it. They like the sense of the fragility of their lives lain next to their own daring. How far will they go? How fast will they be? What happens beyond the point of no return?

It is different for boys. Solitary boys can be loners who vanish for hours on end. But a girl, even the most unloved of girls, must remain within range, within sight. She may sit alone in a hollow in the grass making daisy chains. She may be completely ignored by the other girls, girls with long smooth ponytails who play tetherball and whisper secrets in each other's ears. But she must be there.

Boys can often be seen toiling up and down the side of the valley with their arms full of kindling, stocking the dormitory woodpiles in payment for their transgressions. The boy with the razor is seldom seen at all. He goes to the forest and kneels in the dark humus below the pine trees, sifting through the soil for the ivory gleam of bone. The boy, if he were smarter, if he were less absorbed in his own private reveries, would realize that his companion is not quite right, that she is not abiding by the rules. Bad things will come of this ritual, of this unlikely bond between boy and girl, of these moments spent in a darkening forest. The girl knows this. But she comes again and again. Both of them do.

Sometimes Soren dreams of dying, of his soul rising out of his still body like a bird. A live bird, with hollow bones and a tiny beating heart and feathers at its throat. Not like the birds his brother Gabe kills with a slingshot. Not like those limp bundles with their skulls crushed, their breasts caved in, feathers soaked in dark blood. "A bird's eyes take up a third of its skull," Gabe told him once, slicing through a woodpecker's scalp with his knife and peeling the skin away. A bizarre beaked creature with enormous dark eyes remained. Its sorrowing eyes stared naked and unprotected at Soren in a red mask of sinew and muscle like an exposed soul.

He loves his brother. He always has. He was mad with grief when Gabe first went away to school. He would stand and wait at the end of the driveway every afternoon until his mother came outside and found him. "Come inside and play," she would say. "I'll show you the school holidays again on the calendar." But the black boxes she checked off so carefully each morning meant nothing to him and he waited every day until finally his father's car came winding up the side of the mountain with Gabe leaning out of the window. And then he was so happy he thought he might faint. He pleaded to be allowed to attend boarding school early until his parents acquiesced, just so he could be near him, just so he could hear him laugh. He was sure that Jesus looked just like Gabe, he was sure that Gabe looked just like Jesus.

Even now, now that he knows Gabe is nothing like Jesus, he still loves him. Sometimes, when he is entering the dining hall, being jostled and prodded by the other boys, he will feel Gabe's large hand on his shoulder and his heart will leap like a wild thing. "Hey, kid," his brother always says, and every time Soren looks up slowly, savoring it, and says, "Hey, Gabe," and then his brother leans over and scoops him right up, even though he is not a small boy anymore. Gabe lifts him out of the children's line and into his own. "Stick with me, kid," Gabe says. "Try and look old." The boys around him, Gabe's friends, always laugh. They laugh at everything Gabe says. The other younger boys fall silent and watch in envy when Soren is with Gabe, but he does not care. He does not care about anything then; he is perfectly happy, standing with his brother in the dining hall line. Then they reach the food counters and the hall monitor notices him and sends Soren back to his own line, no matter how well Gabe pleads and smiles. Even so, it is enough for Soren, and when he is ordered away he always turns to Gabe and gives him a thumbs up and says, "Better luck next time." And then they part.

He still loves Gabe. But in the afternoons after school when Gabe sometimes comes looking for him, Soren does not want to be found at all. His brother kills things. His brother stalks and traps small animals. He enjoys this. Then he skins them and roasts their flesh over smoky fires with other wiry boys who act as if he is a god, although not a god like Jesus.

One day at school Gabe and his friends had come and stolen him away into the forest. "Time to become a man, kid," Gabe had said. "Are you ready for it?" Soren had thought he was. All that long way down the side of the Great Rift Valley, pushing through briars, leaping over gullies, watching the older boys fiddle with their slingshots and hurl stones into trees to flush the birds, he had thought that he was ready.

"We're going to Hyrax Cliffs to check the traps," Gabe said, and Soren had nodded eagerly. "You know what a hyrax is, right?" Soren did. When he still was a small boy, he had extended a lollipop towards a hyrax in a game park and it had bitten his thumb. He did not remember much about the creature itself, but he had a searing recollection of the fiery injections in his belly to protect him from rabies.

The forest gave way abruptly to a vast ledge of bare rock. The change between the shelter of the trees and the open space unsettled Soren. They were standing on the very top of a cliff. The stone was bleached and gray and stank of baboon dung. "Check the traps," Gabe murmured, and the boys fanned out and scattered into the trees. They were all strangely silent. Soren sat down cross-legged on the rock face to wait for them. The stone was hot beneath his bare legs and he liked this. He sat for a long time, drowsy and warm, until the brush behind him rustled and Gabe emerged. His cheeks were flushed and his eyes bright, and he carried a dik-dik by the legs. He dropped it at Soren's feet. Soren reached out his hand and touched its soft coat. The tiny antelope was dead. Its skull had been bashed in and blood from the wound pooled around Soren's feet. The creature's hooves were smaller than Soren's thumb. "It was a fighter," Gabe said cheerfully. "Half out of its mind and impossible to hold down." He looked down at Soren. "All right, kid," he said. "Your turn." And he tugged Soren to his feet and led him to the edge of the great rock. For one stunned moment, Soren thought that Gabe was going to push him off the cliff. Instead, Gabe lifted him down onto a ledge that ran along the length of the cliff. The other boys had returned, some bearing trophies. They ran to the edge and fell upon their stomachs to watch. Gabe led Soren along the ledge to a cleft in the rock. "Hyraxes like rifts in the rock," Gabe explained. "Best place in the world for a snare." He stepped back and helped Soren step into the cleft.

At Soren's feet stretched a long thin wire tied with a noose. A hyrax lay trapped in the noose. Soren had never seen an animal trapped in a snare. The hyrax's tongue was swollen and gray. Its paws pushed feebly at the bloody noose around its neck where it had torn its flesh trying to wrench free. Its eyes were dull and unfocused, but it continued to twitch spasmodically, fighting for life. "Sometimes they get away," one of the boys said from somewhere above his head. "But nothing gets out of Gabe's snares."

Gabe tapped his shoulder and pressed his knife into his hand. "Go on, kid. Kill it." Soren did not refuse. He had never refused his brother anything. He reached out his hand and cut the throat of the tormented creature. It was not so very difficult. The hyrax was already near death. He just finished it. The creature shuddered then fell still; its blood spattered upon his hand. Something inside Soren's chest wrenched and tore. He thought he might faint. Gabe spun Soren around to face him. "Good boy," Gabe said, and reached out and lightly, oh so lightly, touched Soren's chest over his heart, over the torn place, almost as if he knew.

Then, somehow, Soren was back out on the ledge and the boys were lifting him up, whooping. They snatched the limp bundle from Gabe's hands and dipped their fingers in the blood and wiped it across Soren's cheeks. "You're a man," they said. Gabe grinned.

Something was hurting him. He thought it might be his heart. He looked down to find the knife still in his hand, his fingers wrapped tightly around it. He turned away from his brother and saw that he was standing on the very edge of the cliff. A dead tree jutted out of the side of the rock face below him. Its limbs beckoned like broken bones. He knew what he should do. He knew that he should fall. But he did not want to die. So he cut himself instead across the inner skin of his forearm, with the knife he had used to cut the hyrax's throat. The flesh parted so easily, stinging. The blood welled up, an atonement. "I'm sorry," Soren whispered.

He has cut himself ever since that time. It is not something one can do every day, lest an adult notice. On most days he simply searches for and collects the bones of small forest creatures: dik-diks, duikers, birds, hyraxes, voles and shrews. This began in guilt but now simply gives him pleasure. He keeps them on a shelf above his bed: lines of tiny ribcages, delicate skulls, jawbones and incisors, and all the indeterminate bones of leg and forearm. He finds and keeps their bones. But he also offers, carefully and methodically, his pain. He cuts for Gabe's sake and not his own, for he has not hunted again. He knows it is not sufficient, but he gives his blood for all the creatures starving and choking in the snares of his sibling. He dreams about those creatures at night, dreams of their bright eyes, their glossy coats and delicate paws. They do not seem angry with him, only fearful. He reaches out and tries to offer them lollipops but they turn and run away into the shadows. He looks down and sees that there is still blood on his hands, even after all this time. He looks up and sees Gabe standing in front of him, grinning. "Hey, kid," Gabe says. "Time to become a man." And then he wakes in the silent dormitory and cries a little, quietly, so that none of the other boys will hear him.

Nights are Sarah's downfall as well. As long as there is still light, she can endure anything. She studies the other girls. Under the harsh fluorescent light of the study cubicles the girls sit in their nightgowns at the desks, their bare feet twisting on the metal legs of the chairs above the cold linoleum. None of them ever remember to wear their slippers, no matter how often the dorm parents chide. They pass notes back and forth surreptitiously between their desks and practice their curly signatures.

In the warm lamplight of the dorm parents' quarters upstairs, they play with each other's hair. They take turns with the hairbrushes and the rubber bands, brushing and braiding and twisting while the dorm father reads from the Bible and the dorm mother stirs cocoa over the stove. If the dorm father were a sardonic man, he would read the biblical passages that speak of hair: Absalom hanging by his black curls in the thicket, Delilah sawing through Samson's long mane, the sinful woman wiping Christ's feet with her long repentant tresses. But he is not a man of much wit, so he reads the Epistles to them instead. A woman's hair is her glory, the Apostle Paul proclaimed, and on this the girls would agree. Occasionally one of them will take a brush to Sarah's hair. But she wears it short and she has grown accustomed to sitting outside of those intimate inner circles.

In the dim glow of the bare bulb hanging above the shower room the girls double up in square porcelain tubs and scrub each other's backs. Sometimes they steal a towel and make the hapless victim run back to her room naked and dripping. They say that they inform the boys of these towel thefts beforehand, that the boys are waiting outside in the dark night with their faces pressed against the windows, fogging up the glass. Sarah knows that the girls are not this organized. Sometimes one of them will climb into one of the dryers lined up against the wall and the others will spin her around until she begs for mercy. This makes them all hysterical, although they are careful to listen for the shuffling steps of the dorm mother.

In the bright sunlight of the recess hour, the girls do gymnastics on the edge of the field. The girls know that the boys watch them, although they seldom acknowledge this. They arrange themselves in circles and stand upon their hands with their feet pointed straight into the air towards heaven. They do star jumps and chains of somersaults that leave grass stains all down their shorts and some of them can even do round-offs and back walkovers. It is as if the red earth below the green grass is as yielding as a trampoline. Gravity seems to have no hold on them at all. They hang by their knees from the monkey bars and flip down to the ground below, their hair swishing through the air. For a season they practice pyramids, lithe towers of girls balancing upon each other's shoulders and thighs and knees. They like to pretend that they are the Tower of Babel. On a prearranged signal they all tumble free to the earth below, each one shouting words in a different language.

Sarah is not so different from these girls. But they possess something she lacks; they know some secret she does not know. Their cheerfulness does not seem feigned. Perhaps they are secretly miserable. Yet they are braver somehow. Unlike her, they are able to refrain from weeping when the darkness comes, and they resent her bitterly for this failing. During Sarah's first few weeks at boarding school, the dorm mother would carry her away into her own quarters and rock her while she wept. But her sympathy ebbed as the weeks became months and now she issues hearty warnings instead as her plump hand hovers over the light switch. "Let's not have any crying tonight, my girl," she says. "Think of your roommates." How could Sarah not think of her roommates, whose eyes are fixed upon her bed as soon as they adjust to the dark? Waiting anxiously, angrily, for her to fail.

She tries. As the darkness fills the room, she lies with her arms folded across her chest. She pretends she is dead. The dead do not weep. The sheets are rough against her skin but she imagines that she is lying in a teakwood coffin, the wood smooth against her cold flesh. She holds her breath and listens to her heart slowly beating; she waits for it to stop. She imagines the red earth cut open like a box waiting for her coffin to be lowered into it like an offering. But then, inevitably, she spoils it. She sees her mother standing by her graveside, dressed all in black. Her mother tries to smile but instead she falls to her knees and cries out like she did the first time Sarah went away.

The week before Sarah entered boarding school her mother packed her daughter's belongings in steamer trunks. She folded two sets of towels and pillowcases and sheets as if Sarah were married and moving away. She assembled the clothing prescribed by the school's dress code. Each item bore a small tag with Sarah's name upon it. Her mother had sat next to a dim lamp every night for a month, lips pursed, sewing those name tags into every piece of clothing Sarah owned. Each sock, each pair of panties, each washcloth in the trunks bore the work of her mother's needle. Sarah sewed in one tag herself, but the stitches were crooked and her mother tore it out and started over again. "I'll do them all," she said to Sarah. "I don't mind doing them." She told Sarah that she must be brave, that she must be good. She told Sarah that when the day came on which Sarah must go away that they must both be very brave, as if Sarah were a soldier going away to war. She would salute

Sarah, she said, and kiss her on the forehead once and smile, and then turn and walk up the steps back into the house.

A neighbor had offered to take Sarah to boarding school. Sarah had never met this woman. She stood with her mother on the close-cropped lawn and waited. Her mother was wearing black that day. Perhaps mothers wear black when their children go off to war. Sarah does not know. When the neighbor's car pulled into the graveled driveway, her mother squeezed Sarah's hand and gave a strange little smile and said, "Well, then." She stepped forward to greet the neighbor woman and Sarah began to forget how to breathe. Her throat was tight and strange.

Her mother loaded the trunks in the neighbor's car. Her mother saluted her and bent down to kiss her on the forehead. Sarah felt as if someone had both hands around her throat, squeezing it. She tried to speak but she could not say a word. "Well, then," Sarah's mother said, but then she forgot how to be brave. She began to sob. She fell to her knees on that perfectly manicured lawn and pushed Sarah roughly into the arms of the strange woman, her fingers pressing hard into Sarah's thin arms. Later Sarah will guard those bruises as if they are kisses. When they begin to fade Sarah will panic, when they are gone she will die inside. "Take her," her mother sobbed to the stranger. "Take her. I can't let her go." The woman gathered Sarah's body, rigid with shock, into her arms and carried her to the passenger seat of the waiting car. Unknown children in the backseat watched Sarah's mother double over on the manicured lawn. Their eyes protruded like fisheyes. Sarah stared silently as the car lurched into reverse and pulled away from her kneeling mother. Her mother's hands clawed the brilliant green grass and the red earth. Her mother lay there weeping as if she were broken and let Sarah go. The other woman chattered to Sarah as if nothing were wrong. Her children shifted restlessly in their seats. How wonderful Sarah's new dorm mother is, the woman said. What an adventure Sarah will soon be having. The other children love the boarding school. Her son loves it, doesn't he? Her son looked disdainfully at Sarah. What a lovely large tuck box her mother has packed for her. She will be able to eat some of it every afternoon after school at three. She will be able to trade the treats packed by her mother with her little friends. She is a lucky girl.

Sarah thinks of her mother crying like a broken winged crow. She thinks of her mother, who lets Sarah be taken away, who sends her away, again and again. Rage and desperate loneliness well up inside of her and a whimper escapes Sarah's throat in the dark dormitory room. Each holiday she pleads with her mother, she prays to whichever god will listen, although none of them ever do. "Don't make me go back," she begs. "Let me stay with you." And her mother shakes her head and wipes her wet eyes with angry hands and says, "I promised myself I wouldn't cry this time." Sarah does not hate her. She knows what this is like.

Every night Sarah lies on her mattress and shakes with her sobs. The other girls turn their backs to her, harsh words upon their lips. They jam their fists into their ears and burrow into their blankets, but to no avail. Her grief follows them. They cannot escape her and the hot tears rise in their own eyes. All the girls in the room lie weeping nightly for their absent mothers and they hate the girl who makes them weep, who makes them remember, who wakes their longing and their sorrow.

"You are just a little crybaby," one spits at her in the cold light of morning.

"You cry too," Sarah says, helplessly.

"Only if you start it, you baby," the other girl cries, and spins on her heel and strides away.

Sarah wonders if this is true. She wonders whether, if by some miracle she could stay dry-eyed, the other girls would fall asleep as peacefully as they braid each other's hair during their nightly rituals. She wonders if she is truly to blame. It does not matter. There is nothing she can do. She can endure anything if it is light, but the boy's razor helps. Nothing can make the ache around her heart fade, nothing except for the sight of her mother standing in the doorway of the dormitory to take her home for the school holidays. Nothing can make the pain go away, but she can replace that great pain with another one, small sharp and stinging, and for this reason Sarah leaves the school grounds to stand with the boy on an old cistern in the woods and takes a razor to her skin.

Soren does not always go to the forest. He likes to hide in a culvert that runs beneath the road beside the prayer chapel. He leans back against the curved walls and stares open-eyed into the darkness. Occasionally a car passes over the road above and the entire culvert trembles, dust sifting down upon his head as if he is in a miner's tunnel. Its rough concrete sides are threaded with tiny cracks. Yet it holds. Soren has read that South African miners keep canaries in cages as early warning systems. If the canary topples from its perch, then the air has gone bad and all the dirt-streaked men scramble back up to the surface. Soren wonders what it must be like for the canaries who live deep beneath the earth. Do they mind it or have they forgotten what the sun looks like at all? Do they still sing? He likes to sing, softly, when he is lying in the culvert. His voice becomes more resonant; it drifts back at him off the walls. He is a canary singing gently under the earth.

He has hidden some things in this culvert, but he tries to keep it simple. He also keeps track of the seasons. When the rains come, runoff from higher in the valley churns through his hiding place in a fast-flowing stream, red from the oxides in the earth and full of pine cones and grass. Once Soren came and found all of the belongings he had stored in the culvert scattered in the mud behind the prayer chapel, lying right up against the cabin walls for any passerby to see. His heart rose up in his throat until he had gathered everything up and stolen away. There are so few places to hide in a boarding school. Children crawl over the landscape like ants—scaling every tree, burrowing into every hole, swimming in each water tank. Finding a secret place is like finding a treasure in a field.

He is better than many of the children at finding hiding places. He has had more practice. When he and his sibling still lived at home, Gabe would go off on solitary hunting trips and Soren would play by himself on the grounds of their farm. He was more afraid of nature then, so he often played near or inside the house. He would find the most hidden of places and he would very carefully slip into them. It was very important to not disturb the outside of these places. He would try and erase his tracks as he crept into them. It was best of all if they were dark, because then he could light a candle on an upturned tin can. And then he would sit—underneath the leaning mattress in the attic, in the middle of the kai apple hedge, in the skeleton of scaffolding beneath the staircase— watching the candle burn and thinking to himself.

When Gabe came home, he would come and find him. He would stalk Soren. He would follow his tracks, brushing his fingers over broken twigs, crushed moss, telltale piles of dislodged dust, the scuffmarks of a small boy's shoe. He would creep right up to where Soren was sitting and peel open his hiding place like a fruit. He would poke his head into the hedge, he would yank the leaning mattress away from the wall, he would jump up and catch Soren's dangling foot. "Found you, kid!" he would crow. Soren was startled witless every time. And every time, for one brief moment, he felt a flash of resentment at being found. Caught. Invaded. Then his love of Gabe would roll over him like an ocean and he would drown.

One day on the way to the culvert, Soren stumbles upon four men standing in the science teacher's yard. They are all gathered around something, something large and struggling, and Soren sees an enormous feathered arm flap between their knees. He tries to slip by unnoticed but the science teacher has seen him out of the corner of his eye. "Come here, boy, and lend a hand," he calls.

Soren's heart sinks but he shuffles over obediently. The men are standing around a vulture with a broken wing. Beside them on the grass lies a pile of bandages and some lightweight rods. The men are debating and dancing slightly to stay out of range of the bird's fierce thrusts with beak and claw. Soren has never been so close to such an enormous wild creature. Its head and neck are featherless and an ugly shade of pink. Its feathers are storm-cloud gray. Its great hooked beak hisses angrily and its eyes are hot and feral. Soren can hardly breathe. It is a splendid and terrible bird. Gabe could never kill this creature. Its hoarse cry would knock Gabe spinning on his back like a beetle. Its burning eye would judge all Gabe's sins in an instant and pronounce condemnation. Its beak would crush Gabe's traps like twigs, swallow his knife whole, snap off each of his fingers at the root, tear great tufts of hair from Gabe's blonde head.

The men reach a decision and step in. The science teacher catches the vulture at the nape of the neck as two other men secure those slashing legs. The vulture hisses in rage as the science teacher slips a noose around its beak and pulls it tight. The draft from its beating wings blows Soren's hair back from his forehead. The last man secures the healthy wing. The teacher gestures to Soren. "I need you to hold its head for me so I can splint the wing."

Soren's hands are trembling, but he obeys. He steps in close to the enraged bird and puts his hands around the vulture's head, just above the neck. The teacher releases his hold on the bird and quickly arranges the bandages and rods on the grass. The neck of the vulture is covered with leathery and pebbled skin, but it is as strong as the muscles in Gabe's arms. The vulture writhes in Soren's hands, and his body bucks as if he is riding a runaway horse. "Hold it steady, boy," the men say to Soren. "Don't let go." The teacher kneels in front of the vulture as if he is going to embrace it and begins to splint the bird's wing. The vulture hisses and fights. The splinting seems to take a very long time. Soren's fingers ache from the effort of holding the neck upright, of keeping that hooked beak away from the science teacher's bent head.

"I can't hold it," Soren thinks. "They shouldn't have asked me. I can't hold it."

And then the science teacher speaks to that enormous ugly angry bird. He croons to it. He says, more gently than Soren believed was possible for a man to speak, "Hold still, baby." The torn place in Soren's heart suddenly throbs. He will not let go of the vulture; he will not fail. He will stand here for as long as he is needed. He closes his eyes and it is Gabe kneeling in front of the vulture, binding its wing. Gabe smiles up at him, his hands full of bandages. "Hold her still, kid," he says. Soren will. He will hold onto the life thrashing beneath their hands for as long as he lives.

Large hands close over his and he opens his eyes, startled. The science teacher is looking down at him. "That was well done, young man," he says. "I've got her now." Soren nods, stunned, and staggers away. Behind him on the grass, the vulture snaps the twine around its beak and cries out in an indignant tongue to the cloudless sky. It is a wild thing finding itself in a dark mine it cannot understand, surrounded by men with dirt on their faces. It does not know that these are good men, but Soren does. He begins to run down the hill, faster and faster, beating the air with his arms as if he too has wings, as if he too can fly if he picks up enough speed. He flies down the valley to the dining hall to find the brother that he loves. He knows that somewhere in Gabe's heart is a man who will kneel before a vulture and bind its wounds. He knows this because Gabe loves him, and he is not strong. He is like a bird, like a small forest creature. He is a canary singing under the earth and he believes that Gabe will throw down his pick-axe and fling open the door of the cage and hold him against his breast as they ride up the mineshaft towards the light. He flies down the hill to sing Gabe the song he knows how to sing.

If a boy her own size torments a girl, there are things she can do. She can scratch him or slap him or pinch him or even kick him. She can shame him before the other boys or accuse him of misbehavior during school hours when a teacher is present. She can even take a complaint to the dorm parents, who may act upon it. Boys are paddled far more often than girls. But paddling is not common even so. There are so many ways to punish a child. Carrying wood is favored, as is collecting trash on the school grounds. Tuck boxes can be locked away, chores can be doubled, extra homework can be assigned. In the world at the top of the valley, where the primary students live, the girls are treated gingerly by the boys. Sarah does not fear boys her own age.

Unfortunately, the dining hall is situated lower in the valley, on the grounds of the secondary school. It simplifies the logistics of the boarding school for all of the pupils to eat in one building. The primary and the secondary school students have separate dining rooms reached by a single hallway. A cursory barrier of welded pipe runs down the center of this hallway. The older students queue on the left side of the pipe until they reach the counters where the food is served. The primary school children enter the passageway on the right side of the pipe. At its very end lies the entrance to their dining room. Every evening at five o'clock in this hallway, things occur.

The girls do not run races on the playing fields merely for pleasure. They are also interested in becoming fast. A well-timed sprint may carry a girl all the way down the long length of the hallway into the inner dining room where a monitor stands to observe misbehavior. If no one is watching for her, if no one is waiting, the older boys may be reduced to tall blurs shouting in her wake. "Hey, girlie!" they shout. Or, "Come back and talk to us, honey!" These secondary school boys are enormous. Their arms go on forever. If they hold a girl against the concrete wall at arm's length, there is no way of reaching him with nails or flying feet. All a girl has is her voice. This is what pleases these boys most: waiting to hear what a captive girl will say. Will she curse them? Will she plead for mercy? Will she speak in tongues? If she cries, they will release her more quickly. Some girls cry. Most of them do not. They hate these boys. They will not give their tormentors the satisfaction of seeing them weep.

The running technique has its drawbacks. If too many girls are getting by them, the boys will trip one. Sometimes they stand back and watch the girl fall, but this is risky. Injury brings attention. More often, one boy will do the tripping and another will stoop down below the dividing pipe and catch the falling girl. She will fall directly into his arms like an eager young lover while the other boys erupt into clamorous applause. "I saved you, girlie," the boy will say to the girl trapped in his arms. "What do you say?" If she thanks him, he will grin and let her go. Some of the girls trade stories amongst themselves of being touched or kissed, but usually they do not discuss these episodes. They would rather not speak of them at all. If a girl at this boarding school stumbled upon a magic lamp and was offered three wishes by a genie, she would make those older boys vanish completely, as if they had never existed at all. Or she would wish for them to diminish in size, to end up as small as rabbits or cats, and then she would carry them up the valley and keep them in cages and never feed them enough. Or she would shorten their arms, leaving them just long enough to raise a fork to their lips and clap their hands lightly with the tips of their fingers. She might also, if she had a wish left, remove their voice boxes, so that they could never say girlie again. There are endless variations on these wishes. The fields have been scoured but unfortunately no lamps have been found. Some nights in their study cubicles they draw treasure maps of the mission station and speculate on possible locations, but they know it is just a child's game. And in the stories it is always Arabic boys who find such lamps. Nevertheless, they tape the maps in the backs of their closets behind their Sunday dresses, as if they are talismans or good luck charms. So far they have proved largely ineffectual.

Some nights there are sporting events and the older boys are not present when the younger children enter for supper. Some nights there are older girls standing between the boys in the line, and the boys flirt with them instead. Some nights it is better to be late and some nights it is safer to be early. Not knowing which kind of a night it is can drive a girl mad.

Sarah is always late for dinner. She intends, sometimes, to try the early run, but her steps slow as she descends the hill. Often she begins with a crowd of girls and then lags behind. She lets things distract her: stones, pinecones, cicadas shrilling on the trunks of trees. For a while she stopped going to dinner at all, a brilliant tactic that was foiled by the instigation of an attendance list of the primary school students. Children must be fed three square meals a day, including two glasses of milk.

Sarah is always late and usually alone when she enters the dining hall. Her legs become heavier and heavier as she nears the entranceway. It is like a dream, like those terrible dreams where her legs are asleep and she cannot wake them, or she discovers she is paralyzed from the waist down or that her legs are encased in quicklime. She cannot move, or she can hardly move, and there is always something running hard on her heels. Something coming closer. Usually, after the futile struggle, she wakes in terror just as the thing lunges for her. She wakes before she is devoured. This does not work in the dining hall. But she must eat dinner every night and so she enters the dining hall, slowly.

Sarah does not run past the boys. There is no point in it. Nothing does any good at all, not if he is there, the tall boy with the blonde hair and the enormous hands. If he is not there, they do not bother with her. If he is not there she walks by with her head down and they let her pass as if she is invisible. After all, she is such a small girl, just a small plain uninteresting girl. She tried so hard to be unworthy of their notice. Yet one day she failed and most evenings now she pays for this failure.

She does not know what she did to attract his attention the first time, but she knows what keeps it. It is her fear and her hatred. These things excite him. When he sees her, he swings himself under the bar and kneels in front of her, blocking her way. "Speak to me," he pleads. She will not. He clutches his heart and throws back his head. "She's cold, she's cold, she's breaking my heart!" The other boys, for there are always other boys, love this. They laugh and shout encouragement. "Just one word," he begs. "Just one kiss." She will not look at him, so he reaches out and catches her chin and forces it up until she meets his eyes. His hands are very strong. If he were ever truly angry with her, she knows he could break her bones. "Not even one word?" he whispers. His eyes gleam. She will not speak to him. It is the only resistance she dares offer. She will not speak but she trembles. She cannot help this trembling. Because of it, he calls her Rabbit. He loves her, he says. He cannot live without her.

Sarah looks down at her feet and trudges into the dining hall. For two days now, the boy has not been present. For two days now, she has walked all the way down the hallway to the children's line unnoticed. Unmolested. Unharmed. She does not expect her luck to hold. He has hidden himself between the other boys. She does not see him. But she hears him. She hears his voice. "Rabbit," he whispers. "Raaaabit." She stops, dazed. She does not know whether she has passed by him. She does not whether he is ahead of her or already behind her. She does not know if this disembodied voice is all he has in mind for the evening. And then his hand grips her shoulder and he spins her around to face him.

He is kneeling, which is normal. He has one hand behind his back, "Did you think I'd forgotten you, Rabbit?" he asks. There is something different about him tonight, something terrible, and so she shakes her head in response. No, she did not think he had forgotten her.

He cradles the back of her skull with his free hand the way her mother does. But she must not think of her mother now. She must not think of her at all. Sarah begins to tremble. He pulls her closer to him. "Tonight's a big night for me, Rabbit. Don't you want to hear about it?" She nods.

He sighs. "You know, Rabbit, sometimes I think you don't care at all.

Sometimes I think you'd be perfectly happy to never see me again." He pulls right up against him until his forehead is touching hers and she can feel his breath upon her face. "I have a surprise for you, Rabbit," he whispers.

She will not cry. She will not. She pretends she is dead. The dead do not weep. She imagines that her flesh is cold but his breath is hot on her face, his fingers are warm on her head.

"Be very brave, Rabbit," he tells her and then he draws his hand out from behind his back and in it is a dead thing. In his hand is a black crow with broken wings and a crushed skull. She had imagined that she would die and her mother sob beside her body but no, she has gotten it wrong, all wrong, her mother is the one who is dead, her arms broken, her skull crushed in, and Sarah is the one on her knees by the graveside, screaming and screaming.

Soren runs into the hallway and sees Gabe on his knees shaking the girl who comes to the forest with him. The girl is screaming and Gabe is shouting and shaking her and on the floor between them lies one of Gabe's birds and Soren runs right up to him and pushes him with all of his might.

"Stop it, Gabe! Stop it, stop it!" He is screaming too. He is screaming and hitting Gabe with both hands, small feeble blows, but Gabe releases the girl. She stumbles away from him and runs out of the dining hall. Gabe stares after her, then looks at Soren.

"She your girlfriend?" he asks.

He cannot stop screaming. "Don't you ever touch her again! Don't you ever!"

"Whoa, kid—" Gabe reaches out his hand but Soren runs from him.

He finds her crouched by the cistern in the woods. She has already found the razorblade. There are bloody streaks all up and down the length of her legs and arms. She is striped with blood, she is awash in it. Soren kneels down before her.

The girl's teeth chatter and she rubs her hands up and down her arms, wetting them with the blood. "I'm dead," she says. "I'm already dead. I want to be dead."

Soren wants to talk to her. He wants to tell her about the vulture, about how the man knelt before it and bound its wing, he wants to teach her how to hide, how to find secret places, he wants to tell her that his brother will never hurt her again. He does not know how to do this. Her eyes are hooded and blank. Her trembling skin is cool and clammy to his touch. She is the canary in the cage. She has toppled over because the air has gone bad. They are far below the surface of the known world, and all is dark and strange. The Tower of Babel has fallen and they do not speak the same language.

He pries the razorblade out of her hand and searches for a tongue she will understand.

"Don't ever use it like that again," he says and then he rises to gather moss from the cedar trees. He will need a great deal to bind up her wounds.

THE GOAL OF THIS INTRODUCTION is *not* to analyze the story but to point to questions posed by the story, relevant to an understanding of being male or female in a terribly complicated, always, in some way, cross-cultural world. Think of these as open-ended queries, reasons for starting and continuing the journey into a greater understanding of the role gender plays in identity and culture.

৯◦Many of us know persons who practice self-destructive behaviors: anorexics, bulimics, over-exercisers, addicts, suicidals, cutters. This story introduces a pair of cutters, surprisingly male and female. What purpose does self-immolation fulfill in their lives, or any life, for that matter, and how does their friendship perpetuate both self-immolation and resistance?

৯◦Many of us know boys who, in trying to live up to the honor codes of fathers, older siblings, and friends, get drawn into patterns of violence that disturb them deeply. How can this fierce loyalty be reconciled with the hate it seems to demand, and that may well shadow the primary relationship itself?

৯◦Many of us know women who have been religiously configured, whether that configuration comes from forced veiling, cliterodectomy, enforced codes of modesty, or compelling systems of guilt. Many of us also know women who have been sexually abused, whether that abuse comes from verbal harassment, physical rape, forced affection for older males, or, again, impossible codes of modesty and the resulting guilt. Often women, like the girl in this story, suffer from an almost palimpsestic layering of these factors. What should be the role of mothers and "other mother" figures in helping girls and women to resist, find voice and claim their own bodies and souls?

৯◦Many of us have been caught in cultural cross-fires, whether it be the discrepancy between place of origin and present environment, between home/church and school, between mother's and father's ancestry, between personal ethnic background and the backgrounds of friends. How does one ideology, in this case, Christian boarding school or village/home life, influence the other? More important, how does one context become "privileged" over the other?

৯◦Many of us know broken persons who have been almost miraculously healed by relationships and events. At the same time, we realize that healing, like life itself, is an ongoing process with many stops along the way. (Maybe it is our brokenness and need for healing that keep us in religious community, as well as sending us forth when religion becomes the oppressor.) What signs and sources of healing are possible in a complex context like the one articulated in "Blood," and in our own lives?

❧ Race, class and gender stereotypes must continually be deconstructed in order for life to assume its essential vitality. What stereotypes are being disrupted in this story—by actions of the characters, by strategies of the writer, and by the complexities of language itself? Equally important, what reconfigurations of reality are taking the place of these dead metaphors? And how might this "death-rebirth" dynamic reflect the transformations in our own lives?

We hope that the more you explore the various sections in this book, the more you will return to pondering this story and the very real questions it asks. In addition, we hope that the impact this story makes on you, whatever that impact might be, will help you to think critically about the pieces you read. For this journey toward informed selfhood should be wildly dialogic and hopefully endless.

As a final send off, even a blessing for the way, we offer Denise Levertov's poem "A Gift" which speaks for itself.

A Gift

Denise Levertov

Just when you seem to yourself
nothing but a flimsy web
of questions, you are given
the questions of others to hold
in the emptiness of your hands,
songbird eggs that can still hatch
if you keep them warm,
butterflies opening and closing themselves
in your cupped palms, trusting you not to injure
their scintillant fur, their dust.
You are given the questions of others
as if they were answers
to all you ask. Yes perhaps
this gift is your answer.

II. Transforming Paradigms

WOMEN'S STUDIES IS NOT ONLY about unmasking what has been invisible in the curriculum of the academy, the theologies handed down to us and the culture surrounding us. Women's Studies, as Martha Nussbaum will point out later in this anthology, calls for a transformation of the very paradigms that have shaped both the academy and our common (and radically diverse) lives.   In this section we include writers who call for transformations in psychology, theology, and even in the construction of feminist thought. Each writer expresses hope that such transformations are not only possible, but already in evidence, even if only a hint of change can be detected. As readers we are invited to participate in these transformations.

bell hooks' call for all feminist movements to be transformative requires an inclusive and deepening sense of feminism. Rather than assume sexism lies at the root of all other oppressions, she holds that at the heart of all forms of oppression, whether race, class or gender, we find domination—the belief in superiority and inferiority and the right of whoever is superior to hold power over those who are not. bell hooks also asserts that we cannot divide the world simply into oppressors and victims; instead, we must face the truth that all of us have the capacity to wound, violate and control others, as we often do. Even as we have violence done to us, we do violence to others.

Above all else, she wants feminist movements to progress from academic, conference and book encounters back to grassroots, small group encounters where genuine critical thinking can take place; for example, among working class people in open (and often uncomfortable) dialogue with theorists. Perhaps then we could actually name "the realities that divide us, make us different, stand us in opposition, and work to reconcile and resolve these issues." This "face-to-face solidarity" would make actual the potential of feminist movements to revolutionize our personal and collective experiences in the world. It might even make possible love; a word bell hooks retrieves from sentimentality and overuse to mean an empowering source to sustain us through terribly difficult, albeit authentic, transformations. Quoting Paulo Freire "that true revolutionaries must perceive the revolution, because of its creative and liberating nature, as an act of love," she says we must begin to document and affirm each other whenever differences are authentically addressed and constructively transformed. We need these love stories "so that we are not broken in this process, so that we do not despair." Hopefully, the articles included in this section, calling for and pointing out needed paradigm shifts and transformations, begin to do what bell hooks calls for.

Carol Gilligan invites us to listen to the voices of the adolescent girls she has come to know over years of study. These voices call into question traditional theories of adolescent development and have begun to transform gender theory for women and men. The crisis for girls coming of age is by now well known and even contested, and just as there is no universal experience of womanhood, no universal experience of girlhood exists. Still, over the course of her research, Carol Gilligan maintains she has been radicalized by remembering her own adolescence and by discovering the persistent desire of girls to stay in authentic relationships, contradicting traditional theory which makes separation necessary for normal development into adulthood. Girls coming of age find their authentic relationships hard to maintain, and Gilligan's research indicates that often by late adolescence they have given up on openness and honesty in favor of idealized relationships, or if they keep their voices, as girls of color often do, they may drop out of school or other institutions silencing them. But, at core, girls resist these losses and can rediscover voice and constructive agency if encouraged by parents, older women, or other adults who remain in relationship to them while they renegotiate their childhood connections.

And so we come to Sally Smits, who embodies in her letters to her father both the longing for genuine connection and the resistance to silencing so hopeful if gender is to be transformed. A college sophomore at the time of the writing, Sally articulates both her desire to tell her father who she is and her sense of risk in that telling, even when her father has encouraged Sally's voice and person. Reclaiming (rather than forgetting) her regression into silence and her eventual regaining of voice and anger means she stays more consciously aware of her resistance to cultural expectations than many girls can. We will meet Sally again in a later section of the anthology where she tries to speak to her father about her most painful experience of anorexia, an indicator of how difficult coming of age can be for girls, even those as courageous as Sally.

The abundance of recent writings about how gender construction has wounded boys and men seems to indicate that perhaps the cultural discussion of what has been happening to girls has given us permission to question what has been happening to boys. Years ago Carol Gilligan, in *Mapping the Moral Domain*, drew the connection: "...listening to girls and women, we have come to think differently about boys and men."

Thus we include Mary Stewart Van Leeuwen's article on boys' development and what might be needed for boys coming of age to experience their full personhood. Schooled in the "Boy Code," named by Joseph Pollack in *Real Boys*, males learn early on they must avoid anything considered sissy stuff, become paragons of stability and self-reliance, and at all costs compete for the limited commodity of being on top, a position always in danger of slippage if one is not masculine enough, not willing to take dangerous risks, or if one shows a wider range of emotions than anger, the acceptable way of expressing fear or sadness. Van Leeuwen is not offering a universal experience of boyhood; indeed she finds hope in studies done with highly involved wage-earning mothers and stay-at-home fathers whose children seem freer of gender rigidity, more able to do "border work," able both to nurture and explore, and relate comfortably with same and cross gender friends. Hope of transformation comes as boys are allowed freedom to stay attached to caretakers even after they begin school, are not shamed for expressing a wide range of feelings, and have in their life mentors and role models of both genders who can advocate for their full personhood.

Shifting now from human relations to theology, we find Katherine Bloomquist questioning traditional images of God by asking, "Who is the God in whom we can believe?" Openly calling for a gracious and liberating God who empowers women, Bloomquist shows us how the domination bell hooks diagnoses in "feminism: a transformational politic," permeates theology. Exploring language for God, Bloomquist shows how symbols "bespeak a whole social structure," a hierarchical configuration with God at the top, men on the next rung, and women, children, and finally nature following in order below. In bell hooks' description, the superior has the right to rule over the inferior; Bloomquist shows how this has been built into the fabric of patriarchal theology, with God characterized by much of masculinity in the Boy's Code—complete stability, self-reliance, independence which needs no other relationally, the autonomous "sturdy oak," so to speak. Simply trying to retrieve a nonsexist core does not go far enough, she declares; instead theology must be reworked, i.e., we must acknowledge how patriarchy permeates the tradition all the while exploring what has been liberating in it, intent always to transform key resources into "what has not yet been heard." Bloomquist also mentions with great respect theologians who have rejected Christian theology on the grounds that it cannot be redeemed for women. She encourages us to listen intently to their voices, staying face-to-face as it were, refusing to do violence by rejecting them.

Once again, we join Sally Smits as she struggles to find a God whom she can trust and a religious community which can include and empower her. She writes about the issue of ordination for women, and how it felt to be side by side with her father as they both resisted church tradition. On new and shakier ground for her, Sally finds herself asking questions about language for God as an "issue of justice," exploring the mystery of not being able to name God while at the same time needing to image God in inclusive and empowering ways. She recognizes her own anger at the social structure traditional language keeps intact, alongside wonder at the freedom she feels addressing God in new ways.

Our biblical exegesis comes from May Term professor, John Linton. "The Running Father" (Luke 15) relates a story told by Jesus guaranteed to startle his contemporaries and deconstruct our notion of who God might be. Often called the story of "The Prodigal Son," the text is used to show that if we truly repent we will be forgiven. In actuality, the story is not primarily about the boy, who tells us he plans to return as a servant in order to regain the favor of the father he has violated by demanding his inheritance while the father still lives, and then wasting it all away until he is penniless and a stranger even to the pigs he tends. Instead we meet the running patriarch, shameless as he runs (and patriarchs must never run) to embrace his child, the very child who should be publicly beaten, not given a party. Linton introduces us to a lover God who comes to meet us where we are and who calls us into a life we did not know possible. Perhaps we could trust this God.

We finish the section with poetry. Rachel Bennett's "Rafting" paints for us her father's message about desirable sons and lacking daughters, along with adolescent silencing brought about by penetrating gazes and violating hands. Her circumscribed life is radically transformed by a rafting trip which brings her home to her body and her raging voice.

Marge Piercy's "Ruth and Naomi" introduces us to an older and younger woman, whose relationship carries them through terrible loss into a life that can sustain them both. A story of deep connection, its lines have often been borrowed for wedding ceremonies, but we remember that they were exchanged first between women, "Where you go, I will go too..." (Gilligan would be pleased).

feminism

a transformational politic

bell hooks

WE LIVE IN A WORLD IN CRISIS—a world governed by politics of domination, one in which the belief in a notion of superior and inferior, and its concomitant ideology—that the superior should rule over the inferior—effects the lives of all people everywhere, whether poor or privileged, literate or illiterate. Systematic dehumanization, worldwide famine, ecological devastation, industrial contamination, and the possibility of nuclear destruction are realities which remind us daily that we are in crisis. Contemporary feminist thinkers often cite sexual politics as the origin of this crisis. They point to the insistence on difference as that factor which becomes the occasion for separation and domination and suggest that differentiation of status between females and males globally is an indication that patriarchal domination of the planet is the root of the problem. Such an assumption has fostered the notion that elimination of sexist oppression would necessarily lead to the eradication of all forms of domination. It is an argument that has led influential Western white women to feel that feminist movement should be the central political agenda for females globally. Ideologically, thinking in this direction enables Western women, especially privileged white women, to suggest that racism and class exploitation are merely the offspring of the parent system: patriarchy. Within feminist movement in the West, this has led to the assumption that resisting patriarchal domination is a more legitimate feminist action than resisting racism and other forms of domination. Such thinking prevails despite radical critiques made by black women and other women of color who question this proposition. To speculate that an oppositional division between men and women existed in early human communities is to impose on the past, on these non-white groups, a world view that fits all too neatly within contemporary feminist paradigms that name man as the enemy and woman as the victim.

Clearly, differentiation between strong and weak, powerful and powerless, has been a central defining aspect of gender globally, carrying with it the assumption that men should have greater authority than women, and should rule over them. As significant and important as this fact is, it should not obscure the reality that women can and do participate in politics of domination, as perpetrators as well as victims—that we dominate, that we are dominated. If focus on patriarchal domination masks this reality or becomes the means by which women deflect attention from the real conditions and circumstances of our lives, then women cooperate in suppressing and promoting false consciousness, inhibiting our capacity to assume responsibility for transforming ourselves and society.

Thinking speculatively about early human social arrangement, about women and men struggling to survive in small communities, it is likely that the parent-child relationship with its very real imposed survival structure of dependency, of strong and weak, of powerful and powerless, was a site for the construction of a paradigm of domination. While this circumstance of dependency is not necessarily one that leads to domination, it lends itself to the enactment of a social drama wherein domination could easily occur as a means of exercising and maintaining control. This speculation does not place women outside the practice of domination, in the exclusive role of victim. It centrally names women as agents of domination, as potential theoreticians, and creators of a paradigm for social relationships wherein those groups of individuals designated as "strong" exercise power both benevolently and coercively over those designated as "weak."

Emphasizing paradigms of domination that call attention to woman's capacity to dominate is one way to deconstruct and challenge the simplistic notion that man is the enemy, woman the victim; the notion that men have always been the oppressors. Such thinking enables us to examine our role as women in the perpetuation and maintenance of systems of domination. To understand domination, we must understand that our capacity as women and men to be either dominated or dominating is a point of connection, of commonality. Even though I speak from the particular experience of living as a black woman in the United States, a white-supremacist, capitalist, patriarchal society, where small numbers of white men (and honorary "white men") constitute ruling groups, I understand that in many places in the world oppressed and oppressor share the same color. I understand that right here in this room, oppressed and oppressor share the same gender. Right now as I speak, a man who is himself victimized, wounded, hurt by racism and class exploitation is actively dominating a woman in his life—that even as I speak, women who are ourselves exploited, victimized, are dominating children. It is necessary for us to remember, as we think critically about domination, that we all have the capacity to act in ways that oppress, dominate, wound (whether or not that power is institutionalized). It is necessary to remember that it is first the potential oppressor within that we must resist—the potential victim within that we must rescue—otherwise we cannot hope for an end to domination, for liberation.

This knowledge seems especially important at this historical moment when black women and other women of color have worked to create awareness of the ways in which racism empowers white women to act as exploiters and oppressors. Increasingly this fact is considered a reason we should not support feminist struggle even though sexism and sexist oppression is a real issue in our lives as black women (see, for example, Vivian Gordon's *Black Women, Feminism, Black Liberation: Which Way*). It becomes necessary for us to speak continually about the convictions that inform our continued advocacy of feminist struggle. By calling attention to interlocking systems of domination—sex, race, and class—black women and many other groups of women acknowledge the diversity and complexity of female experience, of our relationship to power and domination. The intent is not to dissuade people of color from becoming engaged in feminist movement. Feminist struggle to end patriarchal domination should be of primary importance to women and men globally not because it is the foundation of all other oppressive structures but because it is that form of domination we are most likely to encounter in an ongoing way in everyday life.

Unlike other forms of domination, sexism directly shapes and determines relations of power in our private lives, in familiar social spaces, in that most intimate context—home—and in that most intimate sphere of relations— family. Usually, it is within the family that we witness coercive domination and learn to accept it, whether it be domination of parent over child, or male over female. Even though family relations may be, and most often are, informed by acceptance of a politic of domination, they are simultaneously relations of care and connection. It is this convergence of two contradictory impulses—the urge to promote growth and the urge to inhibit growth—that provides a practical setting for feminist critique, resistance, and transformation.

Growing up in a black, working-class, father-dominated household, I experienced coercive adult male authority as more immediately threatening, as more likely to cause immediate pain than racist oppression or class exploitation. It was equally clear that experiencing exploitation and oppression in the home made one feel all the more powerless when encountering dominating forces outside the home. This is true for many people. If we are unable to resist and end domination in relations where there is care, it seems totally unimaginable that we can resist and end it in other institutionalized relations of power. If we cannot convince the mothers and/or fathers who care not to humiliate and degrade us, how can we imagine convincing or resisting an employer, a lover, a stranger who systematically humiliates and degrades?

Feminist effort to end patriarchal domination should be of primary concern precisely because it insists on the eradication of exploitation and oppression in the family context and in all other intimate relationships. It is that political movement which most radically addresses the person—the personal—citing the need for transformation of self, of relationships, so that we might be better able to act in a revolutionary manner, challenging and resisting domination, transforming the world outside the self. Strategically, feminist movement should be a central component of all other liberation struggles because it challenges each of us to alter our person, our personal engagement (either as victims or perpetrators or both) in a system of domination.

Feminism, as liberation struggle, must exist apart from and as a part of the larger struggle to eradicate domination in all its forms. We must understand that patriarchal domination shares an ideological foundation with racism and other forms of group oppression, that there is no hope that it can be eradicated while these systems remain intact. This knowledge should consistently inform the direction of feminist theory and practice. Unfortunately, racism and class elitism among women has frequently led to the suppression and distortion of this connection so that it is now necessary for feminist thinkers to critique and revise much feminist theory and the direction of feminist movement. This effort at revision is perhaps most evident in the current widespread acknowledgement that sexism, racism, and class exploitation constitute interlocking systems of domination—that sex, race, and class, and not sex alone, determine the nature of any female's identity, status, and circumstance, the degree to which she will or will not be dominated, the extent to which she will have the power to dominate.

While acknowledgement of the complex nature of woman's status (which has been most impressed upon everyone's consciousness by radical women of color) is a significant corrective, it is only a starting point. It provides a frame of reference which must serve as the basis for thoroughly altering and revising feminist theory and practice. It challenges and calls us to re-think popular assumptions about the nature of feminism that have had the deepest impact on a large majority of women, on mass consciousness. It radically calls into question the notion of a fundamentally common female experience which has been seen as the prerequisite for our coming together, for political unity. Recognition of the inter-connectedness of sex, race, and class highlights the diversity of experience, compelling redefinition of the terms for unity. If women do not share "common oppression," what then can serve as a basis for our coming together?

Unlike many feminist comrades, I believe women and men must share a common understanding—a basic knowledge of what feminism is—if it is ever to be a powerful mass-based political movement. In *Feminist Theory: from margin to center*, I suggest that defining feminism broadly as "a movement to end sexism and sexist oppression" would enable us to have a common political goal. We would then have a basis on which to build solidarity. Multiple and contradictory definitions of feminism create confusion and undermine the effort to construct feminist movement so that it addresses everyone. Sharing a common goal does not imply that women and men will not have radically divergent perspectives on how that goal might be reached. Because each individual starts the process of engagement in feminist struggle at a unique level of awareness, very real differences in experience, perspective, and knowledge make developing varied strategies for participation and transformation a necessary agenda.

Feminist thinkers engaged in radically revisioning central tenets of feminist thought must continually emphasize the importance of sex, race and class as factors which *together* determine the social construction of femaleness, as it has been so deeply ingrained in the consciousness of many women active in feminist movement that gender is the sole factor determining destiny. However, the work of education for critical consciousness (usually called consciousness-raising) cannot end there. Much feminist consciousness-raising has in the past focused on identifying the particular ways men oppress and exploit women. Using the paradigm of sex, race, and class means that the focus does not begin with men and what they do to women, but rather with women working to identify both individually and collectively the specific character of our social identity.

Imagine a group of women from diverse backgrounds coming together to talk about feminism. First they concentrate on working out their status in terms of sex, race, and class using this as the standpoint from which they begin discussing patriarchy or their particular relations with individual men. Within the old frame of reference, a discussion might consist solely of talk about their experiences as victims in relationship to male oppressors. Two women—one poor, the other quite wealthy—might describe the process by which they have suffered physical abuse by male partners and find certain commonalities which might serve as a basis for bonding. Yet if these same two women engaged in a discussion of class, not only would the social construction and expression of femaleness differ, so too would their ideas about how to confront and change their circumstances. Broadening the discussion to include an analysis of race and class would expose many additional differences even as commonalities emerged.

Clearly the process of bonding would be more complex, yet this broader discussion might enable the sharing of perspectives and strategies for change that would enrich rather than diminish our understanding of gender. While feminists have increasingly given "lip service" to the idea of diversity, we have not developed strategies of communication and inclusion that allow for the successful enactment of this feminist vision.

Small groups are no longer the central place for feminist consciousness-raising. Much feminist education for critical consciousness takes place in Women's Studies classes or at conferences which focus on gender. Books are a primary source of education which means that already masses of people who do not read have no access. The separation of grassroots ways of sharing feminist thinking across kitchen tables from the spheres where much of that thinking is generated, the academy, undermines feminist movement. It would further feminist movement if new feminist thinking could be once again shared in small group contexts, integrating critical analysis with discussion of personal experience. It would be useful to promote anew the small group setting as an arena for education for critical consciousness, so that women and men might come together in neighborhoods and communities to discuss feminist concerns.

Small groups remain an important place for education for critical consciousness for several reasons. An especially important aspect of the small group setting is the emphasis on communicating feminist thinking, feminist theory, in a manner that can be easily understood. In small groups, individuals do not need to be equally literate or literate at all because the information is primarily shared through conversation, in dialogue which is necessarily a liberatory expression. (Literacy should be a goal for feminists even as we ensure that it not become a requirement for participation in feminist education.) Reforming small groups would subvert the appropriation of feminist thinking by a select group of academic women and men, usually white, usually from privileged class backgrounds.

Small groups of people coming together to engage in feminist discussion, in dialectical struggle make a space where the "personal is political" as a starting point for education for critical consciousness can be extended to include politicization of the self that focusses on creating understanding of the ways sex, race, and class together determine our individual lot and our collective experience. It would further feminist movement if many well known feminist thinkers would participate in small groups, critically reexamining ways their works might be changed by incorporating broader perspectives. All efforts at self-transformation challenge us to engage in ongoing, critical self-examination and reflection about feminist practice, about how we live in the world. This individual commitment, when coupled with engagement in collective discussion, provides a space for critical feedback which strengthens our efforts to change and make ourselves new. It is in this commitment to feminist principles in our words and deeds that the hope of feminist revolution lies.

Working collectively to confront difference, to expand our awareness of sex, race, and class as interlocking systems of domination, of the ways we reinforce and perpetuate these structures, is the context in which we learn the true meaning of solidarity. It is this work that must be the foundation of feminist movement. Without it, we cannot effectively resist patriarchal domination; without it, we remain estranged and alienated from one another. Fear of painful confrontation often leads women and men active in feminist movement to avoid rigorous critical encounter, yet if we cannot engage dialectically in a committed, rigorous, humanizing manner, we cannot hope to change the world. True politicization—coming to critical consciousness—is a difficult, "trying" process, one that demands that we give up set ways of thinking and being, that we shift our paradigms, that we open ourselves to the unknown, the unfamiliar. Undergoing this process, we learn what it means to struggle and in this effort we experience the dignity and integrity of being that comes with revolutionary change. If we do not change our consciousness, we cannot change our actions or demand change from others.

Our renewed commitment to a rigorous process of education for critical consciousness will determine the shape and direction of future feminist movement. Until new perspectives are created, we cannot be living symbols of the power of feminist thinking. Given the privileged lot of many leading feminist thinkers, both in terms of status, class, and race, it is harder these days to convince women of the primacy of this process of politicization. More and more, we seem to form select interest groups composed of individuals who share similar perspectives. This limits our capacity to engage in critical discussion. It is difficult to involve women in new processes of feminist politicization because so many of us think that identifying men as the enemy, resisting male domination, gaining equal access to power and privilege is the end of feminist movement. Not only is it not the end, it is not even the place we want revitalized feminist movement to begin. We want to begin as women seriously addressing ourselves, not solely in relation to men, but in relation to an entire structure of domination of which patriarchy is one part. While the struggle to eradicate sexism and sexist oppression is and should be the primary thrust of feminist movement, to prepare ourselves politically for this effort we must first learn how to be in solidarity, how to struggle with one another.

Only when we confront the realities of sex, race, and class, the ways they divide us, make us different, stand us in opposition, and work to reconcile and resolve these issues will we be able to participate in the making of feminist revolution, in the transformation of the world. Feminism, as Charlotte Bunch emphasizes again and again in *Passionate Politics,* is a transformational politics, a struggle against domination wherein the effort is to change ourselves as well as structures. Speaking about the struggle to confront difference, Bunch asserts:

A crucial point of the process is understanding that reality does not look the same from different people's perspective. It is not surprising that one way feminists have come to understand about differences has been through the love of a person from another culture or race. It takes persistence and motivation—which love often engenders—to get beyond ones ethnocentric assumptions and really learn about other perspectives. In this process and while seeking to eliminate oppression, we also discover new possibilities and insights that come from the experience and survival of other peoples.

Embedded in the commitment to feminist revolution is the challenge to love. Love can be and is an important source of empowerment when we struggle to confront issues of sex, race, and class. Working together to identify and face our differences—to face the ways we dominate and are dominated—to change our actions, we need a mediating force that can sustain us so that we are not broken in this process, so that we do not despair.

Not enough feminist work has focussed on documenting and sharing ways individuals confront differences constructively and successfully. Women and men need to know what is on the other side of the pain experienced in politicization. We need detailed accounts of the ways our lives are fuller and richer as we change and grow politically, as we learn to live each moment as committed feminists, as comrades working to end domination. In reconceptualizing and reformulating strategies for future feminist movement, we need to concentrate on the politicization of love, not just in the context of talking about victimization in intimate relationships, but in a critical discussion where love can be understood as a powerful force that challenges and resists domination. As we work to be loving, to create a culture that celebrates life, that makes love possible, we move against dehumanization, against domination. In *Pedagogy of the Oppressed,* Paulo Freire evokes this power of love, declaring:

> I am more and more convinced that true revolutionaries must perceive the revolution, because of its creative and liberating nature, as an act of love. For me, the revolution, which is not possible without a theory of revolution—and therefore science—is not irreconcilable with love...The distortion imposed on the word "love" by the capitalist world cannot prevent the revolution from being essentially loving in character, nor can it prevent the revolutionaries from affirming their love of life.

That aspect of feminist revolution that calls women to love womanness, that calls men to resist dehumanizing concepts of masculinity, is an essential part of our struggle. It is the process by which we move from seeing ourselves as objects to acting as subjects. When women and men understand that working to eradicate patriarchal domination is a struggle rooted in the longing to make a world where everyone can live fully and freely, then we know our work to be a gesture of love. Let us draw upon that love to heighten our awareness, deepen our compassion, intensify our courage, and strengthen our commitment.

Women's Psychological Development

Implications for Psychotherapy[1]

Carol Gilligan

A PERSISTENT OBSERVATION

Beginning in the nineteenth century, psychiatrists and psychologists have consistently marked adolescence as a particularly difficult time in women's development—a time when girls "are more liable to suffer" (Henry Maudsley, 1879, cited in Showalter, 1985, p. 130). And among the girls who suffer in adolescence are those who seem most psychologically vital. Elaine Showalter quotes the following passage from Josef Breuer as illustrative:

> Adolescents who are later to become hysterical are for the most part lively, gifted, and full of intellectual interests before they fall ill. Their energy of will is often remarkable. They include girls who get out of bed at night so as secretly to carry out some study that their parents have forbidden for fear of their overworking. The capacity for forming sound judgments is certainly not more abundant in them than in other people; but it is rare to find in them simple, dull intellectual inertia or stupidity. (p. 158)

Michelle Fine (1986), studying high school drop outs at the end of the twentieth century, notes that the girls who drop out of inner-city schools—at the time they drop out—are among the least depressed and the brightest. Lively, intelligent, and willful girls at both ends of the century and the social class spectrum thus find themselves in trouble at adolescence. Anne Petersen (1988), reviewing the literature on adolescence, pulls together a series of findings which provide further evidence that girls are likely to experience psychological problems at this time. Adolescence witnesses a marked increase in episodes of depression, eating disorders, poor body image, suicidal thoughts and gestures, and a fall in girls' sense of self-worth. Petersen's review extends the impressions of clinicians across the century that girls at adolescence experience a kind of psychic constraint or narrowing (Freud, 1905, 1933; Horney, 1926; Miller, 1984; Thompson, 1964) and suffer from a range of depressive symptoms, dissociative processes, and "as if" phenomena (Demitrack et al., 1990; Deutsch, 1944; Rutter, 1986).

Epidemiological studies offer further evidence. Elder and Caspi (1990) report that when families are under stress—whether from marital conflict, economic hardship, or fathers going off to war—the children who are most psychologically at risk are boys in childhood and girls at adolescence. Block (1990) reports a sudden drop in girls' resiliency around the age of eleven, with no corresponding finding for boys. Seligman (1991) finds that "girls, at least up to puberty, are more noticeably optimistic than boys," (p. 125) and concludes that "whatever causes the huge difference in depression in adulthood, with women twice as vulnerable as men, it does not have its roots in childhood. Something must happen at or shortly after puberty that causes a flip-flop—and hits girls very hard indeed" (pp. 149-150). And a recent national survey (Greenberg-Lake Analysis Group, 1991) finds that white girls tend to experience a drop in feelings of self-worth around the age of eleven, Latinas experience a more precipitous drop a few years later—around the beginning of high school—and black girls tend to sustain their feelings of self-worth but at the expense, perhaps, of dissociating themselves from school and disagreeing publicly with their teachers.

Taken together, this evidence suggests that girls face a psychological crisis at the time of adolescence—a crisis to which some girls respond by devaluing themselves and feeling themselves to be worthless, while others disagree publicly and dissociate themselves from institutions which devalue them—in this case, the schools. Both solutions, however, are costly for girls. Yet despite this remarkable convergence of clinical observation, developmental findings, and epidemiological data, pointing repeatedly to a striking asymmetry between girls' and boys' development—and one which has clear implications for preventing suffering and fostering development—this persistent observation of difference has, until recently, remained unexplored and unexplained theoretically (see Brown & Gilligan, 1990b; Gilligan, 1990a; Gilligan, Brown, & Rogers, 1990; Rogers, 1990).

GIRLS

Sounds, touching memory, filtering through theory, collecting, like water slowly filling a basin and then suddenly overflowing or rain falling steadily onto the afternoon streets of childhood—girls' voices, shouting, screaming, whispering, speaking, singing, running up and down the octaves of feelings. And the silence. Faces calm, eyes steady, ears open, girls sitting in a circle and then suddenly rising—like a flock of birds. Taking off and then settling, as if by prearrangement. And yet, nothing has been said, nothing is spoken. Only girls' faces and bodies taking in, registering the tides of daily living, following the drifts of thoughts and feelings, picking up the currents of relationship. I wade in.

It is Tuesday afternoon in the beginning of November—just after Halloween. The Theater, Writing, and Outing Club is meeting for the second year—part of a project designed by three women to learn from girls about girls' experience in the time when childhood turns into adolescence and to offer girls in return our help in sustaining and strengthening their voices, their resistance, their courage and their relationships.[2] Ten girls, ages ten and eleven—three African-American, five European-American, one Asian-American, one with a parent from India—and three women (Annie Rogers and myself—European-American psychologists, and Normi Noel, a Canadian-born actor, theater director and voice teacher) stream into the science room of the public school which the girls are attending. The girls have decided this year to teach us what they know.

Two girls stand side-by-side in the center of the clearing we have created. Two other girls—"their thoughts"—stand behind them. The drama begins. One girl says that she wants to play with the other; the other clearly does not want to. As the two girls face into this relational impasse, their "thoughts" articulate the stream of their consciousness—a brilliant rendering of each girls' thoughts and feelings in response to what is happening between them. Finally, the thoughts take over, and speaking now directly to one another, set into motion feelings and thoughts which initially seemed fixed, unchangeable and settled, and in doing so begin to work out the relational problem.

What girls know about relationships and feelings unfolded steadily through our weekly meetings in the second year of the group. The immediate grasp of psychological processes, the keeping of a watchful eye and open ear constantly tuned to the relational surround which we had observed in girls and heard in interview settings (Brown & Gilligan, 1990b; Gilligan, Brown,

& Rogers, 1990), now was dramatized directly for us by girls who seemed to want to leave no question in our minds about the strength of their voices and the depths of their knowing and the intensity of their desire for honest relationships between us. The week Normi introduced neutral masks from Greek theater by demonstrating how a face can mask feelings, each girl, going around one by one in a circle, turned her face into a mask and then named the feelings in the mask and the feelings which the mask was hiding. The feelings masked were feeling "ordinary, nothing special" (covered over by a mask that was "snooty") and feeling angry, not wanting to be with someone, hating someone, being bored (covered over by masks that were "nice," "smiling" and "interested"). "But Normi," eleven year old Joan says at the end of the exercise, "people always mask their feelings."

Girls' facility in turning their faces into the faces of nice, smiling and interested girls was coupled by their ear for false voices—especially the false voices of women in false relationships. On Halloween, when Annie and I brought pieces of costumes, including angel wings for "someone too good to be true," the girls, putting on the wings, instantly raised their voices to the high-pitched breathiness of good-woman conversation, dramatizing both the persona of the too-good-to-be-true woman and the mechanism of disconnection—the use of voice to cover rather than to convey thoughts and feelings and thus to close rather than to open a channel of connection between people. Separating their voices from the well of feelings and thoughts which lies deep in the body, girls did precise imitations of women's greeting rituals and social gestures and in doing so revealed how well they know the timbre and pitch of false female friendships.

Daily, girls take in evidence from the human world around them—the world which is open for psychological observation all day long, every day, "for free." And in this way, girls often see what is not supposed to be seen and hear what supposedly was unspoken. Like anthropologists, they pick up the culture; like sociologists, they observe race, class and sex differences; like psychologists, they come to know what is happening beneath the surface; like naturalists, they collect their observations, laying them out, sorting them out, discussing them between themselves in an ongoing conversation about relationships and people which goes on, on and off, for much of the day, every day.

Eleven-year-old Stephanie, for example, describes herself as a radio—capable of tuning herself into a range of other people:

Sometimes I feel I am a radio. On my dial is one [station] that's sad songs, one that's happy songs, one that's sort of no caring songs....And then if I am with Rita, I turn to the happy songs and the giggly songs; when I am with Irene, I turn to the sad songs and the real songs. And it's just like, I tune myself in.[3]

This relational capacity may well underlie the psychological resiliency which girls show throughout childhood—an ability to tune themselves into the relational world, to connect with different people.

But girls, living intensely in relationships, often face difficult relational problems. Stephanie explains:

I totally disagree with the song, "Don't cry out loud." I totally disagree with it. You should tell everybody how you feel, if it won't hurt their feelings, of course. Just like talking to stuffed animals or things; it just helps you get out your pains....And just after you cry enough—like into your bunny's soft tummy, you just start to love them and you really grow to love them.

Stephanie is clear about the nature of the problem: You should tell people how you feel, if it won't hurt their feelings. But her solution is deeply ambiguous. Telling her pains to her stuffed animals, she leaves it unclear as to whether she comes to love the animals or the people from whom she has kept her sadness.

In this light, it was surprising to discover the readiness with which younger girls—seven and eight-year-olds—tell people how they feel, mark relational violations, and openly respond to what is happening in relationships, even when their response leads them to experience painful feelings or cause others to be upset.[4] This relational honesty is vividly caught in Lyn Mikel Brown's (1989) example of Diane, an eight-year-old whistle-blower in the relational world. When Diane is asked about a time when someone was not being listened to, she speaks of her experience at dinner when her brother and sister interrupt her and "steal [her] mother's attention." Diane's solution is to bring a whistle to dinner and to blow the whistle when she is interrupted. Mother, brother, and sister, she reports, suddenly stopped talking and turned to her, at which point she said, "in a normal voice, 'that's much nicer.'" Karin, her classmate, walks out of the room on the second day when the teacher ignores her hand and calls on others "to do all the hard problems." Karin (see Brown, 1989; Brown & Gilligan, 1990b) knows that people seeing her in the hall will think that she is in trouble, but she also knows "I wasn't in trouble. I just couldn't take it. So I guess I just left." Asked if her teacher knows why she left, Karin makes a fine distinction between knowing and listening, saying "She wouldn't listen to me, but I told her, so I guess she knows."

Girls' willingness to voice painful relational realities is rawly evident as eight-year-old Jesse, in Brown's description (see Brown, *Women, Girls & Psychotherapy*, 1991) tells of the time when she went to play with a friend and the friend had another friend over and they would not play with Jesse. Jesse told her friend that she wasn't having any fun "just sitting there" and that she would go home if they did not play with her, at which point her friend, she reports, said "Just go home." In contrast, Tanya, at thirteen, reveals the treachery which flows from not speaking about painful relational realities. She and another friend backed out of a plan to go to camp with a third girl who was, Tanya says, "supposedly my best friend." When the girl discovers what has happened and asks if she can go to the other camp with them, Tanya says to her, "If you want to; it's up to you," while being perfectly clear that "I didn't want her to come." Tanya feels trapped because "I can't say so….I can't say anything to her. Because she'll be hurt, so I have no idea what to do."

Victoria, at eleven, in the face of such relational treachery, opts for radical isolation—"independence from everyone." Describing her withdrawal from relationships in an effort to stay with her own experience, she is unequivocal in her judgment that what she is doing is harmful: "I try to build, it's kind of bad really to do it, but I try to build a little shield."

～

Learning from girls what girls are doing at the time they reach adolescence, I mark the places that are both familiar to me and surprising. And notice the sensations which bring back memories, like the feeling of moving without hesitation and the sound of a voice speaking directly without qualification— the open sounds of voices coming directly from the center of girls' bodies. Picking up from girls the feeling of moving freely in a girl's body, I find myself running with girls as I remember running in childhood.

And listening to girls' voices, I also begin to listen with girls to the voices which they are taking in. Opening their ears to the world, listening in, eavesdropping on the daily conversations, girls take in voices which silence their relational knowledge. And as their experience and their bodies change with adolescence, girls are more apt to discount the experiences of their childhood or to place a cover over their childhood world so that it remains intact. Yet, closing the door on their childhood, girls are in danger of knocking out what are in effect the T-cells of their psychological immune system—their seemingly effortless ability to tune into the relational world. Voices which intentionally or unintentionally interfere with girls' knowing, or encourage girls to silence themselves, keep girls from picking up or bringing out into the open a series of relational violations which they are acutely keyed into, such as not being listened to, being ignored, being left out, being insulted, being criticized, being spoken about meanly, being humiliated or made fun of, being whispered about, being talked about behind one's back, being betrayed by a friend, or being physically overpowered or hurt.

Tanya, at sixteen, writes a letter to Lyn Mikel Brown—the director of the Harvard-Laurel Project—about her feelings in response to a paper which Lyn and I had written (a paper which she and Lyn had discussed together at some length) (see Brown & Gilligan, 1990a, 1990b). She speaks of "a voice inside" her which "has been muffled." She explains, "The voice that stands up for what I believe in has been buried deep inside of me." Tanya wants to be in honest relationship with people. And yet, taking in what she is hearing about perfect girls whom people seem to love and admire, Tanya finds herself paying attention to voices which impede her relational desires. "I do not want the image of a 'perfect girl' to hinder myself from being a truly effective human being," she writes. "Yet, I still want to be nice, and I never want to cause any problems."

When Nina—a gifted writer—turns twelve, the word "nice" spreads through her conversation, covering over a world of feelings, as the word "interesting" covers thoughts.[5] These two words, which gain currency in girls' conversation, dull the human world which girls live in, and the magnitude of this loss is evident in the change in Nina's description of her stories.

At eleven, Nina tells me that she is writing a story about "someone during the Civil War" and making her story "a little bit sad," because when the father goes to war, the girl "is really upset." Nina explains:

He talks to her before he goes, about how he feels about leaving and that he is just as worried as she is, or more worried and more scared....And, you know, she feels like he's never going to come back, which is possible, but, you know, it's not a fact yet. So she has a very, um, a very strange feeling sometimes.

I ask Nina about this strange feeling, and she offers an extraordinary description of the ways in which feelings layer or cascade, one lying over another or one falling into another like anger lies over sorrow which lies next to shock or surprise, all falling into an ongoing stream of upset feelings, calling forth comfort in the presence of the steady hum of fear and continuing surprise at realizing connection—that "he could feel like this too." Nina says, continuing to describe her story,

> Before he left, she realized that he was not, um, totally powerful, but she didn't, um, feel angry at him for that, but she felt very, um, very sorry, sort of, very sorry for him and very shocked or surprised mainly and still upset that he was leaving. And, um, he was trying to comfort her when he told her about, um, about his, his own fears of going, but really she was just mainly surprised and she hadn't realized that he could feel like this, too...

I ask, "Why hadn't she known this?" And Nina continues her precise laying out of people's feelings and thoughts in response to one another—an exquisite, naturalistic psychological narration of change occurring through relationship, which then suddenly comes to a stop, as the father leaves for the war and the girl, responding to his wish that she not make it any harder for him, stops feeling upset or at least stops showing her upset feelings:

> He had always been there for her, you know. She had been, um, she'd been hurt...and she had been humiliated because she was a girl. And he always understood her and she was very close to him....Her siblings thought it was really brave of him to do it [enlist] right away, but she knew that, he was, he just, if he waited any longer then he wouldn't be able to do it, he wouldn't have enough courage to do it.

And how did she know that?

> She knew because of the way be talked to her...that he was feeling really scared and upset...and he didn't want her to make it any harder or anything. After that, she didn't get so upset, or she didn't show it.

Girls around eleven often come to know their fathers as part of the human world which they take in and listen to, and thus they discover what is often unspoken in this culture: men's humanness—men's vulnerability. Annie Rogers (1990) describes girls' "embodied courage," noticing that voice and body, play and knowledge, tend to be joined in girls prior to adolescence, and that this joining issues forth in a seemingly "ordinary courage"—girls' readiness, in accordance with an old meaning of the word "courage," to "speak one's mind by telling all one's heart" (Rogers, 1990). Courage, however, more often connotes, especially for men, an absence of fear and an overcoming of vulnerability—a psychological and physical disembodiment.

This disconnection is exemplified by the father in Nina's Civil War story as he hurriedly covers over the vulnerability he has exposed, overriding his fear in his determination to do the right thing and enlist in the army. But it also seeps into Nina's stories, so that like the daughter in the story who covers over her feelings so as not to make it any harder, Nina at twelve writes as if she did not know what she knows about people and about psychological processes. In fact, her stories at twelve are less about how people feel than about how things "would feel" if they were "able to see"—like a pen with its cap off. In one story, a lesson in love is reduced to pure adventure as a girl who,

is trying to, well, she falls in love with this boy...and they have these adventures. It starts when they're at a dance and then when she has to leave, his car gets stolen and then they go to the gang....This group has stolen it...and he has to fight one of the guys and then they set off in the car and there's a storm and the car stalls and they have to walk and things like that.

The relational world which Nina previously described is gone, seemingly without leaving a trace. And along with it, Nina, the writer of the Civil War Story, seems to have disappeared. "It's really a good story," she says of her romance adventure, "I can tell. It's a lot better than the ones I wrote a couple of years ago anyway."

Nina's stories about how things would feel if they could see are winning prizes in local story-writing contests, and Nina at twelve dreams of becoming a famous, prize-winning writer or at least winning scholarship money for college. What she loves most—writing and reading—has value in the eyes of other people, and to sell her stories on the open market, she has to pay attention to what others want and value.

Focusing more at age twelve on the value of her stories in the eyes of others than on her own pleasure in writing, which she described at age eleven, Nina seems to have diverted her attention from psychological processes to questions of judgment. Now the people in her stories change inexplicably—shifting from bad to good. For example, in one story "a queen who's really a bad queen" gets assassinated on the anniversary of her coronation. But three generations later, she becomes "a beautiful, wonderful queen." Sensing with me that something is missing in this story—some understanding of or even interest in how the queen changes—Nina offers by way of explanation the following observation: "It's just the way memory covers up the bad things."

"Cover up," girls are told as they reach adolescence, daily, in innumerable ways. Cover your body, cover your feelings, cover your relationships, cover your knowing, cover your voice, and perhaps above all, cover desire (see also Debold & Tolman, 1991; Debold, *Women, Girls & Psychotherapy*, 1991, Tolman, *Women, Girls & Psychotherapy*, 1991). And the wall that keeps memory from seeping through these covers may be the wall with the sign which labels body, feelings, relationships, knowing, voice and desire as bad.

A Theory of Development

If psychological health consists, most simply, of staying in relationship with oneself, with others, and with the world, then psychological problems signify relational crises: losing touch with one's thoughts and feelings, being isolated from others, cut off from reality. The zen of development which makes human growth such a fascinating journey is that relationships which are the channels of growth are also the avenues through which people are psychically wounded. Vulnerability—the opening to experience which is at the heart of development—thus always carries with it the risk of being seriously hurt or diminished, and this play of opening and closing, embodiment and disembodiment, is reflected in the two meanings of the word "courage" (see Rogers, 1990).

The evidence that boys are more likely than girls to suffer psychologically in early childhood whereas girls are more at risk for developing psychological difficulties in adolescence calls for explanation and implies a revision—a new way of speaking about psychological development. This difference, I will suggest, also contains a hope for transformation.

Learning from girls about the relational crisis which girls experience as they approach adolescence—a place where development seems impassable— I offer as a working thesis that adolescence is a comparable time in women's psychological development to early childhood for men. It precipitates a relational crisis which poses an impasse in psychological development, a place where for the sake of relationship (with other people and with the world), one must take oneself out of relationship. Because this separation of self from relationship is psychologically untenable and also essentially confusing (if one is not in one's relationships, then the word "relationships" loses meaning), this division must be resisted and some compromise arrived at.

Freud (1899/1900) suggested as much for boys when he spoke about the "oedipus complex" as a turning point in boys' early childhood and also as the foundation for neurotic suffering and for civilization. The pressure girls are under as they reach adolescence and girls' experience of severe relational crisis similarly marks a turning point or watershed in girls' development. But girls' relationship to the culture is different, and also girls at adolescence are at a very different point in their own development than boys in early childhood—with far more experience of relationships and also perhaps with less incentive to give up relationship as the cost, ironically, of entering society. Consequently, women's psychological development—as others have observed (see Miller, 1986)—is profoundly transformational.

The relational crisis of boys' early childhood and of girls' adolescence is marked by a struggle to stay in relationship—a healthy resistance to disconnections which are psychologically wounding (from the body, from feelings, from relationships, from reality). This struggle takes a variety of forms, but at its center is a resistance to loss—to giving up the reality of relationships for idealizations or, as it is sometimes called, identifications. As young boys are pressured to take on images of heroes, or superheroes, as the grail which informs their quest to inherit their birthright or their manhood, so girls are pressed at adolescence to take on images of perfection as the model of the pure or perfectly good woman: the woman whom everyone will promote and value and want to be with (see Gilligan, 1990a; Brown & Gilligan, 1990b; Jack, 1991).

Children's healthy resistance to disconnection—the intense human desire for relationship which now is generally taken as foundational of psychic life— thus tends to lead children into a political struggle. Boys in early childhood resist leaving the comforts and pleasures, as well as the discomforts and pains, of their relational life: They want to stay with the people who have been with them. And girls at adolescence resist leaving the rich relational tapestry of their childhood. This resistance calls into question the prevailing order of social relationships and calls forth counter-pressures to enforce that order in the name, currently, of psychological health, as well as for the sake of civilization.

Thus at the time of early childhood for boys, when masculinity seems in question, and in early adolescence for girls, when femininity seems on the line, a healthy resistance to disconnections which turns into a political struggle comes under pressure to turn into a psychological resistance—that is, a resistance to knowing what is happening and an impulse to cover the struggle.

Here, the differences observed over the century between the times of seemingly heightened vulnerability or openness to growth and wounding in boys' and girls' lives contains a promise of transformation. If girls can sustain in adolescence a resistance which is more easily overwhelmed in boys' childhood, then women's psychological development will change the prevailing order of relationships. Compared with boys, whose desires for relationship, although strongly felt, tend to be less articulate, more inchoate, more laced with early loss and terror, girls' desires for relationship, leavened through years of childhood experience, tend to be hardier, more easily spoken, better known, more finely textured or differentiated and consequently less frightening although no less painful. Girls' healthy resistance to disconnection which springs up at the edge of adolescence as girls approach a culture of relationships which has been built largely by men thus calls into question what has been accepted as the canonical story of human development: the story which takes separation for granted, the story which seems logical, the story which rejects the possibility of honest or genuine relationship. [...]

NOTES

1. I am most grateful for the support and encouragement of Joan Lipsitz and the Lilly Endowment, the late Lawrence Cremin and the Spencer Foundation, and Wendy Puriefoy and the Boston Foundation. The work described in this paper would not have been possible without grants from the Geraldine Rockefeller Dodge Foundation, the Joseph S. Klingenstein Foundation, the Cleveland Foundation, the Gund Foundation, and Mrs. Marilyn Brachman Hoffman. Lyn Mikel Brown, the director of the Harvard-Laurel Project, and Annie Rogers, the director of the "Strengthening Healthy Resistance and Courage in Girls" project have contributed centrally to my understanding of girls' voices and my thinking about women's psychological development. I wish to thank Lyn and Annie, the other members of the Harvard Project on the Psychology of Women and the Development of Girls—Elizabeth Debold, Judy Dorney, Barbara Miller, Mark Tappan, Jill Taylor, Deborah Tolman and Janie Ward, Sarah Hanson—the project assistant, and all of the girls who

have joined with us in this work and taught us about girls' experience.

2. The Theater, Writing, and Outing Club is a central part of the project, "Strengthening Healthy Resistance and Courage in Girls." This prevention project is designed to help girls sustain their knowledge of relationships and the clarity of their voices into adolescence through theater and writing exercises created to strengthen and expand the range of girls' voices and girls' relationships and outings designed to encourage girls' active responses to the natural and cultural worlds. The project works centrally through developing healthy relationships between girls and women.

3. Stephanie was interviewed by Dr. Sharry Langdale in 1981, along with nine other eleven-year-old girls, and these interviews contributed substantially to a growing interest in the voices of eleven-year-old girls within the ongoing Harvard Project.

4. My analysis of Diane, Karin, Jesse and Victoria draws heavily on Lyn Mikel Brown's work on girls' narratives of relationships (Brown, 1989, *Women, Girls & Psychotheraphy*, 1991; see also Brown & Gilligan, 1990b).

5. In writing about Nina, I draw on conversations with Annie Rogers with whom I read Nina's interviews, as well as on the insights of Kathryn Geismar, Amy Grillo, Sarah Ingersoll, Kate O'Neill, and Heather Thompson—members of the research group on the "Strengthening Healthy Resistance and Courage in Girls" project.

REFERENCES

Belenky, M., Clinchy, B., Goldberger, N., & Tarule, J. (1986). *Women's ways of knowing: the development of self voice, and mind.* New York: Basic.

Block, J. (1990, October). Ego resilience through time: Antecedents and ramifications. In *Resilience and Psychological health.* Symposium of the Boston Psychoanalynic Society, Boston, MA.

Brown, L.M. (1989). *Narratives of relationship: The development of a care voice in girls ages 7 to 16.* Unpublished doctoral dissertation, Harvard University Graduate School of Education, Cambridge, MA.

Brown, L.M. (in press). A problem of vision: The development of voice and relational knowledge in girls ages 7 to 16. *Women's Studies Quarterly.*

Brown, L.M. (1991). Telling a girl's life. *Women & Therapy.*

Brown, L.M., & Gilligan, C. (1990a, August). Listening for self and relational voices: A responsive/resisting reader's guide. In M. Franklin (Chair), *Literary theory as a guide to psychological analysis.* Symposium conducted at the annual meeting of the American Psychological Association, Boston, MA.

Brown, L. M., & Gilligan. C. (1990b). Meeting at the crossroads: The psychology of women and the development of girls. Manuscript submitted for publication.

Debold, E. (1991). The body at play. *Women & Therapy.*

Debold, E., & Tolman, D. (1991, January). Made in whose image? Paper presented at the Ms. Foundation's Fourth Annual Women Managing Wealth Conference, New York.

Demitrack, M., Putnam, F., Brewerton, T., Brandt, H., & Gold, P. (1990). Relation of clinical variables to dissociative phenomena in eating disorders. *The American Journal of Psychiatry, 147*(9), 1184-1188.

Deutsch, H. (1944). *Psychology of women,* Vol. 1. New York: Grune & Stratton.

Elder, G., & Caspi, A. (1990). Studying lives in a changing society: Sociological and personological explorations. In A. Rabin, R. Zucker, R. Emmons, & S. Frank (Eds.), *Studying persons and lives* (pp. 226-228). New York: Springer.

Fine, M. (1986). Why urban adolescents drop into and out of public high school. *Teachers College Record, 87*(3), 393-409.

Freud, S. (1899/1900). The interpretation of dreams. In J. Strachey (Ed. and Trans.), *The standard edition of the complete psychological works of Sigmund Freud* (Vols. IV & V). London: Hogarth Press.

Freud, S. (1933). New introductory lectures on psychoanalysis (Lecture XXXIII: Femininity). In J. Strachey (Ed. and Trans.), *The standard edition of the complete psychological works of Sigmund Freud* (Vol. XXII). London: The Hogarth Press.

Freud, S. (1905). Three essays on the theory of sexuality. In J. Strachey (Ed. and Trans.), *The standard edition of the complete psychological works of Sigmund Freud* (Vol. VII). London: The Hogarth Press.

Gilligan, C. (1982). *In a different voice: Psychological theory and women's development.* Cambridge, MA: Harvard University Press.

Gilligan, C. (1990a). Joining the resistance: Psychology, politics, girls and women. *Michigan Quarterly Review, 29*(4), 501-536.

Gilligan, C. (1990b). Teaching Shakespeare's sister. Notes from the underground of female adolescence. In C. Gilligan, N. Lyons, & T. Hanmer (Eds.), *Making connections: The relational worlds of adolescent* girls at Emma Willard School (pp. 6-29). Cambridge, MA: Harvard University Press.

Gilligan, C., Brown, L.M., & Rogers, A. (1990). Psyche embedded: A place for body, relationships, and culture in personality theory. In A. Rabin, R. Zucker, R. Emmons, & S. Frank (Eds.), *Studying persons and Lives* (pp. 86-147). New York: Springer

Gilligan, C., Lyons, N., & Hanmer, T. (Eds.). (1990). *Making connections: The relational worlds of adolescent girls at Emma Willard School.* Cambridge, MA: Harvard University Press.

Greenberg-Lake Analysis Group Inc. (1991, January). Shortchanging girls, shortchanging America: A nationwide poll to assess self esteem, educational experiences, interest in math and science, and career aspirations of girls and boys ages 9-15. (Available from The American Association of University Women, 515 Second Street NE, Washington, DC 20002).

Hancock, E. (1989). *The girl within: A groundbreaking new approach to female identity.* New York: Fawcett Columbia.

Homey, K. (1926). The flight from womanhood. *International Journal of Psychoanalysis, 7,* 324-339.

Jack, D. (1991). *Silencing the self: depression and women.* Cambridge, MA: Harvard University Press.

Kincaid, J. (1985). *Annie John.* New York: Farrar Straus Giroux.

Kingston, M. H. (1977). *The Woman Warrior.* New York: Alfred A. Knopf.

Miller, J. B. (1984). The development of women's sense of self. *Work in Progress, No. 12.* Wellesley, MA: Stone Center Working Papers Series.

Miller, J. B. (1986). *Toward a New Psychology of Women* (second edition). Boston: Beacon.

Miller, J. B. (1988). Connections, disconnections and violations. *Work in Progress, No. 33.* Wellesley, MA: Stone Center Working Papers Series.

Petersen, A. (1988). Adolescent development. *Annual Review of Psychology 39,* 583-607.

Rich, A. (1979). *On lies, secrets, and silence: Selected prose, 1966-1978.* New York: Norton.

Rogers, A. (1990). The development of courage in girls and women. Unpublished manuscript, Harvard University, Project on the Psychology of Women and the Development of Girls, Cambridge, MA.

Rogers, A. (1991). A feminist poetics of psychotherapy. *Women & Therapy.*

Rutter, M. (1986). The developmental psychopathology of depression: Issues and perspectives. In M. Rutter, C. Izzard, & P. Read (Eds.), *Depression in young people: Developmental and clinical perspectives*. New York: Guilford Press.

Seligman, M. E. P. (1991). *Learned optimism*. New York: Random House.

Showalter, E. (1985). *The Female Malady*. New York: Penguin.

Stone Center Working Papers Series. *Work in Progress*. Wellesley, MA: Wellesley College.

Stern, Lori. (1991). Disavowing the self in female adolescence. *Women & Therapy*.

Thompson, C. (1964). *Interpersonal psychoanalysis*. New York: Basic.

Tolman, D. (1991). Adolescent girls, women and sexuality: Discerning dilemmas of desire. *Women & Therapy*.

Letters to My Father

Sally Smits

Dear Dad,

This first letter is full of heart and hope and disclaimers. Beginning always means that I brim with doubt, but I'll tell you what I know. I know that I am a lucky daughter, that you've been with me and behind me, helping but not holding me back, and you've been doing it all along. I'm not writing to you to try to make you understand something, my ideologies or experiences, my stances or ideas. I'm writing to you because I think you will understand, and I trust your opinion, your thoughts and ideas and mind-workings. I want to explain where I'm standing, but not for defenses or rationalizations. I just want to talk to you.

And I'm writing, this way, because you have always believed that I could build with words, that I could write books, that I could change my days and thoughts into vivid pages. I have not always kept that confidence you have in me—I have struggled and doubted and hurt, and I have not always believed what you told me. I am learning, slowly, now, that my experiences as a woman and a woman-becoming *are* valid and valuable, true in this world. But my voice would not be as strong as it is if you had not taught me early to speak.

Mom and I have something beautiful, too, a relationship that ties me to her in unbreakable ways. You know, from watching us together, how open and giving we are with each other, sharing all the wildflower joy and real sadness that we have. We talk together, a lot and often, trading ideas and plans and thoughts and worries. I'm a very lucky and blessed daughter. With Mom, I have long stretches of time as we walk up to the park or go to breakfast or spend summer vacations together, and she's patient with me as I try to find the words and work out what I mean.

And I would never say that you and I don't have that same strength running in undercurrents through our relationship. It's no less, and I hold it just as close to my heart and soul; it's simply different. I'm lucky to have inherited and been given so much from you, but part of that sparkling similarity means that sometimes, I misunderstand you, or take what you say the wrong way or too personally, and sometimes, I trip over my own words and meanings and intentions. I love talking to you. Just know that when I look down or away, it's because I can't seem to say, out loud, everything that I want to tell you. I can't just say that I'm blessed to have you as a father, or Mom for my mother.

So somehow, in the writing of this, I'd love to tell you who I think I'm becoming, where I've gone to and come from, and who I am now. And I want you to know that you have been a part, a shaper and sculptor, of all three, whether or not you realized it or intended it. It will not be an easy thing, and I can never summarize or explain completely. I worry that I'll misstep or write the wrong thing or leave gaps and holes that you won't be able to fill. But I have to try because I want to tell you all of this, and I want you to understand that I'm just now opening my eyes, seeing how lucky and blessed I really am.

I hope you'll understand that in all my life, I've always looked to you, sometimes for advice, sometimes for assurances. And I know that we didn't get along or agree all the time, but I love you with all my heart, and you've also made me more whole, more confident and loving of myself.

Sally

Dear Dad,

I remember that I asked you once, over the phone, on a gray day two weeks before Christmas break, "Are you ready for your daughter's new-found feminism?"

And you answered, "'New-found?' Since when is it 'new-found?'"

And you were right. As I start paging back through my yearbooks, through years of school and church and struggles and fights and speeches, I realize that somehow, feminism for me has not only been a rational, intellectual pursuit, a theory and a world-view and a critique, but it's also always been with me, like a hunger, like a fire, an underlying knowledge that something is awry in the world, something is not right even in my classrooms. Maybe I got that hunger from you, wanting things to change and move, or maybe you strengthened mine. I don't suppose I always went about activism in the right ways, but somehow, I have always been "about it." I didn't always know why, and I didn't always feel adequate for the task or understand exactly why the issues were important. I call myself by the broad name of feminist now; though in the past years, I didn't have that nametag. I only knew by intuition and gut that something needed to be done, something different than the standard way to handle what was wrong—just swallow.

Do you remember my third grade year? Every day, Nate Sloop, with a brown buzzcut and a cocksure head tilt, would tell me that I played "like a girl," I kicked "like a girl," I was "nasty" and he didn't want my "girl cooties." I glowered at him, I talked back, and I ran after him. One lunch recess, walking through the hallway out to the playground, he was up to his teasing and hassling again, and I was so mad that I told him (loudly) to shut up. I was called back in to write, "I will not say shut up," ten times. Nate had said "shut up," too. He went outside. But I was a nice girl, my teacher told me, and if I didn't have anything nice to say, then I shouldn't say anything at all.

And fourth grade? Andy Lanoha, sweet, athletic, popular and brown-eyed-adorable, told me that I couldn't play floor hockey in p.e. class because my stick was too heavy, or some such junk. I spit in his hair. I spent the next recess writing out the dictionary's definition of "spit" over and over on lined notebook paper.

And the whole year during sixth grade, coming home in tears and frustration, tired of being teased for my shorts, my legs, the books that I read. Carl Oliver, blonde-haired and tall, insulting and sneering, used to ask me when the flood was coming because I wore my pants too high on my waist. He fell on the ground shouting, "earthquake!" whenever my best friend, heavier by sixth-grade standards, walked past. And he would tell me, after I wore my birthday present from Grandma, "If you were president, we'd all have to wear yellow bunny sweatshirts." I fumbled for an answer, some smart remark. But the best day, the one I most remember, was the one when I couldn't answer and just boiled over. I smacked him hard on the back, leaving a clear, red hand-print after he called me the "milk-servant," and jeered that I hadn't counted right, couldn't count. But I had brought enough chocolate milk, and I knew it.

Seventh through ninth grade: regression. Maybe more "peaceable," definitely more confused, less sure of self. Didn't want to beat 'em up, wanted them to like me or "go out" with me. (Where?) Still, in some things, the undercurrents were still there, rising to the surface when I needed them, when they couldn't be pushed down for acceptance's sake.

One day, in gym class, I felt that crunch in my stomach again, without being prepared or knowing why. And all the details are stuck in my head still today. We wore dingy gray shirts and short gray shorts, laced-up tennis shoes and socks scrunched down. Nothing fit any of us quite right, but the theory was that if we were all wearing the same thing, none of us could make fun of anyone else. They were wrong. The gangly or pudgy limbs still stuck out from sleeves and legholes, the sweat collapsed our bangs and soaked through in dark circles on our uniforms. And then there were the movements, the awkward, speed bursts and halts, the squatting defense and the crash-and-burn strategy of the offense. And though he intended some good, our teacher set the rule that a goal scored by a girl would be two points, rather than the traditional, male one point, making girls easy targets for snide comments whenever they missed, and quick rationalizations after one of the teams lost. Well, that team had more girls, and, well, they played like girls. The words from third grade bounced off the blue mats, came back to haunt us. "You kick like a girl."

I was a wild kicker in soccer, since I had limited eye-foot coordination and even less of an idea of what the game was supposed to be. Once in a while, tired of the comments that I couldn't kick, tired of swinging high or wide of the pentagon-splotched ball, I "accidentally" kicked the opposing team member's shins. It was a scary class period. Still, we continued, a collection of running bodies and out-of-breath kids.

Through the next half-hour, the ball rolled all over the floor, off knees and feet, under the bleachers and occasionally into the net, beyond the goalie's stretch. Most of the time, I ran to follow the ball, wanting a chance at it, playing no particular position except defense on my side of the floor, offense on the other. Mostly, I tried to look like I knew where to go, what was happening. Mostly, I didn't. But once, I miraculously ended up a few feet from our goal, in an open space, with one of my male classmates finally conceding that his way was blocked, and mine could lead to a clear goal. He caught my eye and then tapped the ball with his foot around the defense's ankles toward me. Without too much thinking, I angled my foot so the inside curve of my shoe would connect with the ball, and somehow, it changed course and sped toward the corner of the net. It rolled in. I stood amazed. My p.e. teacher stopped the clock, put up one hand to pull in our attention.

"Now, I want you to notice what Sally just did," he began. The tops of my ears burned, excited, unsure, thrilled, embarrassed. "She didn't just stand there, like most girls would have, combing their hair. She went after the ball, scored two for her team."

And then I stood, my whole face red with confused anger. "Combing their hair?" I latched on to those words. "Why on this green earth would I comb my hair in the middle of a game, and not score the goal? And why would any girl, for that matter?" Had I not been so bewildered by this logic, this slipped-in comment, I would have said something to contradict him right there. Instead, all I could do was stand there, suddenly without pride, and glare. I didn't want an extra point. I didn't want a comb. I wanted to play, and not worry what "the boys" thought or what the coach expected or what the generalizations were. I just wanted to play.

I did keep playing sports, three each year in high school, and for each one I pulled my hair off of my face into a rubberband and never really thought about how I looked on the court, around the track. It was one place that sweat and clenched teeth and sprinting were finally acceptable, expected, worth it. It was one place where the girls got together and worked, where we fit together like the mesh of a basketball net. It was one place we had value.

But the third grade words still rang in my ears, never completely silenced or dismissed. I still remember walking through the high school hallway, seeing elaborate banners (or semi-elaborate, poster-painted banners), made by the cheerleaders, touting boys' basketball games and boys' football games, hanging on every wall so the game would not be missed. I remember the guys getting new jackets and sweats, taking our "good" bus (the one that broke down less) to away games, having crowded stands at their home games.

And I remember, too, our "obligation" banners from the cheerleaders, hearing them complain about having to cheer for fewer fans at a girls' game, or about having to cheer for girls' basketball at all. I remember that our team jackets were a generous donation from one of my teammate's parents, and that our parents were sometimes the loneliest of fans.

I remember the convoluted, angry feeling I had, trying to understand what made the difference between two teams playing a sport with the same rules. I remember wondering why one team was school-supported to the hilt, while the other was mostly parent-supported. I really was angry, got up on my small soapbox, and cried out against the small discriminations that loomed even larger behind the banners.

The day was bound to come when I had heard it from too many sides, had been tripped up by too many examples and discriminations, had had it up to here.

Eleventh grade: all of the guys in my class leaning up against their lockers after lunch, lining the hallway. I had just finished a turkey sandwich and a conversation with my basketball teammates about how we should have won the game the night before, how we were sick of people telling us that girls' basketball wasn't worth going to if we couldn't even pull out a win, much less dunk. (How many guys were dunking on our guys' team?) Chris Berge—short, sandy hair cut around in an upside-down bowl, unsure with a high-pitched laugh—decided to make the final comment that would break the camel's back, right as I passed him on my way to my locker. "Girls' basketball? Why would I go to their next game? It was so boring, you couldn't pay me enough to watch." Too much for me to handle, enough to push my limits, enough to bring back my old fiery reactions to "You play like a girl," enough to make me unsure of words but certain of needing to do something. I grabbed his collar (I'd seen this on t.v.), clenched hard and curled my hands down to my wrists, shoved him with all I had into the nearest locker door, told him "never to say that again." And then, unsure of what came next, I watched him slide down to the tiled floor as I uncurled my hands, his eyes a mixture of astonishment and smirk and embarassment.

After that lunch hour, it became a marker and a known fact that I was the "one who beat up Chris Berge," and it became a challenge to the other guys. I took bets that I could beat them in one-on-one games. Too often, I took the bait, the jokes and teasing, that they knew would bring my frustration and anger to a boil. But at least I had done something for myself; I had not backed down. Though I wouldn't recommend throwing punches at everyone who degrades or derides women in sports or women as individuals or as a whole, it's one way to leave a stinging reminder, and once in a while, it's oh, so liberating.

Still, after that day, I earned the term "feminazi" from my male athlete classmates, and I truly stepped into their idea of what would fit the name when I offered my speeches on women's roles in marriage and in the church whenever these topics came up in class. I took my share of insults and jokes, and I made my way trying to separate the simple jests from the more seriously sarcastic, biting comments. And part of me was proud to stand alone, to beat up the boys who ragged on girls' sports, to be the one to speak, though I didn't always know what foundations to stand on or if I was the only one who had ever felt this way.

And part of me loathed that loneliness, that unstable opposing stance. I wanted to be liked, to be dated, to be accepted, to be a fan sitting in the bleachers at the boys' games without noticing their new warm-ups, their in-style uniforms. I wanted to be equal, but I wanted to blend as an equal. I wanted to be equal, but not held separate and away. I didn't want to be intimidating, but I wanted to be truthful. I had learned as I grew up through school grades that nice girls didn't get mad, call someone names, shout or tackle. They get along, they cooperate, they settle things peaceably and with smiles. So I was never sure that the "difficult" part of me was acceptable, allowed. I didn't always understand what to do with this frustrated broiling or this sense of injustice or certainty that things were not right.

So what a liberation when you, my dad, a saving grace in sixth grade and after, told me, "Just go ahead and hit 'em if they (the provoking boys) won't let up. We'll back you up if you get a detention." I knew that my dad was angry on my behalf, but he also knew that he could do nothing that would have a lasting effect. It was more important that he stood behind me, giving me the right to be angry, the right to do something, the right to stop ignoring the hurts and cuts and work to stop them.

From then on, I took with me a lesson, though it's more than a slogan or a poster. And it goes beyond sports and sixth grade now. I still have this anger, but rather than swallowing it whole, I tell myself: carry this anger, this passion and devotion, with you. It doesn't mean that I'm less of a person, or a bad person, or a sick or ungrateful person if I'm angry. You have helped me learn it, sometimes by example, sometimes by reminders. Sometimes, the world is wrong. The "way things are" is not the way they could be/ought to be. People are hurting, and they need our compassion along with our anger if we are to help them. Our anger is our energy, it is our drive, it is our love. We are only angry because we care deeply—if we did not care, we could let the injustice and the pain slip by, slide past us. It would be easy and apathetic and distant. We would shrug it off, claiming that it wasn't our responsibility or that it would change on its own. Anger is a channel for change, a catalyst, and it gives us courage to speak the need. It comes out in tears and shouts and protests and silences and mostly in love and caring. It has been called "prophetic caring," this anger that springs from a deep well of love, this willingness to point out where we have gone wrong, and this willingness to change and correct and break down and build again.

So, what I would say to myself now, if I could go back to stand in the high school hallway? I'd tell myself the same thing that you taught me: that it's all right to be angry and to care about the cuts and knifeblades you feel sharply underneath certain comments. When they tell you that 'you play like a girl,' and when they bait you and try to stir you up, when they make subtle statements and don't even realize what they are saying, know that you don't have to just smile demurely or laugh uncomfortably or say only nice things in return. You have the right to be angry. You have the right to call them on it, to shout it out, to disagree and defend and declare the truth. That girls play right alongside boys, and they do it well. And they are worth respect, as athletes and as people. These barbed-wire undertones do not have to be strung through every high school, and they do not have to be "the way things are."

I'd tell myself: if you need me, I'm here. Not far away, just working in a different place, taking down other sharp fences. And your dad is right there with you, too.

Sally

What Can We Learn from Developmental Psychology?

Mary Stewart Van Leeuwen

Gender Asymmetry

Some years ago a researcher was exploring career aspirations and the way these interacted with children's gender stereotypes. Her method was to ask each of her young respondents what they would do in adulthood if they grew up as a member of the other sex. One little girl confided that her ambition was to "fly like a bird" but that this would probably not happen because she wasn't a boy. And a boy in the same study concluded that if he were a girl he would just grow up "to be nothing."[1]

In a more recent study in Michigan, elementary school children were asked: "If you woke up tomorrow and discovered you were the other gender, how would your life be different?" Most of the girls stated that they'd rather remain female but readily listed positive features of being a boy. ("I could shoot hoops after breakfast," "I'd hunt and fish with my dad," "I'd be picked in gym to demonstrate how to play a game.") But the majority of boys were horrified by even the imaginary prospect of becoming girls. Some envisaged taking their life as a result. ("I would stab myself in the heart fifty times with a dull butter knife," "I'd take a whole bottle of aspirin.") Others portrayed what they saw as the drawbacks—but almost never any advantages—of being female. ("I couldn't play any good sports." "I'd have to stay home," "I'd be weak, a pansy, a wimp.")[2]

Studies like these underline an important point about boys and girls growing up in our culture: their socialization as children is not merely complementary but often *asymmetrical*. That is to say, the amount, the timing and the results of socializing influences directed at boys and girls are not necessarily the same at all ages. For example, in the above-mentioned studies, preadolescent boys and girls both agreed that boys have it better in terms of the kinds of activities they can engage in. As another example, North American parents on average still invest more resources (such as teaching and sports equipment, private schooling, special lessons or summer camp experiences) on behalf of their sons than of their daughters.[3]

However the asymmetry does not always favor boys. It is true that females continue to struggle with various kinds of discrimination, both while growing up and as adults. But at least in the years prior to adolescence girls do not need to be as careful as boys to avoid the clothing, toys and games normally associated with the other sex.[4] Close to two-thirds of U.S. women report that they were tomboys as children, and young tomboys, far from being ostracized, are usually popular with peers of both sexes. Boys on the other hand, are more narrowly socialized into the masculine script, and the social costs of deviating from it are much higher in terms of peer rejection and adult disapproval.

One result of this male gender-role rigidity was described by *Generation X* author Douglas Coupland, who is also a trained artist. "My first day of art school," he recalls wryly, "was the first day in my life I could pick up an object and say 'That's so beautiful' without getting beaten up."[5] In the same vein, therapists Dan Kindlon and Michael Thompson recall a fifty-two-year-old male patient who described his hurt and bewilderment when, on graduating at the top of his class at an elite university, he told his parents he wanted to apply his gifts to teaching. His father's only response was "You mean after all that, you want to be a teacher? Why can't you get a *man's* job?"[6]

Unlike these two men, most boys choose not to pay the price of deviating very far from the requirements of cultural masculinity. In the Michigan study, you will notice that the boys saw the idea of waking up female as not just inconvenient or disadvantageous but a source of panic and even pollution.[7] In part, as I have noted, this is because our society promotes a male culture of honor. [...] In such cultures hegemonic masculinity, though accompanied by power and status, is hard-won, precarious and subject to escalating performance demands. Consequently it is something many males (both younger and older) fear losing. As we will see shortly, this fear begins early in life and leads most boys to base the security of their gender identity as much—if not more—on avoiding the feminine as on embracing the masculine.[8]

But we should also note that children acquire notions about gender even when adults bend over backwards to make sure this doesn't happen. Fifty years ago, under the sway of Freud's dictum that anatomy is destiny, parents worried if their children didn't conform to traditional notions of what males and females should be like. Now, a few decades after the advent of second-wave feminism, some parents are upset—or at least bewildered—when their children do adhere, often quite extremely, to the gender stereotypes their parents were so careful not to teach them. A five-year-old boy whose mother is a practicing physician nonetheless insists that only men can be doctors. A four-year-old girl asserts that it is her mother who vacuums the carpets, even though this task is routinely done by her father. A three-year-old girl is dressed in blue pajamas by her mother one night, only to sneak out of bed and exchange them for her pink pair once her mother has left the room. How do little girls and boys acquire such ideas and behaviors? In part through patterns of role modeling and reinforcement by parents and others, but also through the children's own attempts to make cognitive sense of their social world. Let's look at each of these processes in turn.[9]

Raising Cain

The asymmetry of boys' and girls' paths begins with an obvious but often underappreciated fact: in industrialized societies, from infancy through at least middle childhood, most boys have much less access than girls to same-sex role models. Girls are literally surrounded by adult women from birth on, since most infants are cared for by mothers or other female caretakers, and most preschool and elementary school teachers are women. As a result girls tend to feel reasonably confident that they are "getting it right" in terms of learning their gender script, though sooner or later they also learn that in many ways it is a culturally devalued script relative to boys'.

But with asymmetrical caretaking boys get double messages as well. Most female teachers and caretakers want boys to be culturally masculine but also self controlled and deferential. On the other hand, their fathers and male peers are likely to encourage self-assertion, independence and vigorous play. Thus as psychologist Carole Beal puts it, "the little boy is faced with figuring out whether he should be like Cary Grant or Hulk Hogan."[10] And in contrast to his sister, he has fewer same-sex adults around to reassure him that he's getting his gender script right—or that perhaps it's not such a big deal even if he isn't. Small wonder that panic and fears of pollution surface at the least suggestion of being girlish. The boy is supposedly getting ready to join the more powerful half of the adult human race, but for much of his childhood he lacks close, regular contact with male mentors who can help him on this path or encourage him to seek an alternate one.[11]

Independence training for boys starts young. From the first few weeks of life on, mothers on average look at, hold, touch and cuddle daughters more than sons—even though boys actually startle, cry and fuss more readily than girls during the first months of life.[12] But mothers also cut boys more slack when they resist attempts to control them, in effect allowing sons to set the style of interaction, on the assumption that boys should learn to assert themselves. With girls, by contrast, mothers usually try to create and sustain a more mutual pattern of exchange. We should note that the direction of causality here may run both ways: infant boys do appear to be more stressed than girls by intense social interaction, so in some ways they may he training mothers to keep their distance. But either way it is a mixed blessing: Children's later capacity to express healthy independence depends on large doses of responsive caregiving which help the child feel that the world is predictable and thus worthy of progressively greater risk-taking, both physically and emotionally. At the same time the early concession to boys' self-assertiveness, if not combined with reasonable limits, often means that as they get older they are treated (using terms coined by two therapists who work with boys) either as "Wild Animals" who cannot be controlled or as "Entitled Princes" who should not be.[13]

As early as one year of age, when given the choice boys and girls alike gravitate towards gender-typical toys. Longitudinal studies have shown that this behavior follows, rather than precedes, parents' expressed enthusiasm for the child's interaction with these "appropriate" toys, which suggests that such behavioral tendencies are more the result of nurture than of nature.[14] But again the reactions of parents are not symmetrical: mothers on average are fairly tolerant of cross-gender play in daughters or sons, but fathers are much less so, especially when boys play with "feminine" toys.

In one study, preschool children were taken to a playroom while their parents were being interviewed, and were asked to play with either gender-typical or gender-atypical toys. When a parent later joined the child, his or her reactions were observed. Parents of both sexes reacted positively to daughters' playing with a kitchen set and with only mild negativity when they played with a toy gas station. But boys got mixed messages: Mothers were generally positive toward whatever toy the sons played with, often sitting down and joining them. Most fathers, however, responded positively to sons' playing with "masculine" toys but *very* negatively to play with "feminine" ones: they frowned, made sarcastic comments and in some cases even picked up the child and moved him away from the kitchen set.[15] Again, whatever biological priming boys and girls may bring to their play styles, it is magnified greatly— and asymmetrically—by socialization.

GENDER CHAUVINISM

By the time children are about five years old, much of their play is so thoroughly gender-typed that parents no longer need to monitor it. But gender typing happens not just because children passively absorb parental preferences influential though these are. Once they pass through infancy and early toddlerhood, it also happens because of children's own need to develop a clear self concept. This leads to (among other things) the formation of gender identity which [...] refers to a sense of oneself as being male or female. Once established, gender identity provides a strong motivation to identify with same-sex role models and to learn from them by observation. Moreover, the growing realization that one is either a boy or a girl—and permanently so—becomes a powerful tool with which to make sense of the child's social world. Gender becomes an organizing principle, a cognitive category or (more technically) a schema that children use to understand and judge people's behavior.[16]

The development of a gender identity and a gender schema helps us to understand why many younger children apply gender stereotypes to themselves and others even when adults consciously work against this tendency. Developmental psychologist Carol Beal summarizes it well: "Because gender is thought to be an either-or category, children resist the notion that males and females might sometimes behave in similar ways, are critical of others who deviate from traditional gender roles, and exaggerate the differences between the sexes."[17] Regardless of who does what in their own home, children survey their entire social landscape—including, of course, the media images that surround them—and draw general correlations between perceived sex on the one hand and behavior, appearance and personality traits on the other. They then turn the resulting stereotypes into moral imperatives about what males and females can and should do.

It's as if the child in the preschool and early elementary school years is saying, "Look, I've just figured out this girl-and-boy thing. Don't complicate it by telling me that the boundaries are sometimes movable." This stance highlights the cognitive strength of all stereotypes: they reduce the mental strain that would occur if we were to regard every person and situation as unique. In Hilary Lips's words, both boys and girls at this stage "seem to be trying to solidify a sense of gender identity by renouncing any form of ambiguity."[18] And it is shortly after this that they often become spontaneous gender chauvinists. The early school years are the ones when "boys versus girls" contests are common, when children segregate themselves by sex at tables in the school cafeteria, and when the chant "Girls rule, boys drool" is matched by "Boys reign, girls are a pain." In the continuing process of consolidating gender identity, each sex insists that it is the best.

I must be careful not to overdraw this picture: boys and girls at this age also do a lot of what sociologist Barrie Thorne calls "border work." They make calculated forays into each other's playground territory, engage in ritualized chasing games with each other and even remain happily capable of mixed-sex activities in a variety of settings. This is especially the case when adults take responsibility for organizing such activities (in well-run church youth groups, for example) and when the task is an absorbing one that encourages cooperation and deemphasizes gender, such as producing a school newspaper or play, or participating in a service project.[19] Furthermore adults who want children to focus more on their common humanity than on their gender differences can take heart from the fact that the intolerance for ambiguity may start to decrease as early as seven to ten years of age. Throughout this period children—though girls sooner and more often than boys—begin to think it might he acceptable if they, their friends and their families are not always rigidly gender-typed, and that the extent to which they are might be as much the result of custom as of biology.[20] [...]

Fragile Loyalties

Dan Kindlon and Michael Thompson are psychologists who work in all-boys as well as coed schools in Boston, in addition to having private therapy practices. In their book *Raising Cain* they describe an adult client they call Gary, who recalled cooperating as a boy with a juvenile version of the male culture of honor and in turn becoming its victim. As a fifth-grader Gary had a best friend named Peter, with whom he studied, talked, and played hunting and tracking games in the woods. Peter was a reasonably good athlete but also happened to be the shortest boy in the class. In sixth grade he became the target of teasing, which both boys at first tried to ignore or brush aside. But one day in the locker room several boys formed a ring around Peter and started snapping their towels at his crotch and mocking him. While struggling into his pants and trying to protect his anatomy, Peter glanced over at Gary as he stood by his own locker. He was "not exactly pleading for help, but checking to see what I was going to do. What I did," Gary recalled, "was finish getting dressed and walk out of the locker room. We never talked about it, but that was the end of our friendship. To be honest, he had become a liability for me, and I didn't have the guts to deal with it."[21]

Gary soon acquired a new best friend, Lee, a top student, athlete and school leader with whom he even traded clothing as a symbol of mutual allegiance. But in seventh grade Gary—a Jewish boy in a largely non-Jewish school—began preparing for his bar mitzvah, and though his Jewish identity had not previously been a matter for comment, it now became the butt of jokes. Uncertain whether to ignore these or to fight back, Gary (like Peter before him) looked to his best friend for help, only to see him regularly laughing along with the rest of his mockers. Later, when he invited half a dozen boys, including Lee, to his bar mitzvah, none of them showed up. Lee admitted that he and his classmates had decided that none of them wanted to go to the synagogue because they would have to wear "kike caps" during the service. Gary's conclusion: "That's what becoming a man meant to me when I got Bar Mitzvahed: I realized I was on my own. I never had a best friend again."[22]

The "Boy Code" and the Culture of Honor

Gary, Peter and Lee shared with most other boys in our society a systematic process of induction—some of it deliberate, much of it unwitting—into what psychologist William Pollack calls the "Boy Code."[23] This is a set of requirements for all who aspire to a contemporary version of the male culture of honor. We saw that in its classical form the culture of honor requires a man to resist challenges from other men, while advancing his own prestige and social ranking by a continuous display of cool-headedness, shrewdness, and verbal and physical dominance. In an article that has become something of a classic in men's studies, social scientists Robert Brannon and Deborah David have outlined its four imperatives for boys growing up in North America today.[24]

First, there must he *no sissy stuff.* Any display of behavior or emotion associated with the feminine may become an occasion for shaming or even physical abuse, unless a boy is lucky enough to be raised in a subculture where adults—and especially men—model such emotions and don't punish boys for doing so. Empathy is feminine, so a boy like Gary, though he feels conflicted about it, does not stand up for a friend who is being mocked and abused. Religion is feminine and Jews are a vulnerable minority, so Gary's classmates will not let themselves be seen in "kike caps" even for a short time in a restricted setting. Being small is feminine, so Peter is considered fair game for boys higher up in the pecking order. And since showing distress is feminine, Peter must simply grit his teeth, make light of his torment and hope for a speedy exit from the locker room. In an earlier culture of honor Peter's brothers and other male kin might be a ready-made network to protect or avenge him. In its modern incarnation, even this safety net cannot he counted on, and the "rule of law" that is supposed to have replaced it is often inconsistently enforced by adults responsible for children's welfare. Boys, it is assumed, will sort these things out among themselves.

Recognizing these dark tendencies does not mean we should one-sidedly demonize boys or men. Girls may not be physical bullies as often as boys, but they are quite capable of using ostracism and verbal cruelty to construct their own hierarchies.[25] The difference is that when girls suffer emotional distress, they are not as often discouraged from expressing it. Most parents of both sexes respond with warmth and concern to girls' fears, encouraging them to "talk it out" as an acceptable expression of femininity. But they use fewer emotion-words with sons, expecting them instead to limit their expression of vulnerability. Fathers are especially apt to use scorn and teasing to toughen up their sons in the face of fear or sadness. Indeed one emotion-word that fathers are far more likely to use with sons than with daughters is *disgust.*[26]

This illustrates the second imperative of the Boy Code: he must learn to become *a sturdy oak*—that is, stable, stoical and self-reliant. If he can't always be on top of the heap, he should at least "take it like a man" when adversity comes his way. He should even look for occasions to practice this virtue. In the movie *Lawrence of Arabia* the hero at one point demonstrates how he can let a match burn right down to his fingertips. "Of course it hurts," he says with a smile. "The trick, you see, is not to *care* that it hurts." This, David and Brannon observe, "goes far beyond the mere avoidance of feminine emotionality: it's the cultivation of a stoic, imperturbable persona....A 'real man' never worries about death or loses his manly cool."[27] It also helps to explain why Christianity is so often stereotyped as an unmanly endeavor: to the extent that it calls on men to admit that they are not self-sufficient but need the grace of God and the support of other believers, Christian faith and lifestyle challenge the sturdy oak image.

Closely related to that image is a third imperative. A boy must learn, in David and Brannon's words, to be *a big wheel*—to cultivate success and status and provoke envy and admiration in others. Athletic prowess is perhaps the most acknowledged way to do this, as well as (with the onset of adolescence) the ability to attract girls. But there are class and subcultural differences. The studious boy who would be seen as a masculine cop-out in the inner city will be pressed to study even harder in the suburbs, in order to make it into an elite university and thence to a prestigious and high-paying career. The zealous Christian boy who is the butt of jokes in his public school setting may aspire to become a minister or evangelist who will compete as an adult for fame and followers.

What links these various expressions is something they all share with classic cultures of honor: by definition "big wheel" status is a limited commodity that not every male can achieve, and that even those who do are in constant danger of losing.[28] As one of Kindlon and Thompson's young informants put it, "Everyone thinks you've got it so easy when you're on top, but being on top just means you have to worry all the time about slipping....All it takes is one mistake or a bad day, and all sorts of people are waiting to take you down."[29] Pollack notes that it is this aspect of the code that makes some boys push themselves to unhealthy limits in athletic or other kinds of competition. It is also what leads many boys to prefer girls who massage their egos (in Virginia Woolf's memorable phrase, who "reflect them at twice their natural size") to those who see them in all their human ambiguity and insist on a more genuine partnership.[30]

Lastly, in its extreme form the imperative to be a big wheel becomes, in David and Brannon's words, the mandate to *give 'em hell.* Violence performed by other than legally mandated persons is, of course, officially condemned in Western society. At the same time, it is modeled incessantly in the media and often encouraged in boys with a wink and a nod. At the very least, boys are often urged to defend themselves vigorously when attacked. And given the mystique that violence has in popular culture, "the line between self-defense and aggression for the sheer fun of it is narrow in theory and often ignored in practice, especially among older boys out of sight of adults, where the rule that 'might makes right' usually reigns supreme."[31] Alternately boys may he tempted to engage in behaviors risky to themselves, such as driving too fast or taking drugs, often on an implicit or explicit dare from which they feel they cannot back down.

EMOTIONAL IMPOVERISHMENT

From all this we see that boys are expected to embrace a masculine ideal emphasizing self-reliance, stoicism, competition and power. It is important to point out that these are not inherently pathological traits. In the right contexts and the right amounts, they are virtues *all* human beings can draw on to serve their communities and unfold the potential of creation. What is problematic about them for boys as compared to girls is that they are often emphasized to the exclusion of other equally valuable traits and are linked to performance standards that can never finally he met—if, as the Boy Code holds, it is only by staying on top that one's masculinity can be fully assured. The behavioral rigidity and anxiety this generates are made worse by the fact that most boys have less access than girls to same-sex adult role models— especially to ones who practice a fully human range of emotion and behavior and who refuse to link masculine worth to a never-ending performance treadmill.

In their extreme form such asymmetries contribute to the dramatic social problems we have come to associate more with boys than girls: homicide, suicide, property crime and various forms of violence. And when we nuance this picture by class and ethnicity, it becomes even more complex, since boys of color often face additional challenges from the Boy Code. Many live in situations of limited economic opportunity and thus feel doubly shamed (or tempted) by the code's demand for material success. In neighborhoods of high father absence, there may he few adult males to model alternative ways of being masculine—though many African American churches do a superb job of providing such models for young people willing to take advantage of them.[32] Moreover, in communities where the rule of law has broken down and normal city services are inconsistently provided, the temptation to form gangs and channel one's sense of honor and achievement through them is very strong.[33]

But even for boys who do not resort to such behaviors there is an emotional price to be paid. We have seen that boys are pushed from an early age to suppress fearful or sad feelings and are often shamed when they fail to do so. But they *are* often encouraged to express one strong feeling: anger. Indeed when parents tell their children stories or teach them how to manage conflict, they are likely to stress empathy and harmony for their daughters but the use of anger for their sons.[34] As a result, anger can become the single pathway or "emotional funnel" through which boys channel the forbidden, softer feelings. From his work with men and boys Pollack concludes that "the more tender feelings seem too shameful to show, and thus boys turn to anger.... It is very challenging for most men to express or experience emotions other than anger, since as boys they were encouraged to use their rage to express the full range of their emotional experience."[35]

The long-term physical consequences of such emotional narrowing—increased risk of ulcers, high blood pressure and other somatic problems—are serious enough, but the relational consequences are equally troubling. This past year, for example, I found myself smiling—but rather ruefully—over a news item about dozens of check-out clerks who complained to their grocery store chain owners about the requirement that they make a constant effort to be friendly to customers. Their professional courtesy was frequently interpreted as a sexual invitation by customers of the other sex, whose persistent attentions then became annoying and occasionally even dangerous. Though both sexes had received exactly the same customer service training, only the women clerks faced this problem. This failure on the part of many men to correctly read others' emotional intentions in voice and facial expression—and their tendency to get angry when their mistaken reading is rejected—has also been found in various laboratory studies.[36]

Part of this asymmetry is due to status differences: lower-status groups—including women and, in America, blacks of both sexes—are generally better at decoding nonverbal cues than the higher-status groups to whom they have had to defer for so long. But boys' early training in suppressing or ignoring their own feelings undoubtedly plays a part as well. Clinical psychologist Ronald Levant has coined the term *alexithymia* to describe this truncated ability to feel and express a wide range of human emotions. He has also devised ways for men with stress and relationship problems to relearn how to monitor their bodily states and accurately identify a wider range of feelings.[37] But it would be better for all of us if the emotional narrowing did not occur in the first place.

Raising Real Boys

The psychologists we have met in this chapter who specialize in work with boys show remarkable agreement as to what changes are needed. Boys need freedom to stay attached to parents longer than our culture has allowed them to. They need to be accepted not just for their strengths but with all their fears and doubts, not shamed into denying them or taught always to mask them with anger and bravado, They need academic and cocurricular experiences that challenge but also respect their limits, and that put as much stress on mutual encouragement and skill building as on winning. They need loving but firm limits—to be treated neither as Wild Animals nor Entitled Princes but as persons in whom the fullness of God's image requires wise cultivation.

Many Christian families, churches and parachurch groups, intuitively seeing the New Testament's message of freedom from the male culture of honor, have provided such an environment for boys as well as for girls. Others, interpreting Paul's accommodations to that culture as an unchanging set of gender norms, do not, or do so only ambivalently. Some anxious gender traditionalists worry that the changes suggested above will end up effectively turning boys into girls—although after several decades of gains for women we seldom worry that girls' expanded opportunities are turning them all into men. We might recall that not so very long ago higher education for girls was seen as an activity that would inevitably shrink their ovaries![38]

In point of fact, the psychologists who want to expand boys' emotional and behavioral horizons are aware that boys have some unique developmental challenges that need to he taken seriously but often are not. For example, in early childhood boys can lag behind girls in their acquisition of language skills by as much as one to two years—yet we insist on keeping both sexes to the same timetable in learning to read and write.[39] In addition, many (though not all) young boys seem to thrive in large spaces that allow for physically active team games with clear rules. By contrast, girls often (though again not always—remember all those tomboys!) prefer one-on-one activities confined to smaller spaces. The point is not that one style is better than the other but that individual differences need to be accommodated, even as we challenge children to stretch their horizons to include the activities and learning styles that they usually associate with the other sex.

THE POWER OF NURTURANT FATHERING

At various points in this chapter I have noted that the absence of role-flexible men from boys' lives can lead them to overinvest in the Boy Code in order to convince themselves that they are adequately masculine. What happens when this situation is reversed—when boys have regular access to male caretakers who model a wide range of feeling and behavior, accept the same in boys, and establish age-appropriate boundaries in a consistent and nurturing way? These are questions Yale psychiatrist Kyle Pruett has been asking for over a decade while following almost twenty working-and middle-class families in which fathers have been the primary caretakers of children from infancy on and mothers have been the family's primary wage earners.[40] This ongoing study is significant because it compares fathering styles with mothering styles under roughly comparable conditions—that is, when one parent is the primary caretaker while the other is less accessible due to wage-earning responsibilities. Do fathers act just like mothers in such circumstances? And how does their children's development differ from that of children raised primarily by mothers?

When the firstborns of these families were assessed as infants, they were at or above national norms on standardized cognitive tests and ahead of schedule in personal and social skills. Regardless of sex, they seemed unusually attuned to and comfortable with whatever physical or social environment they were in. By age four, "they were avid explorers of their backyards, bus stops and grocery stores, confident that something interesting would always turn up."[41] Pruett also noted the ease with which they moved between boys' and girls' play: "While their peers were concentrating on joining the 'gender gang' they were moving comfortably back and forth between gender groupings at day care, playgrounds and birthday parties."[42] Their imaginary play was particularly rich with images of caring fathers, yet not to the exclusion of mothers. These children clearly regarded both parents as procreators and nurturers of human beings.

By age eight, most of the children were involved in nurturing activities themselves—raising or breeding a variety of plants and pets, helping to care for younger siblings, taking responsibility for various household chores. Because most of their mothers remained highly involved, Pruett surmised that "having a father *and* a mother devoted to the nurturing of a child was a pervasive culture in these families. Children identified early on with nurturing as a valued, powerful skill and role, and wanted to explore their competence in this area."[43] By ages ten to twelve, they continued to interact comfortably with friends of both genders. At an age when most youngsters are becoming more sexually self-conscious, these children enjoyed cross-sex friendships that included birthday parties and community and religious events, and they preferred friends who shared their less restrictive view of gender roles. Pruett concludes that having two highly involved parents produces "a bedrock trust and comfort with male and female relationships, so that [their] gendered aspects may be less salient than their overall quality."[44] [...]

NOTES

1. Marion N. Libby and Elizabeth Aries, "Gender Differences in Preschool Children's Narrative Fantasy," *Psychology of Women Quarterly* 13 (1989): 293-306. See also Hilary M. Lips, *Sex and Gender: An Introduction,* 3rd ed. (Mountain View, Calif.: Mayfield, 1997), chap. 10.

2. Office for Sex Equity in Education, "Influence of Gender Role Socialization upon the Perceptions of Children." (Lansing: Michigan Department of Education, 1989).

3. Carole R. Beal, *Boys and Girls: The Development of Gender Roles* (New York: McGraw-Hill, 1994), chaps. 1-2.

4. This changes rather drastically in adolescence, however. See for example Mary Pipher, *Reviving Ophelia: Saving the lives of Adolescent Girls* (New York: Grosset/Putnam, 1994), and Jill McLean Taylor, Carol Gilligan and Amy M. Sullivan, *Between Voice and Silence: Women and Girls, Race and Relationship* (Cambridge, Mass.: Harvard University Press, 1995).

5. Quoted in Fred Bernstein, "Blame Canada: Bottling Gen X Style," *New York Times,* March 30, 2000, pp. F1, F8; quotation from p. F8.

6. Dan Kindlon and Michael Thompson, *Raising Cain: Protecting the Emotional Life of Boys* (New York: Ballantine, 1999), p. 112.

7. On boys' treatment of girls and girl-associated things as polluting, see for example Barrie Thorne, "Girls and Boys Together . . . but Mostly Apart: Gender Arrangements in Elementary Schools," in *The Gender and Psychology Reader,* ed. Blythe McVicker Clinchy and Julie K. Norem (New York: New York University Press, 1998), pp. 667-83. Boys' almost panicked resistance to engaging in "girl play" persists even when they are encouraged by influential adults to do so. In one study, preschool children of both sexes were able to select a small toy as a prize, and most selected a gender-typical one. Then the child's favorite teacher was recruited to come and see the toy, but then to give

several strong reasons for trading it in for a gender-atypical one. Both boys and girls resisted this suggestion, but while most girls were content just to say that they preferred the girls' toy, the boys appeared extremely uncomfortable, argued actively with the (favorite) teacher, and even tried to discredit her advice by saying that she must be ill or overworked or she would never have urged them to swap a truck for a necklace! See Dorthea M Ross and Sheila A. Ross, "Resistance by Preschool Boys to Sex-Inappropriate Behavior," *Journal of Educational Psychology* 63 (1972): 342-46.

8. For an earlier analysis of this tendency, see Deborah S. David and Robert Brannon, *The Forty-nine Percent Majority: The Male Sex Role* (Reading, Mass.: Addison-Wesley, 1976). For a variety of more recent reflections, see Larry May, Robert Strickwerda and Patrick D. Hopkins, eds., *Rethinking Masculinity: Philosophical Explorations in Light of* Feminism, 2nd ed. (Lanham, Md.: Rowman and Littlefield, 1996).

9. See also Eleanor E. Maccoby, *The Two Sexes: Growing Up Apart, Coming Together* (Cambridge, Mass.: Harvard University Press, 1998).

10. Beal, *Boys and Girls*, p. 10.

11. For a detailed theoretical treatment of this asymmetry and its consequences for both sexes, see Nancy Chodorow, *The Reproduction of Mothering: Psychoanalysis and the Sociology of Gender* (Berkeley: University of California Press, 1978). For an applied, clinical perspective, see for example Frank Pittman, *Man Enough: Fathers, Sons and the Search for Masculinity* (New York: Putnam, 1993).

12. William Pollack, *Real Boys: Rescuing Our Sons from the Myths of Boyhood* (New York: Random House, 1998), chap. 2.

13. Kindlon and Thompson, *Raising Cain*, chap. 2; Beal, *Boys and Girls*, chap. 3.

14. Eleanor F. Maccoby and Carol N. Jacklin, *The Psychology of Sex Differences* (Stanford, Calif.: Stanford University Press, 1974).

15. Judith H. Langlois and A. Chris Downs, "Mothers, Fathers and Peers as Socialization Agents of Sex-Typed Play Behavior in young Children," *Child Development* 51 (1980): 1217-47. See also Beal, *Boys and Girls*, chap. 5, for related studies.

16. See especially Lawrence Kohlberg, "A Cognitive-Developmental Analysis of Children's Sex-Role Concepts and Attitudes," in *The Development of Sex Differences*, ed. Eleanor F. Maccoby (Stanford, Calif.: Stanford University Press, 1966), pp. 82-173, and Sandra L. Bem, *The Lenses of Gender* (New

Haven, Conn.: Yale University Press, 1993).

17. Beal, *Boys and Girls*, p. 102.

18. Lips, *Sex and Gender*, p. 64.

19. Thorne, "Girls and Boys Together," pp. 678-79.

20. Beale, *Boys and Girls*, chap. 6.

21. Kindlon and Thompson, *Raising Cain*, p. 91.

22. Ibid., p. 91.

23. Pollack. *Real Boys*, chap. 2.

24. Deborah David and Robert Brannon, "The Male Sex Role: Our Cultures Blueprint of Manhood, and What It's Done for Us Lately," in David and Brannon, *Forty-nine Percent Majority*, pp. 1-45.

25. Among others, Margaret Atwood, in her novel *Cat's Eye* (New York: Doubleday. 1989), has painted a graphic picture of little girls' capacity for cruelty. See also Beal, *Boys and Girls*. chap. 7.

26. "Pollack, *Real Boys*, chap. 2.

27. David and Brannon, "Male Sex-Role," p. 25.

28. Ibid., p. 19.

29. Kindlon and Thompson, *Raising Cain*, p. 75.

30. Virginia Woolf. *A Room of One's Own* (1929; reprint, San Diego: Harcourt Brace Jovanovich, 1957); Pollack, *Real Boys* chap. 2.

31. David and Brannon, "Male Sex-Role," p. 29.

32. For some pertinent examples see K. Brynolf Lyon and Archie Smith Jr., eds., *Tending the Flock: Congregations and Family Ministry* (Louisville, Ky.: Westminster John Knox, 1998).

33. See for example Ronald B. Mincy, ed., *Nurturing Young Black Males* (Washington. D.C.: Urban Institute, 1994), and James Garbarino, *Lost Boys: Why Our Sons Turn Violent and How We Can Save Them* (New York: Free Press, 1999).

34. Pollack, *Real Boys*, chap. 2.

35. Ibid., p. 44.

36. See Lips, *Sex and Gender*, chap. 4, for a review of the pertinent research literature.

37. Ronald F. Levant and Gina Kopecky, *Masculinity Reconstructed: Changing the Rules of Manhood at Work, in Relationships and in Family Life* (New York: Dutton, 1995).

38. See for example Barbara Ehrenreich and Deirdre English, *For Her Own Good: 150 Years of the Experts' Advice to Women* (Garden City, N.Y.: Anchor,

1979).

39. Kindlon and Thompson, *Raising Cain,* chap. 2; Pollack, *Real Boys,* chap. 10.

40. Kyle D. Pruett, *The Nurturing Father* (New York: Warner, 1987), and *Fatherneed: Why Father Care Is as Essential as Mother Care for Your Child* (New York: Free Press, 2000). Note that 1999 U.S. Census Bureau data listed some two million fathers as primary caretakers of children in two-parent families.

41. Pruett, *Fatherneed,* p. 62.

42. lbid,. p. 62.

43. Ibid., p. 64.

44. Ibid., p. 72.

Let God be God

The Theological Necessity of Depatriarchalizing God

Karen Bloomquist

FROM A FEMINIST THEOLOGIAL PERSPECTIVE, the question of God and God-language is not an abstract philosophical issue to be debated from a position of disinterested neutrality. It is first and foremost a moral issue, deeply entwined in our relationships with ourselves, others, and the world in which we find ourselves. Because human persons are essentially social, in a way that patriarchal consciousness has often overlooked, we cannot talk about the relationship between God and human persons apart from our relationships with one another, including the social constructs and ideologies by which those relationships are structured.

The past and continuing litany of women who have been silenced, rendered invisible, demeaned, raped, and dismembered provokes what for many feminists is the central God-question: Who is the God in whom we can believe? This theological quest arises out of moral outrage at what has been done to women throughout history in the name of "God," including in our own day. The director of a shelter for battered women told some of our students that in that community the chief instrument used to batter women is the Bible. It is used to justify any means to subordinate women to men. The "God" who has been used to justify or overlook such brutality will simply not suffice. To insist that God is not like that, while "he" continues to be referred to in ways that reinforce the power relations of patriarchy, is contradictory. That there *is* a God who has upheld, redeemed, and sustained women through their pain and struggle is for most women a given. Although some feminists may give attention to atheism as the problem, the God-question for most women is more similar to Luther's well-known quest for a God who is gracious, for a God who is liberative rather than oppressive.

Who is the God in whom women can believe? That is the question. Re-imaging and reworking understandings of God from such a perspective have the potential to become another major "reformation," as threatening to the ecclesial-theological establishment as was the previous one, and themed with the same cry, "Let God be God." That is the real issue at stake.

The failure to recognize what really is at stake in the feminist challenge is revealed in a typical response of many men. They agree (grudgingly perhaps) to "clean up their language" so as not to "offend the women." If the women in "my" congregation or in "my family" are not offended by "my" language, then it is assumed there is no onus to change. The very way in which the issue is set up belies the patriarchal assumptions that are operating. The men are in the positions of authority to be the final arbiters. It is "their" language and "their" women who are at stake, with the ownership assumption only thinly veiled. Attempts are made to "please" and not "offend" the women, that is, basic rules of etiquette must be observed so as to keep the underlying power relations of patriarchy in place.

Furthermore, what this position overlooks is that many women have been as blinded and silenced by the assumptions of a patriarchal system as have men. The complacency of many women with the way the social structure and God-language within it operate, rather than dismissing the need for fundamental change, points instead to the deep and urgent need for such change. Changing the language not only is necessary in those settings where feminists consciously pressure for such but it is especially urgent where there is no such outcry, that is, where patriarchal assumptions continue to silence, mystify, and victimize ordinary women.

What is involved is more than excavating the biblical-theological understandings of God that would counter such misuses. Although nec-essary, this is not sufficient because of how texts, images, and God-language come to function in the subsequent life of a community. Symbols develop a life or history of their own, which must be dealt with as well as the original meaning. The original meaning can help to challenge our contemporary understandings, but the "normative" meaning of a biblical position will result from a dialectic of the original and the present "meaning horizons."[1]

For our purposes here, pervasive in that meaning horizon is the reality of patriarchy. In addition to its narrow definition in terms of the specific *pater familias* structure, patriarchy can more generally be defined as a male-dominant power structure in a society in which all relationships are understood in terms of superiority or inferiority, and social cohesion is assured by the exercise of dominative power.[2] Within patriarchy, males and females are politically differentiated, not as individuals but as members of a social class. Sexual difference becomes the excuse for gender inequality. Females are subjected to the male construct of "femininity," implying females' relinquishment of power or the indirect or manipulative exercise of power.[3] Patriarchy is essentially dualistic and hierarchical. The power and the authority exercised over subordinates are believed to derive from God's will and are exercised in the name of "God." The subordination is difficult to protest without appearing to challenge God "himself." Patriarchy is the basic principle underlying sexism, racism, classism, colonialism, and other institutionalized patterns of inequality. Inequality of power becomes embedded in how we view reality and in how we do theology.

The social structures and ideologies of patriarchy permeate a society's language. Language is not merely an external feature of reality, but as the major traditions of social theory have asserted in recent decades, language is the main bearer and transmitter of the social structure. It encodes our sense of how we are related to others, with patterns of domination and subordination implicit in it. The language itself is revelatory of unjust relations.

God-language bespeaks a whole social structure. In a patriarchal society, the pyramidal structure typically has God on top, then, in hierarchical order, men, women, children, and nature. As a theologian I would insist that God-language does more than legitimize a given social order, but I cannot discount those conscious and unconscious ways in which it does precisely that. Insofar as the social structure has valued males more than females, from a feminist moral perspective it must be challenged. Challenging the God-language operative within that structure is at the core of this moral struggle. As Elisabeth Moltmann-Wendel states:

> The image of God as Father had been useful for forming personality in a patriarchal society. In a hierarchy it offered protection and privacy, trust and security. For a changing society which is apparently fatherless and has undergone a process of internalizing patriarchal laws, images and ideas are needed to replace the restrictive patriarchal morality which puts women in their place.[4]

Tillich's familiar understanding of "symbol" is that it participates in the reality for which it stands and in the power to which it points.[5] The segment of finite reality, in this case male experience, which becomes a vehicle of concrete assertions about God, is affirmed and negated at the same time. Males are like God, but not like God. If God is symbolized as "Father," God is concretized in terms of the human relationship of father and child. *At the same time,* this human relationship is consecrated into a pattern of the divine-human relationship, thereby giving fatherhood theonomous, sacramental depth. If a segment of reality is used as a symbol for God, that realm is elevated into the realm of the holy.[6] Once it becomes "holy," it becomes untouchable, not to be tampered with or changed. In trying to communicate what God is *like,* we use symbols that then tend to be perceived as God-like. If we are to speak of the God revealed through the Bible, we cannot avoid using human vehicles, but a more balanced variety of symbols rather than nearly exclusively male ones can help circumvent the tendency to divinize the male at the expense of the female.

RETRIEVING, REJECTING, REWORKING

There are three basic feminist approaches to our central inquiry: Who is the God in whom we can believe? One is primarily engaged in *retrieving* the nonpatriarchal aspects of our biblical-theological tradition that have been there all along, although often overlooked. Another has *rejected* the historic faith of Jewish and Christian communities, insisting that it is too pervasively and essentially patriarchal to be worth saving. Efforts are devoted instead to retrieving or creating religious traditions that are nonpatriarchal and empowering of women. A third accepts how pervasively patriarchal the tradition is, but insists that it is not essentially so and hence is engaged in the complicated project of *reworking* the symbols and understandings of the faith from out of a nonpatriarchal, that is, feminist, perspective.

Those identifying with the "retrieval" approach would insist that there is basically no incompatibility between women's quest for justice and wholeness and the biblical-theological tradition. The latter inspires and sustains the former. While they acknowledge that sexist biases have tainted many translations, interpretations, and practices, clearing up such biases so that the consistency between the biblical-theological tradition and women's contemporary quest for justice can shine through is seen as a relatively clear, straightforward task. Guiding motifs in this endeavor are the creation of male and female in God's image, the baptismal "new creation" in Jesus Christ, in whom there is neither male nor female,[7] and the recorded accounts of Jesus' amazingly egalitarian dealings with women, which establish for some contemporary interpreters that indeed "Jesus was a feminist."[8] Searching for the women who have been "lost" or overlooked in Bible and church history, and for the hidden feminine images and metaphors for God, is part of the retrieval project.

The basic position here is that there is no inherent problem in "adding women and stirring" because the tradition is at root nonsexist. Although often clouded by patriarchal trappings, these have not distorted the central theological understandings. Clearing up the past misunderstandings that have been perpetuated should be sufficient to enable the Bible's freeing message to transform women today. The God in whom feminists can believe is basically the God whom the church has proclaimed all along. It is mandatory that this God be proclaimed in such a way as to make it totally unambiguous that women are as fully included as are men in the divine intention. It would be helpful if language and imagery for God were more female-oriented, enabling women more readily to relate their experience to God. However, not all retrieval feminists would insist that this is *essential,* because of the central presumption that the God revealed through albeit patriarchal Judaic and Christian traditions has nevertheless, when rightly understood, communicated "good news" for women. Patriarchy, although pervasive, has not infected the basic substance of Christian thought.

This position was characteristic of the beginnings of feminist theology in the early 1970s among especially committed church women, and was the beginning of a contemporary challenging of the ways in which androcentric theological traditions have silenced and rendered women invisible. (The connection between religious thought and male/female power was earlier made by nineteenth-century feminists.) It was the experience of being excluded that provided the motivating impetus for this theological endeavor. The goal was that of clearing away the rubbish in order to uncover the ground on which self-respecting women could stand and be fully "included in" again. The problem was that those of us who engaged in this endeavor in the early 1970s were not yet cognizant of how pervasively the rubbish of patriarchy had penetrated and polluted the ground on which *all* (not only women) depend for their sustenance, necessitating not just a cleanup operation but a major excavation and landscaping project.

This far more radical challenge was set forth by those who now are seen as "post-Christian or post-Jewish" feminist theologians, most notably Mary Daly:

> If God in "his" heaven is a father ruling "his" people, then it is in the "nature" of things and according to divine plan and the order of the universe that society be male-dominated.[9]

What Daly argues is that our entire system of theology and ethics, developed under conditions of male dominance, has been a product of patriarchy and has served sexist interests. The symbols and traditions of Christianity are inherently and essentially sexist. In her later books, she maintains that the tenets and symbols of patriarchal religion have been *consciously* designed to justify male control and to foster hatred toward women.

In response to those feminists who seek to demonstrate what a feminist Jesus was, Naomi Goldenberg replies, "So what?" The point is that regardless of how liberating and egalitarian he was toward women, the Christ symbol since then has become an oppressive symbol for women, such that "he" cannot symbolize liberation for women. What the spokespersons for this "rejecting" approach propose is that women need to make a clear break and enter a new space where harmonious noncontradictory visions and traditions can be spun, whether that means going back to retrieve the Goddess and other religious impulses that have been declared heretical, or developing new myths, language, and traditions.

If we too quickly condemn or undercut these critiques and alternative proposals, we betray our own bondage to patriarchal ways of operating (i.e., by "shooting down the other"). We repeat the age-old way that women have been dealt with, namely, by condemning as heretical those strains which have broken out from under the usual patterns of male dominance. In other words, we prove the point that these radical feminists are trying to make and lend fuel to the argument that the symbols of Christianity are inherently sexist.

The third approach in feminist theology takes seriously the critique that the "rejecting" approach makes of "the tradition." It acknowledges how pervasively patriarchal the tradition is but insists that the tradition has done something else besides legitimating sexism. Those of us identifying with this position find that we have been grasped by a liberating dynamic within the tradition that has somehow broken through in spite of all the patriarchal constructs. There has been something besides patriarchy that has gotten through to women for all these years, convincing some of us that indeed there is Word of *God* and not merely words of *men* embedded in the biblical theological witness.

Therefore the task is that of "reworking" the symbols and understandings of the faith so that they no longer are captive to patriarchal interests. This involves challenging the patriarchal distortions from the inside by using key resources within that tradition itself and yet interpreting these resources so that the tradition begins saying things that haven't been heard before. There is an insistence that no social group can set itself up against others as image and agent of God or use God to justify social domination.[10] The patriarchy of certain metaphors is assumed because of the culture, but the message of the metaphors subverts patriarchy.[11]

This task is empowered by a fundamental faith in a divine power that cannot be confined to any social structure, specifically in a God (or Goddess) who "transcends" patriarchy. As Celie insists in *The Color Purple*, "You have to git man off your eyeball before you can see anything a'tall." Yet the Deity cannot be imaged or spoken of apart from some social assumptions. Ideology and faith are far more deeply intertwined than has usually been assumed. Form and meaning are difficult if not impossible to extricate from one another. But as we begin to interpret the faith through an ideological lens that is an alternative to patriarchy, in the clash between those two world views, what is essential can perhaps be glimpsed.

Reworking the Biblical-Theological Tradition

How have patriarchal assumptions been incorporated into our most basic ways of thinking and talking about God? Understanding the implications of recent feminist scholarship on the origin of patriarchy is important in helping us identify the dimensions of what needs to be addressed in this theological task. The common tenet of such scholarship is that patriarchy emerged in history; it is not an ontological given, despite its seeming universality. Male dominance as a historical phenomenon was based on certain biologically determined givens but became a culturally created and enforced structure over the time span of approximately twenty-five hundred years.[12] By the time men began symbolically to order the universe and the relation of human beings to God, the subordination of women had become "natural" to both men and women.[13]

There are differences in identifying how patriarchy began or what kind of social order it succeeded. A few scholars have posited a prehistorical matriarchy, but many dispute this, suggesting instead a more ambiguous prehistory with no real ascendancy of one gender over the other. The presence of mother-goddess figures in a number of early societies, although suggesting the positive valuation of female power, does not by itself presume a matriarchal social structure.

As to why patriarchy arose, an emerging consensus among a variety of feminist scholars in anthropology, history, and philosophy, as well as theology is that it arose as a compensation for men's physiological inability to give birth. In early societies, giving birth connoted a divine power, especially when the male role in procreation was not yet known. Females, in being able to reproduce themselves, exhibited greater permanence and were experienced as having the key to immortality in a way that males did not. Thus, males experienced females as a substantial ego threat. Azizah al-Hibri, a feminist philosopher, theorizes that males' desire and struggle for the "immortality" that women seemed to have is why males developed ways of appropriating women and their "sacred" life-giving power.[14] He appropriates her, that is, her sexuality and reproduction, such that she becomes commodified, that is, his private property. Maleness came to connote power, strength, and positive agency, so that the male could ensure "his" women and progeny as his own.

In this process, males also acquired hegemony over the symbol system and transformed the major symbols of female power into symbols of male procreativity. For example, the focus shifts to the male's "seed," assumed to be complete in itself needing the female only for incubation. (This continues to be the unexamined premise in some antiabortion positions today.) Although Hebrew religion is often viewed as a move away from the fertility religions of the Canaanites, the suggestion has been set forth that the fertility emphasis still remained, only transformed into male terms, specifically through circumcision as the sign of dedication to the one God and "his" blessing of male procreativity.[15]

The genesis of the Western patriarchal, masculine God occurred alongside the subjugation of women, who, in this new paradigm, were seen as tempting men away from righteousness and the immortality for which women had previously been the agents. Cross-cultural anthropological studies indicate that it is the combination of masculine religious symbols in a society and a climate of social stress and competition that endorses male dominance.[16]

Control and dominance are seen as necessary in the face of fear, conflict, and strife. If a people's identity is forged in less adverse circumstances, and hence less dependent on aggressive acts of men, the gender power relations are likely to be different.[17] Gender power relations change when the situation is such that without change things would come apart, which in our day may suggest a move away from the qualities associated with male dominance.

Perspectives such as these on the origin of gender inequality and of the symbol systems related to such provoke uncomfortable questions of suspicion, especially regarding the structure of theological thought and thus of God-language.

The emergence of Hebrew monotheism, and hence the exclusion of goddess figures, has been linked with the emergence of dualistic under-standings of sexuality.[18] The independent image of women is taken over, even demonized. Male control over women becomes the analogy for divine control over human beings. There is one in charge, and "he" is male. If "he" is the creator of life by himself, within this monotheistic patriarchal framework, creation can only be *ex nihilo*. The point is not that these were conscious, deliberate moves to link the roots of our faith to patriarchal frameworks, nor is it to overlook that some matriarchal qualities did carry over, but it is to suggest that whatever the theological intentions, reinforcing the dynamics of patriarchy was one of the key social functions of the dualistic, hierarchical theological thought and imagery that began to emerge.

Four interrelated aspects of how God is conceptualized are, from a feminist perspective, particularly suspect because they are ways of thinking and talking about God that are essentially patriarchal:

1. In Western theological thought, God is often conceived of *dualistically*. "He" and the world are dichotomized. The transcendent is dichotomized from the immanent, spirit from matter, the creator from creatures, and a masculine God from "feminized" believers. Gender becomes the underlying dualism on which these dichotomies are erected.

There are numerous examples in Scripture where such dichotomies are not seen as necessary in order to communicate who God is and what God is about. A major witness against such dualisms is the incarnation. The uniting of the divine and the human is a radical scandal that the church has always had difficulty with. The "either/or" logic of patriarchal consciousness cannot conceive of a "both/and" option. As Patricia Wilson-Kastner proposes, all the dualisms that divide, separate, cause pain, and support oppression rather than community are gathered together at the cross. Those qualities most incompatible—most dualistic—are paradoxically united in the Crucified One. In redemption dualisms are overcome.[19]

2. *Hierarchical* categories are often viewed as necessary in communicating that God is God, that is, in maintaining God's transcendence. The question is, Can God be God without the necessity of hierarchically ordered relationships? Hierarchy is often viewed as divinely instituted, but many feminists would challenge this. To make God dependent on hierarchical patterns is to limit God to what is humanly contrived. In this sense, insistence on the use of hierarchical patterns in doctrine and language regarding God is itself idolatrous:

> God the monarch, supremely free and sovereign over "his" created, is a conception of domination. Only God is free under this rubric, and the people are "his" property.[20]

The biblical notion of a God who is personally accessible and who enters into loving, steadfast relationships with people can best be communicated through more mutually relational categories. A hierarch tends to be distant, separate, ruling over "his" people in a way that deters the emergence of genuine relation. In contrast, Jesus' experience was of a God who is in intimate, immediate relation with him.

3. Those who would cling to hierarchy as a way of expressing God's transcendence also are challenged by feminist critiques of understandings of God's *power*. For many feminists, power is not a fixed quantity such that one having more power means the other has less power. Power need not be viewed as "control over" but as that which enables and empowers others. The transcendent God is often imaged as a power of hierarchical relation, an almighty God, the essence of whose power is control. That, insists Carter Heyward, is a use of power that is neither creative nor redemptive. A deity who exercises power as control over those who have only to trust and obey blindly is a problematic understanding of transcendence. It results in a Christianity that reflects

> an enormity of control in its preaching and practices—but a dearth of benevolence, justice, and mercy—whether on the mission fields or in the bedroom....Faith in a divine master of domination and control...[serves] to safeguard our claims as those of an all-powerful "God" and our values as reflective of all that he values on earth.[21]

Furthermore, such a use of "transcendence" is contrary to what "transcend" literally means, namely, to cross over, to bridge, or to make connections. A truly transcendent God knows the bounds of no human life or location but is always too actively crossing over boundaries to become any group's source of special privilege. We have "stuck God" with a notion of transcendence that is a projection of those who are used to being in charge.

Consequently, by dichotomizing transcendence and immanence we overlook that transcendence is a relational power that moves to cross over from person to person, race to race, class to class, gender to gender, binding us into one body, breaking down all that would keep us apart. That power is transcendent precisely in its immanence among us.[22]

4. Finally, the net effect of the above three tendencies is to conceive of God in "his" *aloneness,* as if that is what makes God divine:

> If "He" is set apart from human experience (physical, tangible, sensual, painful, humorous, delightful, terrible experience in the world) by the nature of "His" impassivity, then God is completely useless to us. Such a "God" is a destructive, controlling device, manufactured in the minds of men who have bent themselves low before ideals of changeless Truth, deathless Life, pure Spirit, perfect Reason, and other qualities often associated with the patriarchal "God."[23]

Aloneness, impassibility and autonomy are often characterized as the male stereotype in our society. What have we done in so masculinizing God? What God is like becomes equated with what males are conditioned to be like, thereby deluding themselves and others that they are "god-like."

The church's central doctrinal understanding of God—namely the Trinity—is a strong voice against so conceiving God. God as the hierarchical ruler supposedly was repudiated when the church established the doctrine of the coeternality and coequality of the three members of the Trinity. A primary motive in trinitarian formulae was to secure Jesus' divinity. Hence, as Susan Brooks Thistlethwaite analyzes the situation, Christology tended to overtake pneumatology replacing the Spirit with an impersonal, controlling grace that leaves believers passive rather than empowering them. The church becomes a spiritual realm animated by a pacifying and harmonizing Spirit that has no independent identity. Such a spiritual realm becomes privatized and divorced from the messy world and the conflicts in it. Thus we are left with a feminized Spirit to tend to the "private" realm, while Father and Son remain the active agents in the "public" realm.

Let us look more closely at what this gender duality has done to God. The Spirit, subordinate to the Father and even to the Son (in the Western church), confined to maintaining personal relationships with no independent identity of its own, ends up sounding stereotypically feminine in the extreme. Society has tended to assign women the responsibility for maintaining relationships, allowing men to view themselves as self-seeking, competitive, aggressive, and sustained by nurturing women:

> It is then not, perhaps, so curious that theologians have done the same to the Godhead. One aspect of God, an aspect deemed subordinate and peripheral, the Spirit, has been chosen to be responsible for self-giving and for sustaining relationships. But God the "Father" has remained the "Almighty": impassive, remote and unknowable, dominating "his" creation.[24]

Reclaiming the coequality of God the Spirit with God the Creator and Redeemer is necessary if the Spirit is to be seen as free to act in history and to do so through our relationships. God is essentially a relational God—how else could we proclaim "God is love"? God gives and God receives. Such give-and-take relationship is a sign not of weakness but of strength. Because we are culturally so hooked on the myth of the self-contained, self-possessed, autonomous man, such an image has also been projected onto God. Bonding with others, which tends to be associated with women, is seen as a sign of dependence, need, and weakness. Feminists would insist that that "ain't necessarily so!"

Insofar as our culture has devalued what is associated with women, so too we have devalued such in God. It is as a relational God that God's presence becomes most powerful in our lives and history, not as one who controls us but as one who empowers us. We become empowered to seek and live out just relationships that are mutually enriching and fulfilling, not ones that build up one party at the expense of the other.

Glimpses of this kind of relationality seem to be present in the Gospels' portrayal of Jesus. We cannot deny that he was male. He had status and privileges that he would not have had as a female in that society. But at crucial points he is depicted as going against the societal expectations, whether consciously or not. He refused to lord himself over others, particularly over women. The unquestioned connotations of gender, that is, the power of men over women, were challenged through the ways he related to women. He broke taboos prohibiting men from conversing with women to whom they were not related (the woman at the well). He refused to have any woman, including his own mother, identified primarily in terms of her childbearing function.[25] His relationships with women were not limited by women's prescribed role or status in society. His actions suggest a challenging of what is the most universal relationship of domination and submission—that between males and females. It was transformative relationships, not biological or social givens, which were primary in his life and hence in the meaning of who the Christ is for us today. Biology is not destiny. If the seemingly most absolute status began to be transformed through Jesus' historical activity that breaks open new transformative possibilities for us—for men as well as for women.

In the Synoptics we find a Jesus who did not proclaim himself as king but who proclaimed the reign of God. In that promise he focused on the "little ones" whom especially the religious leaders of that day had excluded or trivialized. He called people not to subject themselves to the existing social order of bondage, but pointed instead to a new sense of God's saving activity revealed in their present while pointing to the future. We find a Jesus who willed the wholeness and humanity of everyone and who had a following—a Jesus movement—that was a discipleship of equals. Those who once had no hope now had hope.

Unfortunately these images of Jesus are a far cry from the Christ whom much of the church has proclaimed since then. As the early Christian movement grew and became more established, Christ tended to become a timeless revelation of divine perfection rather than an iconoclastic, prophetic figure to empower people in their present. In the fourth century as the Constantinian era began, Christianity became installed with political power over the world. It became an imperial religion, providing a "sacred canopy" over the existing social order. Understandings of who Christ is became increasingly hierarchical and otherworldly. No longer was Christ viewed as one who frees from oppression. Christ was no longer encountered through slaves and women, but instead his maleness was accentuated in importance, to the point that only males could represent him, as continues to be the case to this day in Roman Catholicism. As Rosemary Radford Ruether contends, Christology became the apex of a system of control over all who are "other" and inferior in some way, particularly women. Christ was increasingly seen as the founder and cosmic governor of existing social hierarchies.

Certainly much of this carried over and continued to influence the Lutheran tradition. But there also is within this tradition a distinctive emphasis with the potential to challenge these tendencies. I refer to the "theology of the cross" emphasis. Luther insisted that God is not known through the visible or analogical means but through invisible and seemingly contradictory means. In what we regard as contrary to the divine—through such experiences as trouble, misery, and weakness—God becomes visible, and not through what human beings have created or assumed to be "of God" (which today would need to include such "isms" as racism and sexism and imperialism). Therefore:

1. The true God is not the omnipotent monarch but the one who divests "himself" of power, who hides under the opposite of what the world recognizes as omnipotence, who is the "crucified God." God is none other than the One manifest on the cross, revolutionizing our idea of God and of power.

2. The good news is not of deliverance *from* the experience of pain and struggle (removing us from it) but of permission to enter it with expectancy, and therefore with freedom. This is not masochism but an insistence that authentic liberation is found as we confront and enter into the negations and contradictions of our lives.

3. A theology of the cross proclaims a God whose will is to *be with us,* radically to identify with us in our concrete, everyday experience—in our suffering, in our femaleness, in our maleness, in the givenness of our particular situation.

4. Consequently, God is not preeminently revealed through the male-ensconced values of our society—especially those of mastery or power over others. The male-centered, patriarchal qualities attached to God are overturned. No more need there be an idolatrous projection upon God of the characteristics of the ruling sexual group. God's "otherness" is in terms of that which the predominant society has devalued.

Jesus is not a model for women to imitate, in some kind of scapegoat, self-sacrificing role. To identify with him in that sense would only increase our victimization and mutilation. We are not to give ourselves up to be crucified for anyone's sake but are "to struggle together against the injustice of all human sacrifice, including our own."[26]

The cross reveals to us intimations of the God who identifies with us in the cruciform sufferings that are already a part of our lives as women and thus encourages us to struggle against them. The cross challenges any triumphalistic link between God and the kind of exclusive "power over others" that controls, limits, and destroys women and others. That kind of power which has given divine sanction to racism, capitalism, imperialism, and sexism is challenged by the cross. Such "power over" has been central to the social understanding of what it means to be male in this society. To the extent that God through the cross is freed up from an identification with such dominating power, God is also freed up from the social criterion of maleness.

The christological symbol of receptivity to God's will and to self-sacrifice, if it had been historically embodied in a woman, would have only reinforced a not too helpful stereotype—that of the self-sacrificing female. If he had been a woman, he would have gotten even less of a hearing in his day than he did! Instead, Jesus, a male, through his interactions with others, helped to break the stereotype of who males are. He challenged the social definitions of power and hence of the power relationship between men and women. Mutual relationships rather than hierarchical relationships are what he lived out and to what he calls us today.

There is a richness in the self-revelation of God in Christ that discloses more inclusiveness than Christianity has dared to preach. An exclusive god created by men and encapsulated in male imagery of power and privilege must be challenged so that the true God can live. God encourages us to resist patriarchy's deathblows, to stand on our feet, empowered by the one we know as Christ who identifies fully with us. One of our students describes in powerfully moving terms her experience of being raped, and as she lay there on the ground fearing that she would be killed, what flashed before her was a vision of Christ—of Christ as a woman—"because only a woman would understand."

God is immanently with us, revealed through our pain and struggle, but "she" is more than immanent, more than female. God is always "other," moving us beyond simple identification with what is, thus endlessly challenging all of our human attempts to nail down God. God is the continually transforming horizon of human existence, calling us to break with patterns of oppression. God is always with us and always other. Salvation in Christ occurs through what happened on the cross, but the new creation that is set loose through the resurrection—the iconoclastic, transforming power of God—creates a new partnership, a new "us," a new church.

NOTES

1. Lisa Sowle Cahill, *Between the Sexes* (Philadelphia: Fortress Press, 1985), 33.

2. Sandra M. Schneiders, *Women and the Word: The Gender of God in the New Testament* (New York: Paulist Press, 1986), 13.

3. Beverly Wildung Harrison, *Making the Connections* (Boston: Beacon Press, 1985), 31.

4. Ibid., 92.

5. Paul Tillich, *Systematic Theology, 3 vols.* (Chicago: University of Chicago Press, 1951-63), 1:239.

6. Ibid., 240-41.

7. Gen. 1:27; Gal. 3:28.

8. E.g., Leonard Swidler, "Jesus Was a Feminist," *Catholic World* 212 (1971), 177-83.

9. Mary Daly, *Beyond God the Father* (Boston: Beacon Press 1973), 13.

10. Rosemary Radford Ruether, *Sexism and God-talk* (Boston: Beacon Press, 1983), 23.

11. Schneiders, *Women and the Word,* 34.

12. Gerda Lerner, *The Creation of Patriarchy* (New York: Oxford University Press, 1986), 42.

13. Ibid., 211.

14. Ibid., 86.

15. Ibid., 192.

16. Peggy Reeves Sanday, *Female Power and Male Dominance* (Cambridge: Cambridge University Press, 1981.), 230.

17. Ibid., 11-12.

18. Elisabeth Moltmann-Wendel, *A Land Flowing with Milk and Honey: Perspectives on Feminist Theology* (New York: Harper & Row, 1986), 55.

19. Patricia Wilson-Kastner, *Faith, Feminism, and the Christ* (Philadelphia: Fortress Press, 1983).

20. Susan Brooks Thistlethwaite, *Metaphors for the Contemporary Church* (New York: Pilgrim Press, 1983), 112.

21. Isabel Carter Heyward, *Our Passion for Justice, Images of Power, Sexuality, and Liberation* (New York, Pilgrim Press, 1984), 244-45.

22. Ibid., 245.

23. Isabel Carter Heyward, *The Redemption of God: A Theology of Mutual Relation* (Washington, D.C.: University Press of America, 1982), 7.

24. Ibid., 116.

25. Luke 11:27-28.
26. Heyward, *The Redemption of God*, 212.

Letters to My Father

Sally Smits

Dear Dad,

I don't know how you have stayed there this long, and I don't know how much longer you can sit in the hard wood pews and listen to some of the damage as it's done, or watch some exclusion or hurt as our church sometimes grips and misuses the power it has.

When Rev. Mel White came to Hope to speak, I love what he told us. He said that sometimes people can "take the Bible literally, but not seriously." I think you take it seriously, Dad, as you open and read, and you seem to be able to keep the whole overarching meaning in the back of your mind, even as we hear the individual passages and proof-texts. You taught me to look at the Bible seriously, too, although not word-for-word literally. You helped me understand that the Bible was not a scientific textbook, nor a table and catalogue of facts, nor a self-help, how-to book. You taught me to read it as though these stories were being passed down to me, from the oral tradition in which they began. You taught me to see it as literature, and as the most amazing, century-spanning story of salvation. The Bible, under that kind of reading lamp, didn't make God any less true or real, but instead it opened up God's creativity and faithfulness, and it gave the Bible a context and a setting and a meaning. The whole book became a woven fabric, stitching the Old and New Testaments together, making the story complete (or nearly complete) rather than fraying in too many directions and instructions. You have repeated the German word for "story of salvation" to me so many times, saying, *"Heilsgeschichte,* Sally—remember that." You reminded me to put the passage back in the place where it came from, sent to the Corinthians or the Israelites, given in the desert or spoken in the Holy City. I am so thankful that, although I'll never understand everything in the Bible, with all of its richness and complexity and tightly woven threads, I at least have a starting place, a foundation. *Heilsgeschichte.*

And this outlook and overview was one of my saving graces as our church fought over the ordination of women, and even as it still simmers. It helped me to hold the Bible close, rather than give up on it and walk away. And this way of seeing opened up God's love for me and other women, too, even as we felt trampled or ignored or shut out of the church, only on account of our gender. I couldn't really understand the confusion or dilemma from where I stood, since the questions for me were these: Do we allow talented, qualified, gifted pastors, all of them, to preach and serve? And do we pay attention to Christ's redemption and restoration? Do we still live by the letter of the law and only use the New Testament freedom when it doesn't require a change in our structures? Do we proof-text and proof-text, find submission, headship, and Adam's finger pointing towards Eve, and then look no further, no deeper? Do we ignore Christ, his treatment of women? And do we take it into our hands to limit his death and resurrection, saying that it was only meant for half of the human race, and that Eve and her daughters must be redeemed some other way before they can use their gifts?

The worst idea I came across in a book I was reading was not one that was perpetuated by our denomination (thankfully), but I think it may hold some unconscious clout in some minds. It stated, quite matter-of-factly, that women should not be ordained because Jesus Christ was a man, and "it would be difficult to see in the minister the image of Christ. For Christ himself was and remains a man."

I stopped reading. I threw the book. How far would we push that assumption? Will we only ordain Jewish men? Only Jewish men who have woodworking skills? Only Jewish carpenter men who are approximately thirty? Only carpenter, thirty-year-old, Jewish men who perform miracles, come of a virgin birth, have plans to be executed? It was too ridiculous. The minister imitates Christ and his life of service and love, just as many in the Christian faith try to do. But to exclude women as pastors and leaders in the church based on Christ's gender? I can't handle that. Christ's humanity, his understanding and connection to us as human while still fully God—this is the important part. All the questions that come to my head, when I search out the whole of all the arguments, are answered with a loud and shouted "no!" Certainly, Christ came for women, and certainly, women have gifts that should not be stifled, stomped out, choked off.

And certainly, you can see that I've already loaded the questions. But they seem to be the ones that I needed to ask in order to challenge the assumptions already made, even if they were made only silently.

This issue of ordination of women, to me, is more than just a question of position or office. It's an issue of whether or not our church values women, whether it sees them as whole members of the body of Christ, or whether it still sees them as less, as missing some of their worth, as lacking some sort of forgiveness or redemption, as secondary humans. It's an issue of justice. I remember when both of us wrote letters to the council, asking, (or demanding), that they consider women fully human, fully capable, fully worthy of complete participation in the church, and that they stop throwing up specific and out-of-context verses as smokescreens to prevent movement ahead, forward. I remember that yours was all in capital, attention-demanding letters. I have never felt so valued as when I realized that not only were you fighting for the "right thing" or the "just cause" or even the survival of the church, but you were also fighting for me and my sister and my mother, three women directly affected by the battle in the church. I remember gathering strength from your anger and loud call for change, while at the same time warming myself up with the kind of love that would stand with me, burn with me. I don't know that I ever told you how much I needed that, how much I needed something to hang onto or someone to hang onto me, telling me that I was worth fighting for. You've done it more than once in my life, and it's only been slowly that I've realized it. Now, I'm beginning to fight for my own self too, and recognize my own value.

Lately, more than just ordination has come up in front of me, stood in my line of vision, and I can't put these issues away in any drawer, either. They are too important to let slide, and I don't think I can just stand in a quiet, dark corner of the church while I wait for change to come. I'm certain that bringing these things up, putting them in church bulletins or on council agendas, will bring divisions and splits and fights again, but I don't think we can continue to glaze over them just for the sake of a false harmony. Besides all of this, they are too connected to the other issues of women in the church, and nothing will be healed or resolved until we've confronted and worked through each of them. I'm too aware, too awake now to let them go, and I care too much about the church and the people in it to decide to stay away. I think you'd tell me, too, not to back away or back down from what I believe. So I'm trying to stand firm, deconstruct but not destroy, and change without too much loss.

Just a while ago, I met an amazing woman, Claire Wolterstorff, and she brought one of these subtle, often underlying issues to my attention in a sharper, clearer light. It is the issue of language, inclusive or exclusive, for people and for God. Most people, when I talk about this, tell me that it doesn't really matter. They're just words. But words, as insults or endearments, as symbols for what we mean and feel, have tremendous power. Claire told me that she sees inclusive language not as some small or insignificant letter-change, but "as an issue of justice."

Maybe I've already told you, or maybe you've already noticed that I can't use "he" for God any longer. Maybe this is stretching my radical roots too deep, but ever since all of the other metaphors and names for God have been given to me, I can't go back to just using one, especially one that, since it is used exclusively, seems to leave women out of God's image entirely. And I have trouble, too, with generalized male words for all people, though this is less controversial or boundary-pushing or powerful than language for God. I wanted to write another letter to the church, maybe for their next council meeting, but my guess is that they'd push it to the side, thinking of it as too unimportant or too insignificant to talk about. But I'd still have things to tell them, and this is what I'd say, anyway. (Do you mind if I scribble it to you first?)

If you are going to call me "brother," then treat me as such.

If you are going to spread the word "mankind" or "men" over me like a suffocating blanket, then you ought to know that I will struggle to breathe.

If you are going to generalize and try to call me just "one of the guys," you shouldn't be surprised if I want to be a part of that "elite" group.

If you make enveloping labels, you must know that they will only be accurate when they do, in fact, include and envelop...

And it would go on from there.

Do you see the same things, Dad? Am I completely off my rocker here? I just can't close my eyes to it anymore. Maybe it was never intentional, but as I look more and more at the dominant labels and names that are scattered through our texts and hymns and stories, in our churches and culture, and even in our everyday lives, I am always surprised at how predominantly male they are. Why shouldn't it change to be more welcoming, less specified and exclusive?

In the first inclusive worship service I'd ever attended, I was taken aback by the use of "her" for God. But I was more surprised at the fact that I'd never heard it before. Where had this been all along? Hidden beneath layers of turning God into a male, making "Father" and "him" the most important metaphors in our language. I am so used to language-with-a-penis (I know that sounds crude, but would you ever say that it's the other way around?), I almost didn't know how to respond to the tables when they were turned or flipped over.

But I found myself thinking that the male terms would be fine if they didn't necessitate subordination. If these general terms truly did include everyone, and if male pronouns and references to God truly did include all facets and aspects of God, then there really would be no problem, and no reason to worry. But they do not. They exclude. They make women less, and outside. So there is a need for language castration, if it's the only way to level us again. I keep wondering how most men would handle being included in "womankind" and joined in the "sisterhood." And if they can't fit comfortably there, why wouldn't they then understand that I don't feel included in "mankind" or initiated into the "brotherhood"?

And I keep wishing that I were able to call God everything at once, more than just "he" or "she," and that labels didn't feel so mutually exclusive, so obstructive, putting up so many walls.

It was and sometimes is the standard opening for a prayer for me, to say "Dear Heavenly Father..." It is so ingrained that my tongue slides easily over it, and I'm already finished with the smooth three words before I realize that I've said them. And I don't mean to say that "Father" as a label and a connection to God is so terrible. Really, it's a beautiful and open way to image and speak about God. My personal connotations, from you and the characteristics and qualities you've shown me, are good, solid, warm, intelligent ones. (What was it like for you, with your father and a relationship that has not always been whole and welcoming? What were your connotations with "father"?) As it was for me, I never stepped beyond my own connotations (it's still difficult, even after noticing my limited names and meanings) and I made "Father" the only possibility and way to see God. I just left out and didn't account for or even realize all "his" other names, and in turn, "his" other possibilities.

Talking about God-language has opened my eyes, or at least begun to open them. Why didn't I ever consider the other possibilities? I know that God does have some fatherly characteristics—we are called "children of God," Jesus used this name in his prayers, and for probably more than centuries we have invoked God and opened dialogue with a phrase or sentence that calls on God as "father."

It is a powerful way to begin speaking, a word that can bring God close and caring, a word of comfort and power—"*Abba.*" But even these associations can fade; it can become too commonplace and easy; and it is so limiting to use only one name. Out of all the possibilities—the words of an entire language—to call on the most powerful Being of the universe, and I can only come up with one or two words? To encase God, to frame God, to limit God, to make God safe. Certainly, these images and words based on "father" give us an entry point to *begin* thinking of God, but they are not the only doors. There are so many other entrances, considerations, names, phrases, parables, stories, images, characteristics, and metaphors that allow us to come closer to fathoming our Creator, our Ruler, our Love, our Mother and our Father.

Maybe the fact that we can never find an adequate name for God shows that we will never be able to wholly grasp who God is and what God does in this world. As I've talked about the ways that naming something can control, or exorcise, or expose and break down, maybe I have come to realize that we can only name God in parts and pieces, never in one word. We come closest in our fractional metaphors and similes. And we've made some stronger and more well-known than others, but none really can imagine all of God. God is beyond our pronouns, adjectives, images. God is not solely father, mother, lover, savior, ruler, or servant, though I wouldn't take any of these away.

Granted, it looks like/feels like shock value to use the feminine or try to start with something "genderless." Maybe our church isn't ready, or will never try. Changing our deepest perceptions and our foundation-words is bound to be frightening and "shocking" at first. But it's also revealing, amazing, deepening, and liberating, and it's closer to truth than we'll be if we simply keep the same vocabulary. If we're going to discover even one hundredth of the mystery of God, we need to start speaking in a way that approaches that mystery, that allows God to be larger than our language.

I don't know how you'll think of this, or if this is over the edge or beyond liberated. What I know is that I haven't ever felt so in awe, or so close to God, as when I began to split wide my ideas about God and who God might be, who God could be, and what God could do. Maybe you won't want a thank you for this, or maybe you will, but I am thankful that I could at least begin with *Heilsgeschichte,* an open and working and liberated view of God's speech and Word. In turn, my faith broadened, deepened, grew and took new root, as I could begin to see God in new ways. And that was a gift. Thank you.

Sally

The Running Father

Luke 15:1-2, 11-32

John Linton

IN MY BIBLE, the caption above this text reads "The Prodigal Son," and that's how we all learned it as children. But I believe Jesus tells us this parable of a father with two lost sons to show us who God is. So, I've titled the story "The Running Father." Let me say why.

Luke gives us a context for the parable by telling us at the start of Luke 15 that tax collectors and sinners are eating with Jesus, causing the Pharisees and scribes to murmur. Tax collectors were contracted by the Roman occupiers to collect a set amount of money, and whatever they could extort above that amount constituted their wages. So, of course, the general population dreaded and hated these tax collectors. The Pharisees, on the other hand, were a well-respected sect, but they lacked the actual status inherited by the aristocracy of priests, born into their privilege. While some Pharisees were also born priests, they were, for the most part, still outsiders. However, by keeping the rules priests kept, they could acquire some of the status priests enjoyed. Rules for maintaining purity were elaborate and complicated with uncleanness measured in the first, second, third, or fourth degrees. For example, if you touched a person unclean in the first degree, you became unclean in the second degree; unless you touched them with a wet hand, in which case you became unclean only to the first degree. I think you get the picture. Given all the complications and the myriad stipulations of ritual purity rules, the Pharisees had to be careful to eat only with others who knew and obeyed the same rules they scrupulously kept. Anyone who did not belong to their diner's club, the Pharisees called, "*Am Haartez*," which means "person" or "persons of the land," in short, just an ordinary person who made no special effort to keep daily purity rules. Nowadays, when we read "sinner" in the text, we attach to it connotations of bad moral behavior, but to the Pharisees it meant persons like ourselves, even though those persons constituted a social caste or class to be avoided as much as possible.

By eating with "sinners," Jesus undermines the power base of the Pharisees. He includes in his table fellowship exactly those persons whom the Pharisees need to exclude in order to guarantee their status. Jesus knows the Pharisees are murmuring about his inclusivity, even though the Pharisees' complaints are not very direct. They merely observe that Jesus is eating with tax collectors and "sinners." The Pharisees tend to be passive aggressive on this score, and Jesus confronts their masked aggression with three parables.

The first two parables are about lost individuals—a lost coin in one case and a lost sheep in the other. Individuals always get lost in the "group think" of communities who need outsiders in order to establish their insider status. So, Jesus tells parables that speak about the joy of including lost individuals. However, the third parable of the chapter underscores this point, and then moves beyond it; the parable of the Running Father shows the Pharisees how their "group think" has prevented from being in touch with themselves as individuals.

The younger brother represents the "sinners" and tax collectors. The older brother represents the Pharisees. Both brothers are out of touch with their father and at odds with each other. Both brothers seem unaware of negative feelings for their father. Both brothers are out of touch with their true selves. The older brother cannot rejoice at his younger brother's homecoming because his identity is based on excluding his younger brother. The father of the parable is with both boys in such a way as to foster reconciliation in their dysfunctional family. Of course, the father represents God. Let's review some of the story's details in light of their cultural context in order to unpack these ideas.

At the start of the parable, the younger son wants his inheritance now. Cultural anthropologists tell us that in Mediterranean culture, asking for an inheritance before the death of a parent was equivalent to asking them to drop dead; sons should never inherit property or money until their father died. Again by cultural standards, the elder son should have talked the younger boy into staying home and then facilitated reconnection with their father. He fails to do his cultural duty on both accounts. By agreeing to let the younger son go he also is telling his father to drop dead. We know this because the elder son also receives his inheritance before his father dies, "He divided his living between them."

The father does something unheard of: he distributes his substance without making provision for himself, becoming unnecessarily vulnerable to the vicissitudes of old age. Culturally speaking, the father should have retaliated by disowning or punishing his sons for breaking a cultural taboo, or at the very least, protected himself with a document obligating his children to take care of him in his dotage. The text makes no mention of any such protection. The father seems literally to be giving his life away.

The young buck heads off to a faraway place where he finally ends up feeding pigs, especially degrading work for a young Jew. In response to his dire need, "no one gave him anything," a direct contrast to his almost prodigal father who gave away his own living. For a Jewish son to lose his inheritance to Gentiles would be shameful, so it might not be safe to come back to his hometown where many would be slow to forget his complete disregard for village and family honor.

However, he begins to feel a lack. The text says, "He began to be in need." And so he begins to get in touch. Then the text says, "He comes to himself." That describes something very simple and basic. It dawns on the kid, somewhere deep down, that something fed him or gave him life in the past, and now he is in dire need of that something. Remembering he once had it gives him hope to imagine it possible again.

But even in returning, the younger son is still out of touch. "Make me a hired servant," he murmurs as he walks home. It's his strategy to get in good with life again. Perhaps he can pay his father back by working for wages. That way he won't have to live at home with his elder brother; he can live with the hired help. To be sure, the villagers' humiliations will be enough to face. But perhaps he will eventually be able to please his father once again. Conceptually, the younger boy is off track, but at least he is listening to his body. If, like me, you spend a good deal of your time tying to get your ideas straight, take notice—according to the parable, we can be on the right road and still have goofy ideas. We don't have to have our ideas straight in order to experience God. So, the murmuring son nears his village, probably with some hesitation and ambivalence, since we also know that the village would be justified in beating a disrespectful son who has disgraced his father. He rehearses his speech, but he never gets to use all of it.

That's because his father runs to greet his son. According to cultural anthropologists, men of importance living in the Mediterranean basin do not run in public. They have someone else do the running for them. They are too dignified to run.

But this father is willing to make a fool of himself in front of all the villagers who've gathered to watch. He is willing to run the gauntlet of village disapproval. The text tells us that, moved "in his guts" with compassion, he runs to fall on his son's neck and embrace him, kissing his lost child over and over again. He endures something culturally shameful because, as he exclaims to his servants, "this my son, was dead and now is alive; he was lost, and is found." He is so happy to see his child going in the right direction for a change. Again the anthropologists say the cultural message is clear: the father is conveying to the villagers his willingness to reintegrate his son at the expense of his own honor. This father loves and accepts his younger son in a way that the younger son cannot love and accept himself.

So, upon return, the father gives his younger son an identity that the younger son never dreamed he had. You have probably met people, if you aren't one yourself, who have murmured for decades, "make me a hired servant." The younger son begins the speech he rehearsed but is cut off by his father before he even gets to the "make me a hired servant" bit. Like the lost son, it's difficult for many of us to feel an organic connection to God. On the other hand, some well-meaning Pharisees claimed a connection they didn't have. Both sons in the parable seem unaware of their ambivalent feelings for their father. According to the parable, redemption lies in the direction of becoming conscious of these negative feelings and allowing them to surface.

God is something of a party animal in this parable. It's the robe, and the ring, and the fatted calf, and the invitation to all the villagers (who've watched him run down the road, robes flying) to come celebrate his returned child. I do love this about the Gospel: it wouldn't be bad if it were true. The God of the parable wants to celebrate the recovery of our place in the family. God is closer to us than we are to ourselves and coming to God is a coming to ourselves.

Now let's think a bit about the elder son. He too is out of touch. The preparation of the fatted calf begins before the son and the rest of the villagers have come in from the fields. Lack of refrigeration meant that meat after slaughter had to be immediately prepared, so as the elder son returns home, music from a party already in process greets him. You would think that after a long day in the field, he would welcome a surprise party promising to last well into the night, but he is suspicious. Inquiring about the music, he learns it marks his brother's return. So, he refuses to come in, snubbing his father and the other party goers who expect him to assume his role as master of ceremonies. His father leaves the party to entreat him to come in, an exact parallel to his earlier running to embrace his younger son. Instead of berating the older boy for not doing his duty as host of the party, his father walks outside, signaling the entire village that he will take responsibility for his eldest son's rude behavior even at the cost of losing dignity in their eyes. Joining his older child, he implores, "Son, you are always with me, and all that is mine is yours," as if to say, can you not understand grace? Can you not celebrate this resurrection with me? The elder son is sitting on a bit of anger, and it spills out as he accuses his father. Not even able to call his sibling, "Brother," he slanders his younger brother when he says to their father, "This son of yours has spent his inheritance with harlots." While everyone knows he disgraced the village, his father, and that he ended up resorting to pig's food, sleeping with "harlots" isn't actually part of the story. The older son does not know this to be true. Is he projecting or what?

The elder son's ambivalence about his father surfaces as well. You can feel his resentment burn when he finds out his brother is sumptuously feasting on a calf while he has never partied with as much as a goat. The elder boy might have talked around town about his father's generosity, but in his heart he feared his Dad was stingy and unwilling to grant him his heart's desires. In short, the elder son had never been able to feel his father's joy, not then and not now.

The parable speaks about a relationship both children have trouble participating in. Their morbid rivalry blinds the brothers to what they already have in their father. They both are sustained in life by a parent who views them in a way they cannot see themselves. There is something "organic" going on all around them, but they have trouble seeing, let alone being a part of it.

One does not have to be much of a feminist to take offense at this parable. On the surface, it appears to be another story about guys, told by a guy to a bunch of guys. One can imagine a feminist wondering if these boys have a mother and the father a wife. Perhaps a feminist would rewrite the story from the perspective of what the parable has left out. But profoundly and surprisingly, despite its all male cast, we find in this odd parable a deconstruction of the notion of "father" as it was accepted by Jesus' contemporaries. The father in the parable is willing to dispossess himself of his substance before death. In a culture based on honor, he willingly humiliates himself for the sake of inclusion. He treats both the younger and elder son in an egalitarian fashion offensive to hierarchy. Such actions would have shocked every father listening to Jesus' words, because they show an almost cavalier attitude towards the institution of fatherhood as they understood it. I might add that mothers and children would also have been startled by this father who refuses to abide by patriarchal rules.

Furthermore, death is circulating in the family and village of the parable. Both boys appear to be parricides because they are, first of all, involved in fratricidal rivalry. The rivalry is apparent in the younger son's intention to live outside of his brother's house upon return and his desire to take his inheritance to a far country in the first place. In the cultural context both actions insult his older brother. Brothers should dwell together on the family land upon the demise of the patriarch. On the other hand, the elder son's refusal to come to the feast and be the master of ceremonies not only insults his father but unmasks his hatred for his younger brother. What I am suggesting is that Jesus might be describing the kind of dysfunction typical of patriarchal families. The boys jockeying for position, despite the cultural expectation that the older boy will rule the roost with a double portion of the inheritance (laws obviously aimed at minimizing rivalry yet often stirring it up), not really knowing what they truly need—all are criticisms feminists make of patriarchy. The father in the parable, attempting to subvert fraternal violence by active love, goes against the hierarchal distribution of limited goods. As a parent, he desires closeness, relationship and connection, quite unlike the aloof, distant, law enforcing father of patriarchy often targeted by feminists for criticism. Perhaps the parable even suggests that we ought to look for examples of real fathers among those who are the victims of fraternal violence caused by the inevitable rivalry of hierarchy.

Feminists have called attention to how death dealing patriarchy can be to both women and men, to those marginalized and to those on center stage. In this story, patriarchy does not work for either brother. The father who does not pay much attention to patriarchal protocol is the person working for reconciliation. His principal work, if we can call it that, consists in border crossings (transgressions of what the culture considers well behaved). Our work today as we bear witness to the enlivening presence of God may consist of similar border crossings, for example, the use of feminine images and language for God.

Our parable is operating on at least two levels. Not only does it call attention to the Pharisees' behavior toward outsiders (sinners and tax collectors), but it does so by narrating to the Pharisees a believable scenario, a scenario they might well have recognized. Sibling rivalry or an estranged son must have felt like a well-known death to some of Jesus' listeners. We can feel Jesus entreating the Pharisees, much like the father of the parable entreating the elder son, to come in. Wouldn't the Pharisees feel joy if their family problems were resolved? And what is this business with Pharisees and sinners: is it a replay of their own family problems anted up to a collective level? The Gospel of this parable is *in concreto*. The father of the parable is not an idea. He divides his substance, runs, kisses, and entreats. He gives a ring, a robe, a fatted calf and throws an extravagant party. These are real events in his children's lives. He seeks them in their lostness, culturally inscribed, and meets them in their lostness, by transgressing cultural inscriptions. We can imagine that if Mediterranean culture were matriarchal instead of patriarchal, Jesus might have told the story with a mother and daughters as protagonists. Perhaps in that case, the second person of Trinity would have been a woman accompanied by her twelve female sidekicks. Additionally, it is easy to imagine how a matriarchy could foster rivalry leading to matricide.

Returning to our situation, if the parable is true, then the God coming toward us is already a reality. We do not "think" this God; instead we recognize God already present with us. This God willingly runs on the way to meet us, to carry our shame for us, and in the process of embracing us, heal us of our shame and return us to ourselves. Of course, a direct experience of God may not be the only way we come to awareness. The younger son sees his father running and feels the embrace and the kisses. These are not ideas or words. Perhaps in your own experience, someone has loved you in a specific way that exceeds our culture's expectations. If so, they incarnated the Gospel for you, whether or not you recognized it at the time. They encouraged you to accept the world as a friendly little place despite your fears and perhaps your shame. I hope you can relax into those experiences as you become empowered to discern them—because they are the arms of God.[1]

NOTES

1. For the anthropological insights and scholarship, I am especially grateful to Bruce Malina, *Social-Science Commentary on the Synoptic Gospels*, and Kenneth Bailey, *Poet and Peasant* and *Through Peasant Eyes: A literary-Cultural Approach to the Parables in Luke*. Of course, my use of their work should not imply their agreement with any of my ideas.

Rafting

September 19, 1997

Rachel Bennett

My weighty body was
never that of a boy.
i never knew the tricks
that all boys know…
and i still don't.

"You are a girl"
Daddy tells me.
"I wanted a boy
but you are a girl."
i understand this—
my seven year old mind
never learned anything
as well as it learned this:

girls don't
girls can't
girls aren't.
especially when they
are clumsy
or fat

especially when they
have asthma
or funny legs
or big breasts.

speaking of breasts—
i learned some of
boys' secrets.
i learned their
hunger for my body
hunger that ate me and
swallowed me whole.
i learned the pressure
of their hands, their arms,
i learned the disrobing
intrusion of their knowing gaze.
i learned violation.

so while i was
being devoured
i stopped eating.
maybe if i become
the boy i never was but the boy i always
wished i was…
but that didn't work either.

so i have simply learned
to walk eyes
averted or
cast down.
i walk out of lighted doors
toward lighted doors
i avoid bushes, trees,
and tall, dark, silent types.
i try not to watch the tv screen
telling me my experiences of
terror

are necessary to glamorize-
especially if taken "in context".

and yet...
i spent saturday
pummeling the water
in my rage
staying in the raft
"going all the way"
giving myself the
luxury of strength
giving my body
the freedom of a voice.
and now it won't stop
talking.
my shoulder is sweetly sore
and my hand has beautiful blue bruises
my weakness is beginning to leave me
all because I let myself sit
on a raft in a raging river
and raged right back
and now i never want to stop talking.

The Book of Ruth and Naomi

Marge Piercy

When you pick up the Tanakh and read
the Book of Ruth, it is a shock
how little it resembles memory.
It's concerned with inheritance,
lands, men's names, how women
must wiggle and wobble to live.

Yet women have kept it dear
for the beloved elder who
cherished Ruth, more friend than
daughter. Daughters leave. Ruth
brought even the baby she made
with Boaz home as a gift.

Where you go, I will go too,
your people shall be my people.
I will be a Jew for you,
for what is yours I will love
as I love you, oh Naomi
my mother, my sister, my heart.

Show me a woman who does not dream
a double, heart's twin, a sister
of the mind in whose ear she can whisper,
whose hair she can braid as her life
twists its pleasure and pain and shame.

Show me a woman who does not hide
in the locket of bone that deep
eye beam of fiercely gentle love
she had once from mother, daughter,
sister; once like a warm moon
that radiance aligned the tides
of her blood into potent order.

At the season of first fruits we recall
those travelers, co-conspirators, scavengers
making do with leftovers and mill ends,
whose friendship was stronger than fear,
stronger than hunger, who walked together
the road of shards, hands joined.

III. Voices at the [Kitchen, Seminar, Communion] Table

MANY INTERESTING THINGS happen around tables—good things and bad things. Probably every reader has experienced at least one excruciating holiday dinner when the extended family, representing multiple political orientations and religious persuasions, has gathered for the first time in months around the groaning board, and someone, unwisely, brings up an incendiary theological or political issue. Diversity of opinion is off and running, and not in a particularly healthy fashion. Or, perhaps, a deadly silence falls over the table, letting everyone know that active disagreement is in *very* bad taste. The gravy congeals along with everyone's festive spirit, and the gathered company is aware, once again, not only that they are not ONE, but that difference itself is an enemy.

At other tables—peace tables, seminar tables, communion tables—folks approach the gathering knowing full well they are fragmented, angry and of diverse opinion, so they come seeking deeper understanding and, possibly, reconciliation. Kitchen tables are perhaps the coziest tables of all. Here women often gather, in intimacy and warmth, to share their stories, joys and griefs. Paule Marshall, African American writer, says that it was her mother's kitchen table conversations with other working black women at the end of the day that gave her her love for language, for it's many textures and moods and meanings. Later in this collection, Egyptian writer Leila Ahmed will describe such an exchange as the "harem experience."

A goal for this collection of texts, and for women's studies seminars everywhere, is to model the best possible "table talk"—to be places where women and men from many different geographies, theologies, ethnicities, age groups, economic classes, and political ideologies can really talk with and listen to each other. Where their ideas do not have to merge for the dialogue to be called good. Where they can laugh at their own parochialism and learn from those they've been taught to distrust. Where politeness does not necessitate avoidance of difference or appropriate confrontation. Where tough-minded debate is not considered abusive and where emotions are part of the intellectual process—of the very upheaval of thought, as Martha Nussbaum declares in her recent book, *Upheavals of Thought: The Intelligence of the Emotions*. Claiming that experience is the *starting point* of rational investigation, she concludes that, as moral persons, we simply "have to grapple with the messy material of grief and love, anger and fear, and the role these tumultuous experiences play in thought about the good and the just."

This section begins with Nussbaum's essay "Women's Studies" from

Cultivating Humanity: A Classical Defense of Reform in Liberal Education
where she lays out the history of women's studies in the academy, arguing for
a substantial place at the curricular table for this important discipline—after
all, women *do* represent half of the human race and more than half of the
college and university student population. She is arguing on the basis of
simple justice for those who have been shut out of the libraries and lecture
halls and psychological studies of the past, and she is arguing on the basis
of empirical data. By illustrating what serious consideration of female
anatomy, psychology and cultural contributions has recently added to many
of the established disciplines, she makes it quite clear that women's studies,
by its interdisciplinary nature, both undergirds and transforms the work the
academy has always done.

From this broadly based argument for acceptance of female thinking and
research about women's lives, we move toward an earnest exchange of racial
voices. In "Can We be Different But Not Alienated?" Katie Cannon and
Carter Heyward might well be sitting at a kitchen table, their brows furrowed
and their tea turning cold as they struggle to understand and articulate the
barriers to their intimacy, even as they recognize that it is their very desire for
intimacy that pulled them into conversation in the first place. They discuss
racial difference, abuse, anger, and, most earnestly of all, God's role in their
lives, never veering into false affirmation of one another, nor into competitive
rancor. It is the passion and the honesty of their open display of difference
that makes us, the readers, believe in their continued friendship and hope for
such a "mirror" in our own lives.

Toinette Eugene, both Catholic and black, follows this exchange with
her analysis of how and why African American women often choose to
be known as womanists rather than feminists. Taking us back through the
history of black women's experience in slavery, northern migration, and the
African American church, she illustrates how alien a separatist feminism is
to their way of living and surviving in the world. Black women were often
the prophets for the anti-slave church and the protectors of the community at
large. Mothering was not simply a biological fact, but had to do with taking
in and nurturing those in need. Sisterhood and solidarity were necessities
of life, not political add-ons. The community could not break into male and
female, single and married, mothers and non-mothers and survive. She
argues that these values continue to prevail in the black community in a way
that cannot be replicated by the dominant white community, although like

any set of distinctions, the definitions blur around the edges where poverty and abuse marginalize persons regardless of race. Where this occurs, the womanist voice demands justice and liberation for all. Alice Walker's original definition of womanist accompanies Eugene's essay because of its apt beauty and because Eugene uses it as an important point of reference.

Making a similar cultural move in her writings, Cuban theologian Ada Maria Isasi-Diaz lays out feminist theology for Latin women as *mujerista* theology, that which celebrates the cultural history of women from the Caribbean and Latin America countries. Again, not refuting the validity of the feminist agenda, she wants to make sure that the unique history of *Latinas* and the unique demands on their lives not remain nameless. One of the values she claims for *mujerista* feminist thinking is the necessary connection between theory and praxis. Coming from a marginalized cultural situation, *Latinas* cannot depend on critical thinking alone to solve problems, but must take action in the community and on behalf of the community. Thus, once again, the maternal becomes a matter of community survival, not simply biological continuance. One has only to think of the Mothers of the Disappeared, those wonderfully strong gatherings of women in black that have converged outside of military jails in Argentina, and Chile and El Salvador, carrying pictures of their murdered and imprisoned children, to know what she means. And so, in this essay, she works with the concept of solidarity as a description of the fierce love that draws communities, even communities of difference, together in the love of God to protect "the least of these" and to stand firm for justice.

Then Roxanane Dunbar-Ortiz, coming from a very different margin, that of poor white communities in Oklahoma—the Okies—lays out for us the terrible struggle to get out of poverty while avoiding the guilt of turning one's back on those left behind. With breathtaking honesty she tells how she "married out" at eighteen and spent the next six years trying to prove that she truly belonged in the upper middle-class "tribe" she had joined. Sadly, it is the women in her husband's family who make this particularly hard for her. Ultimately, assimilation proves not to be worth the effort, and her own solidarity with family and early friends emerges as part of a spiritual journey toward wholeness on which she seems to encounter few helpful religious markers. Instead she finds solace in the world of thought, becoming an academic who can write about the history of her people, and in activism, where Dunbar-Ortiz can commit herself to justice movements that will serve them. In her narrative she illustrates that survival—dare we say salvation—can come in many forms, and although she does not address theology or feminism(s) directly in this piece, the dynamics are easy to spot.

This section draws to a close with a biblical meditation by Nancy Linton, co-founder of the Women's Studies May Term, describing another woman living on the margins of respectable society: the infamous "woman taken in adultery." In this exegesis, Linton shows how the Pharisees' test of Jesus' acumen could well be a set-up; the woman, unlike her partner, is terribly vulnerable—female, either unmarried or adulterous, sexually promiscuous. Linton goes on to illustrate how Jesus calls the Pharisees to join in personhood with the woman they have previously "othered" by making them see that they too are vulnerable. And so they exit silently, leaving the woman to Jesus' respectful mercy.

Julia Kasdorf provides a poetic endnote by writing about her "tribe," the Mennonites, and some of the strong women they have produced. One could well imagine sitting around a kitchen table with these women, hearing their stories and learning from their history, not always liking it or wanting to live it, but acknowledging with gratitude its place in the vast colorful story of women's surviving and thriving. Finally, Pat Barker reminds us that "sisterhood" should never be taken lightly or assumed. If it doesn't come with respect for difference and disdain for racial stereotypes, it just won't fly.

Women's Studies

Martha Nussbaum

[W]e may safely assert that the knowledge which men can acquire of women, even as they have been and are, without reference to what they might be, is wretchedly imperfect and superficial, and always will be so, until women themselves have told all that they have to tell.
—John Stuart Mill, *The Subjection of Women* (1869)

AT THE UNIVERSITY OF NEVADA AT RENO, there is a change in the syllabus of the general education course on great books of ancient Greece. Deborah Achtenberg of Philosophy has persuaded the faculty committee to add the poetry of Sappho, together with background readings on the situation of women in the ancient Greek world. These readings present absorbing new research about daily life and the household, data that would not have been available from the great books themselves or from focusing on the events of political history. The faculty learn how scholars have reconstructed women's lives by combining data from visual art, archaeology, tax records, "documentary papyri" such as laundry lists, and little-known medical treatises.

At Stanford University, students of political theorist Susan Moller Okin, chair of the university's Ethics Program, learn to examine texts and issues in Western political thought through what Okin calls "the prism of gender." Okin argues that the most influential contemporary American theories of political justice have neglected women's situation in society and the distribution of resources and opportunities within the family. They have done so, for the most part, because they have simply assumed that the family is an institution characterized by bonds of love and affection, and that it would injure those bonds even to raise questions of justice about its internal operations. Students learn that John Stuart Mill presented powerful arguments against this failure to consider family justice, arguments that have, says Okin, been wrongly neglected. How can we expect to produce a nation of just citizens, Okin asks with Mill, if they have not learned justice in the place that is the source of their most powerful moral instruction?[1]

At Harvard University, students in an economics course on hunger and famine taught by economist Amartya Sen learn how to look at the distribution of food through "the prism of gender." With Sen, they estimate the number of females in the world who are likely to have died because of their sex—whether through sex-selective infanticide or through receiving nutrition and health care unequal to that given to males. In the world as a whole, the number of these "missing women," Sen argues, is approximately 100 million.[2] Sen shows that the family, which can be a source of love, care, and even justice, can also be a place in which women are slowly or quickly killed. He notes how frequently estimates of a nation's general prosperity fail to ask how women are doing, remarking that dominant economic models of the family discourage the investigator from posing that question.

At Brown University, students who sign up for the popular course "Biology of Gender" learn from Professor Anne Fausto-Sterling that many of the experiments purporting to discover innate differences between men and women have scientific defects that call their conclusions into question. They study the results of experiments showing how early cultural norms of gender shape the lives of infants. Infants labeled male are bounced and tossed in the air; the same infants, when believed to be female, are cuddled and held tightly. Even an infant's crying is described differently—as anger when the observer thinks the baby is male, as fear when the observer believes it is a female. Fausto-Sterling (like John Stuart Mill) argues that the pervasive influence of these cultural patterns makes it impossible for us, so far, to know what, if any, natural differences exist between women and men.[3]

Caroline Bynum, professor of religious studies at Columbia University, speaks at a memorial service for David Herlihy. Herlihy was professor of history at Bryn Mawr, Harvard, and finally Brown; at his death in 1991, he was president of the American Historical Association. Describing barriers to the study of women's history created by dominant models of research,

Bynum shows how Herlihy broke down those barriers through his fundamental work on medieval property rights. Forging new demographic and statistical techniques, he made it possible to learn about the lives of people who did not play a big role on the political stage. Herlihy, she says, took those steps when it was unfashionable to do so, a religious Catholic inspired by a medieval ideal of spiritual friendship between men and women.

New scholarship about women's lives is changing the academy. Highly diverse, filled with debate and contention, scholarship about and by women pervades curricula, transforming not only the content but often also the methodology of established courses. These changes are controversial. Critics of women's studies often look back to an earlier era when there seemed to be a general consensus about what the traditional academic disciplines were doing and what their methods were. If women entered these disciplines at all, they did so without questioning the traditional methodology and subject matter of the disciplines. They did not demand that they be allowed to do research on the lives of women, and thus these lives remained largely unstudied, in disciplines ranging from art history to classics to psychology and history.

But there were large gaps in the disciplines, gaps created by a failure to study women with the seriousness with which men's lives had long been studied. What Mill observed in 1869 was still true a hundred years later: we knew very little about the history of women, about their psychology, their bodies, their religious attitudes, their philosophical ideas. The very generalizations about women's "nature" that Mill mocked as inadequate and lacking a basis in true research still dominated many discussions—when women were discussed at all.

Mill predicted that this situation would not change until women themselves did research and told their own story. He might have been proved wrong. The imagination can cross boundaries of gender and class and race, and David Herlihy's idea of "spiritual friendship" between women and men can be realized. But the absence of women in the academy was in fact accompanied by a culpable failure to study the lives of those who had been excluded from academic citizenship. Gaps in knowledge and understanding undermined both teaching and research concerning one-half of the human race. These gaps hindered students in their civil, political, and familial lives.

Nor could these gaps be addressed by simply plugging some new information about women into the existing research paradigms and the curricula stemming from them. In many cases the defects were methodological as well, and the remedy required rethinking how to gather reliable information about the lives of those who were marginalized in a nation's culture, economy, or religious history. For example, as Caroline Bynum argued, historical research focusing on large-scale political events, and using the techniques appropriate to study such events, proved unable to provide a rich account of the lives of women. In order to discover what work women did, how much property they controlled, how children were raised, what they thought about politics or religion, new techniques, both narrative and demographic, needed to be forged.

Again, when the gross national product of a modern nation is reported in fields such as public policy and economics, domestic labor is not counted as productive labor.[4] And yet domestic labor is essential to understanding a nation's overall economy and the quality of life of its members. Without new methods of inquiry, it was difficult to take account of this labor or to estimate its importance. There were similar failures in biology and medicine, in psychology, in philosophy, in art history, in many other fields. Families, and the work women do in them, were often assumed, but at the same time ignored. Mill's criticism was still valid.

As Okim argued, the family is one of the most important topics studied by political science and economics, since its influence on human development is pervasive and deep. The most influential economic model of the family has been that proposed by Nobel prize-winning economist Gary Becker.[5] This model is widely used to make predictions, to chart the direction of public policy, and even to gather information. A prominent assumption of this model is that the male head of household is a beneficent altruist who adequately represents the interests of all his family members and can be relied on to distribute resources fairly. Relying on this assumption, users of the model do not ask how each particular member of the family is doing. When gathering information, they ask only about households. A recent attempt to study the situation of widows in India, for example, found that there were no data on widows' nutritional or health status because the data did not disaggregate households into their members.[6]

The assumption, however, is false. Conflicts of interest over occupational choice, division of labor, basic nutrition, and health are pervasive parts of family life the world over.[7] A closer look at the family reveals that in many parts of the world girls are fed less well than boys, less frequently taken to the doctor when ill, less well educated, less well protected from violence—all this if they are permitted to survive infancy in the first place. To reveal these facts, new methods needed to be devised.

The silence about women in the academy was not a benign or neutral silence. It supported, as it was supported by, the exclusion of women from the dignities of the scholarly community. Treating women as of such little account that they were not worth studying was a way of denying respect to women's lives; this denial of respect went hand in hand with the denial of academic employment. Worse still, the silence concealed evils in the larger world, ranging from unequal opportunity to domestic abuse and malnutrition.

Women had many urgent and justified grievances, in short, against traditional male research and teaching. These failures were failures in scholarship for all, since all need to know the truth. Men should have been asking these questions and doing this research, and in some cases they did. But on the whole, correction of these deficiencies in scholarship awaited the arrival of women in the disciplines in sufficient numbers to influence the direction and character of research, seeing traditional topics through "the prism of gender."

Already in the fourth century B.C., Plato recognized that an unbiased look at the reality of women's lives was an uphill struggle, in a culture long accustomed to restrict women to a domestic role. Socrates says to Glaucon in the *Republic* that most Athenians will find it ridiculous to think of women doing exercise out of doors, or studying philosophy—and therefore they will avoid asking sincerely and objectively whether women have the capacity to do these things. Any question that challenges deeply rooted habits seems threatening, especially when the challenge is to entrenched structures of power. Socrates reminds Glaucon, however, that many things we now know to be fruitful seemed absurd when they were first introduced—for example, the custom of public exercising that is now at the heart of Greek culture. When we reflected well about that change, however, "the appearance of absurdity ebbed away under the influence of reason's judgment about the best." He later reminds Glaucon that rational reflection can be crippled by habit even at the level of language: if they do not use both the masculine and the feminine forms of the participle when they talk about rulers (equivalent to our practice of saying "he or she"), they will be likely to forget what they have agreed, that women should have the opportunity to attain the highest functions in the city. Reason can falter through a failure of imagination.[8]

Women's studies, at its best, makes just such an appeal to reason. It asks the scholarly community not to surrender to the tyranny of habit and to habitual ideas of what is "natural," but to look for the truth in all its forms, using arguments that have been carefully sifted for bias. In this way, it has opened up many fruitful lines of research.

WOMEN'S STUDIES AND THE EXCLUSION OF WOMEN

Mill suggested, correctly, that ignorance about women's lives was supported by the exclusion of women from the academy. In 1969, one hundred years after the publication of Mill's call for women's studies, there were two tenured women on the faculty at Harvard University, one in a chair endowed through Radcliffe for a woman. This was typical in the elite universities that trained young scholars. Women were allowed to dine at the Faculty Club only in a small side room. Until 1967 they had been forbidden to use Lamont Library, where reserve books for undergraduate courses were kept; their own separate facility (with separate though not entirely equal resources) was almost a mile from most classrooms. A female teaching assistant, assigned to teach a section of a large course in a seminar room inside Lamont, asked what she should do about the fact that women were forbidden to enter the building. She was told, "Go around to the side entrance, and do not use the elevator." Harvard, which had taken a strong stand on racial integration in university facilities since 1923, had no hesitation in denying the equal use of its facilities to women.

Nor were women equal in graduate student financing. They could not hold prestigious traveling fellowships that helped graduate students with their research. Until 1971 they could not hold the three-year Junior Fellowship, which freed a small group of young scholars for interdisciplinary study. Married women had to declare their husband's income when filling out their expense account for a fellowship, but married men did not have to declare their wife's income.

Lives of young female scholars were difficult in other ways. The university, like most at that time, had no grievance procedure for sexual harassment, and few women escaped some form of unwelcome pressure by their male supervisors and instructors. If a woman wore fashionable clothing and looked attractive, she was blamed for the aggressive behavior her appearance elicited. If a man looked good, however, it was assumed that women would behave like professionals and avoid aggressive behavior. (This asymmetry still exists.) Job placement was governed by male networks and word of mouth rather than by public advertisement and procedures embodying a notion of fair search. As a result, women were usually not recommended for jobs at the all-male Ivy League schools, and in many cases were low on the list of students to be placed, regardless of merit, often with the argument that they did not need to support a family whereas male students did. The first faculty committee formed at Harvard to consider the interests and grievances of women—headed by Caroline Bynum, then a powerless, untenured faculty member—led to charges that its members were unscholarly "agitators."

During this period Harvard began to consider fully integrating women into its undergraduate student body. For some time Radcliffe students had attended Harvard classes. Radcliffe had never had a separate faculty, so the separate identity of Radcliffe in the early 1970s served above all as a quota system for admissions. Radcliffe had a separate admissions office and a limit on its numbers, which ensured a roughly four-to-one male-to-female ratio. It was well known that the academic credentials of students admitted to Radcliffe were on average stronger than those of Harvard students. Thus full coeducation basically meant fewer places for men and more for women. While this discussion was in progress, a master of one of the Harvard residence halls received a letter from an alumnus asking for his view about equal admissions. His reply, published widely (presumably because the recipient found it somewhat shocking, a sign of better times to come), stated that Harvard should not be producing housewives and mothers the way Wellesley did, it should be producing male leaders. This statement, once published, was much criticized; and yet there was widespread awareness that it expressed a view that was commonly held though rarely uttered in public.

In such a climate, it is not surprising that there were few courses at Harvard that touched on women's lives, as there were few in any institution of that time. Female students and scholars, in general, and indeed all scholars and students, received the message that women's lives were not the stuff that serious scholarship was made of. This situation was typical in the academy.

By 1980, when Harvard created a committee on women's studies, many things had changed. Several Ivy League institutions had begun to study the problem of sexual harassment. Once sex-blind admissions were adopted in most Ivy League institutions, the numbers of men and women in the student bodies rapidly became roughly equal. The number of women in graduate school and in at least the lower levels of many university and college faculties was increasing. Most of the fellowships that had previously been closed to women were opened.

Since the late 1960s, women had already been developing courses on women's issues in many disciplines; in some cases men had joined in this effort. Many of these courses were linked to the consciousness-raising efforts of the women's movement, just as the far-from-neutral status quo ante reflected a male political consciousness skeptical of women's full intellectual and civil equality. Yet there was no single political line that was espoused by these early teachers of women's studies—though all were committed to full equality for women in citizenship and opportunity. Then as now, the women's movement was full of debate, containing liberals and Marxists, communitarian defenders of caring and family along with advocates of gender separateness and self-sufficiency.[9] Even core values such as equality of opportunity were understood in different ways, as was the relation between feminism and sexuality.

At this time the increased number of women on college and university faculties, and of men concerned with women's issues, made it possible to develop new areas of research about women and to transform departmental curricula accordingly. Women's studies developed more rapidly in some departments than in others: history, for example, was one of the earliest. Many colleges and universities began interdisciplinary programs in women's studies, some offering undergraduate majors. Then as now, women's studies is carried on chiefly within traditional departments. Special programs tend to be poorly funded, and make few appointments on their own. An accurate account of what is going on in women's studies should therefore look both at departments and at the specialized programs, whose primary function is to stimulate interdisciplinary research and dialogue. Most courses that make up most undergraduate majors in women's studies are departmental courses, although they may be cross-listed in a special program.

Early proponents of women's studies had to confront a number of objections. The most common, then as now, was that these studies were motivated by a political agenda. Yet opponents could not truthfully assert that the old organization of study was apolitical; in countless ways, the traditional focus of scholarship reflected the highly political judgment that it was more important and more interesting to study the activities, bodies, and experiences of men. If opponents, recognizing this fact, continued to oppose women's studies on account of its political character, they would have to do so by making a substantive argument to show that the goals allegedly promoted by women's studies were bad goals, something that on the whole male scholars did not publicly do. Even if an objector were willing to argue that women should be confined to their traditional domestic roles and should not be allowed to take on an expanded role in the professions, it was hard to see how that conservative position could justify scholarly omissions and distortions of the type that new women's scholarship revealed. The best way to answer the charge of a suspect political motivation was, therefore, to keep producing good, truth-revealing work. That remains the best answer today, and it is because women's studies has proved its credentials in many areas that it has had a major influence not only on the academy but also on the law and on many other areas of our lives.

The second common objection, a more substantial one, was that women's studies does not form a single discipline with a single methodology. This was of course not a valid objection to pursuing women's studies within each department. Nor could it plausibly be thought a valid objection to the collaborative pursuit of research and scholarship at the faculty or graduate level, since it is well known that one discipline frequently learns from another. Psychologists cooperate with sociologists and biologists, philosophers with economists and political scientists, historians with specialists in music and art. Fields such as comparative literature, public policy, environmental studies, and classics are interdisciplinary in their very nature. On the other hand, such possibilities of fruitful collaboration do not suggest that each interdisciplinary focus should generate its own doctoral program. Women's studies in particular is such a vast field that it seemed then, and usually seems now, imprudent to offer a Ph.D. in it, both because the student in such a program might not have mastery of any single discipline and because he or she would not find a job. Interdisciplinary doctoral programs such as the University of Chicago's conservative Committee on Social Thought have sometimes generated exciting work; and yet their students almost always enter the academic job market at a disadvantage, encountering skepticism about whether they have really mastered any single set of techniques. Women's studies is in comparable position.

Skepticism about disciplinary unity was less acute when the topic under discussion was an undergraduate major or concentration, but it still had some validity. The student who pursued a major in this "field" might not be mastering any recognized body of knowledge or preparing for any future career or job. Undergraduate programs in general, however, do not necessarily prepare students for a job; the whole point of a liberal arts education is to enrich the life of a citizen in far-reaching ways. Nonetheless, a student completing a major in women's studies should exhibit mastery of some structured body of knowledge. This problem also plagues many established disciplines. Classics, as currently practiced in the academy, is not a structured body of knowledge. The undergraduate classics major frequently emerges with a smattering of language, history, archaeology, philosophy, literature, and history of science, ranging over two cultures and twelve centuries. The new discipline of women's studies focused attention on this issue of disciplinary unity from the start. The most fruitful approach has been to base the interdisciplinary field firmly between the disciplines rather than apart from them. This type of interdisciplinarity required most faculty to be jointly appointed in an established discipline and, frequently, students to have a dual major, one of which is in a more established field. This practice had and has the additional advantage of integrating the new studies into the traditional disciplines and thereby transforming them.

WOMEN'S STUDIES AND THE DISCIPLINES

By now, new scholarship about women's lives has transformed virtually every major discipline in the undergraduate curriculum in the social sciences and the humanities.[10] Transformations in the *content* of the disciplines are ubiquitous and easy to understand. Students now read more literary works by female writers, more religious texts by female thinkers, more about women's lives in various periods of history. Classes in biology are more likely to use a female body as an example of the human body alongside a male body, classes in psychology to use women as subjects alongside men. But the more profound contribution of women's studies, and the one that has proved more controversial, is its challenge to traditional methods of inquiry. Women's studies has asked new questions of the old data, sought new data in ways that require new methods, in some cases rejected the old methods as inadequate. These are the issues on which critics of women's studies focus, holding that a radical fringe has assailed standards in ways that damage scholarly inquiry. Any defense of women's studies should begin, then, by arguing that many of these transformations have been highly beneficial to the search for truth.

Philosophical theories of justice, like economic theories of distribution, have rarely considered the family as an institution to which basic insights about distributive justice and injustice must apply. Philosophers in women's studies have forced the field to confront this issue, challenging the reasons usually given for this neglect. Far from being a realm of love "beyond justice," the family, these scholars show, is a place where gross violations of justice frequently occur, as well as defects in moral development that mar children's capacity for just citizenship. Far from being a realm that exists "by nature," unaffected by legal and institutional factors, the family is shaped in countless ways by laws regulating marriage, divorce, and childrearing, and by general economic policies that govern people's opportunities and living standards.

Contemporary theorists of the family such as Jean Hampton, Virginia Held, Susan Moller Okin, and John Rawls—working, by and large, in close connection to the tradition of Kantian liberalism—have asked how legal changes could promote respect for women's worth and autonomy, and ensure norms of fair equality of opportunity; others have addressed issues of child welfare and the legal definition of parental responsibility.[11]

The new focus on women's lives has also opened other fruitful areas of inquiry neglected by conventional male philosophy. New attention has been given to important human phenomena such as love and imagination, and to the role they play in a truly rational judgment. Emotions such as love of a child, fear for that child's welfare, grief at the death of a parent are held to be not mindless unreasoning forces, but intelligent ways of recognizing the importance of what is occurring. A person who does not respond emotionally could properly be criticized, not only as callous, but also as not fully rational. These ideas about emotion and judgment are not altogether new in the history of Western philosophy. Some of them, for example, were adumbrated by Aristotle, who, despite his misogynistic attitude toward real-life women, said many things that contemporary feminists find appealing.[12] Philosophers such as Rousseau and John Dewey also played a part in their development. Nor do all feminist philosophers hold a single position on these issues; they disagree strongly not only about the proper analysis of emotions but also about how reliable emotions are. But before women's studies began to influence philosophy there was little support for this whole line of inquiry; it would have been scorned as soft and slightly embarrassing. Feminist scholars deserve most of the credit for restoring these topics to the agenda of the profession.[13] In a related domain, the explanation of scientific rationality, feminists have again broken new ground, insisting on the role of affiliation and cooperation in the process of knowledge acquisition. Again, these claims are not altogether new in the history of thought: many of them, for example, can be found in the work of David Hume.[14] But feminist thought has played a major role in their contemporary articulation.

Not all challenges to traditional professional philosophy have been equally successful. Some challenges to notions of objectivity and rationality have been unconvincing—especially when they have suggested that the very norm of objectivity, of a judgment free from bias and distortion, is a mythical male ideal that we should jettison. Feminist argument, from Plato onward, has depended on the ability to distinguish between a judgment that is truly objective and truly rational, and one that is tainted by bias and prejudice. That distinction is not always easy to discern; philosophers will rightly differ not only about where to draw the line but also about what concepts are useful in articulating a norm of objectivity (whether, for example, an emotion-based judgment is by definition nonobjective). They will also differ about whether an objective judgment should be said to require truths that are altogether independent of human experience and history (most thinkers today would deny this). But our best accounts of the limits of human understanding do not imply that we should abandon our norms of rationality and objective truth. The Society for Analytical Feminism, a satellite organization of the American Philosophical Association, has actively promoted rigorous debate about these questions; two of its leading members have recently published an excellent anthology showing the importance for feminism of ideas of truth, objectivity, and rationality.[15] The profession now has a lively exchange about these matters in which no starting point, methodological or empirical, remains unchallenged.

In classics, until 1975, there was no reliable history of the lives of women in the ancient world. Many of the most important sources for these lives were neglected and unedited texts and documents. History was written primarily as political history, including the history of personal connections among influential males. The techniques most often used by ancient historians, which focused on textual and inscriptional evidence, were insufficient to write the lives of women. The reading of documentary papyri is a highly specialized skill possessed by only a handful of experts, none of whom had been interested enough in women to use it extensively to that end. Yet two decades later we know a great deal about the lives of women in ancient Greece and Rome. Sarah Pomeroy's pioneering work on women's lives in ancient Greece derived, in the first instance, from her expert training in the reading of papyri.[16] But she and her followers have also had to correlate these findings with the reconstruction of data about propertyholding and inheritance, with evidence about religious cult practices, and with the evidence of visual art and archaeology. Each piece of evidence representing women had to be carefully sifted for its origins, since little of it will have been written by women. Such work, like work on ancient homosexuality, requires scholars who can go back to the beginning, assuming that nothing is really known, and forge techniques by which real knowledge can be gained. Since this work has produced new questions in a field that for a long time lacked new challenges, it has become a focal point for young scholars. The new edition of the *Oxford Classical Dictionary*, a standard (and very main-stream) reference work, now has an editor for women's subjects in order to ensure that this new scholarship is integrated into articles on many different topics.

"The prism of gender" in classics has revised many established ideas about the ancient world, including standard characterizations of the ancient economy. Before scholars in women's studies came on the scene, the dominant methodological approaches to the study of the ancient economy, whether Marxist or neoclassical, failed to take into account the central role of the household and its "domestic economy." As Sarah Pomeroy characterizes the situation, the economy of the household was standardly treated "as part of a primitive world predating the formation of the polis?"[17] This approach was anachronistic, distorting the reality of ancient Greece to make it fit modern categories. And yet it took the dogged effort of scholars in women's studies, insisting on a focus on women's experience, to gain recognition for questions that are now acknowledged to be central to the proper study of the ancient world.

The new focus on women's lives requires new paradigms of instruction in the undergraduate curriculum. A course focused on "great books" of the ancient world will rightly be seen as unable to convey an accurate and complete sense of what the ancient Greek and Roman world was like. To give a full picture, teachers will need to go beyond the most famous literary and philosophical texts, consulting sourcebooks and other presentations of data in order to discover the lives of ancient women. Even specialized courses in the literature or art or philosophy of the ancient world should set the texts in their historical context, which contained women as well as men.

In anthropology, women's lives have been a focus of research since the days of Margaret Mead, and the field was among the earliest to understand the importance of taking women's points of view into account when describing a society. Recent research in social anthropology has emphasized the importance of the concepts of emotion used by a society, asking how fear and anger and love function in transactions between people and in their dealings with the natural world.[18] This new methodological emphasis has involved correction of some common male paradigms of rationality. These tended to contrast emotion with reason in an excessively simple way, denying that emotions could ever be sources of information. Anthropologists—led by those with a feminist orientation, such as Catherine Lutz and the late Michelle Rosaldo—were quick to see the extent to which a culture's norms of appropriate anger, shame, grief, and love expressed evaluations, not simply unintelligent biological reactions.[19] They proposed a new research project for observers of society: the precise description of the society's emotion taxonomy and its relation to behavior and to social norms. This new research focus has led to corresponding transformations in the understanding of social dynamics.

In physical anthropology, feminist scholars have again produced new methods and questions. When researchers describe the behavior of a primate species, they often use human concepts. Behavior becomes intelligible to them on the basis of their own experience; thus they project onto the primate's behavior perceptions conditioned by the habitual norms of their world. This approach does not always lead to good data-gathering. Male primatologists depicted primate gender roles in a manner strongly influenced by their assumptions about human female roles: the female primate, they repeatedly said, was "coy" in her courting behavior, reserving her sexual favors for the male who won the courting competition. This projection led to distortion. It had long been known that females in other animal species—birds, cats, certain fish—accept multiple sexual partners, though this phenomenon had been ignored in most studies—largely, concludes primatologist Sarah Blaffer Hrdy, "because theoretically the phenomenon should not have existed and therefore there was little theoretical infrastructure for studying it." Only when a substantial number of female researchers got involved in primate research was it noticed that similar promiscuous behavior is present in quite a few primate species. Female sexual initiative, female promiscuity, and other forms of female control are ubiquitous features of primate life. Indeed, Hrdy concludes, it seems likely "that a polyandrous component is at the core of the breeding systems of most troop-dwelling primates: females mate with many males, each of whom may contribute a little bit toward the survival of the offspring." It took the perspective of female researchers to notice aspects of primate behavior that had been there all the time. These findings have thrown sexual selection theory into a state of upheaval, previous male bias has been generally acknowledged, and new research has focused intensively on female reproductive strategies.[20]

What explains the fact that it took "the prism of gender" to introduce these observations? Some studies, Hrdy notes, indicate that female researchers are simply better field observers—on average, they perform better on tests measuring recognition and tracking of particular species members over time, an ability crucial to the detection of polyandry. But Hrdy concludes that the most important factor is that females were more capable of imaginative empathy with the female primates being studied, more capable of supplying an imaginative narrative that put together pieces of observed behavior in a coherent way. (She stresses that this could lead to error, and suggests that the best strategy for avoiding error is to establish a diverse and mutually critical research community.) We may add, as well, that male researchers may have had a strong desire to imagine the "natural order" in a certain way, with females firmly relegated to a position of chaste domesticity, and this narrative bias may simply have marred their vision. As Hrdy says: "When generalizations persist for decades after evidence invalidating them is also known, can there be much doubt that some bias was involved?"[21]

Dutch researcher Frans de Waal has recently added to these criticisms evidence that the very selection of species to describe displayed a bias in favor of familiar human gender roles. Chimps, whose society is to at least some extent patriarchal, with male sexual initiative, have been extensively researched and form a primary basis for accounts of our own alleged sociobiological evolutionary heritage. But the bonobos of Zaire, who are just as close to us genetically as chimps, show an altogether different pattern: female initiative in sexual matters, a society kept at peace by constant sexual activity and surprisingly deficient in aggression. Bonobos were not discovered until 1929, but soon after that a great deal was known about them, including their remarkable closeness to humans—they share about 98 percent of our genetic makeup. Sociobiologists in the 1970s, however, made chimps their species of choice. As a result of this deliberate decision, writes de Waal, "male superiority remained the natural state of affairs," since chimp males "reign supremely and often brutally." Not so the bonobo, whose whole physical style, graceful and nonaggressive, differs sharply from that of the chimp—in the way, says de Waal, that a Concorde differs from a Boeing 747. As intelligent as chimpanzees, bonobos appear to have a more sensitive temperament, and are unusually imaginative in play and joking. Most striking are the ubiquity of sexual contact and its diversity—including frequent male-male, female-female, and male-female contact, and, in terms of acts, oral sex and prolonged kissing in addition to the more usual primate repertoire of vaginal and anal acts. De Waal writes that our view of our evolutionary heritage would have been utterly different had bonobos, rather than chimps, been the species of choice for researchers: we would have believed "that early hominids lived in female-centered societies, in which sex served important social functions and in which warfare was rare or absent."[22] Once again, scientific methods that claimed to be objective really were not objective and did not attain the whole truth—or even amass the entirety of the data.

These are only three fields out of the dozens in the humanities and social sciences. Similar stories could be told about every other field. In religious studies, women's studies has produced new accounts of women's religious lives in ancient societies, new proposals in religious ethics emphasizing the roles of compassion and care, new theological accounts of divinity. In psychology, "the prism of gender" has opened up new avenues of research into the social learning of gender roles, the psychology of the emotions, and the attitudes of the two sexes to intimacy. In history, the new attention to women's lives has prompted a shift in paradigms of research and teaching: at this point social history focused on daily life is at least as creative and lively a field as political history. Like Socrates' gadfly, women's studies has challenged every discipline to wake up, to confront new arguments. Usually this has led to profound transformations, both in the content of knowledge and in methodology. [...]

NOTES

1. See Susan Moller Okin, *Justice, Gender, and the Family* (New York: Basic Books, 1989).

2. See Amartya Sen, "More than 100 Million Women Are Missing," *New*

York Review of Books, Christmas issue 1990, pp. 61-66; Martha C. Nussbaum and Jonathan Glover, eds., *Women, Culture, and Development* (Oxford: Clarendon Press, 1995); Jean Drèze and Amartya Sen, *Hunger and Public Action* (Oxford: Clarendon Press, 1989).

3. See Anne Fausto-Sterling, *Myths of Gender*, 2nd ed. (New York: Basic Books, 1985).

4. See the United Nations' *Human Development Report* (New York: United Nations Development Programme, 1994), which estimates that if it were counted as output in national income accounts, global output would rise by 20 to 30 percent.

5. Gary Becker, *A Treatise on the Family*, rev. ed. (Cambridge, Mass.: Harvard University Press, 1991). See critical discussion in Okin, *Justice, Gender, and the Family*, and in Nussbaum and Glover, *Women, Culture, and Development*.

6. Martha Chen, lecture at Brown University, spring 1995.

7. See Amariya Sen, "Gender and Cooperative Conflicts," in *Persistent Inequalities*, ed. Irene Tinker (New York: Oxford University Press, 1990), pp. 123-149.

8. See the very end of Book VII.

9. The area of caring and family ethics, by now a major component of philosophical women's studies, developed slightly later than some of the others, although it was preceded, in the 1970s, by a general revival of interest in the topics of friendship and emotion. See, for example, Sara Ruddick, "Maternal Thinking," *Feminist Studies* 6 (1980): 342-367; Laurence Blum, *Friendship, Altruism, and Morality* (London: Routledge, 1980); Joyce Trebilcot, ed., *Mothering: Essays in Feminist Theory* (Totowa, N.J.: Rowman and Allanheld, 1984); Carol Gilligan, *In a Different Voice* (Cambridge, Mass.: Harvard University Press, 1982); Nel Noddings, *Caring* (Berkeley: University of California Press, 1984); Christina Huff Summers, "Filial Morality," *Journal of Philosophy* 83 (1986): 439-456.

10. See the excellent disciplinary surveys in Domna C. Stanton and Abigail J. Stewart, eds., *Feminisms in the Academy* (Ann Arbor: University of Michigan Press, 1995).

11. Jean Hampton, "Feminist Contractarianism," in *A Mind of One's Own: Feminist Essays on Reason and Objectivity*, ed. Louise B. Antony and Charlotte Witt (Boulder: Westview Press, 1992), pp. 227-255; Virginia Held, *Feminist Morality: Transforming Culture, Society, and Politics* (Chicago: University

of Chicago Press, 1993); John Rawls, *A Theory of Justice* (Cambridge, Mass.: Harvard University Press, 1991) and "Political Liberalism: Women and the Family" (manuscript).

12. See Marcia Homiak, "Feminism and Aristotle's Rational Ideal," in Antony and Witt, *A Mind of One's Own*; Nancy Sherman, *The Fabric of Character: Aristotle's Theory of Virtue* (Oxford: Clarendon Press, 1989); Linda Hirshman, "The Book of 'A,'" *Texas Law Review* 70 (1992): 971-1012.

13. See Helen Longino: "To See Feelingly: Reason, Passion, and Dialogue in Feminist Philosophy," in Stewart and Stanton, *Feminisms in the Academy*, pp. 19-45.

14. See Annette Baler, "flume: The Reflective Woman's Epistemologist?" in Antony and Witt, *A Mind of One's Own*, pp. 35-48; Helen Longino, "Essential Tensions-Phase Two: Feminist, Philosophical, and Social Studies of Science," ibid., pp. 257-272.

15. Antony and Witt, *A Mind of One's Own*, reviewed in Martha C. Nussbaum, "Feminist Philosophers," *New York Review of Books*, October 20, 1994, pp. 5963.

16. Sarah Pomeroy, *Goddesses, Whores, Wives, and Slaves* (New York: Schocken, 1975); idem, *Xenophon's Oeconomicus* (Oxford: Oxford University Press, 1994).

17. See Sarah Pomeroy, "The Contribution of Women to the Greek Domestic Economy," in Stewart and Stanton, *Feminisms in the Academy*, pp. 180-195.

18. See especially Catherine Lutz, *Unnatural Emotions: Everyday Sentiments on a Micronesian Atoll and Their Challenge to Western Theory* (Chicago: University of Chicago Press, 1988).

19. See ibid. and Michelle Z. Rosaldo, *Knowledge and Passion: Ilongot Notions of Self and Social Life* (Cambridge: Cambridge University Press, 1980).

20. Sarah Blaffer Hrdy, "Empathy, Polyandry, and the Myth of the Coy Female," in *Feminist Approaches to Science*, ed. Ruth Bleier (New York. Teachers College Press, 1991), 119-146, with bibliography; quotations on pp. 124, 125.

21. Ibid., pp. 134, 137.

22. Frans de Waal, "Bonobo Sex and Society," *Scientific American*, March 1995, p. 88.

Can We Be Different But Not Alienated?

An Exchange of Letters

Katie G. Cannon and Carter Heyward

> I will flow, not censor or edit, but let the innermost part of me speak.
> —Katie Cannon

> I'm pulled between excitement and anxiety over what you say.
> —Carter Heyward

[...] A LITTLE BACKGROUND: Katie refers to *The Color Purple* by Alice Walker.[1] At Kate's suggestion, Carter had read this novel, and the two of them had discussed its theological value as a narrative of a rural black woman who is cut off from all love, relationality, and God until she has a friend who takes her seriously.

October 31, 1982

Dear Carter,

I will respond to the parts of the outline you've asked me to think about by writing a letter much like Celie in *The Color Purple* wrote letters to God and Nettie. By this I mean that I will flow, not censor or edit, but let the innermost part of me speak.

Can we be different but not alienated? Only if there is mutuality in our relating. The analogy for me is the difference between the miracle of dialogue and bilateral conversations. When two parties, people, races, nations, etc., are dialoguing, they respect whatever their intellect, spirit, culture, and traditions tell them is sound in each other, with an attitude of openness for growth and change that comes with the moving of God's spirit. The open-flowing energy between the two removes alienation. But when one of the parties tries to listen only long enough to tell the others what to do, to control, to obtain power or superiority, the result has to be alienation. It is like what Alice Walker says about Church. We come to Church to share with others the God we have found in ourselves, not to find God.

When we, as various people, can claim the beauty of our innerselves, then we do not have to exploit, oppress, disenfranchise other people in some kind of hierarchical, vertical, sadomasochistic pecking order.

Racism, sexism, class elitism are all false, institutionalized systems of the abortive search for somebodiness (meaning). Therefore, in such systems there cannot be acceptance of difference. Difference is interpreted by those in power as *less than.* Conformity is the norm, and anyone who cannot be bleached out and neutered has to be isolated, alienated, and eventually exterminated. It is no mere coincidence that hard and destructive drugs flow freely in our black communities. The self-defense that comes from the side of the oppressed is to maintain the alienation that is already in place, because history bears out that whenever any of us try to heal the breach, they either get co-opted and become a token pet in the system or they get assassinated as a threat to the status quo: academic excellence, national security, etc.

As Zora Neale Hurston says, our survival in the black community is to let those researchers probe—but *not* to give them the information, because the very data shared will be used as the boomerang to destroy us.[2] The beauty of living is appreciating the various differences in God's creation, but, for those in power and control, that very difference is the seed of negation that demands a spontaneity in relating which they refuse to give. Race/class and gender oppressions are based on removing the intelligence, the source of feelings, aspirations, and achievements of those who are different by closeting, categorizing, burying, and cremating them, so that those who reap the privileges of superiority and supremacy do not have to confront their futile and anachronistic gestures of success, progress, or their inability to live any other way.

The particular relation between white and black women. My mama always says that black people must remember that all white people have white mamas. She makes several points with this proverb.

First, the hand that rocks the cradle is the hand that rules the world. We may question the validity and truth of such assumptions, but we cannot deny the impact that racist child-rearing practices have had on sustaining and perpetuating white supremacy.

Second, the volatile relationship between the majority of white women and the majority of women of color has to do with the pedestaled position that white women allow themselves to be placed upon, always at the expense of other women. When white women buy into the privileges of white supremacy and the illusive protectiveness of their superiority, women of color are forced to pick up their slack.

Third, white women are the only ones to guarantee the purity of the white race. They are the white man's most important treasure. George Frederickson makes a strong historical case for white supremacy in South Africa and in the United States, with the bottom-line motivation for the oppression of people of color: white men protecting the virtue and virginity of white women, resulting in the objectification of white women and all others.[3]

Fourth, white women in particular are always seeking blessings of assurance from women of color. By this I mean that, even as a teenager when I worked as a domestic, I was asked by the white kids that I tended to, who were sometimes my age and sometimes older, for advice. (My confusion was always about the injustice of why, if we were the same age, I was their caretaker.) They would sometimes ask me what I thought about washing their hair with beer and other white folk phenomena. Learning, knowing, and remembering my place was critical to my job security. If I responded "What in the hell do I care?" or any milder version of that feeling, I would have been written off as uppity and therefore disrespectful—and fired. If I dumbed-up and numbed-out, ignoring them completely, just continuing my menial, low-paying work, such silence would have been read either the same way or as reinforcing my so-called inferiority and ignorance. It really was that precarious situation my mama describes: when you have your head in the lion's mouth, you have to treat the lion very gently.

Economic/work relationships cannot be minimized in discussing and understanding the relationship between white women and women of color. Also this same kind of blessing of assurance has been manifested in my experience with white women when they don't want to participate in an equal, reciprocal process of give and take.

I remember once at a party lots of folks relaxing and having a good time. Black and white together. My conversation with a white woman appeared to be fairly open and honest. She said that she had always been taught that black people had a foul odor and asked for permission to smell me. (I didn't even flinch. I just registered the request in my category of weird-things-white-people-do.) After she sniffed and smelled and got her nose full of me, she concluded that all that time she had been living with a racist myth, which, as far as she could tell from her experiment with me, was not true.

I then reciprocated the experiment by saying that I, too, had heard some smell-myths about white people. I had been taught that when white people wash their hair or get wet, they smell like dogs. I then proceeded to smell her. She jumped back, appalled, infuriated. How dare I have the audacity to smell her. This is when I was shocked. It was good enough for me to be the object of her examination, but it was not OK when the tables were turned.

And that white woman, huffing and puffing, got up and stormed out of the party. This is often what white women do when they're not in front of the line, calling the shots, or in charge of the dynamics between themselves and women of color. They take their toys, their funds, their programs, their printing press, and go home, where they can perch on a ledge and not have their boat rocked. This in itself is privilege.

My relationship with white feminists and women of color, who may or may not be feminists, is radically different. White feminists are aware of racism. White feminists are aware of their own subjugation and oppression as females. White feminists are beginning to claim their biases, their elitist values, and their assumptions about life. And not only are they aware; they are engaged, actively, in justice-making. This, to me, is the hope. White feminists and women of color are changing the directions and the quality of their relations to each other.

White women who are not about the above, even if they call themselves feminists, are not feminists to me, but only white women with white mamas perpetuating systems of oppression by continuing to participate in them.

I believe that, as women, we need each other. We need to cross race lines and class lines, join forces to stop this messing up of lives by the racist, patriarchal systems and structures steeped in a greed for power and domination, all toward the maximizing of profits.

White feminists are standing over against their privileges inherent in an oppressive system to be in mutual relation with others. Women of color often need to test and retest the authenticity of white women's willingness to relate. The question before us is whether our timing and tolerance will sustain the processes of change.

I wholeheartedly believe that "godding is relating."[4] I only know the essential nature of God when I as an individual, and my people as a race, are not permitted—but command by the respect of our very being—space to engage in the most rigorously honest confrontation. When we confront and are confronted so that all might have life and have life more abundantly—this is what it's all about. And this is why, when I hear of "postfeminist" movements, I quake and shake.[5] The hands that rocked the cradle now cradle the rock, so that, together, we can change the powers and principalities of this world.

Studying our lives in relation to the lives of other women. I respond to this by adapting a metaphor of Amari Baraka:[6]

A black woman is locked up in one room of a large house by an oppressor (white male/female and/or racial/ethnic male) who never enters that room. When the isolated woman finally comes out, she is able to talk about the whole house, whereas her oppressor who imprisoned her is not.

Women who are in touch with their oppression may be more fit to handle the totality of the ethical ambiguities in their lives than their oppressors. Since the oppression of women is the oldest oppression, and since no anthropologist, feminist or otherwise, has ever come up with convincing evidence of a culture in which some form of male dominance does not exist, we, as women, have a wealth of wisdom in our stories, many which have never been told.

The metaphor about the woman in the locked room depicts the "epistemological privilege" of *women of color.* Langston Hughes sums it up in his book *The Ways of White Folks.*[7] The class and economic location of women of color affords them the inside scoop on the nemeses, the jugular veins, and the Achilles' heels of those in power. But the catch-22 is that by the time they get through slaving, with no reflective time for analysis, they don't know how to fight, only how to stay alive. The privilege to reflect in order to prevail beyond survival is not granted to them, so their epistemological privilege either lies dormant, in some kind of state of denial or self-delusion, or it is acted out in ways that get black women beaten up, incarcerated, mutilated. How to channel this wisdom is the essential concern of the ongoing survival of women of color.

Do black women and white women experience a common dilemma? A common possibility? I wholeheartedly respond, Yes. The difference is that white women tend to have more layers of veneer with which they deny our common bond. Racism as idolatry teaches them that they are somebody in spite of the violence in the home, the beatings, rapes, incest, conspiracies of silence, because their white skin makes them better than any black person. The "culture of inequality" teaches them that if they obtain certain material objects, they are far superior to those who have not obtained them. Not until white women and women of color are aware and willing to accept our common dilemma can there be any possible common action for liberative change.

A demon that divides us. You asked about these demons. I've mentioned some, but one that we have to name is the hidden injuries of class.[8] The more economic security one has, the more one can buy illusive myths and distance herself from reality. In other words, money can give those who have it the false security and illusory worth that their personhood is more valuable because of their finances. They then set up and manipulate systems to undergird their uniqueness so that those at the bottom of the pyramid also get on the treadmill of wanting that same shallowness always available in the shadows of the golden ghettoes. A case in point is professionalism. The more one goes to school, the more elite one is supposed to be. The farce of so many of our systems cannot be exposed because those of us struggling for upward mobility, once we see the light, cannot speak; or else we have nothing to sustain our energy and effort after the sacrifices that have put us where we are. So many of our class locations are based on the story line of the emperor who has no clothes. But who will dare name this?—because the namer will be discredited either as a liar and a fool, or as a failure who has a bone to pick, or as a traitor to the guild. A few of us marginated people are tolerated to show the equality of the system, but only a limited quota can survive.

I'll stop here because my brain needs to rest.

Kate

[...]

November 18, 1982

Dear Kate,

I've reread your letters many times, and only now, having had them with me for several weeks, can I begin to try to articulate a response, and not only a response to you but to myself. Responding to my own feelings, questions, confusions, and delights. Even now I'm pulled between excitement and anxiety over what you say, what I read, what we're doing, especially as women of different colors. You see, I find that I want to be a color! I'd always, even as a little girl, thought there was something weird about the implication that white people have no color—unlike "colored" people. White seemed to me to be a color, but then someone told me that whiteness is the absence of color—sort of like evil is the absence of good? I have serious reservations about whether this is true ethically and politically. Isn't it crucial for white people to own up to our whiteness (read: privilege in a racist society) and to acknowledge the difference our color makes?

I don't think this is nitpicking but rather that it's one more example of racial privilege looked at through the lens of liberalism—color doesn't make any difference and shouldn't matter; we shouldn't even notice it—because, in the world of God, color (like sex, etc.) is transcended, a nonissue, a nonreality. That sounds to me like the sort of logic that could only bounce out of the brain of a race/a people that thinks of itself as "colorless," folks like my people who distance ourselves from the difference color makes.

I'm excited to be writing this to you, Kate, because I like you and I know you like me, which makes it a little easier to speak my mind. But I would be lying if I said that I'm comfortable discussing race—even with you, or maybe especially with you. My fear is that you'll leave; that you'll notice my racism—which I certainly notice—and that you'll leave, close the door.

Surely I've told you about Bessie. Bessie was our maid. I was about four years old, living with Mamma and Daddy; at the time still the only child. Bessie came every several days, maybe once a week, to clean the house and cook fried chicken, my favorite food, and look after me. And I adored her. Sometimes she'd take me to the movie theater in Hendersonville, North Carolina, where "colored" people had to sit in the balcony and white people downstairs. I can remember begging her to let me go with her to the balcony! And I remember asking Mamma and Daddy why we never went to Bessie's house, except to drop her off at the end of the driveway; and why Bessie's house looked so poor, like a shack, and ours didn't. My memory is fuzzy, but I think I recall both my parents' very pained and strained expressions as they tried to explain racism to a four-year-old white child. I will go to my grave grateful that they told me racism was wrong and that it was not God's will and that we, all of us, were living in a sinful society. Those were the lessons my parents tried to teach, and they were, even then, considered by most folks who knew them to be moderate to liberal white southerners.

But they didn't try to teach me, explicitly, that we should do something about ending racism. I suppose, like most, they didn't know what to do. They felt powerless. They did tell me that I must always be kind to colored people and respect them as God's children. And they also told me that I should never ever call a colored person a nigger—that this was a bad word that only ignorant and racist white people used (notice the class bias of dominant white culture here—white folks' sense of "poor white trash").

But one day my friend Elliott (a white girl) and I were playing jump rope in the front yard and Bessie was watching over us. And I began that infamous little jingle: "Eenie, meenie, miny mo, catch a nigger by its toe." I still to this day have no sense of whether I knew what I was saying, whether I was making the connection between "nigger" and "colored person" or between "nigger" and Bessie; but Bessie walked into the house, got her coat and walked out again, slowly down the driveway. I never saw her again.

That was 1950. Mamma and Daddy explained to me that I had hurt Bessie's feelings and that it was wrong for me to have done it, but that Bessie shouldn't have taken such offense at a five-year-old girl. Recollecting this story is still painful for me, and I haven't fully unloaded it. I do know that it represents my fear—but of what? Of someone leaving? But who? Necessarily a black person? Or might it be anyone? And as I've gotten older, the story has begun to make me angry—to put me in touch with my feelings of having been betrayed—by Bessie. My fantasy now is not to watch silently as she walks down the driveway, but to run after her and ask her to stop, turn around, come back—even demand—that she tell me why she's going, what she feels like, and that, even at age five, if I could do something about it, I would. I also want her to know that I'm sorry, that I am ashamed, that I didn't know what I was doing—at least not consciously or willfully.

It is almost more than I can bear to imagine that Bessie didn't give a damn about me, and yet now, over thirty years later, I can say, for certain, that if I were black, a black woman, I would be burning with an unquenchable fire of rage against white people—including the five-year-old girls and boys I had been expected to nurture at the expense of my own.

As I've told you before, sexism makes racism all the more complicated for me to try to sort out—especially my own attitudes and actions. Sometimes I think that if there were only black women and white women in the world (and of course women of other colors too), racism wouldn't be a problem—for *me,* that is. I don't mean to be idealizing womanhood, because I don't believe women are morally superior to men. What I do mean is that, for me, it's in relation to black men that I get confused about the ways in which I am or am not racist. I do not like for any man of any color or ethnic group to harass me sexually. My experience has been that in relation to most (not all) white men who've come on to me sexually, when I brush them off or say no, they back off and rather quietly get out of my way. In relation to black men (again, not all of them) who've come on to me, when I say no or brush them off, there's usually a big scene about my being racist or about chocolate being better than vanilla—"if only you weren't too hung up to taste it"—and on it goes.

Furthermore, since I came out as a lesbian, I've felt (paranoid or not) that a good many black men have wanted to do to me what the guys in Brewster Place did to one of "The Two."[9] I'll never forget the contemptuous look in the eyes of Mr. —— when a gay man and I gave a five-minute speech on behalf of lesbians and gays at the Theology in the Americas Conference in 1980. He and a dozen or so other black men, together with the men in the Native American group, were the only people, out of some six hundred, who chose to sit there with stone faces after the gay/lesbian presentation rather than to rise and applaud. I understand this from a sociological, historical perspective, of course. But even to write about it makes me angry. And I find that at times—much to my chagrin, actually—my image of black men is of people I cannot trust, people who scare me, people who'll use me—whether physically, professionally, whatever—to bolster themselves. It's really clear to me that these feelings of mine combine simple truth-telling (black men and white women have at best a strained relationship historically that none of us individually can transcend absolutely) and flashy remnants of my own racism (really believing that black men are more violent than white men; being afraid, for example, that a black male mugger would kill me whereas a white male mugger would simply take my money...).

I didn't mean to go on about my relations with black men—that's not exactly the point of this correspondence. And yet, it does relate to us, you and me, does it not?

Can we be different but not alienated? I agree totally, Kate, that the answer lies in the quality of our relation; whether real dialogue, the "miracle of dialogue" as you say, is possible and desired between us and around us, among our sisters, black and white. The problem with white liberalism (I don't know about black liberalism) is that liberal white men and women do not advocate real relation, not mutual relation, but rather a patronizing sort of relation based on hand-me-down affections. White liberals "love" black people; white liberal men "love" all women (white women and women of color)—as long as we're not threatening to change the name of the power game. There's really not much difference between white liberals and white conservatives when it comes to race relations or any relations. There may be a different attitude or worldview—but the actions seem to me, when all is said and done, pretty much the same.

I would distinguish between conservatives and reactionaries. Conservatives are very much like liberals—it's just that their patronizing is attached more explicitly to the value of the past. But both liberal and conservative white people (and I suppose their black clones) really don't want to see things shaken up. Change? Maybe, very gradually, very cautiously, and very amicably. No disruptions, no riots, no violence. Whereas reactionaries in white communities are today in this country very much an incarnation of fascism. They do want to see things change and they do want to see things shaken up—and all in the service of what they believe either once was (the American Dream) or what ought to be—because it's God's will (Moral Majority, for example).

The point of this little digression is that, in my opinion, among us white people, we have very few models of mutual relation—people helping show the way. Most of the white people I know (myself included) grew up as more or less liberal—and, as such, really not very relational in any authentic sense. Even our primary, most intimate relations—parent-child, spouse-spouse, lover-lover, friend-friend—have been characterized more by a "let me give you what's good for you" attitude and less by a "let's try to see what's good for ourselves and then work together for what we see" way of being together. As far as I am concerned, the former is destructive of human well-being, whether between two lovers or two races of people. The latter may be redemptive, or so it seems to me. And it seems to me that that's exactly what we need to be about, we white women and women of color.

Women of color and white women need to own up to our own respective situations, getting ourselves together *as white* women or *as black* women or *as Hispanic* women—so our racial/ethnic womanness and particularity is clear. We need to be clear about who we are *as a people*—which is why white people like me have to own up to our whiteness and not be always bouncing ourselves off people who are black or brown or yellow, as if somehow we are looking to you for our definition—which could only be a sham.

We have to work together—as we are doing right now on this project. I don't believe these two steps of being separate, and also working together, follow in any neat sequence. Rather they can go on simultaneously under the right conditions, sometimes in crisis situations in which solidarity becomes mandatory; or through friendship when solidarity has become thinkable or at least a common dream.

It seems to me that we can work together only if we are willing to risk being candid with each other—about what we need, how we affect each other, how we experience the difference our race makes even in the instant we are acting together for what we believe is our common good.

As you know—I've heard you discuss this—being candid is more difficult for white liberal women than for just about anyone else, because (1) liberals don't like conflict; (2) whites don't like to get in touch with the difference our race makes; and (3) women, white women at least, have been cultivated to be reconcilers—although I should add that such attitudes are also class related. The sort of candor that involves conflict is especially hard for white, upper-middle-strata, liberal women like me raised to think that we must be "ladies." I thought a lot about this when Grace Kelly died. When I was a child, she was my role model of what a "lady" should be; in recent years, I had grown to find Grace Kelly a rather dreary archetype of passivity, a woman who did not interest me in any way, except that once upon a time I had wanted to be like her.

And so what is it I'm afraid of? What do I fear my candor may unleash or cause? Several things: I've already mentioned my fear that you, rather than struggling through issues with me, will simply walk away—not because you won't want to have anything to do with me but rather because I will have become a source of great pain for you, a pain you won't feel that you should have to bear. I'm also afraid that you'd be right to leave, to say "To hell with you," because I'm afraid that my own racism is deeper and more pervasive than I realize, and such that no black person would really want to be with me if ever she were to see this nasty wad of remnant racism, from generations past and present, which I have swallowed, and which, like a giant furball, has infected my gut.

And why am I afaid that I'm the most racist person in the Northeast? Because it's clear to me that racism is far more pervasive, far more odious, far more sinful and outrageous than any of us white children were ever taught to believe or imagine, even those of us who had white "ladies and gentlemen" for parents. Racism is so obnoxious, so unspeakably devastating to each white personality and psyche, that I, no less than any white sister or brother, must surely have been infected by this gross malaise in ways that I still cannot comprehend.

Yes, indeed, every white person has a white mama—and a white papa too. And while I do hear the particular poignancy and responsibility in the black mama-child relation you articulate, Kate, it's the white daddy/white papa/ white father image, symbol, and reality that cuts to the core of what I see the problem to be in the white world I know. It's interesting, isn't it, that the white woman would say, "But let's talk about the white father instead"? Interesting to me—in that it may have something to do with some of the tensions between black and white women. Something we need to sort out?

You see, for me, in my white culture it's the *father* who's been responsible for a kind of headship of family, which the mother simply passes on, passively. She is to nurture and coddle the father's values—including racism. This sounds simplistic, if what I am saying is interpreted on the basis of individual personalities, because, within lots of families—including my own—individual white mothers are as assertive and strong as white fathers. But among white folks in my world, the prevailing, *public* assumption is that father does indeed know best—and even in families where there is no father at home, or in which the mother personally rules the roost, there looms large this image of "the man"/"the father"/"God," in whose service this life is being lived. Which makes for a complex and often intense relation between the white mother and the white child.

Often this means that the white mama must be manipulative if she's ever to have her own way, because wives and mothers do not live for themselves. To be manipulative is to be indirect, circuitous. It means that the mama must never let the daddy think that the children love her more, even if they do. Because, in fact, she is simply the channel through which the children's feelings get passed to daddy. Which means, again, that the mother must be coy, mysterious, enigmatic when it comes to appropriating the child's feelings for her; moreover, it means that she seldom ever really feels loved by the children—even though they may adore her. What this means is that many white mamas live frantic emotional lives in relation to their children—trying always not to love them too much, but at the same time desperate to feel loved by them. And so it is that white mothers "hang on" or "won't let go"—or so the stories suggest, and I think, to be honest, it is often true.

And while black mamas have to teach their kids how to survive in a racist world, white mamas—if they are women of goodwill—have to teach their kids something similar: on one hand, how to reject patriarchal values of racism, sexism, and economic greed; and, on the other hand, how to pretend to accept these values in order not to be destroyed. So white mothers, if they believe in justice, and white fathers too, if they advocate justice, find themselves in the roles of teaching schizophrenia to the kids in order to help them learn to cope humanely and responsibly in—and still survive—a racist, sexist, classist, warmongering situation.

I'll probably write to you more later. Right now I'm spent. Your words bear witness to some deep and abiding truths—and I don't often speak of "eternals." Thank you for the gift of you.

Carter

November 20, 1982

Dear Carter,

I feel so grateful for the honesty of sharing that is occurring in these letters. It reminds me of my childhood, when I habitually watched Red Buttons on TV. I gathered a host of imaginary friends around me for comfort, all named HiHi, HoHo, HeHe, based on the characters I remembered that Red Buttons talked about a great deal. My sister, Sara, who is twenty-three months older than I, refused to play with me because I insisted that my imaginary friends be allowed to play too. At that point she announced to the world (which consisted of my younger sister, Doris, and the neighborhood children, all blood relatives) that I was crazy. But I didn't realty care, because my imaginary friends were with me through thick and thin, they never left; and when I raised questions about the fundamental order of life, especially as to what the curse of blackness was all about, they (the imaginary friends) raised the same question. I knew in my heart of hearts that they knew I wasn't crazy, just extremely delicate and sensitive.

I feel that you are one of those imaginary friends who is now present in the flesh. The bond between us has been there before we were born. I just remembered I wrote a poem about such a bond on the day that the Feminist Theological Institute came into existence—November 22, 1980.

Strolling down the sidewalk
    a woman-pair
Holding quadraphonic conversations
    in our heads
Sure of words
    not sure of the genus of our souls
Agonizing the same truths
Embedded in the common womb
    of wrestling supplications
Posing difficult questions
    with piercing X-ray vision
        inherent in the friendship

before the beginning.

The poem goes on, but the point I am making is that the covenant of relating is mutual. I know that if I tried to lift or erase the fear you have about your racism hanging out that I would be trespassing on God's territory. However, I do believe that only in experiencing the new heaven and the new earth do we develop convictions about what is really possible as well as renewed commitment to keep the covenant alive and ever-expanding.

I don't know whether you are familiar with Lillian Smith's book, *Killers of the Dream,* written in the 1940s and revised and reissued in 1961.[10] I urge you to read it and add it to our book discussion for the collective, along with *The Color Purple.* We discussed Smith's book in the RSAC (Race, Sex, and Class) meeting yesterday.[11] I only wish that more women in my age group had been present. There was such a need for reality checking with counterparts of my generation, and maybe that day will come soon. What you talked about in your last letter resonated exactly with Lillian Smith's discussion of her childhood. For instance, she says:

The mother who taught me what I know of tenderness and love and compassion taught me also the bleak rituals of keeping Negroes in their "place." The father who rebuked me for an air of superiority toward schoolmates from the mill and rounded out his rebuke by gravely reminding me that "all men are brothers," trained me in the steel-rigid decorum I must demand of every colored male. They who so gravely taught me to split my body from my mind and both from my "soul," taught me also to split my conscience from my acts and Christianity from southern tradition.[12]

I need to respond to another issue you raised. Carter, I ask that you separate your experience of black men from everything else right now because as long as those two (men, plus all else) stay tangled inside you, we cannot get on with the conversation that will take both of our lifetimes, and then some, to complete anyway. You and I have shared with each other the experience of being molested as children.[13] It just dawned on me that when you shared your experience with me, I identified so readily with what happened to you that it may be that only in my imagination did I share my experience with you! Do you recall my telling you about being repeatedly molested by an older boy when I was about five years of age? If you don't recall it, then it is probably because I told it to you when you still existed only in your "imaginary" state!

Your fear, feelings, and response to black men are not abstract racist ideology and doctrine but come from that place inside of you that has not healed from violation. I say that from my own space/place. The teenage boy who molested me several times died soon afterwards and I believed, until my early adulthood, that God did that especially for me, that I was special and that if someone hurts Kate, I could ask "Friend-God" to zap that person—and in seconds my will would be done. That theological narrowness of imagining a controlled/controlling God has changed for me, but it sustained me through some of the abuse I endured from men, including that childhood violation.

Think about the incident with your heart, not your mind. Here's a little white girl who shared what she thought was harmless. Then when she spoke of it, she had to endure the response of angry, frightened parents and the retaliation by the white community to the black man. And, all along, Carter gets lost in the shuffle, denying the good feeling, feeling unclean, having confused-as-hell feelings, assuring everybody that she is okay, and remembering we must love "those" people. No wonder your fear of black males is deep and still confusing to you: but it is like I said in our discussion of *The Color Purple: rebirth is only possible when we face terror face to face.* That experience was terror in your life, just as my experience of being molested was. It wreaked havoc in our psyches. What I have learned in facing terror, sometimes day by day, is that I don't go to certain people for affirmation, especially to those who remind me of the boy who molested me.

I hope that the challenge I am presenting to you is not too threatening. I hope that it is simple and clear to you. I think of the pain of violation like the woman in the scriptures who had the issue of blood for seven long years. (Remember all that the number seven symbolizes in the Bible, especially that seven means "complete.") Think of the woman as bleeding away her life energy and life substance, that they flowed from her in wasteful ways. The story affirms that the woman was healed by her awareness of her situation, an acceptance of the help that was available, and the courage to take the action to touch God in the person of Jesus. And even though Jesus was being pressed by the crowd, he knew that he had been touched by this woman in a significant way.

It is like all the healing-touching between Celie and Shug in *The Color Purple*. The people who hurt you in all kinds of ways cannot do the healing. Nor can those who act like our violators act today. For you still to worry so much about black men or the Native American men who did not stand in support of the lesbian/gay presentation at TIA meeting is to long for and look for healing from the source from whence it will not and cannot come. To focus on the walking dead means that you may miss out on the powerful healing touch and touching healing of the six hundred people who stood with you in love and commitment and cheered.

I want to say more about this healing at some later date. For now I will close with a story that I heard recently. Before doing that I affirm that I enter this covenant of friendship with you because I am thoroughly convinced that I cannot be all that I can be as a black woman if I dismiss you from the community of humanity just because you are a white woman. I cannot be in an I-It relationship with anyone and call myself Christian. And the more I-Thous in my life, the more I feel, experience, and know the Eternal Thou who lives and breathes in each one of us in beautiful and unique ways. (I never thought I would reach the day when I'd say that I need white people in my life, just like I need black people and the other people in the world because we are all part of the whole!) On with the story.

As a child, I was a lover of baby dolls. I yearned to the point of experiencing physical pain in my body for a black doll. I always got white dolls because they were more plentiful and cheaper. But my sister, Doris, who is thirteen months younger than I, got a beautiful black doll one Christmas, and the next year we used it for Jesus in the Christmas play at the church. Back in 1956—57 that was a revolutionary, radical thing to do, but we did it, and it felt so good to me, to know that this little black female doll symbolized the boy

Jesus. After that point I didn't care whether I got a black doll, because if the baby Jesus was black, then the boy Jesus and the grownup Jesus could also be black, and it all started to make sense in my little ever-churched Sunday school mind. Of course I only acknowledged this radical truth to HiHi, HoHo, and HeHe, and they, of course, agreed with me. (Believe it or not, this is not the story I started out to tell. The above story is the one that flowed from the miracle of dialogue. Now, for the story I heard recently...)

A woman was asked by her therapist to imagine that she was a child in a crib who had pushed her favorite toy onto the floor so that it rolled out of sight. When no one came to return this beloved object of pleasure to her, what, she was asked, would she do? The young woman started crying, saying no one had ever been there for her. She insisted that people, places, and things had rolled out of her sight and life repeatedly, and, as a result, she was now terrified to trust anyone to be there with and for her. When we have been intentionally or unintentionally hurt by others, it is not enough to have had someone there to return our lost toy on several occasions, randomly, at their convenience. It would not be enough to assure the wounded child that there is somebody who cares. The sexual abuse against you and me, Carter, caused a part of us to roll out of sight. Even though we have done a lot to put ourselves together again, the healing only happens for each of us, I believe, when we embrace God in ourselves and each other. When I touch other individuals, they feel touched by me, and in a miraculous way the healing happens, slowly but surely. The issue of blood stops flowing out of me. Instead it flows through me, in new and invigorating ways, so that I can be present when the next touch connects with me. When my blood stays inside me, flowing in me, I am more sensitive to the press from the crowd, and I am also in tune with myself to know when "somebody has touched me. And, oh, what joy floods my soul, something happened, and now I know, somebody touched me and made me whole." (This is a paraphrase of a popular gospel song in the black church tradition.)

Have a great Thanksgiving.
Kate

NOTES

1. Alice Walker, *The Color Purple* (New York: Harcourt Brace Jovanovich, 1982).

2. Zora Neale Hurston, *Mules and Men* (Philadelphia: Lippincott, 1935; reprint ed., New York: Collier Books, 1970), pp. 18-19.

3. George Frederickson, *White Supremacy: A Comparative Study in American and South African History* (New York: Oxford University Press, 1981).

4. See Carter Heyward, *The Redemption of God*, especially pages 25-59 and 149-72, for the source of my use of the term "godding."—KGC

5. Cherrie Moraga, and Gloria Anzaldúa, eds., *This Bridge Called My Back: Writings by Radical Women of Color* (Watertown, Mass.: Persephone Press, 1981), pp. 27-37, 71-75, 94, 101.

6. See Amari Baraka, "Philistinism and the Negro Writer," in *Anger and Beyond: The Negro Writer in the United States*, ed. by Hetbert Hill (New York Harper & Row, 1966).

7. Langston Hughes, *The Ways of White Folks* (New York: Knopf, 1934).

8. See Richard Sennett and Jonathan Cobb, *The Hidden Injuries of Class* (New York: Vintage Books, 1972).

9. Gloria Naylor, *The Women of Brewster Place* (New York: Viking Press, 1982), pp. 129-73.

10. Lillian Eugenia Smith, *Killers of the Dream*, rev. ed. (New York: W.W. Norton & Co., 1961).

11. RSAC is a network of professional women in New York City, mostly denominational executives, who have been meeting for the past ten years to discuss, analyze, and strategize around issues related to the intersection of race, sex, and class.

12. Smith, *Killers of the Dream*, p. 27.

13. This reference is to an incident in Carter's childhood when she was molested by the black yardman who was employed by her family. As Carter recalls. "I was five or six and I liked Jeff. I knew he wouldn't hurt me and his fondling of me in the garage never bothered me. What did bother me was the reaction of the police captain, and all the other white men when my parents called them. I couldn't understand why all the fuss. What had Jeff done that was so wrong? And I felt guilty because I had told on him."

Definition of Womanist

Womanist 1. From *womanish*. (Opp. of "girlish," i.e., frivolous, irresponsible, not serious.) A black feminist or feminist of color. From the black folk expression of mothers to female children, "You acting womanish," i.e., like a woman. Usually referring to outrageous, audacious, courageous or *willful* behavior. Wanting to know more and in greater depth than is considered "good" for one. Interested in grown-up doings. Acting grown up. Being grown up. Interchangeable with another black folk expression: "You trying to be grown." Responsible. In charge. *Serious.*

~

2. *Also:* A woman who loves other women, sexually and/or nonsexually. Appreciates and prefers women's culture, women's emotional flexibility (values tears as natural counterbalance of laughter), and women's strength. Sometimes loves individual men, sexually and/or nonsexually. Committed to survival and wholeness of entire people, male *and* female. Not a separatist, except periodically, for health. Traditionally universalist, as in "Mama, why are we brown, pink, and yellow, and our cousins are white, beige, and black?" Ans.: "Well, you know the colored race is just like a flower garden, with every color flower represented." Traditionally capable, as in: "Mama, I'm walking to Canada and I'm taking you and a bunch of other slaves with me." Reply: "It wouldn't be the first time."

~

3. Loves music. Loves dance. Loves the moon. *Loves* the Spirit. Loves love and food and roundness. Loves struggle. *Loves* the Folk. Loves herself. *Regardless.*

~

4. Womanist is to feminist as purple is to lavender.

From Alice Walker, *In Search of our Mothers' Gardens* (New York: Harcourt Brace Jovanovich, 1983.)

Moral Values and Black Womanists

Toinette M. Eugene

I come out of a tradition where those things are valued; where you talk about a woman with big legs and big hips and black skin. I come out of a black community where it was all right to have hips and be heavy. You didn't feel that people didn't like you. The values that [imply] you must be skinny come from another culture....Those are not the values that I was given by the women who served as my models. I refuse to be judged by the values of another culture. I am a Black woman, and I will stand as best as I can in that imagery.*

THE VALUES BLACK WOMEN have derived for themselves and have offered as options to the black community as well as to the members of a broader, dominant society cannot be understood or adequately explained apart from the historical context in which black women have found themselves as moral agents. Moreover, the moral values that black women have provided as a legacy to the black community as well as to the feminist movement in American society suggest a distinctive religious consciousness and documentable religious traditions which have been irrepressible in redeeming and transforming an entire human environment.

The central theses of this essay, which traces specific moral values and black feminism to their root causality within black religious traditions, are also theses derived in part from the highest expressions of moral and faith development as described particularly in the theoretical research and publications of Carol Gilligan and James Fowler.[1]

* Bernice Reagon, *Black Women and Liberation Movements*.

By drawing upon this psychological research and by reviewing black religious history, this essay asserts that public activism and private endurance are paradigmatic of black women's value indicators in both the black religious traditions and in feminist communities. Social activism, self-sacrifice, and other similar value indicators may be verified in the lives of Mary McLeod Bethune and Nannie Helen Burroughs, to name but two exemplary models. Nevertheless, these value measures and these valuable models represent more than unusual courage and strength; they also represent realistic responses to economic deprivation and political and social inequality. Black women have been forced to perform labor and to take risks that few white women have been called upon to do, either in the name of religious traditions or in behalf of the survival of their race.

Black women, however, are not special specimens of womanhood; rather, they are women who have been given less protected and more burdensome positions in society. As Michelle Wallace has so poignantly pointed out, this has resulted in the "myth of the superwoman," which is not a description of black women but, rather, a measure of the difference between what is regularly expected of white women and what is essentially required of black women.[2]

It is obvious that black women have experienced oppressive structures of racism, class bias, and male supremacy in both religion and society in this country. What is not always so obvious to a dominant white-world view, and even to feminist theological understandings, is that Afro-American culture and religion have generated alternative interrelated notions of womanhood contradictory to those of mainstream American economics, society, and theology.[3] These alternative experiences, visions, and images of womanhood have been forged out of the furnace of a moral value system endemic to the black church.

This essay will explore aspects of the moral consciousness and value system that guides black women in their ongoing struggle for survival through a commentary on black religious traditions in which black women share. Within this commentary some reflections will also be offered regarding black women's perspectives on feminism as a white women's movement and on feminist theologies.

Black Women and Moral Values During Slavery

Historically, the black church has been the fiery furnace through which systematic faith affirmations and liberating principles for biblical interpretation have been developed by black people. Within this "invisible institution," hidden from the observation of slave masters, black women, along with black men, developed an extensive moral value system and religious life of their own. In the language of moral-development theorist Carol Gilligan, they established and operated out of a web or network of relationships and intimacy with others in community.[4] The moral values of care, compassion, and cooperation with other black and oppressed persons served as criteria for decisions and actions intended to lay hold of the good, the true, and the beautiful.

The biblical interpretations of the antebellum black church which provided black people with webs of relationships centering on the God of justice and of liberation made slaves incontestably discontented with their servile condition. In the case of black women whose bodies and spirits were wantonly violated by the immoral sexual advances of white masters, the moral value system of black people in this period encouraged slave women to eliminate the sources of their oppression in order to maintain and sustain their fragile nexus with God, community, and self as valued and trusted friends. Paula Giddings, in her text, *When and Where I Enter: The Impact of Black Women on Race and Sex in America,* reports on the moral resistance black slave women offered:

> So, by the early eighteenth century an incredible social, legal, racial structure was put in place. Women were firmly stratified in the roles that Plato envisioned. Blacks were chattel, White men could impregnate a Black woman with impunity, and she alone could give birth to a slave. Blacks constituted a permanent labor force and metaphor that were perpetuated through the Black woman's womb. And all of this was done within the context of the Church, the operating laws of capitalism, and the psychological needs of White males. Subsequent history would be a variation on the same theme.
>
> In its infancy slavery was particularly harsh. Physical abuse, dismemberment, and torture were common....Partly as a result, in the eighteenth century, slave masters did not underestimate the will of their slaves to rebel, even their female slaves. Black women proved especially adept at poisoning their masters, a skill undoubtedly imported from Africa. Incendiarism was another favorite method; it required neither brute physical strength nor direct confrontation. But Black women used every means available to resist slavery—as men did—and if caught, they

were punished just as harshly.[5]

In the midst of this dehumanizing slave environment, black families survived. They overcame the slaveholders' attempts to reduce them to so many subhuman labor units, managing to create an ongoing system of family arrangements and kin networks. Domestic life became critically important, for it was the only place where slaves had any equality and autonomy as human beings in relation to one another.[6]

Regarding domestic life and labor, Angela Davis, in *Women, Race and Class*, has observed a paradox of great significance for black women and men:

> The salient theme emerging from domestic life in the slave quarters is one of sexual equality. The labor that slaves performed for their own sake and not for the aggrandizement of their masters was carried out on terms of equality. Within the confines of their family and community life, therefore, Black people managed to accomplish a magnificent feat. They transformed that negative equality which emanated from the equal oppression they suffered as slaves into a positive quality: the egalitarianism characterizing their social relations.[7]

Harriet Tubman and countless others provided egalitarian images of slave women as strong, self-reliant, proud of their roots and of their ability to survive, convinced of their right to a place in society through the liberation of all black people. Equally oppressed as laborers, equal to their men in the domestic sphere, they were also equal in their moral resistance to slavery, participating in work stoppages and revolts, fleeing north and helping others to flee.

The ability of black people to cope in a hostile society has endured into the twentieth century; studies of black women in urban situations show that the means by which black families survived slavery still enable black women and their families to survive today.

Within this historical framework of past and present hostility black women have always perceived networks of relationality in the liberation struggle differently from white women. Domesticity has never been seen as entirely oppressive but rather as a vehicle for building family life under slavery; male/female relationships have always been more egalitarian; there has been less emphasis on women's work as different from and inferior to men's; slaves and freed persons, male and female, have consistently tended to rebel against the sexual oppression of black women as well as the emasculation of black men. It is easy to understand why many black people today see the white feminist movement as an attempt to divide black people. Contemporary black feminists caution against espousing the more "radical" white feminist stances because they leave out, as irrelevant, black men, black children, black families. Consequently, a primary moral value for black people is articulated in this overarching and enduring black feminist position: solidarity among black people is essential for survival.

A dramatic statement of black women's unique attitude toward solidarity with black men is found in the 1977 statement of the Combahee River Collective, a black lesbian feminist group from Boston.

> Although we are feminists and lesbians we feel solidarity with progressive Black men and do not advocate the fractionalization that white women who are separatists demand. Our situation as Black people necessitates that we have solidarity around the fact of race....We struggle together with Black men against racism, while we also struggle with Black men about sexism.[8]

These black lesbian feminists explicitly rejected a feminist separatism that equates all oppression with sexual oppression and fails fully to comprehend the reality that black women *and men* are victims of shared racial oppression. Feminist separatism is not a viable political philosophy for most black women. Ethicist Barbara Hilkert Andolsen, in her remarkable assessment of racism and American feminism, *Daughters of Jefferson, Daughters of Bootblacks*, issues a strong caveat to white women who are desirous of understanding the black feminist experience:

> Those of us who are white feminists need to be careful that we do not articulate limited strategies for dealing with sexism as if they were the only legitimate feminist strategies. White feminist separatist theories or strategies that ignore the strong bond forged between many black women and men in a shared struggle against racism do not speak to all women's experience.[9]

White feminists have a responsibility to learn about black women's perspectives on women's issues, to analyze how racist social structures may distort the impact of white feminist proposals, and to support black women in their self-defined struggle for liberation. Black feminists are creating their own analyses of sexism and of the interconnections between racism and sexism. White feminist theologians who are seeking to contribute to an inclusive feminist theology that respects and reflects the diversity of women's experience need to learn from the experiences, moral values, and feminist theology articulated by black women.

There is ample material to draw upon from the insights of the distinctive theological consciousness of black women during slavery. For example, the biblical exegetical abilities of Maria Stewart coupled with her assumptions (what would later be known as modernist thinking) gave black women in 1832 a freer rein to express and act upon ideas that liberated them from the oppression of both sexism and racism.[10] For Stewart, simple logic demanded that in light of the role of women in the past, "God at this eventful period should raise up your females to strive…both in public and private, to assist those who are endeavoring to stop the strong current of prejudice that flows so profusely against us at present."[11] Maria Stewart was sure enough of her moral values to admonish others not to doubt the mission of her gender. "No longer ridicule their efforts," she counseled. "It will be counted as sin."[12]

At a women's rights convention in Akron, Ohio, in 1851, several of the most celebrated examples of early black feminist theological perspectives were rendered by the legendary abolitionist and mystic, Sojourner Truth, in her famous "Ain't I a Woman?" speech. From the very beginning of the conference, the white women were overwhelmed by the jeering ridicule of men who had come to disrupt the meeting. Their most effective antagonist was a clergyman who used both the gender of Jesus and the helplessness of the women to counter their feminist arguments. Sojourner squelched the heckler by correcting his theology first, noting that Jesus came from "God and a woman—man had nothing to do with Him."[13] Second, Truth asserted that women were not inherently weak and helpless.

Raising herself to her full height of six feet, flexing a muscled arm, and bellowing with a voice one observer likened to the apocalyptic thunders, Truth informed the audience that she could outwork, out-eat, and outlast any man. Then she challenged, "Ain't I a Woman?"[14] She spoke of women's strength and moral abilities to set things aright: "If the first woman God ever made was strong enough to turn the world upside down all alone, these women together ought to be able to turn it back, and get it right side up again. And now they are asking to do it, the men better let them."[15] Moral values asserted by black women who give credence to the black Judeo-Christian tradition honor reconciliation as highly as liberation.

The accumulated experiences and expressions of black women during slavery were greatly influenced and nurtured by their webs of relationship with the black church and its biblical interpretations of the salvific power of God. These women who toiled under the lash for their masters, worked for and protected their families, fought against slavery and who were beaten, raped, but never subdued passed on to their nominally free female descendants a rich legacy of their own moral value system. It was a legacy of hard work so decidedly different from a White Anglo-Saxon Protestant (WASP) work ethic; it was a legacy of perseverance and self-reliance, a legacy of tenacity, resistance, and insistence on sexual equality—in short, a legacy of love spelling out standards for a new womanhood.[16]

FEMINIST MORAL VALUES AND BLACK RELIGIOUS TRADITIONS

The institution of chattel slavery in America was destroyed by the most momentous national event of the nineteenth century, the Civil War. Emancipation removed the legal and political slave status from approximately four million black people in the United States, which meant that, in principle, these blacks owned their persons and their labor for the first time. Unfortunately for the vast majority of Afro-Americans, the traditional practices of racial and gender subordination subjected them to incredible suffering after that war.

The black woman began her life of freedom with no vote, no protection, and no equity of any sort. Black women, young and old, were basically on their own. The patterns of exploitation of the black woman as laborer and breeder were only shaken by the Civil War; by no means were they destroyed. Throughout the late nineteenth and early twentieth centuries, black women were severely restricted to the most unskilled, poorly paid, menial work. Virtually no black woman held a job beyond that of a domestic servant or field hand. Keeping house, farming, and bearing and rearing children continued to dominate all aspects of the black woman's life. The systematic oppression and routinized exclusion of black females from other areas of employment served as confirmations for the continuation of the servile status of black women. As Jeanne Noble describes it, "While freedom brought new opportunities for black men, for most women it augmented old problems."[17] After emancipation, racism and male supremacy continued to intersect patriarchal and capitalist structures in definitive ways.

The religious consciousness of the black freedwoman in the latter nineteenth century focused on "uplifting the black community." The black female was taught that her education was meant not only to uplift her but also to prepare her for a life of service in the overall community. There was a general attitude, says Noble, that "Negro women should be trained to teach in order to uplift the masses."[18] This attitude provided an additional impetus for black women, such as Nannie Helen Burroughs, Charlotte Hawkins Brown, and Mary McLeod Bethune, to found schools. Although the curricula of these schools included academic subjects, there were large doses of industrial arts courses, particularly homemaking, and an environment that enforced codes of morality and thrift. It was biblical faith grounded in the prophetic tradition that helped black women devise strategies and tactics to make black people less susceptible to the indignities and proscriptions of an oppressive white social order.

Understanding the prophetic tradition of the Bible and of the black church has empowered black women to fashion a set of moral values on their own terms, as well as mastering, radicalizing, and sometimes destroying the pervasive negative orientations imposed by the values of the larger society. Also, they articulate possibilities for decisions and action which address forthrightly the circumstances that inescapably shape black life.

Flowing from black women's biblical faith grounded in the prophetic tradition, many black women have been inspired by the Bethune and Burroughs models to hold in high regard a diaconal model of black feminist theology which is extremely consistent with their experience and identity. Without necessarily rejecting white feminist models of theology that focus principally or only on mutuality and equality as essential components of liberation, the preferential choice made by many black feminists is for a theology of servant leadership that was espoused by Christ. This biblical model of feminist liberation theology is principally focused on solidarity with those who suffer or who are marginalized in any way. A much greater examination, integration, and expression of this black feminist perspective and alternative to "mainstream" models of feminist liberation theology is needed.[19]

Rosemary Ruether has been in the forefront among feminist theologians who have insisted that the eradication of racism must be a major priority. She has produced particularly illuminating analyses of the interconnections between racism and sexism.[20] When discussing the future of feminist theory in the academic world, Ruether acknowledges that she speaks from a "white Western Christian context," and she calls for an inclusive feminist theology that must emerge out of "a network of solidarity" existing among many feminist communities "engaged in the critique of patriarchalism in distinct cultural and religious contexts," rather than "one dominant form of feminism that claims to speak for the whole of womankind."[21]

In contrast, black theologian Delores Williams has observed that although Ruether rightly emphasizes the increasing numbers of women students in theological schools and lauds the "enormous amount of solid work in all fields of feminist theology that has been accomplished in these past fifteen years," Ruether does not remind her audience that the work has been done by and on behalf of white women.[22] Black women are a tiny percentage among the graduate students in religion; they are an even smaller percentage of the faculties in departments of religion and seminaries. As of yet, there is no "enormous amount" of published work on black feminist theology to offset, or to dialogue with, the claims Ruether cavalierly makes about feminist theology as if black perspectives on feminist theologies were abundantly or equally included.

During the mass migration of southern blacks to the North (1910-1925), tens of thousands of black women and men left home, seeking social democracy and economic opportunity. During this colossal movement of black people, the black church continued to serve as the focal point and center for maintaining the moral value system and the network of relationships which sustained community life.

Not surprisingly, this accelerated movement of blacks out of the South impinged on the black woman's reality in very definite ways. Black women migrated north in greater numbers than black men. Economic necessity dictated that most black women who immigrated to the urban centers find work immediately. In order to survive themselves and to provide for their families, black women once again found only drudge work available to them.

The interaction of race and sex on the labor market exacted a heavy toll on the black woman, making all aspects of migration a problem of paramount religious significance. Her experience as a wife and a mother, responsible for transmitting the moral values, culture, and customs of the black community to her children, served as a decisive factor in determining how the Bible was read and understood. Simultaneously while the black woman was trying to organize family life according to black traditional roles, the white male-dominated industrial society required that she serve as a catalyst in their labor transition process. Her own unfamiliarities and adaptation difficulties had to be repressed because she was responsible for making a home in crowded substandard housing, finding inner-city schools that propagated literacy for her children, and earning enough income for her family to cover the most elementary needs.

The moral and religious value system of the black church served as a sustaining force and as an interpretive principle that guided migrant black women in facing life squarely, in acknowledging its raw coarseness. The white elitist attributes of passive gentleness and an enervative delicacy, considered particularly appropriate to womanhood, proved nonfunctional in the pragmatic survival of black women. Cultivating conventional amenities was not a luxury afforded them. Instead, black women are aware that their very lives depended upon their being able to decipher the various sounds in the larger world, to hold in check the nightmare figures of terror, to fight for basic freedoms against the sadistic law enforcement agencies in their communities, to resist the temptation to capitulate to the demands of the *status quo*, to find meaning in the most despotic circumstances, and to create something where nothing existed before. The expression of a moral value system for black women meant and required a "sheroic" self-sacrifice and self-giving that could not ever afford shyness, silence, softness, or diffidence as a response indicating subservience.

From the period of black urban migration through World Wars I and II, black women who were rooted in the strong moral values and prophetic traditions of the black church became religious crusaders for justice. Mary McLeod Bethune and her associates recorded and talked about the grimness of struggle among the least visible people in the society. Bethune was adamant about the unheralded achievements of black women, always encouraging them to "go to the front and take our rightful place; fight our battles and claim our victories."[23] She believed in black women's "possibilities," moral values, and their place on this earth. "Next to God," she once said, "we are indebted to women, first for life itself, and then for making it worth having."[24]

In response to the hostile environment, deteriorating conditions, and the enduring humiliation of the social ostracism experienced by black people especially during these war years, Bethune and company exposed the most serious and unyielding problem of the twentieth century—the single most determining factor of black existence in America—the question of color. In their strategic attacks against the ideological supremacy of racist practices and values, they appealed to the religious traditions of black people that began in their invisible church during slavery.

From the period of urbanization of World War II to the present, black women still find that their situation is a struggle to survive collectively and individually against the harsh historical realities and pervasive adversities of today's world. Federal government programs, civil rights movements, and voter-education programs have all had a positive impact on the black woman's situation, but they have not been able to offset the negative effects of inherent inequities that are inextricably tied to the history and ideological hegemony of racism, sexism, and class privilege.[25]

Precisely because of this reality and overwhelmingly oppressive national ideology, Rosemary Ruether warns white feminists to give explicit attention to the ways in which they are involved in race and class privilege. If they do not, she says, they risk social encapsulation.

> Any woman's movement which is only concerned about sexism and not other forms of oppression, must remain a woman's movement of the white upper class, for it is only this group of women whose only problem is the problem of being women, since in every other way, they belong to the ruling class.[26]

Moreover, both black and white feminist groups that do not give explicit attention to the realities yoking racism and sexism will find that they can be easily manipulated by dominant males who appeal to unexamined class and race interests to achieve economic exploitation of all women. Work and dialogue between feminists of color and white feminists in this essential area is, in some sense, just beginning. Meanwhile, black women and their families continue to be enslaved to hunger, disease, and the highest rate of unemployment since the Depression years. Advances in education, housing, health care, and other necessities are deteriorating faster now than ever before.[27]

Both in informal day-to-day life and in the formal organizations and institutions of society, black women are still the victims of the aggravated inequities of the tridimensional phenomenon of race/class/gender oppression. It is in this context that the moral values of black women and the emergence of black feminist consciousness shaped by black biblical and religious traditions must continue to make a decisive difference for a debilitated and nearly dysfunctional human environment.

WOMANIST RELATIONSHIPS, MORAL VALUES AND BIBLICAL TRADITIONS

Because of a social reality, which is so totally demoralizing, and because of the religious traditions from which most black women have come, the Bible has been the highest source of authority in developing and delivering a black moral praxis and a moral theology that is usable in all circumstances. By selectively utilizing the pages of revered Old Testament books, black women have learned how to refute the stereotypes that have depicted black people as ignorant minstrels or vindictive militants. Remembering and retelling the Jesus stories of the New Testament has helped black women to deal with the overwhelming difficulties of overworked and widowed mothers, or underworked and anxious fathers, of sexually exploited and anguished daughters, or prodigal sons, and of dead or dying brothers whose networks of relationality are rooted deeply in the black community. Black feminist consciousness and moral values grow out of and expand upon black, biblical experience and hermeneutics.

Black feminist consciousness may be more accurately identified as black womanist consciousness, to use Alice Walker's concept and definition. In the introduction to *In Search of Our Mothers' Gardens*, Walker proposes several descriptions of the term "womanist," indicating that the word refers primarily to a black feminist and is derived from "womanish," that is, outrageous, audacious, courageous, or willful behavior.[28] To be a faithful womanist, then, or to operate out of this system of black moral value indicators which flow from biblical understandings based on justice and love, is to express in word and deed an alternative ontology or way of living in the world that is endemic to many black women. It is precisely womanist religious responses of endurance, resistance, and resiliency offered in the face of all attempts at personal and institutional domination that may provide a renewed theological legacy of liberation for everyone concerned.

In exploring the implications contained in Walker's richly descriptive prose, it is possible to make some concluding reflections on black moral values and on the contribution of black women's life experiences as they interface with white feminist liberation theologies.

Womanist responses and black moral values are meant to be alternative standards of womanhood and contradictory and paradoxical to those of mainstream American society. Womanist images and black moral values are meant to be paradigmatic of an authentic Christian community of the oppressed that embraces not only the story of the resurrection, but is moreover a referent for the redemptive tribulations through which Jesus as Suffering Servant has come. Womanist moral values are expressed through radical healing and empowering actions with those who are considered as the very least in the reign of God.

Walker adds that a womanist is "committed to the survival and wholeness of entire people, male *and* female. Not a separatist...[she] is traditionally capable."[29] The practical implications of such meanings for interaction and dialogue between black women's moral values and the diverse tenets of white feminist ethics are obvious and challenging. Black womanist moral values can redeem us from naivete regarding the nature and function of liberation as well as deliver us from a simplistic, black pseudo expression of providence, that "de Lawd will provide." Nonetheless, a womanist religious tradition does subscribe to the black folk wisdom that God can make a way out of no way for those, like Zora Neale Hurston and others, who just refuse to resign from the human race.

Womanist moral values of "appreciation for the struggle, a love of the folk, and a love of self—*regardless*"[30] offer to all black people and to all others a continual and open means of interaction between those who claim diverse womanist and feminist identities and experiences, and among all those who have a significant agenda for more authentic theologies of liberation.

NOTES

1. Carol Gilligan, *In a Different Voice: Psychological Theory and Women's Development* (Cambridge: Harvard University Press, 1982), and James W. Fowler, *Stages of Faith: The Psychology of Human Development and the Quest for Meaning* (San Francisco: Harper and Row, 1981).

2. Michelle Wallace, *Black Macho and the Myth of the Superwoman* (New York: Dial Press, 1979).

3. Toinette M. Eugene, "Black Women Contribute Strong Alternate Images," *National Catholic Reporter*, April 13, 1984, p. 4.

4. Carol Gilligan as described in James W. Fowler, *Becoming Adult, Becoming Christian* (San Francisco: Harper and Row, 1984), pp. 39-40.

5. Paula Giddings, *When and Where I Enter: The Impact of Black Women on*

Race and Sex in America (Toronto: Bantam Books, 1984), p. 39.

6. Herbert Gutman, *The Black Family in Slavery and Freedom, 1750-1925* (New York: Pantheon Books, 1976), pp. 356-357.

7. Angela Y. Davis, *Women, Race and Class* (New York: Random House, 1981), p. 18.

8. Combahee River Collective, "A Black Feminist Statement," in *This Bridge Called My Back: Writings by Radical Women of Color*, eds. Cherrie Moraga and Gloria Anzaldua (Watertown, MA: Persephone Press, 1981), p. 213.

9. Barbara Hilkert Andolsen, *Daughters of Jefferson, Daughters of Bootblacks: Racism and American Feminism* (Macon, GA: Mercer University Press, 1986), p. 98.

10. Paula Giddings, *When and Where I Enter*, p. 52.

11. Bert James Lowenberg and Ruth Bogin, eds., *Black Women in Nineteenth Century American Life: Their Words, Their Thoughts, Their Feelings* (University Park and London: The Pennsylvania State University Press, 1976), p. 149.

12. Ibid.

13. Ibid., p. 236.

14. Ibid., p. 235.

15. Ibid., p. 236.

16. Angela Davis, *Women, Race and Class*, p. 29.

17. Jeanne L. Noble, *Beautiful, Also Are the Souls of My Black Sisters: A History of the Black Woman in America* (New York: Prentice Hall, 1978), p. 63.

18. Jeanne L. Noble, as discussed in Paula Giddings, *When and Where I Enter*, p. 101.

19. Toinette M. Eugene, "Black Women Contribute..."

20. Rosemary Ruether has written about racism many times. Two of her more detailed treatments of the topic are "Between the Sons of Whites and the Sons of Blackness: Racism and Sexism in America," in *New Woman/New Earth: Sexist Ideologies and Human Liberation* (New York: Seabury Press, 1975), pp. 115-33, and "Crisis in Sex and Race: Black Theology vs Feminist Theology," *Christianity and Crisis* 34 (15 April 1985): 67-73.

21. Rosemary Ruether, "Feminist Theology: On Becoming the Tradition," *Christianity and Crisis* 45 (4 March 1985): 58.

22. Delores Williams, "The Color of Feminism," *Christianity and Crisis* 45 (29 April 1985): 164-165.

23. Elaine M. Smith, "Mary McLeod Bethune and the National Youth

Administration," *Clio Was a Woman: Studies in the History of American Women*, Mabel E. Deutrich and Virginia C. Purdy, eds. (Washington, D.C.: Howard University Press, 1980), p. 152.

24. Ibid.

25. Angela Davis, *Women, Race and Class*, pp. 231-232.

26. Rosemary Ruether, *New Woman/New Earth*, p. 116.

27. *Facts on US Working Women*, U.S. Department of Labor Women's Bureau, Fact Sheet No. 85-6, July 1985.

28. Alice Walker, *In Search of Our Mothers' Gardens: Womanist Prose* (San Diego: Harcourt Brace Jovanovich, 1983), pp. xi-xii.

29. Ibid., p. xi.

30. Ibid.

Mujerista Theology

I AM A CUBAN ACTIVIST THEOLOGIAN struggling to develop a *Mujerista* theology that is rooted in and has as its source the experience of Hispanic women. I have lived away from my country most of my adult life because of circumstances beyond my control and I think of myself as living in exile. This is the context within which I have struggled to find my voice and my mission. I now know that finding my voice has been part of my mission, a mission which now calls me to struggle to create a platform in the theological world for my voice and the voices of my Hispanic sisters.

As a *Mujerista* I do not see myself as part of a minority group, a marginalized group. It is a fact that at present *Mujeristas*, as well as all Hispanics, have no way of influencing the society in which we live; our values ideals are not part of the norm of society. As a *Mujerista* I believe that we need to change radically the society in which we life. Simply influencing society will not result in the changes that are needed to bring about peace with justice in our world. That is why we *Mujeristas* understand ourselves along the lines of the biblical concept of the "remnant." Like the biblical remnant we are not an integral part of society. Our mission is to challenge oppressive structures which refuse to allow us to be full members of society while preserving our distinctiveness as Hispanic women.

We also apply this understanding of ourselves as a remnant to our theological task and to our role as theologians. We see *Mujerista* theology as a distinctive contribution to the theological enterprise at large which challenges particularly nonliberative theological understandings. For us theology is a praxis—a liberative praxis having as its goal the liberation of Hispanic women which cannot take place at the expense of any other oppressed group. [...]

For me the struggle is life, *la vida es la lucha*. To do *Mujerista* theology is an intrinsic part of my struggle for liberation. To do *Mujerista* theology is to believe that God stands in solidarity with us, Hispanic women.

This definition of *Mujerista* theology comes from an earlier version of "Solidarity" that appeared in *Lift Every Voice: Constructing Christian Theologies from the Underside*, edited by Susan Brooks Thistlethwaite and Mary Potter Engel. (HarperCollins, 1990.)

Solidarity

Love of Neighbor in the Twenty-First Century

Ada Isasi-Diaz

MY NEXT DOOR NEIGHBOR when I lived as a missionary in Perú was a family with four precious children.[1] They lived in a hut-like house with no plumbing and no electricity The father, Cáceres, who worked as a painter when there was work, was an outgoing person who always had time to talk to me as I passed by his house on my way to catch the bus.[2] One day he asked me why I had left Cuba and the United States to become a missionary. I tried to explain to him the sense of vocation that impelled me to live among the poor and to struggle for justice. At the end of our conversation as I was walking away, Cáceres called out to me and said, "Remember, you can always leave this place; we can't." Cáceres's words have stayed with me and have helped me understand several things: my work is not a doing for others but, as far as possible, a being with others. The goal is not to be like the poor and the oppressed (an impossibility), but rather to be in solidarity with them. Cáceres's words were one of the initial reasons why I have been concerned with understanding what solidarity is about and how to live in solidarity with the poor and the oppressed.

Many years after my conversation with Cáceres I was at one of the largest church-oriented women's conferences in the United States. A number of the participants had asked the organizers for an opportunity to address the gathering about a variety of justice issues in which they were involved. At the last plenary session all those who wanted to speak were lined up and allowed to speak for no more than three minutes each. I was struck particularly by a woman who advocated opposition to the Contras in Nicaragua.[3] She asked us "to be in solidarity with the Sandinista government." She herself was totally committed to the Sandinista cause and worked very hard in favor of the people of Nicaragua. She was indeed in solidarity with the struggles of the Nicaraguans against the Contras. What struck me was the response to her plea: applause. As I looked around I suspected that many of the people who had applauded were being very sincere, that they really agreed with what she was saying. But I also suspected and continue to suspect that for the majority of people who are committed to justice, solidarity means agreement with and sympathy for the poor and the oppressed.

After this experience at the women's conference I began to be concerned about how the word "solidarity" is used and misused. I am convinced that its meaning has been coopted. What worries me most is that "solidarity" is understood as a disposition: one can have it for a while, put it aside for whatever reason, and then pick it up again. I am also worried about the fact that "solidarity" has come to mean "agreement with" and that it is given an ephemeral sense of supporting others that has little or nothing to do with liberative praxis.[4]

It is my contention that solidarity, in the original sense of that word, must replace charity as the appropriate Christian behavior—ethical behavior—in our world today. This contention implies a significant paradigmatic shift for Christian behavior, for there is an essential difference between solidarity and charity. Charity, the word used most often when talking about love of neighbor, has been implemented mainly through a one-sided giving, a donation almost always, of what we have in abundance. Obviously that is not all that charity means, but, in general, this is how it is understood and used. I am not saying that giving is not an appropriate, even a necessary way of loving. I do believe, however, that giving is an ethical behavior today only if it is understood and carried out within the context of solidarity.

The paradigmatic shift I am proposing calls for solidarity as the appropriate present-day expression of the gospel mandate that we love our neighbor. This commandment, which encapsulates the gospel message, is the goal of Christianity.[5] I believe salvation depends on love of neighbor, and because love of neighbor today should be expressed through solidarity, solidarity can and should be considered the *sine qua non* of salvation. This means that we have to be very clear about who "our neighbor" is. Our neighbor according to Matthew 25, is the least of our sisters and brothers. Neighbors are the poor, the oppressed, for whom we must have a preferential option. This we cannot have apart from being in solidarity with them.[6]

The Original (True) Meaning of Solidarity

The true meaning of solidarity has been under serious attack; it has been diluted. As proof, notice how fashionable the usage of "solidarity" has become, how easily it rolls off the tongues of all sorts of speakers, how unthreatening it is. If the true meaning of solidarity were understood and intended, visible radical change would be happening in the lives of all of us who endorse it with our applause. Solidarity is not a matter of agreeing with, of supporting, liking, or being inspired by the cause of a group of people. Though all these might be part of solidarity, solidarity goes beyond all of them. Solidarity has to do with understanding the interconnections that exist between oppression and privilege, between the rich and the poor, the oppressed and the oppressors. It also refers to the cohesiveness that needs to exist among communities of struggle.

Solidarity is the union of kindred persons "arising from the common responsibilities and interests, as between classes, peoples, or groups; community of interests, feelings, purposes, or action; social cohesion."[7] Solidarity moves away from the false notion of disinterest, of doing for others in an altruistic fashion. Instead it is grounded in "common responsibilities and interests," which necessarily arouse shared feelings and lead to joint action.

From a Christian perspective the goal of solidarity is to participate in the ongoing process of liberation through which we Christians become a significantly positive force in the unfolding of the "kin-dom" of God.[8] At the center of the unfolding of the kin-dom is the salvific act of God. Salvation and liberation are interconnected. Salvation is gratuitously given by God; it flows from the very essence of God: love. Salvation is worked out through the love between God and each human being and among human beings. This love relationship is the goal of all life—it constitutes the fullness of humanity.[9] Therefore, love sets in motion and sustains the ongoing act of God's salvation in which each person necessarily participates, since love requires, per se, active involvement of those who are in relationship.

Our participation in the act of salvation is what we refer to as liberation. It consists of our work to transform the world. Liberation is both cause and effect of the struggle to have a love relationship with others, including God.

Now, there can be no salvation without liberation, though no single act of liberation can be totally identified with salvation in its fullness. As Gustavo Gutiérrez has said, "Without liberating historical events, there would be no growth of the Kingdom [*sic*]...we can say that the historical, political, liberating event is the growth of the Kingdom [*sic*] and is a salvific event; but it is not the coming of the Kingdom [*sic*], not all of salvation."[10]

The main obstacle to the unfolding of the kin-dom is the alienation from God and from each other experienced by all in and through the oppressive societal categories and structures that cause and sustain oppression.[11] This alienation is what we refer to as sin, both personal sin and structural sin. Sin affects the totality of the person and the relationship with God and with others. Sin always affects society; it is a concrete historical reality brought about and sustained by personal behavior that is institutionalized and sanctioned by societal norms. "Sin appears, therefore, as the fundamental alienation, the root of a situation of injustice and exploitation."[12]

To struggle against oppression, against alienation, is a matter of an ongoing personal conversion that involves effective attempts to change alienating societal structures. This personal conversion cannot happen apart from solidarity with the oppressed. But why are the poor and the oppressed those with whom we must be in solidarity? Why does overcoming alienation demand a preferential option for the oppressed? The reason is not that the poor and the oppressed are morally superior. Those who are oppressed are not personally better or more innocent or purer in their motivations than the rest of us. The preferential option at the heart of solidarity is based on the fact that the point of view of the oppressed, "pierced by suffering and attracted by hope, allows them, in their struggles, to conceive another reality. Because the poor suffer the weight of alienation, they can conceive a different project of hope and provide dynamism to a new way of organizing human life for all."[13] This contribution, which they alone can give, makes it possible for everyone to overcome alienation. The preferential option for the poor and the oppressed makes it possible for the oppressors to overcome alienation, because to be oppressive limits love, and love cannot exist in the midst of alienation. Oppression and poverty must be overcome because they are "a slap in the face of God's sovereignty."[14] The alienation they cause is a denial of God. Gutiérrez refers to the profoundly biblical insight of a Bolivian campesino: "an atheist is someone who fails to practice justice toward the poor."[15]

Who are the poor and oppressed for whom we must opt, with whom we must be in solidarity? They are the ones who are exploited, who suffer systemic violence, the victims of cultural imperialism. The poor and the oppressed are those for whom the struggle for survival is a way of life. To be poor and oppressed means "to die of hunger, to be illiterate, to be exploited by others, not to know that you are being exploited, not to know you are a person."[16] The poor and the oppressed are marginalized, powerless. They are those who suffer from specific forms of oppression—sexism, racism/ethnic prejudice, classism. These specific oppressions, however, are not self-contained realities but are interconnected parts of a worldwide system of domination in which the few oppress the many.[17] This system of domination permeates every aspect of society: ideology, religion, social mores, government, businesses, families, relationships.

Solidarity as Theory and Strategy for Liberation

As an effective way of opposing systems of oppression, we must understand solidarity both as a theory and as a strategy.[18] As a theory solidarity opposes the theory of oppression[19] by reconceptualizing every aspect of society. Control and domination, which I believe are the main characteristics of oppressive structures and relationships, cease to be key elements of societal structures; they cease to be the way people relate to each other. Instead, a new order of relationship makes it possible for a commonality of feelings and interests to flourish and becomes the cornerstone of society, the way it is organized and operates. As a strategy, then, solidarity brings about radical societal change. In our world today, hardly any society is isolated. Therefore, to bring about radical change in one society requires insights and strategies that can effectively undo and replace control and domination with communality of feelings and interests worldwide.

The starting place of solidarity as a theory is not a generalized conception of oppression that easily becomes an abstraction. The starting place of the theory of solidarity has to be the oppression of specific persons, oppression caused or maintained, directly or indirectly, by the privileges of the oppressors. Only because the theory of solidarity is grounded in particular forms of oppression can we claim that solidarity involves understanding and undoing the connections between different forms of oppression. These connections among forms of oppression indicate that there must be commonality of interests among the oppressed, which in turn points to the possibility and need for mutuality among them. If there is no mutuality among the oppressed, they can very easily become tomorrow's oppressors. Without real mutuality we run the risk of not bringing about structural change but rather of promoting participation of the oppressed in present structures.

The theoretical aspect of solidarity is intrinsically linked to solidarity as a strategy.[20] In other words, solidarity on the one hand is a strategy that consists of a praxis of mutuality. On the other hand, solidarity is an understanding and worldview, a theory, about the commonality of interests that links humanity. The praxis of mutuality, the strategic aspect of solidarity, implements the theory of solidarity at the same time that it provides the ground for the reflection needed to elaborate further the theory of solidarity. The theoretical aspect of solidarity provides a goal for the strategy of solidarity: recognition of commonality, of interests. This goal, in turn, becomes an inherent way for evaluating how mutuality is functioning as a strategy. Solidarity as a strategy demands an ever greater clarity about the meaning of "commonality of interests." As a strategy solidarity requires such understanding to be specific and historically rooted. "Commonality of interests" cannot be an abstraction; its specificity is defined by the social, economic, and political circumstances of the persons affected by such commonality or its absence. The inseparable internal relation of theory to strategy that I am claiming for solidarity necessitates a dialogic, circular understanding of the elements of solidarity: commonality of interests and mutuality. Neither of these elements is to be considered more important or more necessary than the other. They are inexorably bound; each of them is always understood in view of the other. There is no separation or opposition, no dichotomy or dialectical relationship between mutuality and commonality of interest.

MUTUALITY AS THE STRATEGY FOR SOLIDARITY

Common interests—that view of the fate of our world that grounds solidarity—are what move Christian behavior from the one-sidedness of charity to mutuality. Common interests and mutuality can make effective in our lives the "love your neighbor as yourself" that is central to the gospel message of love and justice. In our world today the interconnections that exist among nations and peoples in different parts of the planet make obvious the need for embracing commonality of interests as an important goal. Two world wars, multinational corporations, the threat of global annihilation, the global spread of AIDS, the worldwide political influence and control of the superpowers, acid rain, the deterioration of the ozone layer—all these point to the interconnections operating in our world today. The task of those of us interested in making solidarity a reality is to bring about a mutuality among peoples that will make clear such common interests.

First let us look at how to bring about a praxis of mutuality among the oppressed. Mutuality has to be preceded by conscientization. This is a process during which one becomes aware, starting with no more than a moment of insight, that there is something suspicious about one's oppressed condition. Almost anything can create the spark that moves people "from a 'naive awareness,' which does not deal with problems, gives too much value to the past, tends to accept mythical explanations, and tends toward debate, to a 'critical awareness,' which delves into problems, is open to new ideas, replaces magical explanations with real causes, and tends to dialogue."[21] Paulo Freire insists that this process of conscientization involves praxis and is not just an intellectual understanding apart from action.[22] Conscientization makes the oppressed understand the real causes of oppression and the need to engage with others in changing such a situation. This process of conscientization is not something that happens once and for all. Conscientization is a "permanent effort of man [sic] who seeks to situate himself [sic] in time and space, to exercise his [sic] creative potential, and to assume his [sic] responsibilities."[23] Only after the oppressed are conscienticized can mutuality among them begin to develop. Though it is true that many of the oppressed do depend on other oppressed people to survive, frequently the oppressed do not see their common interests because they have to fight each other for the few crumbs that fall from the table of the oppressors. In many ways the oppressed depend for their survival on those who control the society in which they live—their oppressors. To even begin to envision the reality that is possible when they stand in solidarity with each other, the oppressed have to be willing to stop looking for and accepting the "charity" of their oppressors. To turn from the "charity" of the oppressors to solidarity among themselves requires great willingness to take risks. This going beyond the isolated self is followed by creating strategies to carry out their struggle for liberation. Implementing these strategies keeps hope alive and, together with the vision of their own liberation, gives the poor and oppressed the courage to risk that sustains the struggle.

Mutuality of the oppressor with the oppressed also starts with conscientization. To become aware that one is an oppressor does not stop with individual illumination but requires the oppressor to establish dialogue and mutuality with the oppressed.[24] The first word in the dialogue that can bring awareness to the oppressor is uttered by the oppressed. Oppressors who are willing to listen and to be questioned by the oppressed, by the very action of listening begin to leave behind their role as oppressors and to become "friends" of the oppressed.[25] This word spoken by the oppressed is "at times silent, at times muzzled; it is the face of the poor…of oppressed people who suffer violence."[26] This word is often spoken through demonstrations, boycotts, even revolutions. This word imposes itself "ethically, by a kind of categorical imperative, which is well determined and concrete, which the 'friend' as 'friend' listens to freely. This word…appeals to the 'friend's' domination and possession of the world and even of the other, and questions the desire for wealth and power."[27]

This word uttered by the oppressed divests those who allow themselves to be questioned by it of whatever they have totally appropriated. Although the word of the oppressed is seen as a weak word by the powerful, yet this "weak" word has the power to bring judgment. It judges the desire of the oppressor for wealth and power. It is also able to signify effectively the real possibility of liberation for those oppressors who allow themselves to be questioned. The word uttered by the oppressed is efficacious since, when listened to by oppressors, it enables them to make the qualitative jump that pushes them to become "friends," to establish mutuality with the oppressed. This word uttered by the oppressed gives the "friends" the courage to question and judge the structures that they have supported and from which they benefit, thus becoming co-creators with the oppressed of new liberating structures.

"Friends" answer the initial word of the oppressed not only by questioning their own lives but also by responding to the oppressed. Born of the critical consciousness acquired by allowing themselves to be critiqued and by taking responsibility for being oppressors, this response of the "friends" can help the oppressed in their own process of conscientization. Such response can help the oppressed to recognize the oppressor they carry within themselves and to rid themselves of him/her. The mutuality now established can help the oppressed to move away from seeking vengeance and from wanting to exchange places with the oppressors. This response of the "friends" can help the oppressed understand that they must not seek to participate in oppressive structures but rather to change those structures radically.[28]

If we do not recognize the need for the oppressed to learn from the "friends," then we cannot claim that mutuality is at the heart of solidarity. Solidarity requires a true dialogic relationship between oppressed and "friend." Our inability to embrace this mutuality, as described, has to do, I believe, with a romantic view of the oppressed which is sharply divorced from reality. If we fail to recognize that the "friends" need to do more than simply help the oppressed implement their strategies for liberation, no real mutuality, no real solidarity will exist. The process of conversion that becomes an intrinsic part of the lives of the "friends" makes it possible and necessary for them to question the oppressed about their goals. It makes it possible for the "friends" to participate with the oppressed in creating strategies for liberation, in deepening and clarifying the understanding of mutuality that is at the heart of liberation.

The "friends" of the oppressed are often scorned by those in whose circles they once moved because they threaten the powerful. The "friends," once oppressors themselves, know how to thwart control and domination. They are scorned because they know the manipulations and betrayals oppressors must make to stay in power and they can prick the consciences of their previous colleagues in ways the oppressed cannot. The "friends" are able to demystify the world of the oppressors, to expose its weakness and incoherence, to point out its lies.

However, at all times we must remember that it is the word uttered by the oppressed that starts and sustains the dialogic process of mutuality which stands at the heart of solidarity. We must not lose sight and begin to believe it is the "friends" who have initiated and now sustain the process of consdentization of the oppressor, a process that always has to be evolving. We also need to be conscious at all times that the "friends" as well as the oppressed derive their courage, their commitment to the struggle, and their staying power for the long run from a common vision of liberation.

Mutuality among the oppressed and between the oppressed and their "friends" is not simply a matter of reciprocal understanding and support, though that is or could be a very positive side effect. Mutuality as an element of solidarity must push the oppressed and their "friends" to revolutionary politics.[29] Mutuality urges them to envision and work toward alternative nonoppressive systems; otherwise they will not be able to sustain the revolutionary momentum that makes liberation possible.[30] Mutuality must push the oppressed and their "friends" to resist easy, partial solutions which may indeed alleviate oppression but not lead to liberation.

But this does not mean that we can wait until we have a perfect strategy or a perfect moment to act. No strategy is perfect. There are always internal problems and inconsistencies that need to be worked out. All strategies involve risk. This should never keep us from acting; it should never delay our work to try to establish mutuality, to create a community of solidarity committed to change oppressive structures, a community in which no one group of oppressed people will be sacrificed for the sake of another. This is what mutuality, the strategic component of solidarity, will accomplish.

COMMITMENT TO MUTUALITY

Solidarity will not become a reality unless we are totally committed to mutuality. As a matter of fact, I believe that commitment to mutuality is what makes it possible for the oppressed and their "friends" to maintain the revolutionary momentum of the struggle for liberation. Commitment to mutuality means "willingness to do something for or about whatever it is we are committed to (at least to protect it or affirm it when it is threatened)."[31] This is possible only if there is a "sense of being bound to whoever or whatever is the object of [this] commitment."[32] Commitment gives other persons or a worthy cause claim over oneself, thus establishing or strengthening mutuality between the self and the other. Commitment to mutuality results in "a relation of binding and being-bound, giving and being-claimed."[33]

Mutuality that has as its goal embracing commonality of interests demands commitment to action. Without action mutuality becomes a "soft word," a passing whimsical reaction which is often privatized and removed from the public sphere, from the political reality of the struggle for liberation. It is precisely the actions resulting from true commitment that are the framework of mutuality; they are the signs and deeds of mutuality and the efforts that ensure the future of mutuality.[34] It is these actions which express and constitute mutuality and which, in a limited but real way, begin to make liberation present. Actions born out of commitment to mutuality are "eschatological glimpses" which clarify the vision of liberation that will become a reality in the kin-dom of God and which will make faithfulness to the vision possible. Liberation is not a condition that already exists, simply waiting for the oppressed to grasp it. Rather, liberation is a historical possibility that takes form and shape according to the actions of the oppressed and their "friends." Liberative actions born out of commitment to mutuality, therefore, are not only glimpses of the future but eschatological actions making parts of the future present now.

Commitment to mutuality is not a light or easy matter. It involves all aspects of one's life and demands a lifelong permanency. The way in which the commitment is lived out may change. From time to time one may be less passionate about carrying out the implications of mutuality, but somehow to go back and place oneself in a position of control and domination over others is to betray mutuality, to betray others and oneself. Such a betrayal, which most of the time occurs by failing to engage in liberative praxis rather than by formal denunciation, results in the "friends" becoming oppressors once again and in the oppressed losing their vision of liberation. Betrayal, then, effectively delays liberation and, therefore, at the very least makes more difficult the unfolding of the kin-dom of God.[35]

CONCLUSION

More than two-thirds of the people in the world live under terribly oppressive conditions. The way the gospel message to love our neighbor as we love ourselves has been interpreted up to now leads the believer to the practice of charity. But this interpretation does not help oppose oppression; it is not an effective means to bring about radical structural change in society. As we become aware of the alienation that oppression induces, we come to understand that love of neighbor is linked intrinsically and foremost to justice. In order for a person to become fully human, to overcome sin, to move from alienation to a love-relationship with God and with others, justice has to prevail. "As virtue, justice is a trait of character empowering and disposing an agent to act in ways constitutive of human flourishing."[36] This is why the unfolding of the kin-dom of God, which indeed promotes human fulfillment, is made possible only when just structures and situations exist. "This is the reason why the effort to build a just society is liberating."[37] This is why "action on behalf of justice and transformation of the world fully appear...as a constitutive element of the preaching of the Gospel."[38] And, finally, this is why Christianity can be reaffirmed as containing truth, "not because of its origins, but because it liberates people now from specific forms of oppression."[39]

Understanding the centrality of justice has led us to look at other ways of implementing the command to love our neighbors that do not stop with giving. We have come to appreciate the need for radical structural change and the fact that unless we recognize the interdependence of all persons, we face a very bleak future. But recognition of interdependence will not happen apart from a sense of commonality of interest, which in turn will lead us to dis-cover solidarity with the poor and the oppressed and with those committed to justice. Solidarity, then, is a virtue. It is an attitude and disposition that greatly influences how we act. As a virtue solidarity becomes a way of life. It becomes the new way of living out "the love your neighbor as yourself" that up to now has been interpreted as giving out of our largesse. Given the network of oppressive structures in our world today that so control and dominate the vast majority of human beings, the only way we can continue to claim the centrality of love of neighbor for Christians is to redefine what it means and what it demands of us. Solidarity, then, becomes the new way of understanding and living out this commandment of the gospel.

NOTES

1. Originally I dedicated this essay to Blanche Marie Moore, a sister in the Order of St. Ursula who died in the Bronx, New York, on December 10, 1987, as I was writing it. Today I rededicate it to her. Blanche Marie was my high school teacher in Cuba. A person of great strength of character, her dedication and strong will caught my imagination and strongly influenced me. I will always be most grateful to her for imbuing in me a love of reading and studying. *In paradisum perducant te angeli,* Blanche.

2. One year, as his birthday approached, Cáceres came to ask if he could connect an electric wire to our house. He strung it across the street and into his house, providing light so he could party all night long. Knowing we would not sleep at all that night, the eight women of our household settled to listen to the music Cáceres and his friends created, loud singing and banging on pots and pans well into the night. When I left Perú I gave Cáceres my bongos as a token of appreciation for all he had taught me.

3. Just in case we have forgotten, the Contras were an armed, illegal group, heavily supported by the USA, which fought to overturn the Sandinista government, a freely elected, legally constituted government.

4. My concern is similar to that of Paulo Freire many years ago about the use/misuse of the word "conscientization." He stopped using the word; I am choosing to work hard at returning its original meaning to "solidarity."

5. See Isabel Carter Heyward, *The Redemption of God* (Lanham, Md.: University Press of America, 1982), 1-18.

6. In this essay the terms "the poor" and "the oppressed" are at times used interchangeably and at times together. I would have preferred to use the term

"nonperson"—those human beings who are considered less than human by societies based on privileges arrogated by a minority (Gustavo Gutiérrez, *The Power of the Poor in History* [Maryknoll, N.Y.: Orbis Books, 1984], 92). But I am concerned that the ontological meaning of "nonentity" would be read into my use of "nonperson," regardless of the explanation provided. I thought of using only "the oppressed" but felt that "the oppressed" could be seen as a classification, an abstraction, instead of concrete persons.

I then needed to decide what term to add to "the oppressed." I thought of the term I use to identify my own oppression, "Hispanic women," but felt that it was too specific and that what I say here could be understood to apply only to us. I decided to use "the poor" because, though the restricted meaning of the term relates to those who are economically oppressed, it often goes beyond that meaning and closely parallels the meaning of the oppressed even in everyday language. In the Bible, at least in the book of Zephaniah 2:3, 3:12—13, "the poor" are identified with the *anawim*. The *anawim*, the poor, are "the portion of the community...upon which the possible future existence of the community depends (E. Jenni, "Remnant," *The interpreter's Dictionary of the Bible*, ed. George Arthur Buttrick [Nashville: Abingdon, 1965], 32-33). My usage of "the poor" in this chapter definitely includes this meaning.

7. *The Random House Dictionary of the English Language*, 2nd unabridged ed. (New York: Random House, 1987).

8. There are two reasons for not using the regular word employed by English Bibles "kingdom." First, it is obviously a sexist word that presumes that God is male. Second, the concept of kingdom in our world today is both hierarchical and elitist—as is the word "reign." The word "kin-dom" makes it clear that when the fullness of God becomes a day-to-day reality in the world at large, we will all be sisters and brothers—kin to each other; we will indeed be the family of God.

9. Gustavo Gutiérrez, *A Theology of Liberation* (Maryknoll, N.Y.: Orbis Books, 1973), 159.

10. Ibid., 177.

11. Rebecca S. Chopp, *Praxis of Suffering* (Maryknoll, N.Y.: Orbis Books, 1986), 25.

12. Gutiérrez, *A Theology of Liberation*, 175.

13. José Miguez Bonino, "Nueva tendencias en teología," *Pasos* no. 9 (1987): 22.

14. Gutiérrez, *The Power of the Poor in History*, 140.

15. Ibid.

16. Gutierrez, *A Theology of Liberation*, 289.

17. I use these three "isms" as inclusive categories and paradigms of oppression. Under sexism, for example, I include heterosexism. Under classism I include militarism, etc.

18. I use "strategy" instead of "practice" here because of my insistence on the intrinsic unity between reflection and practice. I also use strategy because it carries with it the implication of political effectiveness which is intrinsic to solidarity as a praxis of liberation.

19. Janice Raymond, *A Passion for Friends* (Boston: Beacon Press, 1986), 22.

20. Ibid., 214-15.

21. Gutiérrez, *A Theology of Liberation*, 92.

22. Paulo Freire, *Pedagogy of the Oppressed* (New York: Seabury Press, 1973), 3.

23. Gutiérrez, *A Theology of Liberation*, 92.

24. I have based this section about the relationship between the oppressor and the "friend" on Juan Carlos Scannone, *Teología de la liberatión y praxis popular* (Salamanca: Ediciones Sígueme, 1976), 133-86.

25. Scannone uses the word "brother." I have used "friend" in translating into English in order to avoid a sexist term.

26. Ibid.

27. Scannone, *Teología de la liberatión y praxis popular*, 164. In translating I have used inclusive language even though the original does not.

28. Karen Lebacqz, *Justice in an Unjust World* (Minneapolis: Fortress Press, 1987), 110-11.

29. bell hooks, *Feminist Theory: From Margin to Center* (Boston: South End Press, 1984), 159.

30. Ibid.

31. Margaret Farley, *Personal Commitments* (San Francisco: Harper & Row, 1986), 14.

32. Ibid., 15.

33. Ibid., 18-19.

34. See Farley, *Personal Commitments*, 36.

35. I find Gutiérrez wavering when he comes to this issue of the relationship between liberation and the kin-dom of God. In *A Theology of Liberation* he says, "it is only in the temporal, earthly, historical event that we can open

up to the future complete fulfillment" (167). But Gutiérrez later insists on a different understanding: "nor does it mean that this just society constitutes a 'necessary condition' for the arrival of the Kingdom, nor that they are closely linked, nor that they converge" (231). I too waver on this issue. Does betrayal of mutuality, because it delays liberation, impede or merely make it more difficult for the kin-dom of God to unfold?

36. William Werpehowski, "Justice," in James F. Childress and John Macquarrie, eds., *The Westminster Dictionary of Christian Ethics* (Philadelphia: Westminster Press, 1986), 338.

37. Gutiérrez, *A Theology of Liberation*, 177.

38. Synod of Bishops Second General Assembly, November 30, 1971, "Justice in the World," in Joseph Gremillion, ed. *The Gospel of Peace and Justice* (Maryknoll, N.Y.: Orbis Books, 1976), 514.

39. Sharon D. Welch, *Communities of Resistance and Solidarity* (Maryknoll, N.Y.: Orbit Books, 1985), 53.

Bloody Footprints

Reflections on Growing up Poor White

Roxanne A. Dunbar

I have forsaken mine house, I have left mine heritage....Mine heritage is unto me as a lion in the forest; it crieth out against me: therefore have I hated it. Mine heritage is unto me as a speckled bird, the birds round about are against her.

—Jeremiah 12: 7-9

I wish someone would look up the names on the roster of Washington's army at Valley Forge and trace the bloody footprints of their descendants across the North American continent until they were washed up and washed out on the shore of the Pacific. What an all-American Odyssey it would make! What a great history of the Rise and Fall of American Civilization.

—Oscar Ameringer, Socialist organizer, pre-World War 1, Oklahoma

Labor cannot emancipate itself in the white skin where in the black it is branded.

—Karl Marx, *Capital*

WHITE TRASH. I believe the first time I heard that term was when I saw *Gone With the Wind*, referring to some pretty creepy people, dirt poor, sneaking, conniving, violent tenant farmers, or migrant cotton pickers maybe. At the time I saw that blockbuster picture show my father was alternately a tenant farmer, migrant cotton picker, and ranch hand, but I did not for one minute identify with those whom the planters and the enslaved Africans termed white trash in that movie.

Oh no, I identified with Scarlett, with the O'Hara family, the original Scots Irish settlers, agrarian masters of the savage indigenous Irish who brought their skills of civilization (read colonization) to America to take the land from the savage indigenous Indians. The fact that my father's ancestors were original Scots Irish old settlers was what made me feel superior, even though my family surely could have fit the moniker, white trash. And those characterized as white trash in *Gone With the Wind* were surely also mostly descendants of Scots Irish old settlers. Their sons would die fighting to defend the very institution, slavery, which kept them poor. Their/our greatest heroes—Jesse James, the Younger and the Dalton brothers, Belle Starr—had been Confederate irregulars during the war and mythologized outlaws afterwards.

Once I asked my part Irish—part Native American mother, who had grown up orphaned and homeless in foster homes as a servant and in a reformatory, why my father's family name, Dunbar, was shared by a black person. In my high school English class we had just read some poems by the African American poet Paul Laurence Dunbar. I hoped my mother would say he was a relative of ours. But she said that my Dunbar ancestors were "Scotch Irish" and had once owned huge plantations and many slaves and that slaves took the names of the masters.

"How do we know we're related to the masters and not the slaves?" I asked.

"Because you are white," she answered, closing the discussion forever. Because I was white I was a descendant of the masters, whatever my economic or social situation, and it did not matter that my mother was a "half-breed."

My mother had married up, snagging a descendant of the old settler class. Never mind that he was a migrant cow puncher, then sharecropper. Upon marriage to him my mother became white, or at least her children would.

～

False consciousness. I learned this term much later, when a college Marxist friend, herself a child of blue-collar Greek immigrants, accused me of being a "class traitor," then apologized, amending her analysis to my having "false consciousness." I can't recall what the dispute was about but am certain she was right. At the time I thought she was a fanatic.

～

Poor, rural whites (the original white trash) have lived by dreams, at least the ones I come from did and, in a perverse way, still do, albeit reacting to "broken dreams." (Someone or some force has hijacked their country and now controls the government—Jews through the supposed "Zionist Occupation Government," the Federal Reserve, Communists, Liberals, the United Nations, Gays and Feminists, Satan, etc.). Certainly it can be argued that all the immigrants from all over the world who have been drawn by the "American dream" from then to now believed and continue to believe in "it"—the American dream. But there is a distinct difference between the post industrial revolution, mostly urban immigrants who created the concept of "a nation of immigrants," and the original rural frontier settlers. The latter were landless or land-poor peasants given "free" (stolen) land on the edge of the colonies (later the states of the U.S. Republic). The price they had to pay for land and potential wealth was blood—to drive out the indigenous farmers, the Indians. They lived in terror, isolated, surrounded.

Of course, some made it and some didn't. Those who made it, like Andrew Jackson, were able to purchase, or sire, African slaves and become a wealthy planter and even a general and the president of the United States. Those who didn't make it, and even some of those who did, moved on, shed blood opening new lands, usually lost again, and moved on again. Foot soldiers of empire I call them/us. They unleashed rivers of blood, torrents of blood, unimaginable violence, murder, slaughter, which we refuse to acknowledge and confront but which cannot be dislodged from our collective memory. In the process of that struggle the trekker, the frontier settler, imagined himself and his progeny transformed into the native Americans, the true Americans. *Blood-right*, it could be called.

I come from a segment of white trash called "Okies."[1] They were the white, rural Oklahomans (and other southWesterners) who migrated to find work (and the American dream) in California during the Dust Bowl and Depression in the thirties and during World War II to work in defense plants. Before, during, and after that dramatic exodus, the people who came to be known as Okies formed a social construct and cultural identity which obliterated class and class consciousness. They were the end-of-the-line colonial trekkers—the majority of them also poor white—like the Boers of South Africa, many of the French "Pied Noir" of Algeria, failed British farmers in Kenya, Rhodesia, and for that matter the Hispanic poor of northern New Mexico and more recent trekkers to the rain forests of Central America and Brazil—marginal people, border people, people on the edges of empire who can topple off with the slightest gust from transnational capital.

The Okies are those tough, land-poor losers whose last great hope in the American dream was born and died with the "opening" (theft from the Indians) of Oklahoma and Indian territories to white settlement at the end of the nineteenth century. Their great shame, like all white trash and colonial dregs, is poverty; that is, "failure" within a system which purports to favor them. As with the toss of the dice or spread of the cards, some win and some lose; the majority lose, and they are "white trash," colonialism's riffraff. So they are to blame for their failure, if not then who or what is? The system, of course. And that cannot be; even those losers themselves find blaming the system unacceptable, if not blasphemous.[2]

Unfortunately, and significantly, the story of those frontier settlers (Daniel Boone, et. al.) is ordinarily rationalized or romanticized by historians and popular culture, even by Marxists.[3] In looking at other cultures of colonialism, U.S. patriots—left and right—have little problem in acknowledging that in other locales colonialism/capitalism chews up and spits out its own settler/cannon fodder, and these become despicable pariahs. The difference with the United States is, first, we refuse or are reluctant to treat our history as a process of colonialism, although leftists acknowledge U.S. imperialism (post 1898). Since we are indoctrinated from birth in the ideology of "manifest destiny," we find it nearly impossible to truly distance ourselves from that false ideology. Instead, both right and left, whether the right-wing militias or Jesse Jackson, and mainstream politicians, too, mouth the same platitudes, repeating the origin myth, all claiming to try to recapture the "original" motivations of the "founding fathers," the "true" meaning of the Text, that is, the Constitution, each claiming to be the "true patriot" while the other is the "traitor" to the "origin" of our blessed, surely near-perfect Republic. And the "pioneer"[4] (colonial settler actually) is a sacred symbol of Jeffersonian and Jacksonian democracy, an "empire for democracy," as Jefferson put it. Imprinted in our minds is the covered wagon as the expression of the courage and willfulness of the "pioneer." Even those who condemn and name the genocide against the Native Nations and Africans forced into bondage hang on to the origin myth and particularly the figure of the frontier settler.

We dregs of colonialism, those who did not and do not "make it," being the majority in some places (like most of the United States) are potentially dangerous to the ruling class: WE ARE THE PROOF OF THE LIE OF THE AMERICAN DREAM. However, self-blame, a sprinkling of white-skin privilege with license to violence against minorities, scapegoating, and serving as cops and in the military (give them a gun and point to the enemy) conspire to neutralize or redirect our anger. But above all it's that dream and the ideology, the "sacred" origin myth—the religion of "Americanism"—which keeps us doped and harmless, that and alcohol and drugs and cheap consumer items, especially sex and violence. But without the dream/ideology none of the other tricks would work.

~

For most of my adult life I have devoted myself to social justice movements, identifying more as a child of the sixties than a child of my family. Yet during all that time I have tried to figure out the role we (white trash, poor whites, Okies) play.

The first thing I did when I made the decision to commit my life to political radicalism was to sit down for two months, twelve to fifteen hours each day, seven days a week (I was living on a student loan supposedly writing my history doctoral dissertation, which I did eventually) to write what I called my "life history." Trained as a historian I applied those research skills and knowledge to myself and my family as a case study. At the time I was influenced by psychoanalytical theory and practices, particularly Jacques Lacan and R.D. Laing. I believed that as a historian I had to do the same kind of historical self-analysis that a psychoanalyst does in personal analysis. That is, I had to master my own life history and reveal who I was in writing any other history.

I was, after all, a child of the times—"the personal is political"—so my methodology turned out to be widespread among the social rebels who were a formidable force at that time; surely that methodology is one of the most important and lasting contributions to come out of those turbulent years. But I rarely met anyone from my own background. All I could figure out to do was reject and condemn my people, my history, as middle class white radicals were doing.

On the night of the assassination of Martin Luther King, alienation from my own past and from everything about the United States and its history ravaged my mind. I wrote what I called "Dirge for White America My Home," filled with hatred:

I can only wish to see your surly redneck contemptible Smile
Turn to terror when you find yourself surrounded by Panthers
Or shot down by a woman too good to even spit on you after
You kick a Black kid or attack or hiss at a woman alone.

Maybe in that one minute you will regain your Humanity
And beg to die in your self-revealed Maddening horror.
I depart the dead body of my people and lead a Revolution
Against you. SLAVERY WILL BE NO MORE.
3 April 1968 Berkeley.[5]

Of course this vitriolic negation of my people was also a negation of myself and was by no means the final word. My ambivalence to my heritage remains alive and well—maddening as ever—today in my middle age.

The poor whites (white trash) I come from, Okies and their descendants, were those who formed the popular base for the post-World War II rise of the hard right in Orange County, California, Richard Nixon the anti-Communist was their man. They were the "little people" and "silent majority" addressed by Richard Nixon as President, then by Ronald Reagan. They were among the bigots, including my father, who supported George Wallace. During the 1980s, they helped swell the ranks of the Christian Coalition, promoting antiabortion and anti-gay initiatives. They fall in and out of the owning and working class, unreliable in union struggles. Depending on economic times they may be self-employed or reluctantly working for a boss, but their dream is always to acquire land. We are descendants of peasants and cling to that world view mixed with a common history of struggle to acquire land, blood for land, to seize the promised land, implement the Covenant. We are the true Chosen People.[6]

A populist tradition is associated with poor whites,[7] yet often my people hate the rich only out of envy. Hostile to "big government," they are in the vanguard of defending their country claiming to want to "save" it. As Okie country artist, Merle Haggard, sings: "When you're runnin' down my country, hoss, you're walkin' on the fightin' side of me." Many have been eager cannon fodder as well as officers in America's foreign wars. They believe they are the designated beneficiaries of the theft of land from Indians and to the booty of empire and the whole world is a stage.

In the end the only advantage for most has been the color of their skin and the white supremacy, particularly toward African Americans, that pervades the culture; what they are *not*—black, Asian, foreign born—is as important as what they are—white, "true" Americans—in their sense of propriety and self-esteem.

When Richard Nixon died in the spring of 1994, television cameras focused on his Orange County home. Clusters of simple white people gathered silently, placing flowers, lingering. Soon thousands had gathered, Nixon's "silent majority," trekkers and their descendants paying tribute to their favorite son, his political base for forty-five years. He had won his first political race for Helen Gahagan Douglas's seat in Congress by red-baiting her. A former actress, Helen Gahagan Douglas had been in the forefront of publicizing the plight of the Dust Bowl Okies and was their champion in Congress. All that might appear harmless enough, reflecting the last gasps of a dinosaur. But why did President Clinton order flags at half staff and attend the funeral along with every other notable? The polls took note of those milling white mourners.

The most painful part of my quest for identity has been the juggling of my poor white experience and my knowledge of the power of white privilege in this society. Becoming an internationally oriented social activist, a scholar and a writer, I largely evaded coming to terms with "white trash," which is fundamentally a class question. Although my means of escape is not typical of people from my kind of background, it comes down to the same resolution—escape poverty, leave that life behind. Novelist Ken Kesey puts the dilemma succinctly:

> Let me tell you what being an Okie means: Being an Okie means being the first of your whole family to finish high school let alone go on to college…Being an Okie means getting rooted out of an area and having to hustle for a toehold in some new area…Being an Okie means running the risk of striving out from under a layer of heartless sonsabitches only to discover you have become a redneck of bitterness worse than those you strove against.

Survival dynamics are acknowledged and well-known about African Americans, Latinos, Native Americans, and ethnic communities in the United States, but are hardly known to exist with poor whites. That hasn't always been so; during the three periods of leftist surges this century (the nineteen-teens, the thirties and the sixties), great attention and tribute were paid to the internal dynamics of poor white families and communities to the point of romanticization. Because social and economic status are so shaky for poor whites and self-blame or scapegoating so prevalent, class consciousness is damaged. The false consciousness of poor whites in the U.S. is an example, in Marxian terms, of "superstructure" (ideology) overriding "economic base," or economic self-interest.

Despite fantasies of becoming a movie or sports star and get rich fast schemes, the two most successful means of class-climbing among poor whites, like other poor groups, is marrying up and/or education. Marrying out and up is probably more possible for women than men and is certainly something my mother preached to my sister and me. Indeed marriage was my way out of my class and into the middle class. It was during those six years of marriage and that transformation that I slowly comprehended the class question.

I was eighteen and he was nineteen when we married. Jimmy had grown up on the family estate outside Oklahoma City. The house, which his father had built himself, was out of an English novel—a rambling five-bedroom, two-bath, native-stone mansion with a stone, wood-burning fireplace, thick carpets, fine antiques, chandeliers, and cut-glass crystal and bone china displayed in mahogany "breakfronts," as they called the glass-front display cabinets. The place was surrounded by a stream and woods and gardens. At the end of a long stone path was a huge stone patio and barbecue pit. There were even two oil wells.

As Jimmy showed me around the first time he took me to meet his family, I kept saying to myself: "This is where Jimmy grew up," followed by "Why does he love me?" I couldn't even comprehend such a life. The land had been homesteaded by his mother's Scots Irish family who farmed it. When his mother married his carpenter father, who was descended from Dutch Protestants, they lived there, then inherited the land. They were simple farming people, potentially poor whites, but during the Depression and World War II the construction company Jimmy's father worked for grew huge and rich off government contracts, and he climbed from journeyman carpenter to chief superintendent. After the war he sold some of the land to the state to build the Tulsa Turnpike, invested in real estate (slumlord), then built the new house before Jimmy was born. Jimmy grew up rich. The only blight on his and the family's life was that his mother—he called her "an angel"—had died just before I met him.

Jimmy's father fit my image of a patriarch or an English country gentleman out of one of my favorite novels at the time, *The Forsythe Saga*, a man of property. He wore a fine cashmere overcoat and a fur cap. I had never seen anyone with a fur cap. He greeted me by shaking my hand. He was different from any man I'd ever met. A strange thought passed through my mind as I walked down the aisle holding my father's arm. Initially

Jimmy's father's construction company grew rich off New Deal WPA construction contracts during the Depression. It occurred to me that my father when he worked for the WPA may have had my new father-in-law for a boss. The thought made me feel like a traitor and haunted me during the marriage.

If my father had asked me, "Do you really want to go through with this?" I would have said, "No Daddy oh no, please take me away." But he did not ask and instead of taking me away he gave me away.

One reason for marrying Jimmy was so I could go to college, or that was his argument in persuading me to marry him right away. His father offered to pay both our college expenses and provide a free place for us to live. Yet within a week after the wedding Jimmy announced that he wanted us to be self-supporting and persuaded me to work and wait to go to college.

"You support me until I graduate then I'll support you to go back to school, it's only three years," he'd argued, adding the clincher: "My sisters think you might be a gold digger just looking for a free ride off the family but if you work they would know that's not true." What Jimmy's older sisters thought of me mattered a great deal, to him and to me. I agreed to work.

Jimmy and I lived in the three-room garage apartment near the "big house." I idolized Jimmy's family and adopted them as my own, especially his sister Helen who lived with her husband in a cottage they built nearby. She called me "a diamond in the rough." I accepted the role and submitted to being polished. Helen said I was from good peasant stock like Tolstoy's characters and embodied the nobility of the peasantry enriched by being part Indian. I shivered with pleasure when she told me those things.

The whole family opposed racism and segregation. Despite his wealth and being a boss Jimmy's father was pro-union and thought racism resulted from the ignorance of poor white people. Even before the Supreme Court decision on school segregation he'd fought for integration, not very successfully, in the Carpenters Union and as a superintendent on jobs had hired black laborers and hod-carriers. He invited his construction workers and their families including the Blacks to his famous barbecues. I imagined that he was like my Wobbly grandfather, although when I asked him once what he thought of the Wobblies he said they had been anarchists and crazy and un-American.

Everyone in the family read *Time* and *The New Republic* and knew all about what was happening in the world. I soaked up everything they said and I read and read.

I began to wonder about the price I had to pay for my new class status when one summer Saturday afternoon Jimmy and I went to drink beer with his sister and her husband in a tavern we hadn't been to before. The barmaid turned out to be a woman I knew growing up, from a very poor white family.

"Darla, what are you doing here, how is your family?" I said. I was so happy to see her.

Darla wore a tight-fitting red sun dress. Her bosom protruded seductively. She looked different, not so much older but somehow hard, her skin rough. Yet she remained strikingly beautiful with her mane of thick black hair, her smoky skin. Darla hesitated and I thought she didn't remember me. I followed her eyes—she was studying my companions.

"Fancy seeing you here, how are you stranger?" she said, a teasing tone in her voice. Then I realized she was shocked because she had known me as a devout teetotaling Baptist. She looked amused and approving.

"I got married, Darla, this is Jimmy, and his sister and brother-in-law," I said.

Jimmy looked up at her sideways and said, "Howdy do," Suddenly I was aware that Jimmy did not approve of Darla. He glared at me as if I were a stranger, or a traitor.

When Darla returned to serve us she handed me a slip of paper with her phone number on it. "Give me a call, I'm off now." She left with a man who had been sitting at the bar.

"You got some outstanding old friends, Roxie," Jimmy said, not with a smile.

"She's from my hometown. I used to baby-sit for her, you remember me telling you about her." I heard apology in my voice, and shame.

Later when we were alone Jimmy said, "You're not going to call that woman, are you?"

"I thought I might, why not?" I said.

"She's a prostitute," he said.

"She's my friend," I said.

"Not any more. You associate with low-life like that and you will become like them," he said.

I said nothing and never called Darla and never saw her again.

Other contradictions arose which disturbed me—for instance, when Jimmy and I drove to Colorado to see the scenery, my first trip outside Oklahoma. All along the highways were broken-down cars and pickups with women and children and old people sitting in the shade while a man worked under the hood. They beckoned for us to stop and help. Jimmy passed them by.

"Why, don't we stop?" I asked. No one in my family would ever have passed up a stranded motorist, but then we never strayed far from home.

"They're hustlers, rob you blind, highway bandits," Jimmy said.

"How do you know?"

"I just know, they use the kids and old people for bait to get you to stop, then rob you, they're transients, fruit pickers, white trash."

I stared at the sad faces as we passed by and tried to see the con artists and criminals behind the masks. But they merely looked familiar, like my own relatives.

Yet we got plenty of help on the highway. Practically everything that could go wrong with a car plagued ours—the radiator burst, the regulator busted, the carburetor spewed gas, even the ignition wire broke, flat tires on several occasions. Each time we broke down, always in the middle of nowhere, someone stopped to help us or gave Jimmy a ride to the next station.

"How come they don't think we're highway robbers?" I asked. The people who stopped to help us were invariably driving old cars or pickups and looked a lot like the people who tried to get us to stop. New cars whizzed on by.

"They can tell," Jimmy said.

I began to suffer frightening symptoms. For no apparent reason I would be overcome with a blinding white rage. I could see and hear and control my movements, and it seemed to me that I chose to scream or to run and hide or to kick a chair or slam a door. Yet I couldn't prevent or stop it. The fits would last from a few minutes to hours. Inside the fit I felt terror and sometimes a strange euphoria, a feeling of safety. The first time it happened I thought Jimmy would leave me but he wrote me a page-long note saying I was too good for the evil world around me, that I had a pure mind and soul, that I was perfect except for that tiny flaw in my personality which came from my inferior background, and that it was his destiny and mission in life to protect and care for me.

On other occasions Jimmy would shake me awake, saying I was grinding my teeth. Once he recorded it for me to hear. The sound was loud and eerie. Insomnia plagued me. I was afraid to go to sleep not knowing what I would do. Control became the center of my life and I would go long periods without fits or nocturnal sounds. During those times I had blinding, disabling migraine headaches and nausea.

Jimmy and his family believed in inherited traits, either through genes or socialization. They never let me forget, by so carefully helping me, how much I had to overcome with my poor upbringing, the possibility that I was a "bad seed."

One autumn day in my third year of marriage I was home sick with the flu and found myself the only person on the grounds. I had never been alone there before. The place was so serene and lovely, the oak leaves bright yellow, a maple tree flaming red, the blackjacks burnished copper. The huge lawn that sloped down to the creek was still a carpet of green thanks to the sprinkler system.

I sat down on the stone bench in the patio that was halfway between the creek and the big house. Even though I was only thirty-five miles from where I grew up it was so different, rolling hills with trees rather than flat and barren, no cannibalized old cars and junk around.

"How lucky I am," I said aloud and felt like yelling it since no one would hear. I could never have dreamed of being a part of that kind of life three years before. Jimmy's family had taken me in as one of their own. Forever and ever I would be safe and secure and loved. I loved my sisters-in-law and father-in-law as if they were my own flesh. I would never be poor or want for anything again. I tingled with happiness, tears of joy streaming down my face.

The sound of a car startled me out of my reverie. The mail carrier. He always brought everyone's mail to the big house and put it on the back porch where we could each fish out our own. I strolled up the hill to check. Rifling through the pile I saw a letter to Helen from the sister who had moved to California. The letter was barely sealed, just at the tip. I stuck my little finger under the flap and it popped open. I slipped the letter out of the envelope and unfolded the two pages.

My eyes fell on the middle of the first page and the words hit me like a blast of icy wind: *I think you are right that it remains to be seen if Roxie will drag Jimmy down to her level or if he can pull her up to his. Coming from her background she may be beyond rescue. I wish Jimmy would leave her.*

I had to sit down to keep from falling from dizziness. I could not believe what I was reading, and that there had been other letters and conversations, letters about me ruining Jimmy.

The letter was almost entirely about me, mostly a discussion of the condition of "white trash," whether it was genetic or social, and the "complication" that I was part Indian. I read the letter a second time telling myself they were concerned about me because they loved me and wanted to help me. But it wasn't there, only concern for Jimmy and the wish that I would disappear or had never appeared. The letter ended by saying that Jimmy had met me at a vulnerable time in his life just after their mother's death, and I being a gold-digger and devious had entrapped him and pressured for a quick marriage.

I felt like running, packing a suitcase and leaving without a word. I would not be able to tell Jimmy, because he would know I'd opened the letter. I vowed to remain quiet, to finish what I'd started, sending Jimmy to school. He would graduate in three months, then I would insist that we leave. I would carry out my part of the bargain and I would not lose Jimmy. And so we did move to San Francisco; my husband sent me through college, where I learned, among other things, about being a class traitor. I went my own way, away from him, and threw myself into the struggles of my generation, determined never to forsake my class again.

NOTES

1. See my research essay, "One or Two Things I Know about Us: Cues in American Culture," in *Radical History Review* 59:4-34 (1994). My immediate family did not join the exodus—my father says we were too poor to make the trip—to California; although many from my extended family did, and eventually three of the four of us children moved to California. California was definitely "the promised land" of my childhood.

2. The militia movement and other right-wing populist groups are using the term "the system" to identify their enemy—international capital, politics and military, the IRS, FBI, SATF, etc. See the "bible" of this anti-government network: Andrew Macdonald (William L. Pierce), *The Turner Diaries* (Hillsboro, WV: National Vanguard Books, 1978).

3. There are signs of change in mainstream culture. In 1993, the Pulitzer Prize for drama was awarded to the eight-hour play *The Kentucky Cycle*, which is significant because it is the true history of the fate of the frontier settlers, and because it won the prestigious award. Kevin Costner, himself a son of poor white Okie migrants, bought the film rights and is producing it for HBO.

4. "Even in those early years of settlership, however, forces were at work which helped to produce in the collective consciousness of the invaders a strange new self-image. In the first place, their land seizures were fiercely resisted by the peoples whom they first encountered....Thus began a tribal resistance to colonization...in the course of which [the settlers] even when victorious, came to regard themselves as physically and culturally isolated and hemmed in. Their symbol for this sense of isolation became...a defensive circle of covered wagons."

The above is from a study of Boer nationalism in South Africa (Anthony Holiday, "White Nationalism in South Africa as Movement and System," in Maria van Diepen, ed., *The National Question in South Africa* (London: Zed Press, 1988: 79). Certainly we have more in common with the Boers than the Bolivars.

5. Published in *No More Fun and Games: A Journal of Female Liberation* 1:1 (August 1968).

6. "Three ideas seem closely linked to the idea of a 'chosen people.' The first is that this chosen people is endowed with the 'divine mission' of guiding and civilizing...The second is that this 'chosen people' cannot and must not interbreed with other peoples...The third is that the 'chosen people's' right of ownership over the land is inalienable, because it is the 'promised' land given by God." (Marianne Cornevin, *Apartheid: Power and Historical Falsification*, Paris: UNESCO, 1980: 33).

7. My grandfather Dunbar was a Wobbly (Industrial Workers of the World—IWW) in Western Oklahoma and a life-long socialist, as were a large number of trekker descendants who ended up losers on the last frontier. My father is named after the founders of the IWW—Moyer Haywood Pettibone Dunbar. See my research essay, "One or Two Things I Know About Us," cited above. For the most comprehensive study of agrarian socialism in Oklahoma, see James Green, *Grass-Roots Socialism: Radical Movements in the Southwest 1895-1943* (Baton Rouge: Louisiana State University Press, 1978).

Our Sister,
the Woman Caught in Adultery...

Our Brothers, the Pharisees Caught by Jesus

John 8:1-11

Nancy Linton

RECONCILIATION IS HARD and justice is messy. But here's a text where justice happens, and reconciliation, though not complete, begins. Often called, "The woman taken in adultery," I think a better way to name it would be: "Our Sister, the Woman Caught in Adultery, and Our Brothers, the Pharisees, Caught by Jesus." Then we might be able to put ourselves into this text—to see ourselves in both the woman and the Pharisees.

Let's start with the Pharisees and scribes who confidently barge into the temple—right into the middle of a circle of people where Jesus sits teaching. Why? The text says they are "leading" (I suspect a euphemism for "dragging") a woman they caught in the act of adultery. They push her into the circle, making her "stand" in front of Jesus, exposed to everyone's glaring stares. Then, as one religious authority to another, they ask Jesus a question which sounds terribly like a pronouncement: "Teacher, *this woman* has been caught in the act of adultery. Now in the law Moses commanded us to stone *such*. What do you say about *her*?"

To them, privileged by gender and their religious class, she is a "such," one of those "kind" of women; so they do not bother to say her name (in

215

all likelihood they do not know it). Today we call this "Othering," masking over someone's face, by racism, or classism, or sexism, masking over the face of someone radically different from us but also radically like us. Then, for example, I, as a white middle-class woman can stereotype or objectify that person, and not have to own my privilege, or look into his or her eyes to discover our shared and embodied experience of suffering, mystery, joy, and vulnerability.

She is nameless, but the Pharisees do drop the name of Moses. Evoking his name they believe lends authority to their position and proves their right to act as experts on the law. In reality, they intend to trap Jesus, and this woman serves both object and means by which they can pull it off. Considering her inferior, they feel no need to address or attend to her.

Obviously, the entire scene describes a set-up. If she was caught in the act of adultery, there must have been a man caught with her too—so where is he? Not here...hmmm...he must have been in on the scheme too. And if not in on the set-up, he must have either paid them off, or pleaded his loss of honor, his reputation as a married man. So they excused him and dragged her in.

And what about this law of Moses quoted? It's found in Deut. 22:22 and it "commands" that in this situation, both man and woman be stoned. Terribly harsh, it wasn't followed in Jesus' day, or probably even in Old Testament days. Still, the twisting of it is obvious—pretending this woman committed adultery all by herself. Why doesn't Jesus call them on their hypocrisy about the law? Why doesn't Jesus attack these patriarchs and demand justice on the spot? I would have! I would have yelled, "Where is the guy, you jerks?" I would have shouted for fairness—Come on, if you're going to play this game, stick by the law!

Jesus seems to ignore the issue. Where is his sense of justice? In other biblical texts Jesus directly confronts the system. Remember the day he drove the moneychangers out of the temple—whip in hand, pushing over their tables, and protesting angrily their making God's house a capitalist venture? But I wonder what would have happened if Jesus had immediately called their bluff? Would the Pharisees have admitted they didn't really intend stoning her after all and leave with their sense of superiority only slightly tarnished? Perhaps Jesus does justice in such a unique way that it cannot be predicted from one context to another.

The difference here, I think, is the woman standing in front of him, eyes downcast, exposed to her superiors and this crowd. Reconciliation will be complicated. The Pharisees will have to come to the point where they cannot "Other" the woman. That means they will have to face themselves in their privilege and hypocrisy. But our sister, the woman, also needs reconciliation—in her own alienating sexuality, and in her marginalization. I'm beginning to think that the really radical one is Jesus. He will manage to topple the hierarchy, bringing the Pharisees to the same level, eye-to-eye with the woman—while addressing each of them as persons. Look how he does it...

In no hurry, Jesus stoops down and begins to write. We will never know what he was writing—there has been so much speculation...but we do know that once before God wrote with a finger...God wrote the commandments. Actually, God never wished to write them down. God intended to talk with the children of Israel; but God's voice, they wailed, hurt their ears. So they sent Moses trekking up the mountain to bring the law down. Humans seem to opt against relationship; instead they want rules and programs for their lives.

Still seeking relationship and not rules, the giver of the law once again writes with a finger—*ignoring* the law misused by our law experts. Writing, not up on a smoke-filled mountain, but bent down in the dirt. Not above us, but right down here in relationship with us. Emmanuel—God with us. And very soon, this writer of the law will die, fulfilling the law in love—taking it, in short, much more seriously and humanly, then our brothers, the Pharisees, do.

They are bugged at his writing. This is taking too long! They persist, questioning, "Moses commanded us to stone such. So how do you see it?" To them it's a mind-game by which they can catch Jesus either way. If he agrees to the stoning, he will be in trouble with the Romans who alone have power to condemn a person to death. If he disagrees, they can say he is a liberal, too easy on the law. In my anger, I would have tried to play the law game back on them—forcing them to bring the man, or admit it was a test, or perhaps throwing stones at them! My guess is that Jesus is angry too. The Greek indicates that he writes "with great intensity." But Jesus can love in his anger. And his love is more radical and healing than my anger alone could ever be.

The Pharisees and scribes had no clue that meeting God would entail meeting themselves in a way they never imagined. Jesus stands slowly, looking directly into their faces. "Let him who is without sin among you be the first to throw a stone at her." With this simple line, Jesus makes them be persons. He takes away their abstract law where persons are objects and rules are principles to be followed. Our brothers, the Pharisees, must see themselves truly, and in turn, discover the woman as a person, one who cannot be dismissed or demeaned. What goes through their minds, their beings, as their once cock-sure eyes turn inward?

Jesus bends down again to write—no more spoken words. The text says, "When they heard it, they went away, one by one, beginning with the oldest"—quietly, I imagine.

Do they leave different persons? I think so. Are they closer to the kingdom of God—oh yes, before they thought they owned it. They march in perfectly comfortable, playing the role of judge; they slip out quietly, understanding only God can stand in that place. Experiencing dis-ease, perhaps for the first time in their lives, they are closer to reconciliation with God, themselves and the woman whom they dragged in.

Do they see our woman as a person and not just one of the "such as these?" Well, no one throws a stone at her. But reconciliation is just beginning, because no one, from the youngest to the oldest, is able to step into the circle, take our sister's hand, and stand in solidarity with her. That's sad, because they miss the real healing. They don't get to hear Jesus say, "Neither do I condemn you..." They miss not only witnessing forgiveness, they miss receiving it.

And how about our sister, taken in adultery? We don't know her name, but Jesus attends carefully to her. We know because the text makes a point of telling us his body language. While he stands up to confront the Pharisees eye to eye, he stays squatting as he speaks to her, looking up into her face. Not wanting to marginalize or shame her more, he stays down, looking up at the person who has been dragged in and looked down upon. When I first read this text, I wondered why she didn't slip away when the Pharisees and scribes quietly left. I thought perhaps she was bewildered. Or that shame paralyzed her so she could not move. Or perhaps, she felt she could not leave before being dismissed. But now, I think she knew instinctively that she was safer here with this man, who attended to her person.

So she stays. Jesus is left alone with the woman (literally: "alone in the middle"). Rightly so, since he is the only one without sin—the only one who could stay and cast the first stone. But how strange is this law-writer, this God who once wrote with a finger on a mountain, and now writes here in the dirt, this one who could throw the stone. This God would rather die than do so; and indeed will...for her...and very soon.

"Woman" (ah—Jesus addresses her directly, and as a person) "Woman, where are they? Has no one condemned you?"

"No one, Lord."

It's important that our sister speak these words herself and out loud. So many voices, including, most likely, her own, have condemned her. Now she says: "No one condemns me."

Is reconciliation dawning for her?

She waits...

"Neither do I condemn you...go, and (literally) *from this now,* no longer sin."

The order of Jesus' words to her is crucial. First, comes "Neither do I condemn you," then the second part, "Go, and from this now, no longer sin."

How different from the way I grew up. I was *taught* that God freely forgave me, and in my head I believed it. But in my guts, I knew forgiveness was conditional. It depended first on how sincerely I repented. That included intending never to do it again—I felt I had to promise God that I wouldn't. If I did the behavior again, it meant that I had not really been sorry for my sin in the first place, I had treated it lightly; and so, God didn't really forgive me at all. The forgiveness I was asking for always hung on whether or not I would repeat the sin in the future. Psychologically this felt terrible...like I had to earn forgiveness by penance or good behavior. Taken to its ultimate extreme, it sounds absurd: the only way to truly deserve being forgiven is to never sin again—in which case you don't need to be forgiven.

This way of thinking also implies a steady progression upwards, where behavior becomes more and more perfect—like climbing a set of stairs. But in reality, the pressure to appear more and more together means that we are not free to say our real alienation. We develop finely-tuned false selves to hide the core of shame we experience in our real self.

This is tragic. It's tragic because if something remains so shameful we cannot talk about it, we cannot work through it and experience healing. And it's tragic because it results in self-alienation, alienation from others, and certainly alienation from God. This is the real definition of sin—alienation— not the behaviors which we try so valiantly to exorcise.

If Jesus had been operating in the behavior-forgiveness mode of my childhood, I believe he would have first asked the woman if she was truly sorry about her sexual behavior. Next, he would have asked her if she intended to stay out of adulterous relationships. Only if she answered "Yes" in both cases, would he have pronounced her forgiven.

Instead, Jesus does the opposite. He first pronounces her forgiven, without any conditions being required or met on her part. By doing so, Jesus addresses the real issue of alienation which lies beneath her behavior.

Alienation? Yes, our woman taken in adultery obviously relates sexually in an alienated way. She has promiscuous relationships, predictable enough to allow her to be caught. Catching someone in the middle of intercourse would otherwise be rather complicated, even impossible. She did not know well the man with whom she was having sex, and she certainly wasn't in a committed love relationship, or he would have been with her in crisis. My guess is that this woman experienced not only alienation, but also a great deal of shame in her life.

Jesus knew her, and he knew that freeing her from her accusers was not all that was required. Oh, it was a needed first step because it moved her accusers to her level—they were no longer judging superiors—and I bet she had had a lot of judging superiors. But, in reality, it only temporarily relieved the pressure.

For real healing to occur, shame must be openly approached, validated— and the person who is ashamed needs to hear the other say, "Yes, I see you, and I see that you are ashamed, and I am not ashamed of you." That is precisely what Jesus does. He addresses her real self: "Neither do I condemn you."

What difference in our lives would it make if we heard God's forgiveness pronounced to us *first*, always preceding our behavior? Then how would we hear the second part of Jesus' statement to our sister? "Go, and from this now, no longer sin." I believe we could hear it, not as a command which she must obey if we wants to stay in God's good graces, but as permission and freedom to move in a healing relationship which already exists—"from this now." Let me explain.

In order to love, to not experience her sexuality in an alienating way, this woman needs to be healed of and freed from the shame that binds her. I don't think she hears the "Go, and from this now, do not sin again" as a burden—or as an expectation that she is actually supposed to be perfect in her behavior. Instead, I think she hears the good news, that the binding and obsessive patterns of shame are broken. She is free to live in response to being forgiven, always in response—never in order to be forgiven. Would her behavior be affected? Certainly, in a way radically different from the years of trying to stop her addictive behaviors *in order* to be a respectable person.

And I don't believe that if Jesus had met her a few years down the road and the process of her healing had been slow (as it often is with issues of sexual addiction), I don't think he would have condemned her then, making his forgiveness dependent on her behavior. I believe he would have said to her again, "Neither do I condemn you, go, and from this now, no longer sin." And she would have heard it again, only more deeply.

This story ends just where I wish it would keep going. I want to know what happened to our sister, the woman taken in adultery—how did her own reconciliation to God and herself take shape in her life, the lives of her family, her ability to speak her own name and her experience? What about our brothers, the Pharisees, who quietly walked away to ponder their own need for forgiveness? Did they ever come to believe, and did they ever, the youngest or oldest, meet her again, this time calling her by name, asking forgiveness for the violence they had done her? Did they ever ask her to tell them her story in her own voice?

We don't know. That's the frustration, and the puzzle and the beauty of the biblical stories. Unfinished, and begging for completion, just like our lives. Precisely so it can ask each of us, as readers, how we would respond. We are invited into the text to ponder who we are in the story—whether we would step into the circle, in what ways we turn away from those different from us. How would we be if we experienced God forgiving us unconditionally?

We desperately need reconciliation within ourselves, with each other, and in our world, where privilege of race, class, and gender often do not get unmade.

If I knew I was forgiven, always, perhaps I could own my privilege as a white woman; perhaps I could admit my bent to "Other" persons different from myself. Perhaps then, I could participate in the reconciliation, in breaking down of walls of hostility, which Jesus has already accomplished on the cross. Perhaps my life might be radically changed in ordinary ways by the text in Galatians 3, which we often say, but seldom hear:

There is no longer Jew or Greek, there is no longer slave or free, there is no longer male and female, for all of you are one in Christ Jesus. (Galatians 3:28)

Thinking of Certain Mennonite Women

Julia Kasdorf

When I think I can't bear to trace
one more sorrow back to its source,

I think of Lois those summer evenings,
when, supper dishes done, she'd climb

a windmill and cling beneath its great blades,
drawing water from under her father's fields.

She'd stay there until the sun went down
on barn roof, garden, and the one paved road

pointing toward town. When I am afraid
to set out once more alone, I see Julie

pumping her legs so hard she believes
she will fly off the swing set and land

gently on the lawn. I see her let go,
braids streaking behind, then see her knees

shredded on gravel, stuck to stockings
each time she kneels to pray at a pew.

When I can't tell my own desire
from the wishes of others, I remember

my mom, too young to know or care better,
flinging her jumper, blouse, socks, and slip

into the wind, dancing for flower beds
until her mother discovers. When I wonder

how I should live this only one life,
I think of how they tell these stories:

honestly, without explanation,
to whomever will listen.

For the White Person Who Wants to Know How to be My Friend

Pat Parker

The first thing you do is to forget that i'm Black.
Second, you must never forget that i'm Black.

You should be able to dig Aretha,
but don't play her every time i come over.
And if you decide to play Beethoven—don't tell me
his life story. They made us take music appreciation too.

Eat soul food if you like it, but don't expect me
to locate your restaurants
or cook it for you.

And if some Black person insults you,
mugs you, rapes your sister, rapes you,
rips your house or is just being an ass—
please, do not apologize to me
for wanting to do them bodily harm.
It makes me wonder if you're foolish.

And even if you really believe Blacks are better lovers than
whites—don't tell me. I start thinking of charging stud fees.

In other words—if you really want to be my friend—*don't*
make a labor of it. I'm lazy. Remember.

IV. At Home In The Body

No body, no voice; no voice, no body. That's what I know in my bones.

—Nancy Mairs

WE SHOULD BE ABLE TO BE AT HOME in our bodies, we live in bodies after all. The authors included in this section can help us understand what conspires to estrange us from our bodies, how that divorcing silences our voices, and how we can and do struggle to speak, experience wholeness, and relate to a world which needs to hear our voices and be loved by our radically diverse embodied selves.

We begin with Rita Brock who explicates for us Katherine Bloomquist's intention to rework theological tradition. In the "Greening of the Soul" Brock brings to voice what has not yet been heard in traditional theology. She characterizes theology as a web, rather than a hierarchy and moves from fall/redemption as the central focus of theology to an affirmation of creation as good and our lives lived in response and gratitude to a God whose love creates and continuously repairs the web of materiality and oppressive relations that constitute our world. Lives of response and gratitude open us to a "greening" (a "flourishing" according to Sallie McFague's article also in this section) and simultaneously to a passion for working to heal each other, the means by which God's love affirms and restores a suffering world. Responding to such a world is no light or sentimental matter; to encounter pain we cannot prevent, or injury resulting from injustice, evokes passionate outrage and calls for a fearless love which "opens us to injury" and keeps us cognizant of our own vulnerability as well as our capacity to dominate or violate others. Response also moves us to confront systemic social forces, not only personal violations. Still, the intent of the creating *Ruah* (Spirit) God empowers us to "work and hope in the face of despair and destruction" toward restoring the web of relations so that all persons might experience their potential to create, celebrate and care for each other in safe and healthy environs, equally cared for and restored. Brock concludes her essay with covenant and communion table imagery, transforming them into web imagery, with God as source of life and community and Jesus' life and death a call to participate in a world "torn and rewoven" and "continually made new by God's love."

In the next essay, Nancy Mairs, asked to speak on coping with Multiple Sclerosis and her voice as a writer, sees no real connection between the two until she allows things to "simmer." In the process she discovers that M.S. "rammed" her back into a body she had been trained to believe she should rise above. And not only rise above, but also stay suspicious and silently ashamed of. (Mairs points out that *pudendum* in Latin comes from the infinitive "to be ashamed.") As her body gradually disintegrates into a "crippled" body, Mairs writes, "somehow over the years, I've learned how to set shame aside and do what I have do. Here, I think is where my voice comes in." And we do hear her embodied voice. Her courage, bluntness and humor call us home to our own bodies and encourage us to speak out loud against whatever tries to silence us. Mairs tells us this "terrifying work" is not only an antidote for her shame, but a way to speak what others know but have been unable to voice. Her words invite us to join her in breaking silence and coming into voice.

Sally Smits, whose voice we heard earlier, writes now about her painful struggle with anorexia, an eating disorder theorists and Sally describe as complicated, multi-layered and very difficult to speak about or overcome. While Sally's words stand on their own, it might be helpful to mention briefly the work of Susan Bordo, feminist philosopher and author of *Unbearable Weight; Feminism, Western Culture and The Body* as one way to speak about anorexia. Bordo suggests that at critical points in history, when traditional gender roles for women and men are in flux, women internalize and act out the contradictions of the conflict in their bodies, embodying as it were the crystallization of a culture's illness as a way both to resist and simultaneously comply with the feminine ideal at stake. For example, she describes 19th century hysteria as a way for women idealized into the role of "angel in the house" to push to the extreme delicateness, sexual passivity, and fragility, thus disrupting the entire Victorian household. Anorexia, according to Bordo, may be the attempt to embody an impossible contradiction characterizing our present culture as well. At the same time a woman learns to develop an other-oriented emotional economy—where self-nurturance and self-feeding are considered greedy and selfish—a successful woman must be master of her own destiny, autonomous, able to move and have control. At a time when femininity still means not taking up too much space, not being too loud, or too sexual, anorexia may allow a woman to go along with the ideal, growing smaller and more androgynous, while at the same time her disruptive body proclaims, "You must see me now; I will not live in a culture which does not allow me to speak and move freely." Sally articulates this space, all the while recognizing the complexity and convolutions of her own experience. If it is true, as a number of theorists claim, that most women in current culture are eating disordered, hopefully readers will find themselves in her words and take courage to move toward wholeness as Sally has done.

Julia Kasdorf, author of "Writing Like a Mennonite," finds in her personal story of silencing from childhood abuse a parallel to her Mennonite history and the stories of her "quiet ancestors" whose collective stories of persecution and martyrdom permeated her childhood. She remembers leaving the home of an abusive neighbor consoling herself, "Well, that was not so bad. It was only my body," a "wonderful splintering trick" she believes she learned from her martyr ancestors. Only in adulthood, as she begins to learn and name her earlier experience of trauma, does she begin to heal. At first she stays in the safety of writing, even though publishing her poem, "The Interesting Thing," changes (violently she suggests) her parents' awareness of her childhood innocence. However, she recognizes that her writing, so important in integrating the trauma which had rendered what happened to her person unspeakable, was partial at best: "I bore witness in writing until I could speak."

Finally, as we move into theology, we find Sallie McFague's "God as Mother" transformative of the ways we image God. We are made in the image of God, so it would seem quite logical to our author to assume that since "we" includes male and female, language for God might reflect both genders. But, language for God bespeaks a patriarchal social structure kept intact by masking over awareness that male metaphors for God are not actually neutral. Female metaphors shock us into awareness, not because they are inherently more sexual than masculine metaphors; they "jolt us into awareness that there is no gender-neutral language if we take ourselves as the model of talk about God, because we are sexual beings."

So McFague calls for an understanding of God as mother, not only in order to correct our overuse of father imagery, but because she feels mother imagery might enhance our awareness of God as creator and justice doer. She also argues that using female pronouns only in instances where culturally feminine characteristics are attributed to God simply strengthens the confining gender binaries already intact. So she encourages the use of female pronouns for God across gender metaphors, and male pronouns likewise. She also explores the well-known word for love, *agape*, to transform our understanding from an impartial to an inclusive love and from a disinterested love to a love passionately interested in every being: a love which could be paraphrased, "I'm so glad you're here and I want you to thrive." This mothering love can, of course, be embodied by both women and men, and this love on God's part would be both creative (with implications for ecology and "greening" of the world and souls) as well as sustaining of all who are vulnerable, unable to feed themselves, and in need of nurturing and justice. Parenting, McFague points out, has to do not only with feelings of love but also with the will and commitment to see a child grow into adulthood and thrive in every possible way. And opening ourselves to imagery of God as birthgiver and feeder would emphasize the interrelatedness of all life and call attention to concrete bodies and to the basic needs of all persons.

As we encounter Jennifer Sanborn's letters to her mother we find Sallie McFague's theology concretized and embodied in the love and loss experienced by Jennifer after the death of the person whose body she knew best. The person who knew her intimately, advocated for her unconditionally, and who knew just how to keep Jennifer's uniqueness intact is gone, and even though her mother prepared her for her death, Jennifer will not be consoled. Grieving must be treasured and journeyed through, not avoided and masked over. Only, years later, does she find the courage to become a parent to the child she now loves and longs to see thrive, and so love continues with all its vulnerability, risk taking, sorrows and joy.

Marcia Bailey, minister and theologian, meditates on the woman whom exegetes have often described as "the woman with the issue of blood." No need to comment on our culture's fear of women's bodies, or sexuality; she is never referred to as "the woman who menstruated for twelve years." (In fact, a college student once admitted he thought this woman had a deep cut on her arm or leg which refused to heal.) Marcia spends her menstrual week with this courageous woman to discover her own spiral of healing into hope, laughter, and the discovery of her own face.

We close with poems by Julia Kasdorf. "The Sun Lover" introduces us to a young girl coming of age and opening to her own sexual desire, while, "Ladies Night at the Turkish and Russian Baths" takes us into the safe company of older women, at home in their bodies and aching for touch and intimacy which they freely grant each other. One senses in these poems that Julia Kasdorf has also come home.

The Greening of the Soul

A Feminist Theological Paradigm of the Web of Life

Rita Nakashima Brock

INTRODUCTION

A pastor once reported that when his congregation introduced inclusive language into its worship services [...] one of those most resistant to changing language about God was a feminist elder of his congregation, whom I will call Mary. When asked her reasons for resisting, she gave vague replies about not tampering with tradition, even though it had been demonstrated to her that female images for God were found in the tradition and the Bible. He was surprised at her resistance. Eventually, she confessed that she believed God *had* to be male because no mother would do to her son what God did to Jesus. Mary knew it was not a very sophisticated reason, but her gut feeling was that something was wrong with the idea of a loving parent who had the power to save a child and did not, or who sent the child to suffer. The idea of such a God offended her deeply.

A quick glance through the theologies of the tradition have made not a few feminists allergic to, if not downright appalled by androcentric definitions of God, human nature, salvation, and love. What we have been told to believe often does not reflect the needs and life experiences of many women. But we have not been satisfied to see ourselves simply as victims of theology. We have sought instead to create women-centered, as well as inclusive, theologies.

What sorts of theology might emerge if a variety of women wrote it out of our experiences of life and of God? Fortunately, we have examples, both from the past and from current work in feminist/womauist/mujerista theologies. Listen to Hildegard of Bingen, an eleventh-century abbess, scholar, and mystical visionary.

> Glance at the sun. See the moon and stars. Gaze at the beauty of earth's greenings. Now, think. What delight God gives to humankind with all these things.

> There is no creation that does not have a radiance. Be it greenness or seed, blossom or beauty. It could not be creation without it.

> God says: I am the supreme fire; not deadly, but rather, enkindling every spark of life. I am the breeze that nurtures all things green. I call forth tears, the aroma of holy work. I am the yearning for good.

> Good People, most royal greening verdancy, rooted in the sun, you shine so finely, it surpasses understanding. You are encircled by the arms of the mystery of God. And so, humankind full of all creative possibilities, is God's work. Humankind alone, is called to assist God.

> The first seed of the longing for Justice blows through the soul like the wind. The taste for good will plays in it like a breeze. The consummation of this seed is a greening in the soul that is like that of the ripening world. Now the soul honors God by the doing of just deeds. The soul is only as strong as its works. (Uhlen: 26, 31, 45, 90, 106, and 123)

Hildegard seems startlingly well grounded in the beauty, generosity, and power of earthly creation. She regards human life positively, as good. Yet, only recently has Christian theology begun creating ideas that highlight this concept of "greening," of respect for God's creation of the natural world and its goodness. For example, the World Council of Churches' call to affirm the goodness and integrity of creation came in the 1980s, a time when eco-feminism became strong. Until that decade, much contemporary theology was influenced by the development of Enlightenment science, with its ideas about rationality, objectivity, and human progress. Hence, theologians had done little reflection on and promotion of life-sustaining relationships with the natural world because it was seen as a machine, like a clock, that could be worked on, manipulated, and controlled for human progress. And, like nature with which we were associated, women were relegated to an inferior status. In addition, the mid-twentieth-century revival of Reformed Protestant theology in the neoorthodox movement emphatically split revelation from nature (partly as a response to the Nazi use of genetics and "nature") and was deeply suspicious of any theology that emphasized the immanence of God or that was called "natural." Yet, a woman's voice from the eleventh century speaks of a deep love and respect for creation, as well as for humankind as part of that creation and as caretakers of love and justice. I find in her voice an echo of my own deep love for nature, in its beauty and its sometimes frightening power, and a basic sense that human life is a gift and rare opportunity. Such values are of bedrock importance in East Asian cultures and reflect the first six years of my life in a Japanese family in Japan and Okinawa. These values are found in many non-European cultures and are also profoundly biblical, as Hildegard knew.

If we begin with Hildegard's fundamental affirmation of life as a blessing and of the responsibility given to us to nurture and protect it, where might our theological musings lead us? In the following paradigm of feminist theology, I suggest one direction our musings might lead, if the starting point of our theology is this "greening," this affirmation of the web of life, the verdancy created by God. To begin with creation and human participation in creativity means we begin not with the fall or doctrines of sin, but with interconnected life—with the goodness of living and our responsibility for loving care. This hearkening back to Hildegard is an important reminder to Protestant women of our legacy from Catholic women in our tradition, a legacy that continues today in Catholic feminist theologians such as Rosemary Radford Ruether, Elisabeth Schüssler Fiorenza, and Elizabeth Johnson, who continue to bring much to the feminist theological table.

While the exact ideas below are mine and no one else's, many of their themes, images, and issues reflect a movement within feminist theology away from traditional fall/redemption or sin/salvation theologies. These traditional, atonement-based theologies focus on the fall or sin and our need to be saved from sin. They begin with a negative assessment of human nature as the central point for theological systems. The central focus of my theology is the affirmation of creation as good, the beginning point of the Bible, given to us in the first story of creation.

This deep intuition that creation (the natural world) is good and that human beings are not born sinful may come more easily to women who feel a responsibility and commitment to nurturing life and caring for families. Women with such responsibilities often find ourselves affirming life as we are immersed in daily life—giving tasks: fixing dinner for a family, wiping the fevered brow of a son, washing the old frail body of a grandmother, holding a weeping friend, making love to our life-partner, or teaching words to a toddler. We respect especially the life-giving survival skills that women have developed while living under adverse circumstances such as slavery, poverty, racism, and domestic violence. The appreciation for the natural world also runs deeply in the history of women in the U.S. The diaries of nineteenth-century women crossing the prairies of the Western frontier, despite the hardships and dangers of travel, mention the beauty of the natural environment more often than any other subject. They were awestruck at the sight of so much natural splendor.

Many feminist/womanist/mujerista theologians share these beginning life-affirming premises, which move us to ache for justice and liberation for all the suffering people of the world and to work for more whole relationships to each other and to the earth, which we depend on for life and which gives us so much beauty. While I am focusing on North American theologies, these new women's theologies also point us toward the suffering of the Two-Thirds World, especially our sisters there, and to the poor in our midst as we struggle to create a just and safe world for all.

The theological picture of the web of life described below will, I hope, provide a framework for understanding how theology might work from some women's perspectives and prompt readers to explore other models. To illustrate how this web works in a new way, the second part of this chapter uses the framework to reflect on how we might understand our relationship to God in the image of the birther of creation. As one way of experiencing God's creativity and care, I propose we examine the image of God as Mother.

A Feminist Theology: The Web of Life

Visualize the theology below as a great, intricate web. The power that creates and repairs it is the love of God. "God is love" is the central affirmation of Christian faith without which divine grace and creativity cannot be understood. We affirm that God creates the world out of this love, just as human life is conceived and nurtured in loving relationship when we live at our best. Without love's power, nothing could exist. Without the web, the weaver has no embodied self-expression, no incarnate manifestation of beauty and shimmering energy. In other words, God loves and needs the work of creating. The world and we are the complex weavings of divine love, found in our works of caring in the world. We need each other to he able to express love fully, and the fullness of God's love is made incarnate in our daily living.

The Web's Central Knot: The Goodness of Creation

The first strands of the web are interlocked into the central knot through which the whole takes shape and is bound together. These fundamental, core strands weave together the goodness and integrity of creation. The love of God is described as *Ruah,* the hovering Breath or Spirit of God in Genesis 1 that creates the world from the waters of the deep. She (*Ruah* is a feminine noun in Hebrew) breathes life into matter, creates the rhythms of time, and quickens the many beings, animate and inanimate. The first principles of this creating are love, beauty, and joy, which are the spiritual core of life and the sources of blessings. This Spirit of creating is later identified as the *wisdom* of God (*Sophia* in Greek and *Hokmah* in Hebrew), who exists at the first moment of creation (Proverbs 8:22—31).

Humankind is inspired by that divine Spirit. We are made in the divine image, female and male as equals, not as opposites, but as beings of like spirit, called by Wisdom to be wise and loving. We are the helpmates of God for creativity and for caring. Through our connection to creating, we find Hildegard's greening of our souls.

If we live, as many Americans do, in suburban and urban dwellings, we are often lulled into a false sense of independence and separation from the natural world. Yet our theological and biblical heritages insist that we are bound to this creation by the very substance of our bodies, by air, water, and sunlight. We live, irrevocably interdependent with the physical universe. Our physical body depends on the environment around us. We are, as Genesis reminds us, made of the earth, of humus, from which we take the word humble. Through care of this earthly body we sustain the dwelling place of God's love and receive the love of others.

Everything that exists, the Bible proclaims, is created by God—even, as the character Shug in *The Color Purple* reminds us, things and people we don't like. When the Bible says all creation is good, it is not speaking of good in a moral sense. There is much violence and struggle in life, so we use "good" to mean that everything that exists is valuable because it exists as part of God's creating. Christians often focus on light, mind, and eternity. We forget that darkness, flesh, and the changing cycles of time are also gifts of life, that light cannot exist without darkness, love without flesh, or beginnings without endings. The delicate balance of the forces of life, not the overwhelming presence of one aspect, gives life a sense of struggle worth the effort, of harmony achieved by the balance of conflicting forces, of wholeness made from healing brokenness, and of creativity born of sweat and work. This sense of creative wholeness, even in the midst of pain and brokenness, reminds us that creation is good and beautiful in its own ways, even when these ways may be mysterious to us.

When we get too focused on light and on a one-sided view of things, we tend to view death as a problem. Yet to be physically alive means to live one's life from the death of living things. As a part of the activity of the world and the rhythms of life, physical death is part of life. Our difficulties with death lie in the thoughtless taking of life and in loneliness and the often painful suffering that accompanies dying. Elderly people abandoned to die alone on our city streets or under the cold, impersonal tools of technology are a judgment about our inability to maintain humane ways of living and dying, not a judgment about death itself. Death is often painful and tragic, but the reality of death is not separate from life and its ongoing, creative process, a process that transcends personal death. Death can come as deliverance from incurable suffering, just as it can feel like the appropriate ending of a long, well-lived life that has finally reached its completion and reward. The tragedy of death is to die alone, unloved, unremembered, without a legacy and without people who care. The evil of death comes from the loss of balance, when violence and poverty inflict death out of time. We balance the sorrow and losses of death and counter its tragedy by our acts of loving and of creativity and out of our work for justice, which show the constant, regenerative work of God's Spirit in our lives and our faithful response. [...]

The Interweaving Strands: Healing and Liberation

The strands that weave the cross patterns in the web and intersect with the radiating strands are healing and liberation. They give strength to the web to withstand both the everyday sorrows and struggles from death and pain, which show us our human limits, and the powers of willful destruction in the world, which are strong. Withstanding deliberately inflicted violence especially requires courage, vision, and a supportive community. The powers of the world that willfully prevent or destroy the fullness of creation must be named and exorcised, for they are legion. Evil is not simply the absence of good, but the active presence of hatred, fear, abuse, and destruction. The Bible uses the image of the casting out of demons to signify liberation, an appropriate metaphor to depict how forces—demons—of destruction can permeate our psyches deeply.

When the demons possess us we are overcome with feelings of powerlessness, and personal healing is crucial to the return of our selves and our powers to care. For example, we know from recent research by psychologists such as Judith Herman that when children are severely abused, especially sexually, they develop important survival mechanisms that disconnect parts of their memory or personalities from conscious knowledge, a process also found often in victims of torture. A person with multiple personality disorder is helpless to know or control all the personalities she or he uses to cope with the evil that has afflicted her/him. And many people are haunted by fears or self-destructive behaviors they cannot locate in any conscious memory of their past. For those so afflicted, healing begins with the return of memory, with safe places to remember, and with the support of those who are not afraid of the suffering of those they love.

Our works to heal each other are the means by which God's love is affirmed and restored to a suffering world, a world often afflicted by pain that we cannot prevent and that comes from injury and injustice. The limits of our human ability to control our lives often become vivid to us in the face of the impersonal fury of hurricanes, floods, earthquakes, hailstorms, tornadoes, and fires. When we know the injury inflicted is deliberately caused, we often feel outrage and fury, which, along with the pain of our injury may also eventually be healed when *kairos*—when the ripe moment—comes. We struggle to heal together because it gives us hope in the midst of pain and tragedy, which constantly eat away at our capacities to care. Our works for healing open doors for grace and generosity to return.

For the fullness of God's creation to be made manifest—for the greening and ripening of creating—all beings must be provided a chance to fulfill their potential to create, to celebrate, and to care. For our lives to be lived at their fullest, human beings require a just, peaceful, and whole world, and a safe, healthy environment. For this, we work and hope in the face of despair and destruction. As the prophet Micah reminds us, we are to do justice, to love mercy, and to be humble when God walks with us. We commit ourselves to healing and liberation because we know the brokenness of human life and its injustices. We are called by God to commit ourselves because we know that through healing and liberation we are led to know grace and generosity. As Hildegard reminds us, "the soul honors God by the doing of just deeds. The soul is only as strong as its works." The works of love and justice that we leave behind are the measure of what we have done with the gift of life bestowed on us.

Our commitments to healing and liberation require risk because the love and trust required to love fearlessly opens us to injury. To remain open and to receive the world's gifts requires us to maintain a capacity for vulnerability, and the tragedies and limits of human life can weaken our trust so that we move from love toward fear and withdrawal. Our vulnerability means we are not completely immune to the forces of evil. Research on human beings under conditions of extreme abuse, torture, imprisonment, and war has taught us that virtually all of us have a breaking point, a point at which we succumb to evil. For those brought to such a breaking point, death can come as mercy and relief; for evil is not simply death per se, but is rather the consequence of misused power and unjust death. Evil is created by powers that cause violence, that create unnecessary suffering and death, and that seek control as an ultimate value; evil is to refuse to help another in pain, to create hatred of others, or to exploit another's vulnerability. Evil is to foster contempt for life, to live by deceit, to choose despair, to separate people from relationships of love and care, and to live by supporting or benefiting from unjust systems while doing nothing to change them. Sometimes, in fact, evil comes from within ourselves because we reproduce our own history of being abused by hurting ourselves or others, we succumb to despair, or we simply fail to help when we should. Wherever we encounter the forces of control, of violence, domination, exploitation, oppression, passive despair, and abuse, we must do what we can to restore the goodness of creating.

To commit ourselves to the work of God's love and justice means taking enormous risks in order to keep healing and liberation alive in the world. We must be aware that the forces of oppression, hate, and violence are strong and canny. They are organized to resist relinquishing their power. In our communities of struggle, we must remain ever alert, open, and careful because sources of evil may not come simply from an external enemy. They may also come from within our communities, from our families, or from within ourselves. We require courage—strength of heart—to challenge evil, even as we remain suspicious of our most self-righteous polemics and defensive postures. Courage enables us to cherish our anger at injustice at the same time we are attuned to the opportunities to heal the pain that lies below anger.

The Christian tendency to focus too narrowly on personal sin and redemption often blinds us to the evil found in organized systems that misuse power to control and destroy. We forget that the greatest forces in our lives, from birth to death, are social forces because love, a social reality, is essential to our survival. Personal sin can pale by comparison to the political and economic forces of injustice in our world that destroy people and relationships. And often, personal behavior is closely tied to the power of such systems. Those forces crush God's creating. In the face of those forces, we are called to work for liberation.

An example of such devastation happened in Argentina in the 1970s when the new military government "disappeared" citizens. Thousands of idealistic young adults, who worked with the poor or were critical of the government's policies, were kidnapped and murdered. Pregnant women were forced to deliver, then killed, and their babies given away to military families and their friends. Many parents and grandparents, ignored by the government, felt desperate and powerless when they tried to get information about their children. But a group of women refused to be intimidated. They started a weekly demonstration in front of government buildings in the capital. They were called the Mothers of the Plaza Del Mayo. By the time the government began to notice the activity of this group of "crazy old women," the world press knew of them and the human rights violations they protested. It became impossible to disappear them all without other governments noticing. When the reign of terror ended, the bones of thousands of tortured and murdered women, men, and youth were found around the country. The Mothers had become a symbol of the conscience of the country, and their activism in solidarity with writers and other activists helped to bring down the government. [...] There are now Mothers groups in many countries in the world where governments torture and kill citizens.

For their sake, for the sake of all the world's mothers, for the sake of all those who suffer now, for the sake of our bruised and poisoned creation, and for the sake of our own desire to live in God's grace and generosity, we are invited by the gospel—by the ever-abundant love of God—to commit our lives to the work of healing and liberation. In our commitment, we must, however, be aware of the ways we benefit from structures of injustice in our own lives. We must seek to make right what we can at the same time we work to heal ourselves. We make right what we can, not because we are to blame or are guilty, but because we commit our heart, mind, soul, and strength to the work of God, to the renewal of God's spirit in our lives. Out of the empowerment of that spirit and of our love, we remain attuned to the suffering of others and to the terrible consequences of injustice. Where we can make a difference, we are called to do so, even when it means an uncomfortable examination of our own lives, our attitudes, our behavior toward others, our lifestyle, and our personal goals. We often miss the mark because of the limits of our lives. However, we continue because we know we are loved, and we seek to increase the work of God's love in the world. And through our just deeds we find the greening of our souls and the renewal of life on earth.

The Web's Anchor: Covenant

The gossamer and resilient web of life—creation/incarnation, grace/ generosity, and healing/liberation—are anchored to the covenant we make with God as the source of life and our community. As human beings and as Christians, we cannot live a creative, gracious, liberating life without a commitment to each other, to our communities, to our history as a religious people (as complex and ambiguous as that is), and to God. We do not commit to a particular creed, a particular statement of faith or formula, to a book, or to a human authority, but to covenant, to relationships—to God and to each other as the body of the risen Christ, the embodied Holy Spirit, which has made us one in our baptism. There is no more powerful or important embodiment of that commitment than the communion table. At that table, the creative love of God joins the elements of nourishment and joy, produced by the earth, with our human lives. The suffering of the world is brought to the table to be embraced by a vision of justice and openness that empowers our hopes for its fulfillment. This incarnational vision affirms the body of Christ as the people of God in brokenness and in resurrection. At the table, we recommit ourselves to loving each other, to remembering our ambiguous and hopeful history, and to working for the healing and liberation of ourselves and those to come.

If we affirm the web of life and images of God as nurturing life, the communion table, where we celebrate the covenant that anchors us, may move us beyond betrayal and sacrifice. The Table may call our attention instead to covenant and the life of Jesus, who worked for healing and justice, as well as to remembrance of his very real death. If the words of institution and invitation to the table were to affirm the kind of theology sketched out above, they might say something like the following:[1]

> We remember that on the evening before Jesus was killed by those who feared him and his ministry, he sat at table with his friends, women, men, and children. They shared in the meal of the Passover, which celebrates the liberation of God's people from slavery. Remembering the brokenness of lives destroyed by the principalities and powers and the risks he took in challenging those powers, Jesus took bread, broke it, and passed it to his friends saying, "This is my body broken for justice, a sign of our work together to make whole a broken world, our body of struggle. Take it all of you and eat. Whenever you break bread together, please remember me."
>
> After dinner, Jesus took a cup of wine and passed it to them, as it is passed to us saying, "This is my life with you and our hope for a renewed creation of healing and love. This cup is for all. In partaking, we affirm our love for each other and our hope for peace and the liberation and healing of God's people throughout the world. Drink it all of you and do this remembering me."
>
> Each time we celebrate this meal together, taking the bread and the cup, we remember the life of Jesus and the lives of all who have risked much for God's love and creation. In taking this meal together, we participate in the Body of the Risen Christ, in the hopes of the cloud of witnesses who have gone before us, and in the hopes of this Community. As we partake, we re-create the Body of the Risen Christ in our work together for Shalom—for justice, healing, and peace.
>
> This is the table of God set for all the people of God. We share an inclusive communion, which means you do not have to be a member of this or any faith community to join us at the table. We believe that Christ sets this table and with Christ we welcome everyone. Come, for the table is ready.

In our words at the table, we affirm that our fragile and strong web remains solidly anchored in its life with God. As it is torn and rewoven, it is continually made new by God's love, which, as its center, radiates outward to all creation. [...]

NOTES

1. This version is paraphrased from worship at Spirit of the Lakes UCC, Minneapolis, Minnesota. The liturgist for the day develops words of remembrance similar to these, which are adapted as new theological insights are learned by the pastor and congregation.

WORKS CONSULTED

Blumenthal, David. 1993. *Facing the Abusing God*. Philadelphia: Westminster Press.

Brock, Rita Nakashima. 1988. *Journeys by Heart: A Christology of Erotic Power*. New York: Crossroad Press.

Doyle, Brendan. 1983. *Meditations with Julian of Norwich*. Sante Fe: Bear & Company.

Greven, Philip. 1991. *Spare the Child: The Religious Roots of Punishment and the Psychological Impact of Child Abuse*. New York: Alfred A. Knopf.

Herman, Judith. 1992. *Trauma and Recovery*. New York: Basic Books.

Hunt, Mary. 1989. *Fierce Tenderness: A Feminist Theology of Friendship*. New York: Crossroad Press.

Isasi-Diaz, Ada Maria. 1993. *En La Lucha: Sisters in the Struggle*. Minneapolis: Fortress Press.

Johnson, Elizabeth. 1992. *She Who Is: The Mystery of God in Feminist Theological Discourse*. New York: Crossroad Press.

"Las Madres, The Mothers of the Plaza Del Mayo." 1986. Documentary film available from Women Make Movies, 225 Lafayette St., New York, NY 10012.212/925-0606.

Noddings, Nel. 1989. *Women and Evil*. Berkeley: University of California Press.

Poling, James. 1991. *The Abuse of Power: A Theological Problem*. Nashville: Abingdon Press.

Ruddick, Sara. 1989. *Maternal Thinking: Toward a Politics of Peace*. Boston: Beacon Press.

Ruether, Rosemary Radford. 1983. *Sexism and God-Talk: Toward a Feminist Theology*. Boston: Beacon Press.

Uhlen, Gabriele. 1983. *Meditations with Hildegard of Bingen*. Sante Fe: Bear & Company.

Walker, Alice. 1981. The *Color Purple*. New York: Harcourt, Brace, Jovanovich.

Williams, Delores. 1993. *Sisters in the Wilderness: The Challenge of Womanist God-Talk*. Maryknoll, NY: Orbis Press.

Carnal Acts

Nancy Mairs

INVITING ME TO SPEAK at her small liberal-arts college during Women's Week, a young woman set me a task: "We would be pleased," she wrote, "if you could talk on how you cope with your MS disability, and also how you discovered your voice as a writer." Oh, Lord, I thought in dismay, how am I going to pull this one off? How can I yoke two such disparate subjects into a coherent presentation, without doing violence to one, or the other, or both, or myself? This is going to take some fancy footwork, and my feet scarcely carry out the basic steps, let alone anything elaborate.

To make matters worse, the assumption underlying each of her questions struck me as suspect. To ask *how* I cope with multiple sclerosis suggests that I *do* cope. Now, "to cope," *Webster's Third* tells me, is "to face or encounter and to find necessary expedients to overcome problems and difficulties." In these terms, I have to confess, I don't feel like much of a coper. I'm likely to deal with my problems and difficulties by squawking and flapping around like that hysterical chicken who was convinced the sky was falling. Never mind that in my case the sky really *is* falling. In response to a clonk on the head, regardless of its origin, one might comport oneself with a grace and courtesy I generally lack.

As for "finding" my voice, the implication is that it was at one time lost or missing. But I don't think it ever was. Ask my mother, who will tell you a little wearily that I was speaking full sentences by the time I was a year old and could never be silenced again. As for its being a writer's voice, it seems to have become one early on. Ask Mother again. At the age of eight I rewrote the Trojan War, she will say, and what Nestor was about to do to Helen at the end doesn't bear discussion in polite company.

Faced with these uncertainties, I took my own teacherly advice, something,

I must confess, I don't always do. "If an idea is giving you trouble," I tell my writing students, "put it on the back burner and let it simmer while you do something else. Go to the movies. Reread a stack of old love letters. Sit in your history class and take detailed notes on the Teapot Dome scandal. If you've got your idea in mind, it will go on cooking at some level no matter what else you're doing." "I've had an idea for my documented essay on the back burner," one of my students once scribbled in her journal, "and I think it's just boiled over!"

I can't claim to have reached such a flash point. But in the weeks I've had the themes "disability" and "voice" sitting around in my head, they seem to have converged on their own, without my having to wrench them together and bind them with hoops of tough rhetoric. They *are* related, indeed interdependent, with an intimacy that has for some reason remained, until now, submerged below the surface of my attention. Forced to juxtapose them, I yank them out of the depths, a little startled to discover how they were intertwined down there out of sight. This kind of discovery can unnerve you at first. You feel like a giant hand that, pulling two swimmers out of the water, two separate heads bobbling on the iridescent swells, finds the two bodies below, legs coiled around each other, in an ecstasy of copulation. You don't quite know where to turn your eyes.

Perhaps the place to start illuminating this erotic connection between who I am and how I speak lies in history. I have known that I have multiple sclerosis for about seventeen years now, though the disease probably started long before. The hypothesis is that the disease process, in which the protective covering of the nerves in the brain and spinal cord is eaten away and replaced by scar tissue, "hard patches," is caused by an autoimmune reaction to a slow-acting virus. Research suggests that I was infected by this virus, which no one has ever seen and which therefore, technically, doesn't even "exist," between the ages of four and fifteen. In effect, living with this mysterious mechanism feels like having your present self, and the past selves it embodies, haunted by a capricious and meanspirited ghost, unseen except for its footprints, which trips you even when you're watching where you're going, knocks glassware out of your hand, squeezes the urine out of your bladder before you reach the bathroom, and weights your whole body with a weariness no amount of rest can relieve. An alien invader must be at work. But of course it's not. It's your own body. That is, it's you.

This, for me, has been the most difficult aspect of adjusting to a chronic incurable degenerative disease: the fact that it has rammed my "self" straight back into the body I had been trained to believe it could, through high-minded acts and aspirations, rise above. The Western tradition of distinguishing the body from the mind and/or the soul is so ancient as to have become part of our collective unconscious, if one is inclined to believe in such a noumenon, or at least to have become an unquestioned element in the social instruction we impose upon infants from birth, in much the same way we inculcate, without reflection, the gender distinctions "female" and "male." I *have* a body, you are likely to say if you talk about embodiment at all; you don't say, I *am* a body. A body is a separate entity possessable by the "I;" the "I" and the body aren't, as the copula would make them, grammatically indistinguishable.

To widen the rift between the self and the body, we treat our bodies as subordinates, inferior in moral status. Open association with them shames us. In fact, we treat our bodies with very much the same distance and ambivalence women have traditionally received from men in our culture. Sometimes this treatment is benevolent, even respectful, but all too often it is tainted by outright sadism. I think of the bodybuilding regimens that have become popular in the last decade or so, with the complicated vacillations they reflect between self-worship and self-degradation: joggers and aerobic dancers and weightlifters all beating their bodies into shape. "No pain, no gain," the saying goes. "Feel the burn." Bodies get treated like wayward women who have to be shown who's boss, even if it means slapping them around a little. I'm not for a moment opposing rugged exercise here. I'm simply questioning the spirit in which it is often undertaken.

Since, as Hélène Cixous points out in her essay on women and writing, "Sorties,"[1] thought has always worked "through dual, hierarchical oppositions" (p. 64), the mind/body split cannot possibly be innocent. The utterance of an "I" immediately calls into being its opposite, the "not-I," Western discourse being unequipped to conceive "that which is neither 'I' nor 'not-I,'" "that which is both 'I' and 'not-I,'" or some other permutation which language doesn't permit me to speak. The "not-I" is, by definition, other. And we've never been too fond of the other. We prefer the same. We tend to ascribe to the other those qualities we prefer not to associate with our selves: it is the hidden, the dark, the secret, the shameful. Thus, when the "I" takes possession of the body, it makes the body into an other, direct object of a transitive verb, with all the other's repudiated and potentially dangerous qualities.

At the least, then, the body had best be viewed with suspicion. And a woman's body is particularly suspect, since so much of it is in fact hidden, dark, secret, carried about on the inside where, even with the aid of a speculum, one can never perceive all of it in the plain light of day, a graspable whole. I, for one, have never understood why anyone would want to carry all that delicate stuff around on the outside. It would make you awfully anxious, I should think, put you constantly on the defensive, create a kind of siege mentality that viewed all other beings, even your own kind, as threats to be warded off with spears and guns and atomic missiles. And you'd never get to experience that inward dreaming that comes when your flesh surrounds all your treasures, holding them close, like a sturdy shuttered house. Be my personal skepticism as it may, however, as a cultural woman I bear just as much shame as any woman for my dark, enfolded secrets. Let the word for my external genitals tell the tale: my pudendum, from the Latin infinitive meaning "to be ashamed."

It's bad enough to carry your genitals like a sealed envelope bearing the cipher that, once unlocked, might loose the chaotic flood of female pleasure—*jouissance*, the French call it—upon the world-of-the-same. But I have an additional reason to feel shame for my body, less explicitly connected with its sexuality: it is a crippled body. Thus it is doubly other, not merely by the homo-sexual standards of patriarchal culture but by the standards of physical desirability erected for every body in our world. Men, who are by definition exonerated from shame in sexual terms (this doesn't mean that an individual man might not experience sexual shame, of course; remember that I'm talking in general about discourse, not folks), may—more likely must—experience bodily shame if they are crippled. I won't presume to speak about the details of their experience, however. I don't know enough. I'll just go on telling what it's like to be a crippled woman, trusting that, since we're fellow creatures who've been living together for some thousands of years now, much of my experience will resonate with theirs.

I was never a beautiful woman, and for that reason I've spent most of my life (together with probably at least 95 percent of the female population of the United States) suffering from the shame of falling short of an unattainable standard. The ideal woman of my generation was...perky, I think you'd say, rather than gorgeous. Blond hair pulled into a bouncing ponytail. Wide blue eyes, a turned-up nose with maybe a scattering of golden freckles across it, a small mouth with full lips over straight white teeth. Her breasts were large but well harnessed high on her chest; her tiny waist flared to hips just wide enough to give the crinolines under her circle skirt a starting outward push. In terms of personality, she was outgoing, even bubbly, not pensive or mysterious. Her milieu was the front fender of a white Corvette convertible, surrounded by teasing crewcuts, dressed in black flats, a sissy blouse, and the letter sweater of the Corvette owner. Needless to say, she never missed a prom.

Ten years or so later, when I first noticed the symptoms that would be diagnosed as MS, I was probably looking my best. Not beautiful still, but the ideal had shifted enough so that my flat chest and narrow hips gave me an elegantly attenuated shape, set off by a thick mass of long, straight, shining hair. I had terrific legs, long and shapely, revealed nearly to the pudendum by the fashionable miniskirts and hot pants I adopted with more enthusiasm than delicacy of taste. Not surprisingly, I suppose, during this time I involved myself in several pretty torrid love affairs.

The beginning of MS wasn't too bad. The first symptom, besides the pernicious fatigue that had begun to devour me, was "foot drop," the inability to raise my left foot at the ankle. As a consequence, I'd started to limp, but I could still wear high heels, and a bit of a limp might seem more intriguing than repulsive. After a few months, when the doctor suggested a cane, a crippled friend gave me quite an elegant wood-and-silver one, which I carried with a fair amount of panache. The real blow to my self-image came when I had to get a brace. As braces go, it's not bad: lightweight plastic molded to my foot and leg, fitting down into an ordinary shoe and secured around my calf by a Velcro strap. It reduces my limp and, more important, the danger of tripping and falling. But it meant the end of high heels. And it's ugly. Not as ugly as I think it is, I gather, but still pretty ugly. It signified for me, and perhaps still does, the permanence and irreversibility of my condition. The brace makes my MS concrete and forces me to wear it on the outside. As soon as I strapped the brace on, I climbed into trousers and stayed there (though not in the same trousers, of course). The idea of going around with my bare brace hanging out seemed almost as indecent as exposing my breasts. Not until 1984, soon after I won the Western States Book Award for poetry, did I put on a skirt short enough to reveal my plasticized leg. The connection between winning a writing award and baring my brace is not merely fortuitous; being affirmed as a writer really did embolden me. Since then, I've grown so accustomed to wearing skirts that I don't think about my brace any more than I think about my cane. I've incorporated them, I suppose: made them, in their necessity, insensate but fundamental parts of my body.

Meanwhile, I had to adjust to the most outward and visible sign of all, a three-wheeled electric scooter called an Amigo. This lessens my fatigue and increases my range terrifically, but it also shouts out to the world, "Here is a woman who can't stand on her own two feet." At the same time, paradoxically, it renders me invisible, reducing me to the height of a seven-year-old, with a child's attendant low status. "Would she like smoking or nonsmoking?" the gate agent assigning me a seat asks the friend traveling with me. In crowds I see nothing but buttocks. I can tell you the name of every type of designer jeans ever sold. The wearers, eyes front, trip over me and fall across my handlebars into my lap. "Hey!" I want to shout to the lofty world. "Down here! There's a person down here!" But I'm not, by their standards, quite a person anymore.

My self-esteem diminishes further as age and illness strip from me the features that made me, for a brief while anyway, a good-looking, even sexy, young woman. No more long, bounding strides: I shuffle along with the timid gait I remember observing, with pity and impatience, in the little old ladies at Boston's Symphony Hall on Friday afternoons. No more lithe, girlish figure: my belly sags from the loss of muscle tone, which also creates all kinds of intestinal disruptions, hopelessly humiliating in a society in which excretory functions remain strictly unspeakable. No more sex, either, if society had its way. The sexuality of the disabled so repulses most people that you can hardly get a doctor, let alone a member of the general population, to consider the issues it raises. Cripples simply aren't supposed to Want It, much less Do It. Fortunately, I've got a husband with a strong libido and a weak sense of social propriety, or else I'd find myself perforce practicing a vow of chastity I never cared to take.

Afflicted by the general shame of having a body at all, and the specific shame of having one weakened and misshapen by disease, I ought not to be able to hold my head up in public. And yet I've gotten into the habit of holding my head up in public, sometimes under excruciating circumstances. Recently, for instance, I had to give a reading at the University of Arizona. Having smashed three of my front teeth in a fall onto the concrete floor of my screened porch, I was in the process of getting them crowned, and the temporary crowns flew out during dinner right before the reading. What to do? I wanted, of course, to rush home and hide till the dental office opened the next morning. But I couldn't very well break my word at this last moment.

So, looking like Hansel and Gretel's witch, and lisping worse than the Wife of Bath, I got up on stage and read. Somehow, over the years, I've learned how to set shame aside and do what I have to do.

Here, I think, is where my "voice" comes in. Because, in spite of my demurral at the beginning, I do in fact cope with my disability at least some of the time. And I do so, I think, by speaking about it, and about the whole experience of being a body, specifically a female body, out loud, in a clear, level tone that drowns out the frantic whispers of my mother, my grandmothers, all the other trainers of wayward childish tongues: "Sssh! Sssh! Nice girls don't talk like that. Don't mention sweat. Don't mention menstrual blood. Don't ask what your grandfather does on his business trips. Don't laugh so loud. You sound like a loon. Keep your voice down. Don't tell. Don't tell. Don't tell." Speaking out loud is an antidote to shame. I want to distinguish clearly here between "shame," as I'm using the word, and "guilt" and "embarrassment," which, though equally painful, are not similarly poisonous. Guilt arises from performing a forbidden act or failing to perform a required one. In either case, the guilty person can, through reparation, erase the offense and start fresh. Embarrassment, less opprobrious though not necessarily less distressing, is generally caused by acting in a socially stupid or awkward way. When I trip and sprawl in public, when I wet myself, when my front teeth fly out, I feel horribly embarrassed, but, like the pain of childbirth, the sensation blurs and dissolves in time. If it didn't, every child would be an only child, and no one would set foot in public after the onset of puberty, when embarrassment erupts like a geyser and bathes one's whole life in its bitter stream. Shame may attach itself to guilt or embarrassment, complicating their resolution, but it is not the same emotion. I feel guilt or embarrassment for something I've done; shame, for who I am. I may stop doing bad or stupid things, but I can't stop being. How then can I help but be ashamed? Of the three conditions, this is the one that cracks and stifles my voice.

I can subvert its power, I've found, by acknowledging who I am, shame and all, and, in doing so, raising what was hidden, dark, secret about my life into the plain light of shared human experience. What we aren't permitted to utter holds us, each isolated from every other, in a kind of solipsistic thrall. Without any way to check our reality against anyone else's, we assume that our fears and shortcomings are ours alone. One of the strangest consequences of publishing a collection of personal essays called *Plaintext* has been the steady trickle of letters and telephone calls saying essentially, in a tone of unmistakable relief, "Oh, me too! Me too!" It's as though the part I thought was solo has turned out to be a chorus. But none of us was singing loud enough for the others to hear.

Singing loud enough demands a particular kind of voice, I think. And I was wrong to suggest, at the beginning, that I've always had my voice. I have indeed always had *a* voice, but it wasn't *this* voice, the one with which I could call up and transform my hidden self from a naughty girl into a woman talking directly to others like herself. Recently, in the process of writing a new book, a memoir entitled *Remembering the Bone House,* I've had occasion to read some of my early writing, from college, high school, even junior high. It's not an experience I recommend to anyone susceptible to shame. Not that the writing was all that bad. I was surprised at how competent a lot of it was. Here was a writer who already knew precisely how the language worked. But the voice...oh, the voice was all wrong: maudlin, rhapsodic, breaking here and there into little shrieks, almost, you might say, hysterical. It was a voice that had shucked off its own body, its own homely life of Cheerios for breakfast and seventy pages of Chaucer to read before the exam on Tuesday and a planter's wart growing painfully on the ball of its foot, and reeled now wraithlike through the air, seeking incarnation only as the heroine who enacts her doomed love for the tall, dark, mysterious stranger. If it didn't get that part, it wouldn't play at all.

Among all these overheated and vaporous imaginings, I must have retained some shred of sense, because I stopped writing prose entirely, except for scholarly papers, for nearly twenty years. I even forgot, not exactly that I had written prose, but at least what kind of prose it was. So when I needed to take up the process again, I could start almost fresh, using the vocal range I'd gotten used to in years of asking the waiter in the Greek restaurant for an extra anchovy on my salad, congratulating the puppy on making a puddle outside rather than inside the patio door, pondering with my daughter the vagaries of female orgasm, saying goodbye to my husband, and hello, and goodbye, and hello. This new voice—thoughtful, affectionate, often amused—was essential because what I needed to write about when I returned to prose was an attempt I'd made not long before to kill myself, and suicide simply refuses to be spoken of authentically in high-flown romantic language. It's too ugly. Too shameful. Too strictly a bodily event. And, yes, too funny as well, though people are sometimes shocked to find humor shoved up against suicide. They don't like the incongruity. But let's face it, life (real life, I mean, not the edited-for-television version) is a cacophonous affair from start to finish. I might have wanted to portray my suicidal self as a languishing maiden, too exquisitely sensitive to sustain life's wounding pressures on her soul. (I didn't want to, as a matter of fact, but I might have.) The truth remained, regardless of my desires, that when my husband lugged me into the emergency room, my hair matted, my face swollen and gray, my nightgown streaked with blood and urine, I was no frail and tender spirit. I was a body, and one in a hell of a mess.

I "should" have kept quiet about that experience. I know the rules of polite discourse. I should have kept my shame, and the nearly lethal sense of isolation and alienation it brought, to myself. And I might have, except for something the psychiatrist in the emergency room had told my husband. "You might as well take her home," he said. "If she wants to kill herself, she'll do it no matter how many precautions we take. They always do." *They* always do. I was one of "them," whoever they were. I was, in this context anyway, not singular, not aberrant, but typical. I think it was this sense of commonality with others I didn't even know, a sense of being returned somehow, in spite of my appalling act, to the human family, that urged me to write that first essay, not merely speaking out but calling out, perhaps. "Here's the way I am," it said. "How about you?" And the answer came, as I've said: "Me too! Me too!"

This has been the kind of work I've continued to do: to scrutinize the details of my own experience and to report what I see, and what I think about what I see, as lucidly and accurately as possible. But because feminine experience has been immemorially devalued and repressed, I continue to find this task terrifying. "Every woman has known the torture of beginning to speak aloud," Cixous writes, "heart beating as if to break, occasionally falling into loss of language, ground and language slipping out from under her, because for woman speaking—even just opening her mouth—in public is something rash, a transgression" (p. 92).

The voice I summon up wants to crack, to whisper, to trail back into silence. "I'm sorry to have nothing more than this to say," it wants to apologize. "I shouldn't be taking up your time. I've never fought in a war, or even in a schoolyard free-for-all. I've never tried to see who could piss farthest up the barn wall. I've never even been to a whorehouse. All the important formative experiences have passed me by. I was raped once. I've borne two children. Milk trickling out of my breasts, blood trickling from between my legs. You don't want to hear about it. Sometimes I'm too scared to leave my house. Not scared *of* anything, just scared: mouth dry, bowels writhing. When the fear got really bad, they locked me up for six months, but that was years ago. I'm getting old now. Misshapen, too. I don't blame you if you can't get it up. No one could possibly desire a body like this. It's not your fault. It's mine. Forgive me. I didn't mean to start crying. I'm sorry…sorry…sorry…."

An easy solace to the anxiety of speaking aloud: this slow subsidence beneath the waves of shame, back into what Cixous calls "this body that has been worse than confiscated, a body replaced with a disturbing stranger, sick or dead, who so often is a bad influence, the cause and place of inhibitions. By censuring the body," she goes on, "breath and speech are censored at the same time" (p. 97). But I am not going back, not going under one more time. To do so would demonstrate a failure of nerve far worse than the depredations of MS have caused. Paradoxically, losing one sort of nerve has given me another. No one is going to take my breath away. No one is going to leave me speechless. To be silent is to comply with the standard of feminine grace. But my crippled body already violates all notions of feminine grace. What more have I got to lose? I've gone beyond shame. I'm shameless, you might say. You know, as in "shameless hussy?" A woman with her bare brace and her tongue hanging out.

I've "found" my voice, then, just where it ought to have been, in the body-warmed breath escaping my lungs and throat. Forced by the exigencies of physical disease to embrace my self in the flesh, I couldn't write bodiless prose. The voice is the creature of the body that produces it. I speak as a crippled woman. At the same time, in the utterance I redeem both "cripple" and "woman" from the shameful silences by which I have often felt surrounded, contained, set apart; I give myself permission to live openly among others, to reach out for them, stroke them with fingers and sighs. No body, no voice; no voice, no body. That's what I know in my bones.

NOTES

1. In *The Newly Born Woman*, translated by Betsy Wing (Minneapolis: University of Minnesota Press, 1986).

Letters to My Father

Sally Smits

Dear Dad,

This could be the hardest letter to write, to try to explain last year, because I can't narrow it down or summarize, and I can't make the hurt vanish or heal immediately, and I still don't have simple answers or conclusions, even after reading so many books and writing so many pages and turning it over and over in my mind.

I'm afraid that I'll make it hurt more. I'm afraid I'll fumble through these explanations and the whole of it will be muddier and murkier than when I started. I'm afraid that you'll still blame yourself, or look for reasons there, I'm afraid that I won't be able to show every contribution and cause, or that I won't find any that make sense as I look back. So take this letter for what it's worth, and please know that I'm a tremendously lucky daughter to have had you and Mom there, hands placed gently on my quaking shoulders, through the long struggle back from my eating disorder. I know, as overused as this phrase is, that I couldn't have made it without you both. And I wish I could change it, fix it, now, though maybe I had to learn this way and learn this much about myself.

If I had the year to begin again, or if I had just a few days from August back again, then I would pull my small, scared self into a tight hug, as you and Mom would have done if I hadn't been in the tiny, far-away town of Holland, Michigan. I'd tell my self: if I could prevent you from tripping into this strange trap, I would. If I could hold you and cover your ears from the subtle, cruel whispers, if I could close your eyes from the constant, flashing images, and if I could draw out your voice from your mouth so that you'd never stop hearing the value and strength that lives in you, needing to he spoken, I would.

But maybe, to explain it now, since I can't change or fix the past year, I can tell you what happened, that I lost myself or hid myself that I lost that feeling that something was wrong with "the way things were," and instead believed that there was something wrong with the way that I was. Maybe the only thing I can tell you is that college can be so hard, and as I lost confidence in my own voice, I had to speak in other, painful ways. As happens to so many women, I took out all the frustrations and fears on my body, making it speak in breaking, silent, hurting words.

As you dropped me off for college, and I stood under a gray sky in a half-empty parking lot, watching the back bumper of our car disappear without me in the backseat, I did feel alone and small and terrified. I sat on a cement curb, my face hidden between my knees, and cried. I did feel lost, overwhelmed by the choices and dark, uncertain waters ahead, and I wasn't sure if I could control any of it. But it wasn't the fact that you had to leave or a lack of strength or love from you that started the spiral of anorexia. I had started slipping, invisibly, before that day. Looking back, healthier and more understanding now, I don't know that anything could have changed unless it had changed inside me first, before I lost faith in myself, before I tried to regain it in a different, pain-filled way.

Now, after going through that year of tangle and fear, and after coming out of it again, I'm much more aware of the danger that's all around women today. I watch carefully the magazine covers, the television shows, the music videos, the advertisements, and I see now the destruction they can perpetuate and reinforce. It seems to me, the more I look at them, the woman we have idealized/idolized today is so close to an impossibility that we need computers, electronics, technology, and stupidity to create her. You, too, have told me this, and you've uncovered and pointed out the lies that speak through some of the advertisements. You won't let these "ideal," constructed women just slide past my eyes, and you stop me before I accept them as normal or the only way to be beautiful. You have told me, too, that if anyone loves me, it won't be because my hipbones are jutting out above the rim of my jeans or because my cheeks are angular or because I slide into a size five instead of a seven or nine.

You deconstruct the "model woman" before I let her become the way I think I ought to be constructed. I'm careful now. I'm paying attention. And this "model woman" comes, I think, in two forms: the sharp-angled, stick-figure, or the voluptuous, curved-and-spilling beauty.

The first, vanishing-thin, somehow constitutes beauty by appearing waif-like, emaciated, spindly. She might be too weak for wind, eyes sunken and rimmed in black, cheeks hollowed and caving in. She must necessarily sacrifice health for beauty, life for fleeting years. She must subsist on lettuce (no dressing, please), caffeine, and apples. The image is starving, painful; it is wearing a skeleton on the outside. It is also dangerous—at this stage of the game, most women lose hair, chip off fingernails, deplete bone structure from lack of protein and fat. Their skin dries out despite bottles of lotion, their bodies shiver and require thick sweaters when the temperature drops below sixty degrees, their regular menstrual cycle disappears, and they can kill off years of their lives without the nutrients they require. And in this country and culture, we put this woman/waif on a pedestal.

So then, there is the other rare and near-impossible woman—she has a thin face with slightly hollowed cheeks, long and never-ending legs that get longer with five-inch heels, a figure that was molded by either steel corsets or an unforgiving hourglass, and a chest that, for most women, would be augmented by inserts, cup-pushers, or wonderbras. Beneath that double-D chest, though, her waist is sliced away to twenty-six, maybe twenty-four inches. She might be two stacked triangles, point to point.

And these two "models," replicas, constructed bodies, are women? I hesitate to say that every woman in one of these two categories is a fake, or a harm to herself, and I know that some women naturally grow up like these paper-doll cover girls. But to set them up as the high-metabolic or corset-perfect ideals, or as the only possible way to look, is unhealthy and unaccepting of so many others. For me, I have to refuse the waif; resist the hourglass. I will take on and take in myself—balanced and whole and shaped as I am. I am not an impossibility any longer, nor am I dangerous to my own health. I am becoming and learning what it is to be a real woman, outside and inside, substantial and strong.

Still, it's not enough to say that I simply gave in to these painted ideals. I know that it was more than culture, more than images and models and plastic Barbie dolls. They were certainly dangerous reinforcements and justifications, helping me along in believing that the airbrushed model was not only possible, she was beautiful and perfect and the way I ought to be.

But being "thin" meant so many things, so many paradoxical, tangled things. It meant finding a slot to fit, an acceptance; it meant vanishing, not being noticed. It meant perfection: the perfect girlfriend/daughter/student/sister/

friend—good enough to live up to standard; it meant becoming small, to find the care and love and wrapping arms that had been there when I was little; it meant grasping a small thread of control over my suddenly overwhelming and chaotic year in college. I've realized, too, as I resonate with authors like Carol Lakey Hess, that it was a way to say that I needed independence, needed to stand alone, needed to be a firm and strong woman, though I couldn't find a way to do that and not hurt anyone in the process of becoming.

And it was a giving, giving, pouring out of myself, never taking, although it never felt like enough. By not eating, by excessive exercise, by denying all food and so denying self, anorexia becomes the metaphor for self-sacrifice, for putting everything ahead of your own needs, ahead of nurturing and taking care of self. In the beginning, it is connected to the guilt and fear that you're failing and letting others down, that you're never meeting their standards or needs or expectations. Some people have defined anorexia as a self-absorbed disease, a focus on self and image. But I don't think that gets to the core of it, the truth of it, because I didn't re-shape and cut away for myself, but for other people. It's most often the people-pleasers and perfectionists that find themselves shrinking away and vanishing because they've given themselves up. Or they've given up on themselves. And self-sacrifice is demanded by anorexia. I know that it was not you who demanded it. Your expectations and standards were not the ones that I was trying to fill, though for a while I believed they were. What I know now is that the standards were ones that I set up, and though they might have been ridiculous or unattainable, I still believed that anything short of them would be failing. I know that you love me, and you didn't expect a solid 4.0 or leadership positions or awards and honors. If you had asked me, straightforward, to explain why I thought I should have these things and still shape a "perfect" body on the side, (though it became center), I would not have been able to explain. It wasn't you that put me to this; it wasn't Mom. Neither of you asked me to give so much, and I know you didn't doubt me. And I know you weren't disappointed in me for anything that I might have called a failure.

And in this giving, this ever-slimming, I was still trying to get in someone's way. I needed someone to notice. I needed, by becoming smaller, to take up more space. Maybe it was resisting change, maybe it was shaking everyone around me to see the changes I'd made, maybe it was a constantly posed question to ask everyone, "Is this what you want, is this who I should be, is this what's required?" And gradually, it became something more—the obsession of assurance and reassurance, that it would be okay if I could just skip breakfast, eat less tonight and tomorrow, eat half, then a quarter, then nothing. And it came to mean more—it was my separated independence. Sometimes, while I was home over breaks, in the safest place, I would long to get back to school, the most off-kilter place, simply to be away from everyone else's control and shoving of food under my nose and onto my plate. In some ways, it was a weakening, a spiraling out of control; in others, it was a strengthening and a "will-to-power" over myself, an extreme self-denial/self/loathing/self-empowerrnent, a personal ritual, a silent assertion.

Anorexia was my personal, carefully guarded paradox. It was not something that could be easily untangled or solved, and only with a tight grip on life, a long learning and rediscovery of love and welcome, and a healing of old fears and doubts could I release it or somehow loosen its grip on me. You and Mom, the two people I call my "secondary therapists," were two of the most important people to stop the fears and downward spiral and help me begin the long climb back up to wholeness, to strength and taking care of myself again. You did notice, and helped me look honestly in the mirror. You both sat with me through tears and apologies, through waves of guilt and the times that I would fold up into myself through the small discoveries and victories and moments of freedom. You waited for me to heal, but more importantly, you waited with me and never let me go through it alone. I still don't understand everything that happened, the process or the pain, and I really can't say why. All I know was that I needed to learn to value myself again, to know that I was giving enough, doing enough, that I was enough, and that I could live fully.

When I had to leave home again after that summer of healing and recovery, I didn't know what would happen as I stood on my own again. Away from the place where I knew love and patience, how could I live and give myself those same gifts? Not that there was complete separation or loss, but there was distance, and there was fear.

That's when I took the class Christian Feminism, and I learned from that theory and philosophy and thought process that it had applications in my own life, and that I had worth as a human being, that I was worth saving. It was like hearing echoes of what you and Mom had told me so often, every Tuesday and Thursday at 9:30.

Maybe one of the most important pieces of that course for me, was the sudden opening of my eyes that I was not the only one who had felt lost or at fault for everything, and I was not the only one who had lost her voice and then scrambled to regain it. And I could finally find that feeling again, that intuition that told me something outside of me was awry and skewed in the world. It wasn't only my flaws and faults that would let people down, and knowing this, I could reclaim my own value, no matter how much I had thought I wasn't worth it before.

This course gave me the sudden knowledge, too, that I am not alone in a strong stance, nor in fighting, wavering, and then pushing ahead again. I am not standing isolated when I begin to believe in women, in myself. I am breaking new ground for myself, but some foundations have already been laid.

Before this course, I hesitated and faltered at the word "feminist" because of it's burning and biting connotations. But now, I see feminism as a return to myself. It is not a removal from who I am; instead, it is a reinforcement. It is a support and also a challenge to remain true to the person, the woman, who is now surfacing. This woman is one you've believed in all along, I think, and now I'm ready to listen and accept. I'm trying, at least. Thanks for your patience, for waiting and holding on, for not letting go even when I tried to peel off your fingers. And thanks for letting go just enough so that I could learn this on my own.

Sally

Writing Like a Mennonite

Julia Kasdorf

Others were tortured, refusing to accept release, in order to obtain a better resurrection. Others suffered mocking and flogging, and even chains and imprisonment. They were stoned to death, they were sawn in two, they were killed by the sword; they went about in skins of sheep and goats, destitute, persecuted, tormented—of whom the world was not worthy. They wandered in deserts and mountains, and in caves and holes in the ground.

Hebrews 11:35—38 (NRSV Inclusive Version)

LONG AGO SOMEONE CALLED MENNONITES *die Stillen im Lande* (the quiet in the land), a phrase that conveys the sense of a silent and defenseless community set against a noisy, violent world—and, at least for some, the name stuck. The phrase probably comes from Psalm 35:20, which is a complaint against an articulate enemy who uses language to persecute voiceless pacifists: "For they do not speak peace, but they conceive deceitful words against those who are quiet in the land" (NRSV). Until the traditional Anabaptist principles of nonresistance and community led some Mennonite people to become engaged with the antiwar and civil rights movements of the 1960s, Mennonites considered silence to be an appropriate attitude toward the wider world and a necessary means of survival in it—whether they inhabited deeply rooted farm communities in Pennsylvania or endured migrations across Europe or between the Americas. This attitude was borne of actual experience: Anabaptist migrant groups in Europe were often allowed to settle in new areas only if they promised not to proselytize or testify to their beliefs. They could live on the land as long as they remained

259

quiet. In early America, a similar habit persisted.

Silence and seclusion became a strategy of living peaceably with the wider world as well as a means of keeping peace within the community. In the Pennsylvania Amish-Mennonite ethos I know, seductive and eloquent discourse was distrusted and considered a possible form of coercion. The choices a person made in daily life wrote the text that mattered most. Conflicts in family or community seemed to be smothered in silence, and because disturbing or minority views were rarely expressed in public, they could exist in their own quiet space on the margins, a kind of "don't ask, don't tell" policy for differences of many kinds. If deviant members refused to keep quiet, conflict could be fractious and bitter. In *Disquiet in the Land: Cultural Conflict in American Mennonite Communities,* Fred Kniss catalogues 208 examples of quarrels over issues ranging from the implementation of Sunday schools and participation in military service, to dress and language use in Mennonite Church communities in four eastern states between 1870 and 1985.[1] He concludes that conflicts often spring from two competing impulses in Mennonite life and thought: traditionalism, with its emphasis on moral, biblical, and collective authority; and communalism, expressed by pacifism, concern for justice, congregationalism, and mutual aid. A vivid example of this tension can be seen in current debates about how to respond to churches that openly accept gay and lesbian members: traditionalists opt for expulsion and excommunication, while some communalists argue for dialogue or even inclusion. Whereas schism can tear a community limb from limb and leave lasting scars for decades, at least it provides a means for both groups of people to disagree and still retain their sense of belonging to a fragment of the original community. For an individual, the cost of articulating a dissenting view is much greater. Rather than stir up trouble, draw unnecessary attention to themselves, or risk ostracism, individuals—especially if they were women— have often chosen to keep their most troubling thoughts to themselves.

I have another, more visceral sense of silence. I am still a child—at seven, at ten, and at fifteen—walking home from the school bus. The kindly grandfather figure of the neighborhood waves to me as he does every day, that gesture not so much a greeting as a way to lure me to his porch. Most days I resist, wave sweetly, and keep walking up the hill toward home as if I do not understand his desire. I am torn between not wanting to visit him and wanting to be good and obedient to a grown-up whom my family respects. So other days I comply, as I do this day. He leads me through the screen door to steps that descend to the cellar, where he will show me an elaborate miniature railroad set up for Christmas or a lathe where he turns wooden candleholders or the workbench where he grows seedlings each spring. Then he will pin me against a wall and stab his tongue against my teeth, which will be clenched tight, as I try to breathe. His tongue will taste sweet from chewing tobacco; his breath will heave as he presses his body against mine. I will never open my mouth to speak or scream, because I think that if I open my mouth his tongue will shoot down my throat like a snake.

Experience comes to a child simply, literally; only much later does it burst on me as a metaphor that has structured my thought and influenced my perceptions all these years. Now I wonder whether my quiet ancestors kept their mouths clamped shut for fear that another's tongue would plunge down their throats. Is this why the shift from oral German dialects to English or Russian or Spanish or Portuguese has always been so painful in Mennonite communities and families? I wonder if a memory of trauma and fear of violation has kept Mennonites from producing imaginative literature until recently, even though they have been living in literate and safely landed communities in America since colonial times. John Ruth has recounted many other reasons for our failure to write in times past: a legacy of iconoclasm from the Radical Reformation, a distrust of the assimilating influence of education and high culture, a devaluation of the individual voice in the service of the collective religious community, a deep commitment to facts and plain speech, and the folk culture's underlying values of practicality, hard work, and thrift.[2] Nevertheless, as plain dress, a strange dialect, and the geographical separation of valleys or remote prairie villages have delineated safety zones for vulnerable Mennonite bodies in times past, so the absence of literary activity has hidden Mennonite hearts and minds from the curious gaze of others. In the absence of published fiction and poetry, outsiders have no access to the experience and imagination of the community. Perhaps the refusal of previous generations to publish imaginative work was another kind of cultural resistance, borne of distrust and of a fear that literature would somehow expose the interior life of the community—or of the individual— and thereby make them vulnerable to violation.

When the man was done, I would let his wood-framed cellar door slam shut and walk home through the backyards, thinking, "Well, that was not so bad. It was only my body." I think that the martyr stories taught me that wonderful splintering trick: it is only the body. In one of my favorite engravings, it is only the body of Anneken Hendriks tied to a ladder that forever tips headfirst into a fire of the Spanish Inquisition, her hands pressed together in prayer. In another story, Maeyken Wens knows it is only a body that her children will miss after she burns at the stake, her tongue clamped so that she cannot speak. "Fear not them which kill the body," it says in Maeyken's section of the *Martyrs' Mirror,* paraphrasing Matthew 10:28: "And fear not them which kill the body but are not able to kill the soul; but rather fear him which is able to destroy both soul and body in hell."[3] They can burn the body but not the soul. You may gaze at my body, even touch it if you must, but you will not know my soul: my essential self exists safely apart from my body and from you. Therapists call this splintering of consciousness *dissociation* and count it among the common psychological strategies employed by those who survive physical trauma.

Once, after a reading I gave from *Eve's Striptease,* a tall, distinguished-looking woman with silvery hair approached me and simply said, "I had an experience like yours, but I do not speak of it. I stand on my silence." And she seemed to have found solid ground to stand on. Rather than endure the feelings of violation that invariably accompany revelation of childhood sexual mistreatment, she chose to keep a dignified silence. Although sometimes mistaken for compliance, the refusal to speak in defense of oneself can be a fierce form of resistance, as when Jesus refused to speak before Pilot or when he hung on the cross and "opened not his mouth...as a sheep before her shearers is dumb" (Isaiah 53:7). Certainly this stance has helped to consolidate identity and has served as a means of resistance for Mennonites; silence is a worthy weapon for a pacifist body that carries memories of physical violation. Following the literal teachings of Jesus, Mennonites have refused for centuries to defend themselves with any sort of visible force—including the force of language in legal courts. [...]

A poem included in [my] first collection revealed to my family for the first time what had occurred in the home of that elderly neighbor man. My parents' concern about raising us away from the traditional community had been soothed by kind neighbors like him—a Mason, not a Mennonite, yet every bit as generous and kind to my brothers and me as a grandfather might have been. For two decades my silence had protected them and also had protected him. Growing up, I had simply absorbed his assault on my spirit and body and had hidden my knowledge away in some secret place. I wanted to disturb no one. Perhaps even then I sensed that, for my parents, the choice to raise children away from their community of origin was a risk. My silence supported their hope that life is more complex than the dualism that would divide experience between the safety of the sect and the danger of the world. Indeed, within that one man I knew both kindness and coercion, a contradiction that to this day I cannot explain and must simply accept. Several times in college I had tried to write about it—once as a poem, once as a narrative sketch—but both pieces remained undeveloped. It was not until the summer I was twenty-six, at the MacDowell artists' colony in New Hampshire for the first time, that I wrote "The Interesting Thing," a poem I included in my book.

To bring this kind of information to light, even in writing, is never simple. When an ancient violation is finally named, people are at a loss about what to do: what to remember and what to forget, whether there is any way to make amends, or whether retribution will only continue a cycle of violation. It is difficult to know what brings healing and justice. At the personal level, these questions are complex. At the local and national level, I see them everywhere as my mind's eye moves down the cities of the Eastern Seaboard to the American South, from Haiti to South America, across the ocean to Western Europe and the former Soviet Union and the Balkans, down the coast and around the cape of South Africa, up to the Middle East and across the subcontinent of India and Pakistan, across Burma to Cambodia, Vietnam, and the People's Republic of China. If it is impossible to correct the horrible things that people have done to one another, then why even try? Consider the recent Japanese apology to Korean women pressed into prostitution during World War II or the rehabilitation of the victims of the 1692 Salem witch trials in New England. Do these gestures offer any critique of history's cruel cycles of violence? Do they prevent future abuses? Yet the cost of not remembering and telling those stories—at least for me—is the unconscious repetition of violence, on the self and onto others. [...]

That trauma can both confine one to silence and compel one to find articulation is clear in the brief history of Mennonite literature. Apart from some devotional books, the first, and by far most important work by Mennonite authors is *The Bloody Theater or Martyrs' Mirror of the Defenseless Christians Who Baptized Only Upon Confession of Faith, and Who Suffered and Died for the Testimony of Jesus, Their Savior, from the Time of Christ to the Year A.D. 1660*. First published in 1660 in an edition of 1,000 copies, this enormous book contains texts composed by or about individuals enduring torture, on trial, or awaiting execution. Commonly called only *Martyrs' Mirror,* the book's full title is useful for the way it defines the words *Anabaptist*—a Christian pacifist who practices adult baptism—and *martyr*— one who dies testifying for beliefs. Elsewhere much has been made of the way this title underlines the spectacle of martyrdom, which unfolded in public, according to a civil and religious script.[4] Yet the word which interests me most is *testimony.*

In cases where court records are preserved, the "testimony" of the martyrs in this book is quite literal. Yet all of the 4,011 "died for the testimony of Jesus." In some cases, their testimony is preserved in letters and verse written to relatives and fellow believers. For illiterate people, martyrdom itself became a kind of writing with the body, because the martyrs' words and actions were converted into textual form as a consequence of the physical ordeals they chose to endure. For Anabaptist sisters, martyrdom represented a choice to enact the ultimate sacrifice that placed them on equal ground with their brethren. A third or more of the sixteenth-century martyrs were women, and in some regions during the worst periods of persecution, as many as four in ten of the martyrs were female.[5] For instance, Annekin Hendriks is described in *Martyrs' Mirror* as Anneken de Vlaster, a housewife from Frisia who could neither read nor write. Yet her dramatic death in Amsterdam in October of 1571 ensured that her words were inscribed forever. The fifty-three-year-old woman, who probably worked as a linen weaver, was so loud and verbal about her faith that the authorities stuffed her mouth with gunpowder to keep her from giving "good witness" to spectators at her execution. The account does not say whether her skull mercifully exploded when her ladder-bound body fell into the flames, but we know that she did not silently store her convictions there. Her words and courage inspired Dutch Mennonites to write a hymn that narrates her execution. In addition, fifty-three hymn texts were written by imprisoned Anabaptists awaiting execution and preserved in the *Ausbund,* a 1564 worship book still used by the Amish.

Even after the Anabaptist era, trauma continued to be a means of articulation and inscription at those times when it did not silence the community altogether. Whereas the Mennonites and Amish who migrated to America during the colonial period published next to no literature for a broader audience until well after World War II, those who had migrated to colonies in Russia during the eighteenth century did publish, but mostly after their communities were destroyed. "The tragic upheaval of war and revolution and the destruction of the Mennonite commonwealth in Russia shocked the Mennonite literary imagination into life as nothing had since the age of martyrdom," observed Al Reimer in a 1993 survey of North American Mennonite writing.[6] During the 1920s and 1930s, a few émigré authors, mostly located in the Canadian West, tried to make sense of that traumatic loss by writing and publishing literature, often in *Plautdietsch,* the German-based mother tongue of their Russian childhoods. Like other literatures of loss—Isaac Bashevis Singer's Yiddish novels come to mind—this work preserved the memory of an ethnic homeland, often portrayed as Edenic.

In these literary efforts, and through countless oral repetitions of violence and dislocation narratives that are still repeated in Mennonite communities, I see spontaneous attempts by individuals to heal the consequences of trauma. From the time of Freud's first work with hysterics, and from early research into shell-shock, the inability to speak has been associated with trauma. Almost from the start, doctors believed that the physioneurosis caused by terror could be reversed with words. It seems that while normal memory exists in narrative structures, the memories of trauma lack context or language and persist only as vivid sensations or images. If these memories and feelings can be articulated and shaped into narrative form, they can thereby be integrated into the rest of a life's experience. A 1992 study by Harvard physician Judith Herman links research into private traumas such as domestic violence and public traumas such as terrorism. Herman relates current work with torture survivors in Chile, where therapists have helped victims to write detailed narrative accounts of their mistreatment and then to relive the experiences by speaking them within a supportive community. "The action of telling a story in the safety of a protected relationship can actually produce a change in the abnormal processing of the traumatic memory," she writes.[7] I wonder whether *Martyrs' Mirror* has sometimes served this purpose at a collective level, for it seems that the book was most often printed in conjunction with an impending war, the need for stories felt most keenly in relation to the community's fresh fears of persecution.

It would also follow that in those times when the community has refused to hear traumatic stories, it has hindered healing. I think of the Mennonites who remained in Soviet Russia after the 1920s migrations and who therefore faced the brutalities of Stalin's regime: collectivization, cultural and religious repression, and the systematic deportation or execution of most able-bodied men. By 1941, the invasion of the German army enabled these Mennonite villages, dominated by women then, to open their churches and conduct school in their own language. For a time, the occupying troops took Mennonite women to be their translators, assistants, and mistresses. When the German army began to retreat in 1943, German-speaking people followed the army in a trek toward Germany, certain they would be killed if they did not stay ahead of advancing Russian troops. A number of these women— some with children, some widowed, some separated from husbands who had been deported to labor camps—emigrated to Mennonite communities in Canada. Although many of these women were eventually integrated into the Canadian communities, they were not warmly received on their arrival after the war. Because of their dubious marital status, many were denied membership in Mennonite churches, and no one wanted to listen to their stories of violence, combat, sexual assault, or impropriety. A desire for peace and purity prevented the community from helping these women to heal, their trauma compounded by abandonment and isolation in an era when common wisdom advised survivors to forget the past and count their blessings. Even now, as full members of the community, most of these women have chosen not to speak about their experiences of war or their initial encounters with Canadian Mennonites.

In 1994 Pamela Klassen published a powerful ethnographic study based on the stories of two of these women.[8] Oddly enough, I first read this book while waiting to be called for jury duty, sitting on a mahogany pew in the massive main hail of Brooklyn's criminal court. I was so moved by the tragedy of the women's experience and Klassen's skillful analysis that I wept, my body curled over the paperback, in the din of that chaotic public space. When my name was called to sit for a lawsuit, I told the attorneys that I come from a Mennonite background, and they dismissed me from the case immediately, knowing of the sect's reputation for being nonlitigious, noncooperative, and apart from civil society. [...]

I have begun to question the disturbing consequences of this martyr identity, however, with the assistance of Lois Frey, a Mennonite-turned-Quaker therapist who has studied creativity and trauma for more than twenty years. She believes that trauma either destroys creativity by making a child too afraid to risk new experiences; or, if it is not so overwhelming, trauma may enable a child to grow, both in strength and in creativity, through the various ways she finds of mastering her injury. Frey wonders what causes a child to turn in either of these opposite directions, and a few years ago she turned her attention to Mennonites, whom she believes have inherited "encapsulated trauma." Symptoms of this inheritance that she recognizes in the Mennonite culture of her childhood include splitting of the self, impaired capacity for fantasy and symbolization, literal and concrete thinking, defensive occupation with the mundane, and memory behaviors that tend to repeat the trauma. The response to a memory of trauma is the curtailing of creativity and a self-protective and fearful refusal to take risks. Cautious behaviors that once protected endangered beings thereby "retraumatize" them.

One aspect of the Mennonite inheritance Frey has named the "persecutor/ martyr introject." *Introjection* is a process whereby things from the world— actual persecutors and martyrs, for instance—become embedded in the unconscious as a pattern of behavior persisting for generations. Among Mennonites, Frey believes, a collective history of victimization, social ostracism, and persecution has written a persecutor/martyr script that gets replayed within the community or within a family every time an individual is censored or marginalized. To break beyond the victim/perpetrator introject, one must integrate both identities within the self. Confronting experience through the production of art is one means of escaping the scripted, narrow roles of victim and perpetrator. Moreover, an artwork's ability to express ambiguity and paradox enables an individual to recognize that she is capable of playing both roles. The production of artistic works thus enables a person to integrate the opposite identities into a whole and complex personality capable of confident, public expression.[9]

In many respects, I agree with Frey's assertions, but I am uneasy about the large claims they make for artistic work. It may appear in her public performance that the poet has become confident and capable; the voice in the poem or on stage seems to have mastered the injury—at once immersed in it and in control of it. Louise Glück brilliantly recounts this apparent "revenge on circumstance": "For a brief period, the natural arrangement is reversed: the artist no longer acted upon but acting; the last word, for the moment, seized back from fate or chance. Control of the past: as though the dead martyrs were to stand up in the arena and say, 'Suppose, on the other hand...' No process I can name so completely defeats the authority of event."[10]

Of course, this triumphal moment exists only within the process of writing and within the written text. This is because writing enables the author to transcend the limits of her body and to evade the demands that others may place upon her. A written text cannot be made to change in response to others; it does not fail to speak out of fear, nor can it alter in response to the loving attention of a reader. Moreover, it exists in a time and in a space quite apart from the body of its author. Unbeknownst to me, you read this book, for instance; even after my death, it will exist. Although much is made of the "writer's voice," text is not speech. In fact, as the ultimate disconnection from the life world, the ultimate dissociation, writing may be the most brilliant splintering trick of all. It has taken me some time to grasp the fact that, in this way, my cure has also been my curse.

This split is another way that writing may be bound to violence. In order to write, an author gives up her conversations with the world, withdrawing for a time from the company of those she loves and from the pleasures and pains of living. French novelist, playwright, and mother Hélène Cixous admits, "Between the writer and his or her family the question is always one of departing while remaining present, of being absent while in full presence, of escaping, of abandon. It is both utterly banal and the thing we don't want to know or say. A writer has no children; I have no children when I write."[11]

I think of Maeyken Wens, most disturbing to me of the Anabaptist martyrs because her story glorifies a choice to abandon her children rather than recant. Could she not have practiced some form of the splintering trick: comply with the authorities yet still believe whatever she wanted in silence, for the sake of her sons? As much as I want to argue for the heroic voice, I also regret her choice, unable to imagine what it must have meant in her time. Maeyken Wens's letters to her family are preserved in the *Martyrs' Mirror* but most startling is the written narrative of fifteen-year-old Adriaen. Standing with three-year-old Hans on his arm to witness their mother's execution, Adriaen fainted and only revived when the fire had burned to a smoking heap. Searching the coals of his mother's execution fire, Adriaen found the contraption made of two blades that were screwed together to secure her tongue. Today this relic remains in the possession of Dutch Mennonites in Amsterdam, a phallic-shaped symbol of brutal force and silence, which, like the cross, is transformed by tradition into a beloved emblem of sacrifice and witness. The engraving in *Martyrs' Mirror* shows, not the martyr Maeyken, but an almost comical view of Adriaen's broad behind as he reaches for the tongue screw in the smoldering coals, while Hans, still wearing a baby's dress, looks on.

In an essay about the staggering numbers of Christian martyrs who, during the twentieth century, suffered under regimes on all points of the political spectrum, poet Dana Gioia reveals an etymological fact that I find very interesting. Historically, the word *martyr* carries no trace of suffering or death. Its root means only "witness"—witness to a truth. "The martyr's task is not armed resistance; nor is it even passive suffering," Gioia writes. "Persecution and death are only the by-products of the martyr's true role—to witness the truth uncompromised."[12]

For many people, the deathbed is the only place where they finally can bear to reveal the truths they have silently carried all of their lives. Facing death, they are finally free to speak with the clarity of those Anabaptist martyrs who gave "good witness" when facing the flames of an executioner's fire. Hélène Cixous identifies death—or an awareness of mortality—as the first rung on the ladder of writing.[13] This is the ladder, tipping toward the fire, on which Anneken Hendriks was bound. The author must lean into the scorching truth of her own mortality in order to write. She must write the book that threatens to cost her her life.

The implications of the martyr's example are absolute: one must bear witness to the only truth one sees. It is a matter of consequence that the word *witness* means not only "to see," but also "to speak." To write like a martyr means, not to choose death, but to choose to bear life-giving witness, to communicate the truth of one's own vision or insight, to affirm its value with confidence, no matter how arrogant or disturbing it may be, "and the truth shall make you free" (John 8:32). When my poem about the old neighbor was finally published, it shattered my family's perceptions of a person whom they had known to be only benevolent and generous. That is a violent act. No wonder the one who disturbs a perceived truth is felt to be an aggressor.

I also know that, by speaking of that molestation, I risk becoming defined and marked by its shame. But how different is that experience from any unfortunate thing that happens to a child on her way to becoming an adult? It may be no different, except in the scope of its consequences, from what happened to me at the age of twelve, while hiking a mountain trail at church camp, when a copperhead bite transformed me from a child who could catch garter snakes with her brothers into a child with recurring nightmares of a floor so thick with serpents that it undulated; of copperheads so smart they could read my mind, which was plotting an escape; of snakes that turned and attacked when I opened my mouth to cry for help and no sound came out. Even now, terror rushes through my body whenever a snake flashes on the television screen or I see a patch of snake skin slither under the leaves in my garden. Metaphoric associations aside, does the snake bite brand me in the eyes of my readers any less than the touch of an old man? Or does everything always and only collapse into the shapes of familiar narrative plots?

~

As a community carries memories of trauma, so does an individual's body, often accompanied by deep and contradictory desires to deny and declare the pain.[14] As a little girl, I found in the martyr stories a way to survive: It is only my body you can touch. The split between body and spirit that I learned in such a visceral way exactly parallels the split between experience and words that developed centuries ago with the technology of writing. The disembodied medium of letters has enabled me to loosen from my body's recesses those old wounds, to re-create them on a page, and, eventually, to speak. Yet whatever I learned from my own texts, whatever I am able to say there, is only partial if I cannot also speak with others. "Writing is the only cure," an old maxim says, and I used to believe this, until I realized that writing was only part of a long training for the day when I would be able to talk. I bore on my body a violence until I could write; I bore witness in writing until I could speak.

Among the few material objects I have from that old neighbor man is a huge 1927 unabridged dictionary with elaborate Art Deco ornaments on its spine. On the title page are these words, inscribed in his inky cursive:

This book is my pride and joy
Presented to Julia Spicher
Dec. 6, 1980
Remember me.

It was a gift for my seventeenth birthday. By then I had been scribbling in school tablets for years, writing to make sense of the fragmented and silent parts of my life, removing language from my own body and inscribing it on that safe, quiet space of the page, where I could assemble and view it again. When he gave me that gift with its heartfelt inscription to remember him, did he assume that I would also remain quiet about the liberties he had taken with my body for a decade? That secret may have been more damaging than the touch of a pedophile's hand for the ways it has gagged my mouth and bound my body, isolating me in silence. Did he think I would fail to remember myself?

The tight-lipped survival strategy of my childhood is no longer useful, and in the martyr stories, I now see, not submission and silence, but men and women who spoke with their words and with their bodies, who refused to hold their tongues or keep the peace. Although I have succumbed to both temptations, I now write not for revenge—following popular tales of victim and monster—nor for redemption—following a Christian, paradigm that is often too swift to be true. Following my perpetrator's advice, I write simply to remember and to bear witness.

The meaning of the word *memory* for me is enriched when I see that its tangled Indo-European roots run through the Latin *memor* (mindful); the Greek *martus* (witness), which became *martyr;* as well as the Germanic and Old English *murnam* (to grieve). We write to bring things in mind, to witness, and eventually, to grieve. Thus, I learn to refuse the abusive one within myself who will always beckon me back into that house. Though I may be tempted to be nice and comply, how can I return to that hushed place, when I would rather stay out on the road, offering myself to conversation and relationship as a martyr offers her body to flames? I must find my own life's pleasures, unable to recant or let some other tongue go down my throat.

CAMP HILL, 2000

NOTES

1. Fred Kniss, *Disquiet in the Land: Cultural Conflict in American Mennonite Communities* (New Brunswick, N.J.: Rutgers University Press, 1997).

2. John Ruth in *Mennonite Identity and Literary Art* (Scottdale, Pa.: Herald Press, 1978) outlines the most obvious traditional resistances to literature among Mennonite peoples, including an amnesia of the oral literature resulting from the language shift from Pennsylvania German to English, and numerous religious and cultural scruples. Since the late 1970s, serious, imaginative literature by Mennonite writers has begun to blossom and has enjoyed both a popular reception and scholarly attention from Mennonite readers.

3. Thieleman J. van Braught, *The Bloody Theater or Martyrs' Mirror...,* trans. Joseph F. Sohm (Scottdale, Pa.: Herald Press, 1977), 982.

4. John S. Oyer and Robert S. Kreider, *The Mirror of the Martyrs* (Intercourse, Pa.: Good Books, 1990), 13.

5. C. Arnold Snyder and Linda A. Huebert Hecht, eds., Introduction to *Profiles of Anabaptist Women* (Kitchener, Ont.: Canadian Corporation for

Studies in Religion/Wilfrid Laurier University Press), 12.

6. Al Reimer, *Mennonite Literary Voices: Past and Present* (North Newton, Kans.: Bethel College Press, 1993), 15.

7. Judith Herman, M.D., *Trauma and Recovery* (New York: Basic Books, 1992), 83.

8. Pamela Klassen, *Going by the Moon and the Stars* (Waterloo, Ontario: Wilfrid Laurier University Press, 1994). See Marlene Epp, *Women Without Men: Mennonite Refugees of the Second World War* (Toronto: University of Toronto Press, 2000).

9. For several years during the early 1990s, Lois conducted a small discussion group of Mennonites who had grown up in conservative homes and who are successful in highly creative vocations. We met a few times a year for a full day at a time to reflect on our memories of the community and on the nature of creativity. Her initial hypothesis in this study was that the experience of being culturally marginal enables persons to function more creatively because they are used to being different and coping with issues of loneliness. Her research was reported in a paper delivered at The Quiet in the Land Conference (Millersville University, 1995) and later published as "Creativity: From Victim to Reconstructor," *Mennonot* 7 (spring 1996); 18-20.

10. Louise Glück, "The Idea of Courage," in *Proofs and Theories* (New York: Ecco Press, 1994), 25.

11. Hélène Cixous, *Three Steps on the Ladder of Writing* (New York: Columbia University Press, 1993), 21.

12 .Dana Gioia, "To Witness the Truth Uncompromised: Reflections on the Modern Martyrs," *Image* 13 (Spring 96): 71-73.

13. Cixous, *Three Steps*, 36-37.

14. "The conflict between the will to deny horrible events and the will to proclaim them aloud is the central dialectic of psychological trauma" (Herman, *Trauma and Recovery*, 1).

God as Mother

Sallie McFague

"FATHER-MOTHER GOD, loving me, guard me while I sleep, guide my little feet up to thee." This prayer, which theologian Herbert Richardson reports reciting as a child, impressed upon his young mind that if God is both father and mother, then God is not like anything else he knew.[1] The point is worth emphasizing, for as we begin our experiment with the model of God as mother, we recall that metaphors of God, far from reducing God to what we understand, underscore by their multiplicity and lack of fit the unknowability of God. This crucial characteristic of metaphorical language for God is lost, however, when only one important personal relationship, that of father and child, is allowed to serve as a grid for speaking of the God-human relationship. In fact, by excluding other relationships as metaphors, the model of father becomes idolatrous, for it comes to be viewed as a description of God.[2] Hence, one reason for including maternal language in a tradition where paternal language has prevailed is to underscore what the negative theological tradition has always insisted: God is unlike as well as like our metaphors.[3]

But there are additional reasons for using female as well as male metaphors of God. The most obvious is that since human beings are male and female, if we seek to imagine God "in the image of God"—that is, ourselves—both male and female metaphors should be employed. Because the point is self-evident, one wonders what all the fuss is about when the suggestion is made that God be imaged in female terms or addressed as "she." But fuss there is, and it is best to address it head on. For whatever reasons, Western thought—certainly Western theology—has been deeply infected by both a fear of and a fascination with female sexuality.[4] The most basic reason, it appears, for uneasiness with female metaphors for God is that unlike the male metaphors, whose sexual character is cloaked, the female metaphors seem blatantly sexual and involve the sexuality most feared: female sexuality.

There are at least three points being made here that need to be addressed briefly. First, to speak of God as father has obvious sexual connotations (as is evident in the trinitarian language of the "generation" of the Son from the Father), but given the Hebraic tradition's interest in distinguishing itself from Goddess religions and fertility cults, as well as the early and deep ascetic strain in Christianity, the sexual implications of paternal imagery were masked. This leads into the second point: the blatant sexuality of female metaphors. It is by introducing female metaphors for God that the sexuality of both male and female metaphors becomes evident, though it appears, because we are familiar with the male metaphors, that only the female ones are sexual. In other words, the shock of unconventional language for God— female imagery—jolts us into awareness that there is no gender-neutral language if we take ourselves as the model for talk about God, because we are sexual beings. Hence, traditional language for God is not nonsexual; on the contrary, it is male. The third point, the fear and fascination associated with female sexuality, is related to the first two points: female sexuality would not, I suspect, be so feared or found so fascinating if sexuality, both female and male, had been accepted in a more open and healthy manner both as a human good and as an important way to model the activity of God in relation to the world.[5] It is treated in this fashion in many religions, and Western thought, including Christianity, with its warped view of female sexuality as well as its reluctance to imagine God in female terms, has much to learn from these sources.

The first thing to insist upon, then, is that in spite of Western and Christian uneasiness over female imagery for God, since the *imago dei* is twofold, female as well as male, both kinds of metaphors ought to be used.[6] The question then arises how God should be imaged as both female and male (as well as, of course, beyond both). I would make two points here: first, God should be imagined in female, not feminine, terms, and second, the female metaphors should be inclusive of but not limited to maternal ones. On the first point: the distinction between "female" and "feminine" is important for the first refers to gender while the second refers to qualities conventionally associated with women.[7] The problem with introducing a feminine dimension of God is that it invariably ends with identifying as female those qualities that society has called feminine. Thus, the feminine side of God is taken to comprise the tender, nurturing, passive, healing aspects of divine activity, whereas those activities in which God creates, redeems, establishes peace, administers justice, and so on, are called masculine. Such a division, in extending to the godhead the stereotypes we create in human society, further crystallizes and sanctifies them.[8]

But to image God in female personal terms, as she as well as he, is a very different matter. It is not, at the outset, to identify God with any particular set of characteristics, unless one is slipping in feminine stereotypes under the cover of simple gender appellation. All that has been done is to use a personal pronoun for deity and this, we have insisted, is not only our tradition, the tradition of addressing God as Thou, but desirable and necessary in our time. Since all agents are either male or female, either pronoun and both pronouns can and should be used. If we use only the male pronoun, we fall into idolatry, forgetting that God is beyond male and female—a fact that the use of both pronouns brings home to us as the opening prayer to "Father-Mother God" illustrated. If we refuse to use any pronouns for God, we court the possibility of concealing androcentric assumptions behind abstractions.[9] If we are, then, to be concrete, personal, and nonidolatrous in our talk about God, we have no alternative but to speak of God in female as well as male terms, to use "she" as well as "he," and to realize that in so doing we are not attributing passive and nurturing qualities to God any more than we are attributing active and powerful qualities. Or to say it differently, we are attributing human qualities: we are imaging God on analogy with human beings, and so far that is all that we are doing: God is she and he and neither.

We come now, however, to the second point: female metaphors for God should be inclusive of but not limited to maternal ones. One of the important insights emerging from current research into Goddess religions is that in these traditions all divine activities are imaged by both male and female deities: both Ishtar and Horus, for instance, engage in creating, governing, nurturing, and redeeming.[10] In other words, neither masculine nor feminine characteristics are attributed to deities; rather, divine activities are attributed equivalently to male and female agents. Both male and female deities operate in both the private and the public arena; both engage in activities of power as well as care.[11] The Hebraic-Christian tradition does not, of course, worship multiple deities, but this fact in no way lessens the point being made—that if we accept the reasoning behind addressing God as "she" as well as "he," we should do so in a fashion that does not stereotype divine activities. This is not a new or radical notion in Christianity, despite the fact that the only female "component" in the tradition has been the quasi-divine figure of Mary, whose characteristics have certainly been stereotypically feminine.[12] But an earlier hypostasis of God—Sophia, or Wisdom, in Hebrew religion— was identified not only with the earth and sexuality but also with order and justice.[13] Moreover, medieval piety freely attributed a wide range of activities to God, some in female form, some in male, some in both.[14]

What, then, about the model of God as mother? Is that not stereotyping by suggesting as a major model for God *one* activity of females and the one most closely identified as stereotypically feminine, namely, giving birth to and raising children? My answer is twofold. First, although this particular essay will focus on God as mother in order to balance and provide a new context for interpreting God as father, other divine activities will also be imaged in female form, especially those concerned with creation and justice. Second, although mothering is a female activity, it is not feminine; that is, to give birth to and to feed the young is simply what females do—some may do it in a so-called feminine fashion, and others may not. What is more important for our purposes is that the symbolic material from the birthing and feeding process is very rich and for the most part has been neglected in establishment Christianity. It is also, as I shall try to show, powerful imagery for expressing the interrelatedness of all life, which is a central component in both a holistic sensibility and an understanding of Christian faith as an inclusive vision of fulfillment.

In this essay the model I have employed has sometimes been "God as mother" and sometimes "God as parent;" the emphasis will be on the former, but the latter will have a role as well. Our tradition has thoroughly analyzed the paternal metaphor, albeit mainly in a patriarchal context. The goal of my work will be to investigate the potential of the maternal model but to do so in a fashion that will provide an alternative interpretive context for the paternal model—a parental one. [...]

THE LOVE OF GOD AS MOTHER: AGAPE

Hidden away in the third volume of Paul Tillich's *Systematic Theology* is the suggestion that the symbolic dimension of the "ground of being" "points to the mother-quality of giving birth, carrying, and embracing, and, at the same time, of calling back, resisting independence of the created, and swallowing it."[15] He goes on to say that the uneasy feeling that many Protestants have about the first statement about God—that God is the power of being in all being—arises from the fact that their consciousness is shaped by the demanding father image for whom righteousness and not the gift of life is primary. What the father-God gives is redemption from sins; what the mother-God gives is life itself. But there is another reason that one might feel uneasy about Tillich's suggestion, for it implies divine resistance to independence for created being, whereas Western thought has prized its image of independent individuals who are saved one by one, either by their own moral choices or by divine grace. But what if the power in us, that which gives us our very existence, is not primarily judging individuals but calling us back, wanting to be more fully united with us, or as Tillich graphically puts it, wanting to "swallow" us? Our first reaction is fear of the maternal maw and a cry that we are independent, owing nothing to anyone, ready to face the consequences of our own actions.

But Tillich's symbolic suggestion for imaging the ground of being, the depths of divinity, as mother-love, which both gives life to all and desires reunification with all life, is helpful as we attempt to answer the question of the kind of love implied in the model of God as mother. We have characterized this love as agape, but that designation needs considerable qualification since the usual understanding of agape sees it as totally unmotivated, disinterested love.[16] Obviously, if God as the power of being, God as mother, calls us back and wants to be reunited with us, her love is not totally disinterested. But one must ask, why should we want it to be? The discussions on the nature of divine love, principally in Protestant circles and principally motivated by the desire to expunge any trace of need or interest on the part of God toward creation, paint a picture of God as isolated from creation and in no way dependent on it. As C. S. Lewis says, God is "'at home' in the land of the Trinity," presumably finding relations with the other "persons" sufficiently satisfying so that needing nothing, God loves into existence wholly superfluous creatures.[17] Discussions about agape as definitive of divine love have, unfortunately, usually focused on redemption, not creation, and as a result have stressed the disinterested character of God's love, which can overlook the sin in the sinners and love them anyway.[18] In other words, even though we are worthless, we are loved—but disinterestedly. Needless to say, this is a sterile and unattractive view of divine love and a view that most of us would not settle for even as a description of human love. If, among ourselves, we want to be loved not in spite of who we are but because in some sense we are valuable, desirable, and needed, then is this not the case also with divine love? If God's creative love is agapic love, then is it not a statement to created beings: "It is good that you exist!"?[19] Agape has been characterized as the love that gives (usually in contrast with eros as the love that takes), and as such it belongs with the gift of life, creation. If it is considered in that context instead of the context of redemption, it need not be disinterested; in fact, it should not be.

As "interested," divine agape cannot be isolated from the other forms of love, eros and philia. If, with Tillich, one understands love as the "moving power of life," as that "which drives everything that is towards everything else that is," then elements of need, desire, and mutuality are evident in all forms of love.[20] An understanding of love as unifying and reuniting is basic to an interpretation of Christian faith as destabilizing, inclusive, nonhierarchical fulfillment for all. It is the love that underscores the interdependence of life in all its forms, the desire to be with other beings in both their needs and their joy. Nonetheless, the *depth* of divine love can be characterized as agapic, for the distinctive feature of this love is its impartiality, its willing of existence and fulfillment for all being.

God as the giver of life, as the power of being in all being, can be imaged through the metaphor of mother—and of father. Parental love is the most powerful and intimate experience we have of giving love whose return is not calculated (though a return is appreciated): it is the gift of life as such to others. Parental love wills life and when it comes, exclaims, "It is good that you exist!" Moreover, in addition to being the gift of life, parental love nurtures what it has brought into existence, wanting growth and fulfillment for all. This agapic love is revolutionary, for it loves the weak and vulnerable as well as the strong and beautiful. No human love can, of course, be perfectly just and impartial, but parental love is the best metaphor we have for imaging the creative love of God.

An important caveat is necessary at this point: the parental model in its siding with life as such is not "pro-life" in the sense of being antiabortion. This is the case because of two features of our model: it is concerned with all species, not just human beings (and not with individuals in any species), and it is concerned with the nurture and fulfillment of life, not just with birth. On the first point: whereas we as biological or adoptive parents are interested in only one species—our own—and with particular individuals within that species, God as the mother of the universe is interested in all forms of life.

One indication of human pride is our colossal ego in imagining that of the millions of forms of life in the universe, we are the only ones that matter. Why should our birth, nurture, and fulfillment be the only concern of the power that gives life to all life? God as mother, on the side of life as such, does not therefore mean on the side of only one species or on the side of every individual human birth (or every individual birth in any other species). This first point on the goodness of creation, "It is good that you exist!" must be followed immediately by the second: the household or economy of the universe must be ordered and managed in a way so as to bring about the nurture and fulfillment of life—and again, this cannot mean every individual life that could be brought into existence. In a closed ecological system with limits on natural resources, difficult decisions must be made to insure the continuation, growth, and fulfillment of the many forms of life (not just one form and not all its individuals). Population control, both for our own species and other species, is one such decision. The balance between quantity and quality of life is one that a contemporary sensibility must keep to the forefront. To be on the side of life means participating in the decisions necessary to keep that balance. It cannot mean being "pro-life" in terms of one species or in terms of unlimited numbers, for such a perspective would in the long run mean being against life in its many and varied forms.

Let us now consider our model in more detail: the model of parental love for God's agapic, creative love. Why is this a powerful, attractive model for expressing the Christian faith in our time? If the heart of Christian faith for an ecological, nuclear age must be profound awareness of the preciousness and vulnerability of life as a gift we receive and pass on, with appreciation for its value and desire for its fulfillment it is difficult to think of any metaphors more apt than the parental one. There are three features basic to the parental model which will give flesh to this statement: it brings us closest to the beginnings of life, to the nurture of life, and to the impartial fulfillment of life.

Much of the power in the parental model is its immediate connection with the mystery of new life. Becoming a biological parent is the closest experience most people have to an experience of creation, that is, of bringing into existence. No matter how knowledgeable one is biologically, no matter how aware that human beings by becoming parents are simply doing what all animals do in passing life along, becoming a biological parent is for most people an awesome experience, inspiring feelings of having glimpsed the heart of things. We are, after all, the only creatures who can think about the wonder of existence, the sheer fact that "things are," that the incredible richness and complexity of life in all its forms has existed for millions of years, and that as part of the vast, unfathomable network of life, we both receive it from others and pass it along. At the time of the birth of new life from our bodies, we feel a sense of being co-creators, participating at least passively in the great chain of being. No matter how trite and hackneyed the phrases have become—"the miracle of birth," "the wonder of existence," and so on—on becoming a parent one repeats them again and joins the millions of others who marvel at their role in passing life along.

There are other ways of being parental besides being a biological parent and I want to stress this point at the outset, because much of the case for the models of mother (father), lover, and friend rests or their extensions beyond their physical and immediate base. One can, of course, be an adoptive parent as well as a biological one, but even more important for our purposes is that all human beings have parental inclinations. All human beings have the potential for passing life along, for helping to bring the next generation (of whatever kind of beings) into existence, nurturing and guiding it and working toward its fulfillment. These tendencies are so basic, widespread, and various that it is difficult to catalogue all the ways they are expressed. Some of the ways that come most readily to mind, such as in teaching, medicine, gardening, and social work, are only the tip of the iceberg, for in almost any cultural, political, economic, or social activity, there are aspects of the work that could be called parental.

Having made this point, however, let us return to the base of the model, in the physical act of giving birth. It is from this base that the model derives its power, for here it joins the reservoir of the great symbols of life and of life's continuity: blood, water, breath, sex, and food. In the acts of conception, gestation, and birth all are involved, and it is therefore no surprise that these symbols became the center of most religions, including Christianity, for they have the power to express the renewal and transformation of life—the "second birth"—because they are the basis of our "first birth." And yet, at least in Christianity, our first birth has been strangely neglected; another way of saying this is that creation, the birth of the world and all its beings, has not been permitted the imagery that this tradition uses so freely for the transformation and fulfillment of creation. Why is this the case?

One reason is surely that Christianity, alienated as it always has been from female sexuality, has been willing to image the second, "spiritual," renewal of existence in the birth metaphor, but not the first "physical," coming into existence.[21] In fact as we shall see, in the Hebraic-Christian tradition, creation has been imaginatively pictured as an intellectual, aesthetic "act" of God, accomplished through God's word and wrought by God's "hands" much as a painting is created by an artist or a form by a sculptor. But the model of God as mother suggests a very different kind of creation, one in keeping with the world as God's body but not one that the central tradition has been willing to consider. And it is clearly the parent as mother that is the stronger candidate for an understanding of creation as bodied forth from the divine being, for it is the imagery of gestation, giving birth, and lactation that creates an imaginative picture of creation as profoundly dependent on and cared for by divine life.[22] There simply is no other imagery available to us that has this power for expressing the interdependence and interrelatedness of all life with its ground. All of us, female and male, have the womb as our first home, all of us are born from the bodies of our mothers, all of us are fed by our mothers. What better imagery could there be for expressing the most basic reality of existence: that we live and move and have our being in God?

If the symbol of birth were allowed openly and centrally into the tradition, would this involve a radical theological change? Would it mean a different understanding of God's relation to the world? We will be dealing with that issue soon in more detail, but the simple answer is yes, the view associated with birth symbolism would be different from the distant anthropocentric view in the monarchical model: it would be an intimate view, inclusive of the cosmos, but not one that identifies God and the world. By analogy, mothers, at least good ones, encourage the independence of their offspring, and even though children are products of their parents' bodies, they are often radically different from them.[23]

The power of the parental model for God's creative, agapic love only begins with the birth imagery. Of equal importance is the ability of the model to express the nurturing of life and, to a lesser extent, its impartial fulfillment. It is at these levels that the more complex theological and ethical issues arise, for the divine agapic love that nurtures all creatures is a model of justice at the most basic level of the fair distribution of the necessities of life, and divine agapic love impartially fulfilling all of creation is a model of inclusive justice. In our understanding of Christianity as a destabilizing, inclusive, nonhierarchical vision of fulfillment for all, the parental model of God is especially pertinent as a way of talking about God's "just" love, the love that attends to the most basic needs of all creatures. It is important to look more closely at the way the model expresses the nurture and inclusion of all of life.

Parents feed the young. This is, across the entire range of life, the most basic responsibility of parents, often of fathers as well as of mothers. Among most animals it is instinctual and is often accomplished only at the cost of the health or life of the parent. It is not principally from altruistic motives that parents feed the young but from a base close to the one that brought new life into existence, the source that participates in passing life along. With human parents, the same love that says, "It is good that you exist!" desires that existence to continue, and for many parents in much of the world that is a daily and often, horrendous struggle. There is, perhaps, no picture more powerful to express "giving" love than that of parents wanting, but not having the food, to feed their starving children.[24]

The Christian tradition has paid a lot of attention to food and eating imagery. In fact, one could say that such imagery is probably at the center of the tradition's symbolic power: not only does the New Testament portrait of Jesus of Nazareth paint him as constantly feeding people, and eating with outcasts, but the church has as its central ritual a eucharistic meal reminiscent of the passion and death of Jesus and suggestive of the eschatological banquet yet to come. Christianity may be reticent in regard to birth imagery, especially as associated with natural, female processes, but it has shown no comparable reluctance to use the experience of eating as a symbol of spiritual nourishment. In fact, as many have pointed out, the Christian eucharist has obvious overtones of cannibalism! But the power of the food imagery is precisely in not fearing the physical connection, for the use of food as a symbol of the renewal of life must be grounded in food's basic role as the maintainer of life. Unfortunately, however, although the power of food imagery has been preserved in Christianity, the practical truth that food is basic to all life has often been neglected. A tradition that uses food as a symbol of spiritual renewal has often forgotten what parents know so well: that the young must be fed.

A theology that sees God as the parent who feeds the young and, by extension, the weak and vulnerable understands God as caring about the most basic needs of life in its struggle to continue. One can extend nurture to include much more than attention to physical needs, but one ought not move too quickly, for the concern about life and its continuation that is a basic ingredient in the sensibility needed in our time has too often been neglected by Christianity in its interest in "spiritual" well-being. An evolutionary, ecological sensibility makes no clear distinction between matter and spirit or between body and mind, for life is a continuum and cannot flourish at the so-called higher levels unless supported at all levels. God as parent loves agapically in giving, with no thought of return, the sustenance needed for life to continue. This is creative love, for it provides the conditions minimally necessary for life to go on.

Finally, God as parent wants all to flourish. Divine agapic love is inclusive and hence a model of impartial justice. This is a difficult point to make without falling back into the old view of agape as disinterested; moreover, parental love can model the impartiality of divine love only in a highly qualified way. Yet it is central to the essence of agapic love to stress that it is impartial, or as I would prefer to say, inclusive.[25] This is a better way to express what is at stake than to call the love disinterested, which suggests that God's love is detached, unconcerned, or perfunctory. In fact, the opposite is intended, for agapic love functions in spite of obstacles and in this way can be love of all, whatever the barriers may be. God as mother is parent to all species and wishes all to flourish. We can reflect this inclusiveness in the model of parent only in partial and distorted fashion, for as parents we tend by instinct to focus on our own species and on particular individuals within that species. To be sure, when we extend the model beyond its physical base to include our parental inclinations toward human children not our own, as well as toward life forms not our own, a measure of impartiality, of inclusiveness, emerges, but only as a faint intimation of divine agape. It is imperative to recognize when a model falters. This one falters here.

With most recent understandings of agape, however, our model would have faltered long ago, for if divine love is seen as totally different from all forms of love that we know, as entirely "giving" whereas human love is only "taking," no human love will serve as a metaphor for God's love. But we have maintained that dimensions of divine agapic love, especially those involved in the creating and sustaining of life, can be modeled with great power by parental love. What this model or any model cannot do is express the mystery that all are included, even the last and the least. [...]

NOTES

1. Elizabeth Clark and Herbert Richardson, eds., *Women and Religion* (New York: Harper & Row, 1977), 164-65.

2. For a fuller treatment of this point, see my book *Metaphorical Theology: Models of God in Religious Language* (Philadelphia: Fortress Press, 1982; 2d printing with new preface, 1985), chap. 5.

3. Virginia Mollenkott makes this point eloquently, when after quoting Schubert Ogden's statement that God is "the most truly absolute Thou any mind can conceive," continues, "This *Thou*, this Absolute Relatedness, may be referred to as He, She, or It because this Thou relates to everyone and everything....This *Thou* is a jealous God...jealous...that He/She/It be recognized everywhere in everyone and everything..." (*The Divine Feminine: The Biblical Imagery of God as Female* [New York: Crossroad, 1983], 113-14).

4. For different but complementary views on this point, see Carolyn Merchant, *The Death of Nature: Women, Ecology, and the Scientific Revolution* (New York: Harper & Row, 1980); Brian Easlea, *Fathering the Unthinkable: Masculinity, Scientists, and the Nuclear Arms Race* (London: Pluto, 1983); Rosemary Radford Ruether, *Sexism and God-Talk Toward a Feminist Theology* (Boston: Beacon Press, 1983), chap. 2; Mary Daly, *Gyn/Ecology: The Metaphysics of Radical Feminism* (Boston: Beacon Press, 1978); and Rita M. Gross, "Hindu Female Deities as a Resource for the Contemporary Rediscovery of the Goddess," in *The Book of the Goddess Past and Present: An Introduction to Her Religion*, ed. Carl Olson (New York: Crossroad, 1983).

5. One example of the danger inherent in twisted thinking concerning sexuality surfaces in the birth metaphors used by scientists involved in creating the atomic bomb. Brian Easlea in his book *Fathering the Unthinkable* has collected these materials, and I quote a few. Kenneth Bainbridge, the physicist in charge of the Trinity test "The bomb was [Robert Oppenheimer's] baby" (p. 95). General Farrell: "Atomic fission was almost full grown at birth" (p. 96). Henry Stimson received the following telegram after the Trinity test: "Doctor has just returned most enthusiastic and confident that the little boy is as husky as his big brother" (p. 96), which meant that the plutonium bomb was as good as the uranium. William Laurence, a reporter at the Trinity test: "The big boom came about a hundred seconds after the great flash—the first cry of a new-born world" (p. 96). Easlea traces the history of science as the conquest of female nature—the taming of Mother Nature—back to Francis Bacon and his call to men to unite and, "turning with united forces against the Nature of things, to storm and occupy her castles and strongholds"

(quoted pp. 20-21).

6. Janet Morley, a British theologian, in commenting on the fact that many natural images are used as metaphors of God in the church's hymns (light, sun, sea, rocks, castles, etc.), whereas God is seldom if ever spoken of as mother, wife, sister, midwife, etc., concludes, "Non-human objects may symbolize God's glory, but, by their almost universal absence in this respect, must we conclude that human women cannot?" ("In God's Image?" *Cross Currents* 32 [1982]: 315).

7. Many feminists are concerned to make this distinction. See, e.g., Ruether's rejection of "masculine" and "feminine" characteristics: there is, she says, no evidence that women are caring and nurturing whereas men are not. "We need to affirm...that all humans possess a full and equivalent human nature and personhood, *as male and female*" (*Sexism and God-Talk*, 111).

8. There are two ways that the feminine dimension of God can be imagined, as Elizabeth A. Johnson suggests in her excellent article "The Incomprehensibility of God and the Image of God Male and Female," *Theological Studies* 45 (1984): 441-65. Feminine *qualities* can be given to God so that God the father displays motherly qualities and, hence, God becomes a more holistic "person," having integrated the feminine side into a basically male character. But as Johnson points out, "The female can never appear as an icon of God in all divine fullness equivalent to the male" (p. 456). Or a feminine *aspect* can be attributed to God, and this is usually the Holy Spirit. Here, not only do masculine and feminine stereotypes emerge, but as Johnson notes, given the historically indefinite character of the Holy Spirit we end "with two males and an amorphous third" (p. 458). I would add that even the attempt by process theologians to introduce the feminine dimension of God as God's consequent nature falls into stereotyping, since the qualities associated with God's consequent nature are receptivity, empathy, suffering, and preservation. Two unfortunate examples will illustrate Johnson's main points. Jürgen Moltmann claims that God "is the *motherly Father* of his *only-born Son*, and at the same time the *fatherly Father* of his *only-begotten Son*.... The Son was...made...from the womb of the Father" ("The Motherly Father: Is Trinitarian Patripassionism Replacing Theological Patriarchalism?" in *God As Father?* ed. Johannes-Baptist Metz and Edward Schillebeeckx [New York Seabury Press, 1981], 53). Nonetheless, Moltmann sees this use of feminine terminology only as a way to limit the use of masculine terminology; anything more, he says, would be in danger of "changing over to matriarchal

conceptions" (ibid.). Donald L. Gelpi in his book *The Divine Mother: A Trinitarian Theology of the Holy Spirit* (Washington, D.C.: Univ. Press of America, 1984) elevates all positive feminine qualities to the Divine Mother as Jungian transformational categories (with none of the negative qualities), thus providing an excellent example of the "eternal feminine" sanctified by the Deity—with the dark side repressed.

9. Rosemary Radford Ruether makes this point tellingly with the comment that those unwilling to give up the male monopoly on God-language often reply to objectors, "God is not male. He is Spirit" (*Sexism and God-Talk*, 67). For the most part, I have avoided using personal pronouns for God in this essay—except for the male pronoun in relationship to the monarchical and patriarchal models—until the issue could be clarified. Henceforth, I shall use both male and female pronouns.

10. For a sampling of this literature, see Judith Ochshorn, *The Female Experience and the Nature of the Divine* (Bloomington: Indiana Univ. Press, 1981); Carol Christ, "Symbols of Goddess and God in Feminist Theology," in *The Book of the Goddess*, ed. Olson; Gross, "Hindu Female Deities"; and Ruether, *Sexism and God-Talk*, chap. 2.

11. This point is made by many feminist theologians and is succinctly summarized by Johnson: "...the goddess is not the expression of the feminine dimension of the divine, but the expression of the fullness of divine power and care shown in a female image" ("The Incomprehensibility of God," 461).

12. See, e.g., Rosemary Radford Ruether, *Mary—The Feminine Face of the Church* (Philadelphia: Westminster Press, 1977), and E. Ann Matter, "The Virgin Mary: A Goddess?" in *The Book of the Goddess*, ed. Olson.

13. In Elisabeth Schüssler Fiorenza's study of Sophia in Israelite religion, Sophia is in a symbiotic relationship to God with a variety of appellations (sister, wife, mother, beloved, teacher) and tasks (leading, preaching, teaching, creating, and so on). See *In Memory of Her: A Feminist Theological Reconstruction of Christian Origins* (New York: Crossroad, 1983), 130ff.

14. See Eleanor McLaughlin, "'Christ My Mother': Feminine Naming and Metaphor in Medieval Spirituality," *St. Luke's Journal of Theology* 18 (1975): 356-86; and Caroline Walker Bynum, *Jesus as Mother: Studies in the Spirituality of the High Middle Ages* (Berkeley and Los Angeles: Univ. of California Press, 1982).

15. Paul Tillich, *Systematic Theology*, vol. 3 (Chicago: Univ. of Chicago Press, 1963), 293-94.

16. Anders Nygren, with his much-discussed book *Agape and Eros* (trans. Philip S. Watson [Philadelphia: Westminster Press, 1953]), initiated the twentieth-century conversations on the issue, taking the extreme view that the two kinds of love are totally unrelated and incommensurable, with eros as the corruption of agape—the self-interest that creeps into disinterested love. Gene Outka summarizes the four points in Nygren's position most influential to Protestants: agape is spontaneous and unmotivated; it is indifferent to value; it is creative of value, making the worthless human being worthy; and it is the initiator of fellowship with God (*Agape: An Ethical Analysis* [New Haven: Yale Univ. Press, 1972]). In this picture, God gives all and we take all; moreover, human beings cannot love God but can only serve as a conduit of divine (agapic) love to the neighbors whom we, like God, love in spite of their unlovableness. Nygren's position rests on the worthlessness of human beings; since all worth, all fellowship, must come from God, it is a fellowship based on the pervasiveness of sin, which God overcomes. One of the main critics of Nygren's position is M.C. D'Arcy, a Roman Catholic, according to whom agape and eros exist in balance in human beings (and hence the ideal love relationship is friendship). Were we not capable of giving as well as receiving, says D'Arcy, the human agent would be eliminated and God would be simply loving the divine self through us. See his *The Mind and Heart of Love: Lion and Unicorn—A Study in Eros and Agape* (New York: Henry Holt & Co., 1947).

17. C.S. Lewis, *The Four Loves* (New York: Harcourt Brace & Co., 1960), 176.

18. In Nygren's words, what is critical is to stress the "principle that any thought of valuation whatsoever is out of place in connection with fellowship with God. When God's love is directed to the sinner, then the position is clear; all thought of valuation is excluded in advance; for if God, the Holy One, loves the sinner, it cannot be because of his sin, but in spite of his sin" (*Agape and Eros*, 75-80).

19. This phrase comes from Josef Pieper's book *About Love*, trans. Richard and Clara Winston (Chicago: Franciscan Herald Press, 1974), 22.

20. Paul Tillich, *Love, Power, and Justice: Ontological Analyses and Ethical Applications* (New York: Oxford Univ. Press, 1954), 23.

21. Another reason is the Christ-centeredness of the tradition, which overlooks the first birth because it wants to stress the second birth. In promoting Christ's mission of redemption, the tradition has failed to appreciate the gift of creation.

22. The Hebraic-Christian tradition has carried imagery of gestation, giving birth, and lactation as a leitmotif that emerges only now and then over the centuries. For Hebraic use of the "breasts" and "womb" of God as metaphors of divine compassion and care, see Phyllis Trible, *God and the Rhetoric of Sexuality* (Philadelphia: Fortress Press, 1978), chap. 2. Another instance of such imagery emerges in twelfth-century Cistercian mysticism, which according to Caroline Bynum employed three basic stereotypes of maternal images: the female as generative, as loving and tender, and as nurturing. "For a theology that maintained—over against Cathar dualism—the goodness of creation in all its physicality, a God who is mother and womb as well as father and animator could be a more sweeping and convincing image of creation than a father God alone" (Bynum, *Jesus as Mother,* 134). However, as Bynum points out, this feminization of religious language does not reflect a more positive attitude toward women, nor for the most part was it developed for or by women (with the exception of Julian of Norwich). Much of it is sentimentalized maternal imagery written by cloistered monks who had rejected women and family (see *Jesus as Mother,* 130ff.).

23. Norman Pittenger makes the accompanying theological point: "Thus we wish to speak of God as the everlasting creative agency who works anywhere and everywhere, yet without denying the reality of creaturely freedom—hence we point toward God as Parent" (*The Divine Triunity* [Philadelphia: United Church Press, 1977], 2).

24. The growing worldwide response to starving populations, response beyond anything expected and from all levels of society in all countries, is witness to the basic parental instinct to feed the young, the weak, the vulnerable. It need not (and should not) be named altruism, Christian love, or anything else grand; it is simply what all human beings want to be part of: passing along to others the gift of life.

25. Those who have written in the most balanced way about agape—including Josef Pieper, M.C. D'Arcy, Gene Outka, and Paul Tillich—all insist that although agape is not so completely different that there is nothing that unites the loves, it is different: agape qualifies the other loves, guarding against their distortions (as for Tillich), or it provides a base line (as in Outka's notion of agape as "equal regard," the "regard which is independent and unalterable; and which applies to each neighbor qua human existent" [*Agape*, 13]).

Letters to My Mother

Jennifer Sanborn

THE FOLLOWING LETTERS WERE WRITTEN as an individual project at the Oregon Extension, May-June '94.

Dear Mom,

I was always a stubborn, feisty, independent soul. I imagine, if given the choice, I would have tried to be born feet first—just to do it my own way. How often this must have frustrated you—my need to take the wheel. No one in the family thought I would *ever* learn to ride a bike; I just couldn't be taught! Each time you or Dad took your hand off the seat I'd put my feet down. It's like I was saying, "Okay, enough of this game." Maybe I was afraid of falling—of *failing*—right there in front of you and it was easier to not even try. I did try, though, when your backs were turned. When you and Dad and Heather were inside I'd climb on top of that bike and pedal, coast, and topple. Scratched knees hurt less then scratched pride!

Finally one afternoon in our backyard in Franklin I discovered the feel of riding a bike. I set my blue two-wheeler at the top of the slightest dip in the yard. My bike, by this time, was pleading for the return of training wheels—it had more bruises than I did! Somehow it worked, though. With the momentum from the hill I managed to coast a bit and keep on pedaling—right past Dad's office. He was on the phone and exclaimed quickly and loudly that everyone should get to a window. I felt like I had done it all on my own, but I hadn't really. You and Dad both had given me patient instruction and modeling—and finally you gave me the space to learn on my own if that was my choice.

It was this same pattern when I learned how to drive standard. Mom, can you forgive me for the frustration, the arguments, the tears? Who would have thought that a mechanism—a clutch—could challenge a relationship? Dad didn't even bother trying to teach me this time—early on he recognized the signs of disaster: my unwillingness to listen to directions, my need to succeed on the very first try. He saw a sixteen-year-old who vowed she would be content driving automatic for the rest of her life! You saw a sixteen-year-old who just needed a little space and independence. Eventually we gave up on our drives together and I took a few solo trips, late at night. Once again, when your back turned, all your words found their way into my coordination and I could do it!

I never could make it without your directions....When I was a senior in high school I pleaded for the freedom to drive the off-island car to Boston each weekend for my lessons at the New England Conservatory. You were hesitant—Martha's Vineyard has no highways and it's a far cry from driving in the city. When I hadn't heard back from you with an answer I assumed it was "no." I figured you would come and drive or I would find myself on the bus once again. Imagine my surprise as you handed me the keys early the next morning when you dropped me off at the boat. I was ecstatic—so honored by your trust and confidence. So busy was I musing about the greatness of you and Dad, I didn't even realize that I didn't have any directions. When I had driven in the past, you had been in the passenger seat instructing me as I went along. Quickly I turned back to you and said, "I don't even know how to get there!" You calmly repeated the directions and I scribbled down some numbers. Once again it was your modeling and instructions that brought me safely there and back. Your trust in me—your willingness to set me off on my own—taught me to trust myself. You instilled in me the belief that I am both trustworthy and capable.

I still did not expect to drive alone so soon, though. In a space of minutes I learned that I would have to take the wheel of my life and I only had a month to try and take down the directions. I never wanted to be alone like this—Mom, I never wanted this much space. I know you didn't either. As you prepared for your boat to leave, you gave me the directions: to believe in your presence with me in all the days of my life and to rely on God—to forgive myself in the same graceful manner that I should forgive others—to live as a sister, friend, wife, and mother in the manner you had modeled. I watched you, mom, as you handed me the keys. I watched every ounce of you embrace life even as you relinquished it. It was your time to show me that one day there would again be laughter and celebration, joy and peace—that one day I would return to share with you the details of my trip.

For now, though, there is a lonely stretch of road ahead. I pull over often to write and reread your directions; I couldn't make it without them!

I love you, Jennifer

Dear Mom,

When you were dying, I wrote that I knew what it was to feel my heart breaking. I wrote it partly because I believed it, but also because it just seemed like the right thing to say. At the time I was a bit too numb to actually feel the breaking—the cracking—but I see the remnants of it now. Now I know the truth that I then spoke.

Deep within me there are fault lines—permanent breaks in that which is my earth. Many days there is only slight movement in my depths—slight enough that I might be able to walk through the day without damage control. I know well enough not to be deceived by the quiet, though. I know there will be quakes. I prepare for them—particularly on special days like your birthday, Mother's Day, the anniversary of your death....most any day that intimately involves thoughts of you. I prepare a sort of emergency kit: some kleenex and my journal, a bed and pillow, some special music and some special friends. We sit back and wait for the quaking to begin, but often the tremors are only dull and mildly aching. It's as though my preparations serve almost as precautionary measures.

Like any expert seismologist, my predictions are not always correct; I am often surprised by the quakes. What I'm realizing is that it doesn't take a so-called "special" day to start the tremors; it is often a moment of the ordinary—the everyday. I wake in my bed at home and in my disoriented state imagine that it is your footsteps—not Heather's—that are sounding their way up the stairs. Maybe there's an argument with Matt and I lean toward the phone to call you for advice—with my hand in midair, I realize there will be no more advice. In the grocery store there is a woman who looks just like you from behind. I catch a glimpse and have to stuff the urge to cry out, "Mom!" Sometimes I just want a hug and a hand to smooth my hair and no arms and no hands fit quite like yours. I overhear a friend complain about her mother. I hear the word "mother" in any context—or "cancer" or "death" or "terminal" or "funeral." I hear the exact pitch of the windchimes hanging outside the living room during that month you were dying. One day in the hallway at school I smelled a smell for just a moment—I could not identify it, but I knew it was a smell of your dying. Yes, smells, sounds, touches—these all can start a quake. Then there are the days when the earth is just as startlingly beautiful that I don't know whether to dance in celebration or stomp on the flowers that persist in blooming despite your absence. Yes, sight can start the tremors—and taste, too.

There are times when the plates of my heart shift and chafe against each other to the extent that I think I cannot survive. If alone, I pull in a pillow to try and muffle the pain. If I can, I pull in anyone nearby and try to share the deafening roar.

Broken forever,
Jennifer

Dear Mom,
You had the perfect mother's body. It was like you were born with a lap just right for sitting on and a shoulder for crying on. In a hug your soft arms encircled me in a way no other arms can. Imagine being in a family without touch; I feel like they miss a whole dimension of what it is to be human. We are bodies and we love through these bodies. I loved you in yours....You were a living, breathing, walking, talking, moving body. I once could touch the flesh on your hand, feel the wetness of you cheek after sad and angry tears, gently rest my arm across your shoulders, or stand back to back against you as I tried to prove yet again that I was nearly your height. This was the you that I knew and loved—I loved a mother who would dance with me in the kitchen. (I will never forget how you would dance the Hava-nagila at the boat to keep warm.) I loved a mother who would bound a little when she was excited and walking at the same time. I loved a mother who would let me cut her hair and then put the vacuum hose up to her neck to suck up all the little hairs. We laughed so hard that day—especially when it appeared the skin on your back would be sucked up, too.

Is it little wonder then that I only find small comfort in reminding myself that your spirit still lives with me or to think that you have been given a new body in Heaven? It took me six months to say good-bye to your body—dreams and other deaths pushed the reality of your absence into me. Oh, I could remember your body as it was dying. I remembered your tube-laden arm wrapped around my neck to pull my face in next to yours that first night in the hospital. With my tears running down and falling to your neck I said, "I love you," over and over in your ear. I remembered the day at Mass General when I was nervous to sit next to you on your bed for fear that I would offset your balance. You asked me to sit and then put your head down on my shoulder—a touch that was so tender but also frightening because I did not yet understand who it was that was caught in your sick, little body. I remembered lying against your heart and the few times you had the strength to put your arms around me in a hug. I could even remember putting my hand against your chest waiting for another beat…and realizing there would be none. Then the hour of passing through that room—watching Cathy straighten your head and trying to close your eyes and mouth. They were wrenched open with the effort of trying to find one last breath. I remembered all this.

What I forgot, though, is the next day—driving to the funeral home and standing beside a cold, stiff, grey you covered over in apricot powder. I forgot touching your crossed hands and kissing your frozen lips—and then flinching because I had never felt anything as plastic and unreal. I had forgotten this: that you were no longer real as I knew you. No, I am not a daughter without a mother—you are still with me. But when I stand on the earth that covers your ashes. I realize I am a daughter without a mother's body. And that is worth a lifetime of tears.

Dear Mom,

Soon after your death I received a letter and check in the mail from social security or some such government institution. The check was a sort of survivor's compensation; the letter explained that I received this because I had become an orphan. How can this be with a father who still lives? The World Health Organization defines an orphan as one who has lost both parents *or* one who has lost his or her mother. Sadly, fathers have not often proven quality care-takers. So here I am—an orphan…a child without a living mother.

What is it to be an orphan? What does it mean? It means your older sister buying you a new dress to wear to your mother's memorial service because you don't have enough money in your bank account at school. It means having to make on your own all those official calls to withdraw from school because there's no one to do it for you. It means going downstairs to tuck your mother into bed before you tuck yourself in. It means clearing the bathroom on the day she dies because guests are arriving shortly. It means entertaining these guests once they arrive, with the help of some generous relatives and friends. It means waking up to an alarm clock each morning rather then a cheery voice calling up the stairs. It means losing the large part of the income in a family and worrying about money *a lot.* It means watching your father take a leave of absence just as you start a new job—and you feel as incapacitated as he does. It means watching your father go out with another woman and father her children more than you want him to father you—simply because it is a mother—not a father—that you want. It means feeling badly for even thinking you would rather have your mother. It means having three attendants remain in the operating room while you have moles removed to be checked for skin cancer because they know the word "cancer" is pretty scary for you. It means packing your own clothes for school and driving yourself back to college. It means watching all your roommates' mothers unpack for them as you do it all by yourself. It means asking your roommate to help you make your bed because your mother always did it for you that first night. It means flinching when you meet new people and they ask what your parents do. It means spending parents' weekend with another friend whose parents couldn't make it. It means not spending Thanksgiving, Christmas, or your birthday at home because you can't bear to be there without your mom. It means watching everyone else at school get survival baskets during exam time and feeling ashamed that you didn't get one because your father forgot. It means getting awards that you don't even care about because there's no mother to call and tell. It means *never* calling your mother—with good news or with bad. It means bringing your father and sister to the commencement dinner when everyone else brings his or her father and mother. It means having to write "deceased" after "MOTHER" on all your grad. school applications. It means going to school in your mother's hometown just so you feel like she knows you're going there. It means having someone else's mother make you a dress for graduation. It means having thirteen relatives come to see you graduate because they're trying to make up for the one who is absent. It means that night, when everyone else is out celebrating, crying with your boyfriend because you don't much care for celebrating. It means not knowing how to plan a wedding or care for a baby or do any of the things you always thought your mother would help you do. It means having children with no grandmother.

It means loving your sister, your father, your boyfriend, your relatives, your friends so very, very much but knowing they will never be enough. It means never again being a daughter with you as my living, breathing mother. If that's not enough to make me an orphan, I don't know what is....

Jennifer

Dear Mom,

It's an ironic ritual—to send flowers to a person who has just watched Death move into her home. They were everywhere—roses scenting the air which still clung to last breaths. For a few days the flowers were enjoyed, but then they, too, died and the house was all full of Death again. The small cards from the florist had the signatures of well-intentioned people, but the whole thing seems almost malicious to me: "Just in case you haven't spent enough time watching the life seep out of a fragile living thing, here are some flowers to remind you of what it was like."

There was one delivery that was different—a brown clay pot filled with five plants—plants for me to water and prune, to fertilize and re-pot, to watch grow and live when much of me wanted to shrink and die. These plants, in a way, were my lifeline; I could give them life while I decided if I wanted to give some life to myself. These, too, turned out to be fragile, though. Just this week I found out that they, too, are dead—one long, hot day in the car and they were beyond resuscitation. My only living link to the week of your death, mom. I bit my lip when Helen told me on the phone, holding down sobs that I choked back up once my hand hit the receiver.

Then there were the sunglasses. You know, the ones you bought on your spontaneous trip to Calvin College. I set them on top of a stack of T-shirts while I tried to decide between maroon or pine green. Maroon in hand, I walked away and didn't look back. More than shady protection from that which is too glaring for human vision, these sunglasses were memories embodied. Memories of the dress you stayed up all night sewing, finishing the final hem as your plane descended into Grand Rapids. For weeks you had been scouting out a black dress in Murry's—just waiting for the spring sale. I still have the letter in which you wrote that there were still four dresses left. But, one day, when you entered the store, there were none there. You designed a black silk dress, hoping in some way to make up for the loss of the other. I imagine the sunglasses and the other things you bought were all part of it—you felt as badly! That little shopping trip was something more, too, though. Always you brought us up to be thrifty—to only buy that which we needed. That day you told me that sometimes we can buy things that we just plain want. Those sunglasses, minus the nine months that they spent under the passenger seat in the blue car, have been with me since that weekend, reminding me of the preciousness of mother-daughter time. These things are all I've got left—some pictures, a sweater or two, priceless letters of you words to me, and a pair of sunglasses that I may never see again....

There was one other pair of sunglasses. I bought them in Leslie's, the drugstore you would work in during the crowded Vineyard summers. I bought them to wear to your memorial service, but Heather stepped on them the day before. I forced the frame to reconnect with the lines, but they were still a bit lopsided. I didn't wear them that day. I figured that the thousands of people were going to see broken sunglasses or look into my swollen, red eyes and see a broken me. I hoped that maybe, just maybe, if they saw how I'd been stepped on, they would help to put me back together. I know they tried, but I'm still a bit lopsided, and sometimes I come apart.

Memories embodied—embodied in things and objects, but places, too... like the house that will be mine for only fifty-two more days. It is a house like no other, filled with the ghosts of daughters' adolescence and the echoing laughter of a mother and daughters who learned how to be friends. The kitchen where the women waltzed to the sounds of your final Christmas.... The dining room where we ate ice cream cake and listened to country music dedications on the last birthday of mine you'll ever share....The living room with the piano that I played while I sang away the final two hours of your life....Upstairs—the bedrooms and the beds on which I would lie, clenching my pillow to my face as I tried to block out the sounds of your gagging and retching as that damn cancer pushed even the bile of your stomach out of its way. In this order I will say goodbye to these rooms, leaving for last the room converted for a month from a TV room to a hospital. I will stand in the doorway—the very same doorway where I stood as your skinny little body bucked and reared with Death on its back. I will stand in that room, as I did over a year ago, and I will have to say goodbye once again. Left behind will be the walls which will always speak of a family and a home watching its heart die.

The "experts" could analyze what I've written here—they'd say, "Following the death, the bereaved may become excessively attached to objects or possessions which remind him or her of the dead. He or she might actually come to value these objects as though they are the dead." Experts are never very smart, though, are they? For a time, these objects might have felt like you, but now they feel like me: dead, lost, broken, and deserted.

Missing you....
Jennifer

WHEN I ATTENDED THE FIRST Oregon Extension Women's Studies May Term in 1994, it was only a year after my mother had died swiftly from pancreatic cancer. I used the air, the trees—the space—of Lincoln to write letters to my mother. These letters became my individual project for the term. It was moving and healing to both write them and hear them read aloud to the other searchers and learners there. Eight years later, nine years after I last spoke face to face with my mother, I continue to write to her as a way to share with her my life, my heart, and who I have become.

April 29, 2002

Dear Mom,

Kyra had a tough night last night. Matt left yesterday morning for a conference—his first night away from our girl. I think she must have been missing him, or at least picking up on me missing him. Each time I would attempt to put her down in her crib, she woke with a startle and immediately began to cry. Of course I tried to let her cry and calm herself down, but now that she is pulling up in her crib, this is easier said than done. When she gets tired—I mean, really tired—she loses all coordination and balance. So, combine pulling up in the crib with near-hysterical crying and a loss of coordination. You get the picture—stand and fall, over and over. I kept hearing her head hit the rails as she dropped...and the cries grew louder, I spent much of the night with her in my arms as I rocked back and forth, back and forth, back and forth. I can't remember the last time we had a night like this. In the quiet, as she rested against my chest, I considered every possible cause: teeth, an oncoming cold, a growth spurt, separation anxiety, overtiredness. I decided it was just Kyra missing her daddy, and I pulled her in close.

Truth be told, I did not mind rocking her through the night. Now that our girl is moving about she so rarely cuddles. It was nice to feel her reach for me and melt into me once again. "Where did baby Kyra go?" we ask her. Of course, at eight months, she is still an infant, but some days it seems she resembles more the child she will become than the baby she once was. Those sparkling, inquisitive eyes are the same. New color, but still continually glancing toward us, seeking to catch our eyes for recognition and reassurance. She takes all her cues from us. When she first began crawling and standing, she would turn to us immediately and await our claps and cheers. Then she, too, would smile her large, toothy grin. Her pride in herself draws from our pride. Her joy draws from our joy. So, too, her sadness, I would guess.

I wonder whether she will draw most from my sadness or my joy in experiencing you. I suppose I knew Grandma and Grandpa, your parents, from the contented sound in your voice when you shared stories of them. There was a trust in your memories, a belief in their goodness. It was one night when you cried as I sang at the piano, though, that I understood who they were *to you.* Embarrassed, I asked why you were crying. You replied that you wished they could have lived to hear me sing. I was in that adolescent phase of resisting all intimacy with my family and wanted to escape the closeness of your emotion, so I voiced some weak response that they probably knew—that they could hear from heaven. I can't remember what you said in reply, but I knew from something in your words and your tears that it simply wasn't the same. I suppose we never grow too old to seek the eyes, or ears, of our parents.

I still seek yours. When I first learned that my first child was due to be born so near to your birthday, I somehow believed the birth would signify your return to the world—that when I looked into my girl's eyes I would find you once again. I do see you when Kyra is intent on a task, her tongue hanging out the side of her mouth. You always bit down on your tongue when you were concentrating. I see you more in me, though. My hands have become yours—soft, but lined, with veins rising visibly to the surface. My face seems more yours, too—particularly in pictures of Kyra and me when I am unaware of the camera and absorbed in her perfection. These resemblances aren't you, though, and some days I can't help but feel you more from the absolute absence of you than from the presence of these shared traits.

How will she ever know you? If I tell her how an empty sugar bowl led to candy cane rolls at Christmas, will she know your ingenuity? If I tell her how you would shift from foot to foot when you were waiting for someone, or seemed to bounce when you conducted, will she know your boundless energy? If I tell her how round and soft your body felt when I sought you for a hug, will she know your touch? And, if one day she feels as though she has some sense of you, will she have a sense of who you were *to me*? Can she know that the only experience more defining for me than her birth was your death? Can she somehow understand that my pride, my joy, my sadness will always be seeking reflection in your eyes?

Someday she will hear my cries, and wonder what keeps me from sleep. "I am just missing my mommy," I will say, and she will pull me in close.

I love you.
Jennifer

Hope Birthing Healing

Luke 8:43-48

Marcia B. Bailey

WE ACCOMPANIED EACH OTHER THIS WEEK, and I struggled to hear what she was saying. For a few brief days our bodies aligned themselves in a synchronicity shared across the ages with nothing less than the moon itself. I walked in her crowd and she walked in my neighborhood, as different as we were alike, me, bearing the stains of her public humiliation in private, and she, birthing the secret hope of my wholeness for all the world to see. "Word" in "words" we intermingled, flowing one into the other, filling, shedding, releasing—life.

Sanitized, like me, she had no name by which *I* would call her. Oh, it's not that they didn't *call* her! "Unclean!" "Woman with hemorrhages." Or this: "Woman with the issue of blood." Ah, yes!! There *is* the "issue of blood," you can be sure! The "issue" of life and death. The "issue" of inclusion and exclusion. The "issue" of family and birth-right. The "issue" of privilege and marginalization. Such issues are to be taken seriously. But how?

Publicly, she was exposed as completely as I was hidden. Privately, I suffered alone as she bore her pain where all could see. As surely as I blended in she stood apart, each of us separated from ourselves in deference to the ominous comfort level of the whole. Speak only what we can bear to hear; do only what we can openly view. In this, there is no "whole." What were legislated matters of public discourse for her are private things for us, things we dare not say to one another lest the wonder and the fear, the mystery and the longing propel us on a course for which we find ourselves unprepared. We like it neat and this is messy. We like it tidy and this is definitely unclean.

"If a woman has a discharge of blood for many days, not at the time of her impurity, or if she has a discharge beyond the time of her impurity, all the days of the discharge she shall continue in uncleanness; as in the days of her impurity, she shall be unclean." (Lev 15:25) You see, there were rules! (There usually are!) Rules that labeled her "sinful" and kept her outside the community. Rules that equated the power of creation with the creation of power. Rules that took everything she had and asked for more.

There are *always* rules. Rules that say the poor should remain poor while the rich thrive. Rules that say African-Americans are inferior to white Americans. Rules that make Asians invisible and tell women "that's as far as you can go, honey, get off here." There are rules that say gays and lesbians are accidents of nature and there are rules that insist that no white male "gets it," ever. In the dim light of such a reality I am reminded that those who live by the rules fail to see we who die by the rules, just like they didn't see her that day, among the crowd.

I tried to understand what *compelled* her, after a lifetime of playing by the rules, as I watched her carefully pick her way among the crowd, deftly measuring the distance, choosing exactly when to move forward and when to hang back.

It was clear this woman took herself seriously, a stark contrast to the world that did not. It was clear that this woman was fueled by some passionate fire that burned deep within her. It was clear—as she reached out to touch the edge of Jesus' garment—that this woman had courage. But I was not prepared for her *hope*.

Hers was a hope implanted divinely in the womb of her soul's birth. Hope watered silently by her tears. Hope nurtured secretly by her blood. Compelling, empowering, life-giving, this hope was *God's holy gift*. In it she found the power to break the rules. In it she envisioned herself re-created. In it she understood God's desire for her wholeness. It was far too much and it was not enough.

She reached out and touched Jesus. Divine hope in *human life* meeting divine hope in *human form*! I was not prepared to come face to face with a *hope so great* that it *called healing out* from the Son of God. This woman *surprised* God! And suddenly the rules are changed. And she is changed. And I am changed. As hope gives birth to healing in the very presence of the Living Christ.

And when she saw that she could not remain hidden, she came trembling; and falling down before him, she declared in the presence of all the people why she had touched him and how she had been immediately healed.

Such a *hope* cannot be hidden—not by a dozen years or a thousand years of cultural and societal rules and regulations, not by poverty or isolation, ignorance or fear. "She came trembling"—filled with *joy* and disbelief, *hope* breaking the silence of her pain and suffering, *hope* declaring "why she had touched him"—that the divine gift of hope in us might meet the divine gift of Hope that is God, calling out healing, making *us* whole.

What I saw in her—this sister, this mother, this daughter of mine—struggles to be born in me. What I long to say, her life speaks. This pregnant hope that breaks the rules, that pushes at the edges, that demands wholeness waits to give birth to the healing God intends for *all* of our lives: To liberate us from the fears of others, to teach us to trust ourselves, to weave us into the fabric of relationship and community, to reconcile our bodies and our spirits. Hope beckons to us with such energy and life that if we take it seriously we cannot help but to find more than we lost, to experience healing in spite of our pain.

I watched as he called her "daughter," relieved to hear her finally called by name and wondered for a moment, what would he call me? Instead of a sin offering to mark the ending of her isolation, her homecoming to her own body was her gift of grateful worship, and as she knelt in thanksgiving, he honored her with the blessing of peace.

The healing that our spirits long for is given birth in the divine hope that is tenderly, deliberately set deep within our hearts. The hope for compassionate justice, the hope for genuine loving, the hope for deep and lasting peace moves us closer to our heart's desire to be made whole—to mend our torn and fragmented bodies and spirits, to renew and energize the gift of God within us, to bring to life, hope.

She invites me to share this cycle, this never-ending, upward spiraling. Immediate healing? She smiles. Yes and no. Always yes and no. For although we are confronted over and over again by the same rules, the same grief, the same isolation, the same despair, the same prejudice and presumptions, we are never in the same place as we were before. Infused by this indomitable hope we rise up to begin the cycle again, each time with just a little less pain, a little more hope until that moment when our hope flows unendingly into the hope of God.

I watch as she is swallowed up by the crowd, she so once alone, surrounded; me, so surrounded, now all alone. Wait! My heart cries to her. I know your name. Now I just long to see your face. Laughing now, she turns. It is my own.

The Sun Lover

Julia Kasdorf

The long afternoon after church
a girl lies on the lawn,
glazed thighs slightly parted,
fingers splayed like petals. At sixteen
she is a virgin. While her parents nap
in the quiet house, she knows
the sun is teaching her about love,
how it comes over your body
making every muscle go soft
in its pitiless gaze,

how it penetrates everything,
changing you into something dark
and radiant. She craves it,
knows it is everywhere like God's love,
but difficult to find. She waits,
entirely still, trying to see her eyelids—
not lingering traces, but the lids themselves
luminous and red as the cheeks of the kid
who stuck a flashlight in his mouth at camp.
She squints so the tips of her lashes
flash like iridescent fish scales.

Every hour, she turns over but prefers
to face the sun. All her life
she'll measure loves against this

gentle ravishing. She'll spend afternoons
alone on crowded beaches, and at home
stand naked before mirrors, amazed
by the pale shape of her suit. She'll touch
her cheekbones' tingling pink, and nip
at her lover's shoulder, as if
it were earth she were after.

Ladies' Night at the Turkish and Russian Baths

Julia Kasdorf

Outside, it's any tenement on East Tenth Street;
at the head of the stairs I drop my watch,
keys, wallet into a slender metal box
and take a robe of thin cotton sheeting.
Past the case of smoked fish, I pull off
my clothes among napping strangers and descend
marble steps stained with a century's grit.

In the steam room, an old woman looks up;
slender gourds hang off the cage of her ribs,
and when she wrings the pink cloth on her crotch,
I see a bun, bald as a girl's and think *crone*,
ashamed. She runs weary eyes down my form,
then closes them.

Along the plunge pool, supple women stroke
green mud on their cheekbones and stretch
their legs between plastic palms. Above them,
a compote of brilliant tile fruit and the name
of an Italian mason. I love to think of him
telling his son about this place, or how it was
in the thirties, filled with immigrants
from cold-water flats, one of them

with eyes like Franz Kafka could not afford
to come here, but did, breathing steam for hours,
not needing to remember the names of things,
only sweating out the soot of New York, safe
as I feel in the hot cave where women drape
between streaming spigots. Some murmur,
most are silent, except when one
grabs a bucket and dumps it onto her chest
with a groan. Our eyes meet and we grin,
grateful to show and view the real shapes
of ourselves: so many different breasts
and hips that get smoothed over by clothes,
none of us looking like we're supposed to!

And after, our hair wrapped up in towels,
we climb to a roof that faces the back
of Ninth Street where strangers pass by lit
windows, cooking dinner, opening letters.
We stretch out there on cots, and beside me
tears slide like sweat into the turban
of a stunning young woman. Whatever
the reason, I feel bound to her weeping,
eyes locked on our city's sky
aglow with all that lies beneath it.

V. Post-colonial Crossings

THE TERM POST-COLONIAL came into popular usage with the publication of *The Empire Writes Back: Theory and practice in post-colonial literatures*, by Bill Ashcroft, Gareth Griffiths and Helen Triffen in 1989. Initially defined as "all the culture affected by the imperial process from the moment of colonization to the present day," it refers to the European take-over and control of Asian, African and Middle Eastern territories from the late nineteenth century up until the independence movements of the post-WW II period. But, in common usage, that definition has broadened substantially to include any "cross-cultural" dynamic in the contemporary world resulting from an unjust use of power by one party to take over the physical space, values and "culture" of another. Thus, one could even say that a tyrannical teacher colonizes the minds of his/her students, who then, if they are fortunate, find a way to understand and respond to that take-over in the *post*-colonial period, following an "awakening," breakaway, or successful resistance.

Post-colonial writing arises not only from the urgency to write engendered by the experience of having been colonized, but also from the desire to demonstrate subversive strategies, rhetorical and otherwise, used to expose and resist systems of power. This is the idea of writing back or talking back, something we have all engaged in at some point in relationship to parents or other authority figures.

Paying attention to post-colonial dynamics is especially important for third world women whose lives have been controlled by both imperial (culturally external) and patriarchal (both external and indigenous) systems of power and who are attempting in their writings to give new definitions both to marginality and to empowered and resistant selfhood. In their writings they show us how to do this for ourselves, bringing us into a greater understanding not only of *their* oppressions but also of our own, while they point us to ways of finding liberation from coercive systems and individuals.

We first encounter an essay by Meena Alexander. Born in India, and having lived in Sudan and New York, Alexander asks in all of her writing how one can truly live in a multicultural world without acknowledging the hard overlapping of realities. As she says in "Translated Lives": "The Muslim women raped in Surat, the Hindu women stoned in Jersey City co-exist in time; cleft by space they forge part of the fluid diasporic world, a world in which I must live and move and have my being." Bringing such unspeakable acts into open literary discourse is, for Alexander, both acknowledgment of and resistance to the violence that perpetuates them.

In the essay printed here she takes us into her struggle to learn and accept English, the colonial master's tongue, as the language in which she will write her woman's life and her resistance. She speaks of poetry as a tearing apart and re-stitching of English syntax so that taking on *her* anguish and joy, it can lead her back to the body of her own thought. Thus, she acknowledges the counterviolence needed to correct the violent hegemony of English as it was taught to her by a strict Scottish tutor and at the Diocesan School for British children in Sudan, where she was forbidden to speak Hindi, Tamil, or her mother tongue, Malayalam.

The essay that follows, written by Indian born Ivy George, associate faculty of the Women's Studies May Term, examines cross-cultural systems of economic power that bring third world women to the first world to provide care for children, the sick and the elderly, often leaving their own dependents at home to be taken care of by relatives or by women further down on the economic ladder. Thus, a three-tiered colonization takes place, with poor women exploiting even poorer women, even as they are exploited by the rich and powerful. It is an insidious hierarchy, indeed, one fueled at least in part by the legitimate desire of first world women to seek careers (without making demands on their male partners to share in domestic work). Thus a legitimate desire for independence fosters illegitimate power and often the practice of illegal immigration as well. As an Asian woman caring for her own adopted child in the North American context and wondering what all of this means, George feels a strong tie with these "imported" caregivers and is able to tell their story from a position of empathy as well as her own deep sense of biblical justice.

Moving to a Middle Eastern voice, we find Leila Ahmed, Professor of Women's Studies at Harvard Divinity School and a practicing Muslim, commenting on the genuine nostalgia she feels for the harem—gatherings of women that graced her childhood in Cairo and whose stories, laughter and recitations from the Quran continue to shape her sense of lived rather than prescribed Islam. She reminds us that mosque-centered legalistic Islam is a recent political development, and that traditional oral Islam, handed down from one generation to the other, often through wise mothers and grandmothers, is the Islam that the ordinary Middle-Easterner has known. Women, the carriers of ethical truth, while wanting to protect their world from destructive Western cultural influence and political imperialism, nonetheless recognize that they have been doubly colonized by mullahs and religious fundamentalists. Their resistance to patriarchy, both within and from without their culture, requires the wisdom Ahmed embodies in her writing and teaching.

In the essay that follows, Elizabeth Morgan, co-founder of the Women's Studies May Term, attempts to model a way for first world readers to approach the works of third world women writers with humility and self-reflexive curiosity. Utilizing the work of Algerian novelist, Assia Djebar, she explores the complex reasons for veiling in the Middle East and turns that complexity back on Western culture in an attempt to understand Westerners' desires, both healthy and pathological, to hide themselves from view. Referring to Judeo-Christian religious traditions and to biblical ideas about physical and metaphoric veiling, she claims that Western stereotypes of Middle Eastern women need to be measured against their own histories, ideas and practices. Thus, we may all discover that modesty is a far more complicated concept than we allow ourselves to believe and that we have much to learn through sensitive cross-cultural readings of texts and lives.

Speaking from the Ghanian context, feminist theologians Mercy Oduyoye and Elizabeth Amoah tell us why African women love Jesus. It's nothing short of a miracle that they do, since Jesus was often forced on them by European missionaries and Christian schoolmarms for the duration of the colonial period. But, as merciful evidence that the truth cannot be annihilated by human distortion, they have read the scriptures for themselves and found a Jesus who cares about physical suffering, who triumphs over evil, who enacts the renewal of resurrection, and does not mind doing women's work. He gathers and prepares food (almost totally woman's work in many African cultures), willingly puts his hands in sick beds, and attends to the dying and dead. These writers' gift to us is in allowing us to see Jesus through new eyes, as a nurturing "other mother" who brings out the best in those around him.

Jennifer Davidson, a May Term alumnus and associate faculty, presents the biblical exegisis for this section. She looks at the terrible triangulation that took place between Father Abraham, his wife and his concubine. It is a triangulation defined by misuse of power, racial hatred, and just plain jealousy and pride. When Davidson shows us how each of these persons lives within us, we want to run for shelter. But there is no shelter except in recognition of how we are all victims and victimizers simultaneously; women, so often colonized through the course of history, are in no way free from the temptation to control another's life and fate. From this meditation we can learn humility and our deep need for truth-telling and forgiveness (of ourselves and others).

The two poems completing this section, and the book itself, are appropriately diverse. One of the ways colonialism stays alive in our world is through the prevalence of sweatshops, factories owned by citizens of rich countries but located in poor countries, where textiles and other products are assembled, often by women, for very low wages. "My Mother, Who Came from China Where She Never Saw Snow" brings it all home, for, in this poem, Laureen Mar reminds us that immigrants from poor countries have often found themselves in sweatshops in US cities where, like their sisters in poor countries, they also engage in back breaking work, for very little pay, in unsafe conditions. She presents an ironic American Dream, to be sure. And yet there is an enduring strength and passionate anger in the women she describes.

"I search for myself ..." is of another ilk. Looking for an empowering reflection of herself in the biblical text is truly a cross-cultural trek for poet Lisa Arensen, as she finds one woman after another colonized by oppressive systems and partners. But just as she despairs of finding a self she can fully embrace, she comes upon a poor woman looking for her lost coin, and knows that here is the image of God she desires to emulate, the one who searches for that which has been lost and knows it to be both precious and capable of restoration.

And so we end where we began: If women's studies is about believing that *all* persons are made in the image of God, including those who have been marginalized, sequestered, locked out, sexually abused and underpaid, then, perhaps, only a world where such persons are actively sought, valued and respected can truly be called home. And perhaps being made in the image of God means to be both the lost coin, knowing how it feels to exist in the shadows, and the seeker who brings things to light. To embrace the former is to enter the space of the victim. To embrace the latter is to insist on agency. Both are necessary in the quest for authentic selfhood; each can be a trap. May we keep our hearts open to those who have been unjustly colonized— including ourselves—without losing hope. And may we keep our eyes and ears open for ways of advancing mutuality and respect, without concluding the quest is ended.

Language and Shame

Meena Alexander

IT IS SUMMER IN MANHATTAN and a hot wind blows. The wind blows in through the window. I feel it against my cheek almost as if I were in Khartoum or Tiruvella. I lay out my old journals on the white desk and gaze at them. Time contracts into the scrawl of my teenage years. The journals composed when I was a teenager in Khartoum contain within them a desperate awareness of my femaleness, a sense of shame, of power drawn back that in its very intensity was a threat to the order that governed my young life.

For not only did I bear the shame from the Kerala world within me, but I set by its side the burning horror of clitoridectomy that many of my friends had described. Some like Sarra had spoken proudly, of how, through the liberal education of their fathers, they had escaped it. Others had suffered its brutality and were silent. In my years growing up, from time to time I was filled with the image of what women might suffer—whether through mutilation or through shame—sufferings caused purely by being female. And I felt in a dim, unspoken way that there was a connection between how I came to language and what it meant to be cast out, unhoused.

As a small child in India, I had learnt to speak English along with Malayalam and Hindi. Syllables, phrases, sentences of English flowed along as part of the river of my experience. In Khartoum, however, as a young child of five, cut from the fluidities of my Indian world, I had to learn English all over again. Now it was not just one language spoken among many: it was the most important one and I was an outsider confronting it. No doubt my English tutor, Mrs. McDermott, had a lot to do with my feelings of utter ineptitude when faced with the complexities of her mother tongue. Over and over she made me repeat the words she felt I should learn till their sharpness overwhelmed me, made my mouth hurt.

I see myself, a small child of six, sitting at a polished wooden table with a sheen so bright it reflected all that was cast onto it, an ivory vase with roses, a place mat, a knife, a fork pushed to the side, two faces, one small and dark, the other older and pale. The book I was trying to read was flush against the wood and so didn't make a double image: an old old book with pictures of Tom and Bess, little English children who wore knickerbockers and pinafores, carried caps in their hands and drank milk. They were forever loitering by ponds filled with ducks, racing down lanes towards windmills with red wooden slats. Mrs. McDermott leant forward. Over and over she made me say: "duck," "duck," "pluck," "pluck," "milk," "milk," "silk," "silk." It was hard for her. I pouted, I fidgeted under the table, knocking my knuckles against the wood, then tried over and over. It was a ruinous waste of time but she persisted. I was all wrong, I knew it. And I felt quite ashamed. The trouble was, I knew the words already but in a different way. And she tried her level best to polish out my Indian English and replace it with the right model. From her point of view she did a good job. Traces, perhaps even more than traces, of that speech linger on my tongue. How could she know that more than two decades later, that very diction would work against me, make me an oddity in the eyes of the white MidWestern feminist at a university in the colder reaches of this country who wanted nothing to do with me, who turned and said: "Of course they'll hire you. They'll trot you out because you speak such good English."

In Khartoum, after the year with the Scottish tutor, I enrolled in the Clergy House School, the first non-white child. At first they wouldn't let me into the school: it was officially known as the Diocesan School for British Children. But faced with the wrenching prospect of sending me away to Saint Joseph's in the hills of India, amma spoke to her uncle, C.P. Maathen, who had just come to the Sudan as the first ambassador from India. My great-uncle put in a word with the Anglican bishop and I was let in, by the side door as it were. For the first few months, when great-uncle and his daughter Sheila were living with us in Hai el Matar, while their large house by the Nile was being prepared for them, I rode into Clergy House School in the Indian ambassador's car, with the flag flying high. For great-uncle was there too, busily scanning his papers, running his elegant fingernails over the leather of his briefcase and his folders. When the driver opened the door for me, I hopped out, my lunch box in hand, my cotton frock come all the way from Tiruvella ironed straight, my two plaits neatly arranged on my shoulders. I was miserable in that school for the first two years. My blackness stuck out like a stiff halo all around me. I was imprisoned there, I could not move beyond it. I felt myself grow ugly under their gaze. The only friend I made was Christine from San Francisco. No one would play with her because she was fat, and so Christine and I had our lunch together under the outside staircase and we sat and watched the British and Australians and French and Germans toss their hair and ride on the roundabout in the Sudanese sun. Christine told me about Superman and Supergirl and the great golden bridge in San Francisco, and I remembered her, when years later, driven into Berkeley to give a poetry reading, I passed over that great metallic span and shut my eyes so the sun would not blind me and caught for an instant behind the sun's rays, the looming architecture of the prison of Alcatraz.

It should come as no surprise, then, that for almost a whole year in class I was dumb, I refused to open my mouth. It was my way of resisting. "You were considered very slow, you wouldn't read in class when you were asked to," amma reminded me. "I came to school," she explained, "and told that English woman: 'My child is not slow, just shy.' She let you be. Then it got a little better." I remember amma walking me to the gate to wait for the school bus, helping me over and over with English words so I wouldn't be puzzled or get lost. But when I began to write poetry at ten and eleven, she grew anxious, perhaps justifiably so, about the disclosures that a writing life commits one to, quite contrary to the reticence that femininity requires.

As a child in Khartoum I used to hide out to write, either behind the house where there was a patch of bare wall and the shade of a neem tree, or better still, in the half-darkness of the toilet. I gradually found that the toilet was safer. There I could mind my own business and compose. I also learnt to write in snatches, a skill that has served me well. If someone knocked at the door, I stopped abruptly. I hid my papers under my skirts, tucked my pen into the elastic band of my knickers, and got up anxiously. Gradually, this enforced privacy—for I absorbed, perhaps even in part identified, with amma's disapproval of my poetic efforts—added an aura of something illicit, shameful, to my early sense of scribblings. Schoolwork was seen in a totally different light. Essays, exercises, note-taking, reading and writing about the literary works on the school syllabus, were always encouraged. It was good to excel there, interpreting works that were part of a great literary past. The other writing, in one's own present, was to be tucked away, hidden. I had to be secretive about the writing that came out of my own body, but still a fierce pride clung to it.

Little did I know that years later the hot unease I had first felt as a small child learning to repeat English words, and trying to get them right, that dense tissue of feeling (unease, embarrassment, a fear of being exposed, a shame, finally, of being improper, not quite right, never quite right) would return sharply, enveloping me. Once again I felt that hot scent: forcing me back onto myself, onto a border existence. But this time it was my intellectual work that was called into question, not because of itself, but because of what my body made me: female, Indian, Other.

I was once called into the office of the chairman of my department at the Jesuit university where I worked. He leant forward in his black garb, stiff, quite clear about his own position. "It has been pointed out to me that you do not publish in the area in which you were hired, British Romanticism."

I perked up. "What about that?" I pointed to a book lying on his table. He picked it up, a little puzzled. "Look at the table of contents," I pointed at it with my finger. He glanced at me. I was sitting there, quite proper in my Kashmir silk sari, erect at the edge of the chair. His eyes shifted to the titles of chapters listed in the table of contents. There was a gap there, a split second. I shivered, not because I was cold—it was early fall and quite warm still—but because I suddenly saw something. There was no way the man who sat in front of me could put together my body with any sense of the life of the mind. I had fallen under the Cartesian blade. "Yes, yes," he muttered, looking at the chapters with names like Wordsworth and Coleridge littering them. "Yes, yes."

I stood up. The trouble was what I was, quite literally: female, Indian. Not that I had not published in my designated area, but that I had also published outside that docket. A paper on Jayanta Mahapatra had just come out in London. Some senior colleagues had seen it. Was this stuff really literature? Also, I was active in the reading series, Art Against Apartheid, and my poems were coming out in journals. It was all quite improper. Later, when I was denied tenure in the spring of 1986, when my body was swelling with a second child, going into work I sometimes smelled that old shame. The sharpness of the recollection excited me, but by then I was too tired to sort it out. I left it hanging there in memory.

When I was a child, barbed wire ran across the back of the Tiruvella compound where the cashew nut trees grew, where the mango trees arced their boughs of speckled fruit. In July the cashews started to ripen. First there were streaks of yellow in the soft fruit out of which the nut descended, then as the season gathered force, green turned ocher or red with the sweetness of the cashew sap. This was the signal for the young boys who lived in the railway huts to turn up in little clusters, armed with stones. If I stood quite still in the back bedroom where my grandmother's mirror stood in its rosewood frame, I could hear the sharp sting of stones against the cashew trees. If Bhaskaran or Kittan were not there, I would have to run out and start shouting at the boys, "Stop that, you, how dare you, scoot, scoot," and other such strings of words that rushed out of my mouth.

Once, I grabbed a young urchin by the foot as he tried to slither out from under the barbed wire, a horde of juicy cashew fruits under his armpit. I felt the air from his ankle lashing at my hand. But as his foot slipped out under the barbed wire, I felt another "I" slipping out with the dusty child. After all, why shouldn't he have a few of the fruits? What did he have to eat at night? A mess of gruel and a few chilis with these fruits as supplement, and once a week, if he were lucky, a small slice of fish. Isn't that why his ribs stuck up in hunger? Wasn't that what Ilya and all his friends were talking about when they had those meetings on "The Needs of Our Children?" I was torn in that way by my own behavior. I was a divided child and felt my own precariousness: born to privilege, I clearly had only one foot in my grandfather's garden. I had returned home for the holidays from Khartoum, and what I saw, however intense my vision, was colored by another life.

Quite soon after, my own divided stance was brought home to me. It was the same summer. The children next door were having a birthday party. Their father had returned after several years in the United States, and had invited a colleague, another mathematician, to visit India. The professor had duly arrived with his redheaded wife and freckled, carrot-haired children in tow. It was a miracle. People came from miles around to see them. "How could anyone be that color," people whispered. "An unknown jinni? Too much henna applied raw—what then of the spotty skin?" Some even wondered if it was an advanced European form of leprosy that invaded the bodies of these visitors, but they seemed perfectly healthy and no one lacked body parts. No toes dropping off, nothing like that. At the birthday party, the little American children, three of them, stood in a lonely group by the marigold patch. My friends pushed me forward.

"You go ahead, Meena."

I dug in my toes, quite firmly.

"Why me?" and even as I knew the answer that would come, "No, no," I muttered. "Not me, not me."

"You must." They pushed me on. "You've talked to people like that in Africa."

"Well..."

"No, don't be worried, really," the oldest, Reeni, took me by the hand, almost leading me there. She wanted the birthday party to be a success. The visitors should at least try to play a little, loosen up, share in the sweet papaya that was being brought around. Still I shrank back, not wanting to be picked out, the childhood desire for conformity turned into a prickly fear, for the little boy Bubu was hissing in my ear:

"You speak like that too, *sssss*," he made the sounds with a sharp tongue, "*sssss*, the Madama language." I stood, smiling hesitantly at those children, and even put out my hand, but I resolutely refused to open my mouth.

I knew what I was: a child from Tiruvella. That is what my flesh made of me and I saw no reason to let my mouth betray me. I was well aware, though, that at other times, in other places, I had to rely wholly on the language I had learnt with such pain, to carry me through the invisible barbed wire of a burden I had not chosen. Later, as I became a teenager, I realized the forked power in the tongue I had acquired: English alienated me from what I was born to; it was also the language of intimacy and bore the charged power of writing. Through it, I dared to hope, I might some day unlock the feelings that welled up within me.

～

I was just thirteen when I entered Khartoum University. My father had to get special permission from the University Senate, so that I could enter. I had graduated first in my class from Unity High School and there was nowhere else I could go. In the mid-sixties, politically and pedagogically, Khartoum University was an exciting place to study. Reading groups recited Arabic poetry; drama groups put on everything from Wole Soyinka's *Dance of the Forests*—I remember the great thrill of helping construct the papier-mâché masks for the production—to *Caligula*. There was the energy of trying to figure out Sudan's place in the outburst of power flooding the Arab world. Nasser was at the helm of Egypt and there was a strong sense that the world was changing. At the same time, the issue of an African identity was not lost in the debates the students engaged in. A civil war was smoldering in the south of the Sudan, and southern Sudanese were being tortured and killed by the northern troops. Although General Abboud's so-called "benevolent dictatorship" had prohibited all discussion of the "southern question," the students' union decided to go ahead with its debate on the issue and, when refused permission, hundreds of students took to the streets. The townspeople joined them. Then the tanks started rolling.

I had gone to the street demonstration with my friends, Sarra and Azza Anis. It was my first public march and indeed my introduction to the larger, more vital life of the university. There was tear gas in the air; two students ahead of us, Babiker and Bedri, were shot to death. More and more tanks rolled out of the army barracks and the stench of the tear gas became unbearable. But in the face of overwhelming support for change the army backed down. A bloodless Coup, everyone said, when democracy was restored for a few short years.

Raised by Ilya on the stories of civil disobedience that had finally forced the British to leave India, I was prepared in my own way for the oppositional struggle my friends were embarked on in the Sudan. It seemed to me then, nearly fourteen, that the whole of the known world must be participating in these struggles. My sense of poetry, even in its uttermost privacy, drew strength from struggle, from tumult. I felt that it must be possible for all human beings to struggle towards equality and social justice, to live in a world without unnecessary suffering.

The language I used, English, was part of my reaching out for this new world. It was braided in for me with the Arabic that was all around me, the language that my first poems were translated into, the language in which I first heard words of love and anger. English was woven too with the French I had learnt in school and chattered with my friends, the language of Verlaine and Mallarmé, of the most exquisite lyricism imaginable, of tears, of storms of tears, of betrayal.

> Le ciel est, pardessus le toit
> > Si bleu, si calme!
> Un arbre pardessus le toit
> > Berce sa palme.

I loved those lines, for quite early I understood the necessity of beauty, of an atmosphere of silence, of a void even in which the imagination might blossom. And without the space made for beauty, of what use was the political struggle? The heart would grow hard, numb, turn into a desert stone.

I existed then, in my unfolding sense of what it might mean to speak and write, in the tension between my multiple worlds. In my teenage studies I was deeply attracted to the poetry and prose of the English Romantics, whose intense, even tormented probings into the nature of image and language were underwritten by the call for a revolutionary knowledge. I will never forget the first time I read Coleridge. It was in Khartoum, and I carried with me the magical thought of what he, borrowing from Schlegel, developed as the notion of organic form, the idea that any living existence, a cloud, a plant, a poem, a person, might have its own unique inner teleology, apparent only in the flowering of the fullest form, a logic, a *svadharma,* that could not be questioned. Given this, no one could say: you're all wrong, you don't do things right, you don't get the final syllable in the stanza right. The inner form had a logic so powerful it was best spoken of in the language reserved for passion and it tore through the mesh of decorum, of the principled order the disparate social worlds had established.

Yet even as these liberating thoughts came to me in English, I was well aware that the language itself had to be pierced and punctured lest the thickness of the white skin cover over my atmosphere, my very self. The language I used had to be supple enough to reveal the intricate mesh of otherness in which I lived and moved. My very first poems were composed in French when I was twelve and thirteen: I felt this was the way to attain the heights of lyricism Verlaine had opened up. Slowly I revised my thoughts and turned to English.

In the late sixties, I was part of a small group of poets at Khartoum University. My friends all wrote in Arabic and were strong supporters of the use of contemporary language. They felt that the decorum of the classical meters could only violate the quick of the spoken form, the pressing needs of the poet. These friends easily translated my poems into Arabic. My first publications were these poems printed in the Arabic newspapers in Khartoum. While this gave me a great deal of pleasure, I was also surprisingly compliant about accepting my illiteracy in Arabic. During childhood, I lived in Hai el Matar near the poet and scholar Abdullah Tayib, who had encouraged me to study the great classical poetry in Arabic. Somehow, I was hesitant to learn the script. I wanted only to listen, to let the spoken language wash over me. Dylan Thomas's lines concerning "the force that through the green fuse drives the flower" made utter sense and I held fast to the same impulses that had allowed me to escape my grandmother Mariamma's elaborate mesh of proprieties, and to escape also the study of the Malayalam script.

It seemed to me, then, that one script was enough, the one that I had been forced to learn. And I truly believed that I could translate myself in and out of it, together with all the languages that welled up inside me. Perhaps there was also something else at stake, a greater fragility than I could acknowledge, a need to protect the quick of the self.

Through an inability to read and write the script in Arabic, and even in Malayalam my mother tongue, I maintained an immediacy of sound and sense in those two great languages of my childhood years that enabled me to dissolve and dissipate, if only in a partial, paradoxical fashion, the canonical burden of British English. And so a curious species of linguistic decolonization took place for me, in which my own, often unspoken sense of femaleness played a great part. I set the hierarchies, the scripts aside, and let the treasured orality flow over me. After all, that was how Malayalam had first come to me: in chants, in spoken voices that held a community together. Perhaps deep within me was a fear that learning the script would force me to face up to the hierarchies of a traditional society, the exclusionary nature of its canonical language. Wouldn't that script imprison me? How then would I ever be restored to simplicity, freed of the burdens of counter-memory?

I did not know any women who were writers, at least not firsthand, though indeed, I was aware that such beings existed in the libraries of the world. And it was only dimly, if at all, that I was aware that the illiteracies I clung to helped me steer clear of the elaborate hierarchical machine that set women apart, lower, different from men. In those days, my friends in Khartoum were slipping out of their tobs, or refusing ever to put them on, and struggling against the old strictures that ordained clitoridectomies for women, that barbarous mutilation my two closest girlfriends had escaped. Women were refusing to carry a bride price; almost in jest, they were renting the elaborate gold jewelry needed for weddings, the cost of which would have burdened the family with debt.

They were seeking out the rights of women. I recall a student union election at Khartoum University when, without the slightest hint of irony, an ardent Communist argued that women have souls. The Communists were campaigning for women's equality and won overwhelmingly that year against the Muslim Brothers, their chief opponents. The struggle to modernize was everywhere, and I entered into the exhilaration of it.

I was fascinated by the corrosive magic of the first person singular: its exuberant flights, its sheer falls into despair. Still there was always a desire to tell the stories of my life, to write of Ilya's garden. My experiences as a young child, as a guardian of the cashew nut grove, were sufficiently troublesome to lead me to want to set down those feelings in words. I needed a fictional form that would allow me more than the intensities of the lyric voice: I needed others, many voices, a plot however simple, a form from which history could not be torn out any more than a heart could be torn from a living animal. At thirteen I thought I would write a short story. But in my first attempts the supple skin of language turned into a barbed wire that trapped me.

I was sitting in the stacks at the bottom of Khartoum University Library. The library was made of sandstone. Large columns held it up and made for a delicious coolness in the basement where the stacks were. I could run my palms over the bricks and feel the pleasure of release from the intense heat outside. I had a favorite spot, right by the poems of Sylvia Plath. To my right was the shelf of contemporary poetry in English translation, and my favorites: Yevgeny Yevtushenko, Hans Magnus Enzensberger, Paul Celan. My own scribblings in poetry seemed quite trite, so I turned to my other life, tried to put down the words of the child I was in Tiruvella, years ago and the thoughts of the child he was, whose name I never knew as I gripped his ankle under the barbed wire.

Something tore inside me. No, I wouldn't. I couldn't do it. I could not turn the Malayalam utterances into English. Why would I even want to do it—turn those words of the language where I lived and moved in my inmost being into an English that could never carry that emotion, that would only distort it? But there was more too. How could I translate the words, the feelings of my mother tongue, the only one I had, into the discrepant script of English? English was so powerful, even Celan and Yevtushenko were translated into it. That is how I read them, knew of them. But I could not bear to set myself into that trench, tear myself limb from limb.

And at least two things became clear: one was that I could never write fiction, for that would mean translating the words of the people I knew best, the life and the practices I was closest to; and the other was a sudden bitter realization of the sheer force of English and how I had been made to learn it. I had had no choice in the matter. It was presented to me quite literally as the only way to go. Living in Khartoum as an expatriate Indian child, I had to learn English. How could I possibly have received an Arabic education? What would that have equipped me for? And in any case the Sanskrit and

Malayalam tutors were far away, across the burning waters I had traveled with amma.

Bit by bit I realized that the form of the poem offered something I needed, a translation out of the boundaries of the actual, a dance of words that might free me from my own body. And I took to reading poems day and night so that history might not consume me, render me dumb. But that realization came slowly when, years later in North America, I had to strip my partial knowledge away so that I could learn to write the truth of the body, pitted, flawed, unfinished....

Was English in India a no man's land? No woman's either? I could not be sure in those tumultuous years of the early seventies when I lived and worked there. At the Central Institute of English in Hyderabad where I started work in 1975, there was much discussion of precise speech, correct pronunciation, appropriate usage, the status of English in India, the function of the language, how knowledge imparted in English, including technical knowledge that had to do with modernizing the country, must surely have a trickle-down effect as it was called, from the elite—who unabashedly saw themselves as such—to the rest of country. English then had this superior status in the eyes of some who taught there, superior that is to any Indian language. But there were others who realized that the future of English in India lay in its ability to blend itself with the life all around, the world of the streets, of the marketplaces.

Often I would spend long evenings with my dear friend Susie Tharu, thinking through what it meant to write in India, what sort of art could come out of the streets, the marketplaces. In her company, I learnt to think afresh of aesthetic forms and consider how they are bounded by the public spaces of our lives. Susie too had spent her childhood in Africa—in Uganda, rather than the Sudan—and then, after her studies in Britain, had returned to India. In those days I learnt from her about femaleness, about resistance, and the possibility of political action. In 1979, just before I left Hyderabad, she took me to the first meetings of the women's group, Shree Shakti Sanghatana. Even after I left Hyderabad for New York our friendship, stretched taut by absence, survived, deepened.

In India, my quest to make sense of poetry written in English—what role would it have in terms of Indian literature, who would read it?—took me to Cuttack to meet the poet Jayanta Mahapatra. First, I wrote to Jayanta, whose work I admired; and asked if I might call on him. It was 1976: I was twenty-five years old. I took the train to Cuttack and then set out in one of those high-backed rickshaws in search of Tinkonia Bagicha. The rickshaw driver took me to the gate. I peered in through the bamboo that grew by the house and saw a bay window filled with books and then Jayanta's slight figure dashing out, calling me. I spent several days there, immersed in the life of poetry, feeling the soil under my feet. Jayanta and his wife Runu grew to be dear friends. Through Jayanta, who had lived his whole life in Cuttack, I learnt to understand the poet's bond with place; learnt to understand how the elegaic voice could gather sustenance from the landscape around; learnt, too, how to accept the ravages of time.

The years when I taught at the Central Institute in Hyderabad, 1975 to 1977, were the years of the Emergency in India, when Prime Minister Indira Gandhi withdrew civil liberties and people could be jailed on mere suspicion of an oppositional stance. Behind my office window was a police station and sometimes I could hear the cries and the hoarse whispers of those who were taken there. I wrote a poem about a police station called "Within the Walls," which appeared in the *Democratic World* in Delhi, but the next poem I sent in and they accepted, "Prison Bars," about prisoners being beaten, was never published. Instead, in the spot where it should have been, the magazine maintained a blank white space, the exact size of the poem, a signal of censorship.

In 1977 I moved a few miles away to Hyderabad University, a very new institution, and there, in an atmosphere of academic excitement, I debated the question of poetry all over again, particularly poetry written in English. My special friend there was the poet Arvind Krishna Mehrotra, who was reading *After Babel* in those days and thinking hard about multilingualism and the composition of poetry in English. For my part I could not forget my Khartoum experiences and how English, the language in which I made poems, had come to me.

Colonialism seemed intrinsic to the burden of English in India, and I felt robbed of literacy in my own mother tongue. The English department of Hyderabad University was housed in "The Golden Threshold," home of the poet Sarojini Naidu. Reading Naidu's poetry and her political speeches—she used English for both purposes—I noted how the discourse of her poetry stood at odds with the powerful language of her speeches. The former was pained, contrived, modeled on the poetry of the English Decadents, filled with images of the female body wasting away. Her speeches, in contrast, were impassioned, concerned with the British abuse of power, with the possibility of a new Indian beginning: they were forcefully directed to her audience, a people struggling for national independence.

I was fascinated by how English worked for her, and how in her political speeches the language could be turned to the purposes of decolonization. What would it be like if Naidu as a poet had been able to break free of the restrictive ideology that bound her in? What would she have needed in order to make poems of resistance, poems that voiced the body?

The questions have not left me. They reverberate in my head. Sometimes a voice rises in my dreams, as floodwaters rise, subsiding suddenly. And the parched landscape of Hyderabad, in the season before the rains fall, starts to crackle with flames and the flames become the blue gas flames in the stove in my New York City kitchen and in my dream I have to hold myself back with both hands, tie the end of my sari to the refrigerator handle to prevent me from tumbling over the slopes into the fault lines that split my imagined earth.

"We must imagine the earth again. Poetry must be like bread," Faiz Ahmed Faiz once said to me. I can still see his face, his eyes, that grand old man of letters, eyes green-blue, the color of the sky after rainfall. It was 1977 or perhaps early '78 in Hyderabad. He was in the large, ornate drawing room, in the home of Indira Devi Dharajgir. It was an intimate gathering, and I had been invited to meet Faiz, asked to bring some poems along to recite to him. A musician was there, with a sitar, a tanpura player, to perform some of Faiz's ghazals. Faiz patted the place next to him on the sofa, so that I could sit down. He spoke of the poems he had composed during the Bangladesh War, he spoke of Beirut, then suddenly laughing at some comment about translation and the Third World, said, "English, of course, is the language of love!" We were charmed, feeling that at least some times he must speak to his English wife in that tongue and she, of course, living in Lahore, was surrounded by Urdu. Now, years after his death, I want to turn to him and say, Faiz, how can poetry be like bread? How?

Shelter, unhousedness, the multiple speeches that surround us, broken walls, prison cells. The thoughts turn jagged in me. Everything is overcrowded. Everything is emptied out. I dream of barbed wire.

There are images of barbed wire in the long poem "Night-Scene, the Garden." I started work on the poem in the months after Svati Mariam was born when the experience of childbirth was still with me. In that poem I am haunted by "ferocious alphabets of flesh." They have to do with the female body, but also the limbo the violence of combat breeds: the blasted terrain of the West Bank, houses blown up, olive trees uprooted; the bombed-out streets of Aden I saw as a child; the ravaged hillsides of Sri Lanka; the fields of the Punjab where massacres bloom as millet and wheat once did. These spaces of radical dislocation are bounded by barbed wire. In the poem, though, the barbed wire is at the edge of the Tiruvella garden, quite close to the heart:

My back against barbed wire
snagged and coiled to belly height
on granite posts
glittering to the moon

No man's land
no woman's either
I stand in the middle
of my life...

Out of earth's soft
and turbulent core
a drum sounds
summoning ancestors
They rise
through puffs of grayish dirt
scabbed skins slit
and drop from them

They dance
atop the broken spurts
of stone

They scuff
the drum skins
with their flighty heels.

Men dressed
in immaculate white

bearing spears, and reams
of peeling leaf

Minute inscriptions
of our blood and race

Stumbling behind
in feverish coils
I watch the women come,
eyes averted from the threads
of smoke that spiral
from my face.

Some prise
their stiffening knuckles
from the iron grip
of pots and pans
and kitchen knives
Bolts of unbleached
cloth, embroidery needles,
glitter and crash in heaps.

∽

Slow accoutrements of habit
and of speech,
the lust of grief
the savagery of waste
flicker and burn
along the hedgerows
by the vine.

The lost child
lifts her eyes
to mine.

∽

Come, ferocious alphabets of flesh
Splinter and raze my page

That out of the dumb
and bleeding part of me

I may claim
my heritage.

The green tree
battened on despair
cast free

The green roots kindled
to cacophony.

On Motherhood and Care

Ivy George

FOUR CAMEOS ARE CRITICAL for framing this discussion.

Time: Zero hours in the summers of 2002 and 2004.
Setting: Bahrain, Kuwait, Doha, Dahran or Muscat airports.
Characters: Sri Lankan and Filipina women standing and sitting in corners, slightly at a distance from the traffic of other international passengers. What singles the women out besides their isolated physical location at the airport is the excessive adornment of jewelry on their passenger bodies—layers of 22 carat gold watches, necklaces, bracelets, bangles, rings and earrings, nose rings and anklets. They are otherwise quite simply dressed and appear to be cowering from the crowds. They are isolated among themselves. They seem preoccupied. Their hand luggage is packed chock-full. They have consolidated their recent livelihood.

The social text is clearly legible. They are nannies and domestics en route to their families of origin after having served wealthy Arab or expatriate families in these Gulf countries.

～

Time: Late 1980s and early 1990s.
Setting: Frankfurt airport.
Characters: Thai and Filipina women who are wives and girlfriends of German men seated in the waiting areas. They sit alone or with their partners as if they are roosting. All are quietly waiting.

～

Time: November, 2001.
Setting: The banks of the Tiber river in Italy.
Characters: My family and I are traveling on a major arterial road along the

famed Tiber river through a sparsely populated, quiet and idyllic Umbrian countryside. Suddenly, I see a lone woman in black leather and hair dyed blonde sauntering aimlessly about on the grass and gravel. Her utterly isolated presence is disturbing due to the absence of any human habitation around. She is like a horse put out to pasture for the day. Perplexed, I ask my host for an explanation. The response, "A sex worker from Eastern Europe. The problem is far more serious with West African women." And soon I pass an African woman, all made up, in tight fitting leathers. And another African woman a little later. And another. And another. The wintry winds blowing through the hillsides are relentless on these barely clothed women. They have their mobile phones on them as pimp monitors. And they wait patiently for a trucker or motorist to stop by.

The scene was the same every time I traveled this road. There was something eerie about witnessing this human tragedy played out on this hauntingly stunning Umbrian landscape. It was all so out of joint. The experience remains seared in my memory.

∾

Time: Mid-morning, mid-week, Spring, 2003.
Setting: Manhattan Children's Museum, New York.
Characters: I walk in with my hands linked to my daughter's. As I wind my way through the maze of women and children visiting, I spy a South Asian woman and send out a glance of recognition and solidarity as woman and mother from the same region of the world. She looks away instantly. A few seconds later another such woman comes along and a similar rejection of attention through deflection occurs. This is repeated once or twice more. In a short while I re-encounter the two women and more from the Caribbean, South America, Africa, the Philippines and Sri Lanka in the reading room for a story session. All their children are Euro-American. And then I know. There could be no solidarity here.

∾

I took a circuitous route to motherhood. I was of the age to know that my entrance into motherhood or the abnegation of it would have political consequences for human well being elsewhere. Having a child was not exclusively a private affair as I had been socialized to believe.

Similar to pressures as a single woman towards getting married, I came into pressure as a married woman to have a child. The communications were fairly explicit: continuity, productivity, success, vocation, fulfillment and some of my thoughtful associates would tell me that children are channels of hope in a world scant of it. Knowing well that historical and contemporary forces and fates larger than the self influenced choice and sensibilities, I could not contemplate motherhood lightly. Needless to say it was a lonely and isolating time as I moved among perplexed friends and against an impatient body clock. Ultimately, my mind encircled around a life-long condition of being and knowing: Grief.

I was born into an egregiously unequal society. A world where even as a child I could easily connect the dots between those who had the advantage and those who did not. The house pets, servants, masters and madams, vegetarians and non-vegetarians, Hindus, Muslims and Christians, boys and girls, men and women, tenants and landowners, rural and urban, fair skinned and dark skinned all bore the marks of the social pox of "birth, rank and hereditary influence." This intricate, sometimes subtle, frequently graphic apartheid was the mantle of my social inheritance. Later, events such as my emigration and a loss of place through colonialism and globalization have contributed to this state of grief. An abiding sense of impotence and irrelevance in this social context meant that life changing decisions and choices could not be entered into casually.

By the time I contemplated motherhood I was aware that the line between private matters and public affairs was thin and broken at many points. It had been difficult enough to justify my own existence by virtue of past inheritances, and now my complicity in the world's evils as a citizen of one of the world's most powerful nations was difficult to bear. I could not take responsibility for a child. It would be reckless to do so and I was without confidence. My exposure to some of the world's unrelenting social fissures, to the circumstances of women and children caught in conflict and want, made me aware of the large numbers of children who needed a home and family. The frequent thwarting of adult and child life was too much to live with. Amidst all this, could I provide a home for one child? I was haunted by that possibility. Despite all the corruption that I was besieged by, the values of care and nurture still had a place in the world, and acts of love still brought meaning and purpose to human living. I was persuaded that to welcome a child into this world was in a way a kind of tribute to life at large, a meager response to the brokenness in this world. After all, that most elemental human and ultimately social relationship between a caregiver and child was perhaps the first and sometimes last space for many of us to do life over, to do the world over in a sense.

It was in that spirit that we moved to adopt a child. The idea that women "choose" to have children is a fraught one. While undoubtedly the female body alone can generate and nurture another human life and in that sense a woman's body may be held responsible for this most amazing feat of creation and parturition, it cannot be automatically assumed that she chooses this process. Choice occurs in particular social spaces. Economic well being, the freedom to engage in or refrain from sexual intercourse, opportunities for marriage, access to contraception, the body's ability to conceive and sustain a pregnancy, the freedom not to bear a child, social and economic freedoms to rear a child, adequate health care are some of the many factors that press on a woman's person as she is set to choose. "Choice" then is mediated by multiple social forces and is therefore a contingent act. Similarly, our decision to adopt a child was shaded by social forces, a product of our particular social memory and inheritances referred to earlier. For me, my experiences with grief and shame in a vast circulatory system of evil made it very difficult to contemplate a biological propagation. Continuity did not have much appeal. The past had to be interrupted. It had to be resisted and doing so personally was a challenge to which I wanted to rise. My spouse and I understood this and came to peace easily. I identified somewhat vicariously with men and women who as survivors and perpetrators of horror in war time Europe and under South African apartheid in the twentieth century had similar responses to their social inheritances. A disturbing and far less sanguine example of this psychology where the self does not own or control the body finds witness in Toni Morrison's protagonist Sethe in her classic *Beloved*. At the outer edges of this thinking our move to adopt fell into the realm of an imperative in our lives of compromised living.

The four years since then have moved me to further my understandings of motherhood. One of the significant lessons I have learned is the danger of essentialising the concept of "mother" based on blood and biology as these specifically relate to a woman and her offspring.[1] Many women who are enacting the role of mothers outside this traditional dyad are exempt from the status and many within the dyad are rigidly confined by the static nature of the term. It is important to observe the power of language to represent and impute intrinsic qualities to social phenomena, and the utility of this process to entrenched social systems such as patriarchy. There are several studies that show that the idea of "mother love" is built on an artifice of social construction; that is, far from this being an a priori relationship which can be automatically assumed between woman and child, a variety of social factors have to be present in order to develop this relationship. Instances of large-scale infanticide in Brazil and India attest to this fact.[2] In Western societies, multiple industries from book publishers, to psychotherapists and retail goods stores flourish in the business of preparing and educating women to "mother" adequately and effectively. All over the world (at least until a takeover by the imperium of technology at a later date), the woman-child relationship still seems like an arrangement where there is little choice of the particular child, or person who births or provides care.

Moving the term of "motherhood" from a fixed, nominal category to a descriptor of specific social relations between a woman and a child provides some elasticity and flexibility to include not only adoptive mothers, but also instances of social maternity where aunts, grandmothers, extended family relations and, in some cases, older siblings become providers of prolonged care for children. Such a shift in understanding among governments and non-governmental agencies has a special immediacy for communities ravaged by war and disease and where traditional families have been destroyed. Conversely, women who for physical, psychological, social, political and economic reasons are not able to care for their offspring should also be free from being weighted down by the term. Biological events should not have to define the entirety of these women's lives.

This versatility in the concept of "mother" has been enormously illuminating and liberating for me as I try to be a mother to our daughter. Not a day passes when I do not think of or pray for the woman who gave birth to our child. I hope that she will be freed from the compulsions of biology and culture that have beset her as a result of the incident of childbirth. I hope she will come to understand that the sum of her life is not to be determined by one incident and experience. Our daughter too will have to grow to understand the meaning of a mother only as she experiences it with me.

As I became a mother I moved to occupy a vast, uncharted and unimagined territory of grief and humanhood. At a visceral level I experience deep emotional, psychological and spiritual bonds with this woman who is connected to my daughter. I am moved by the heroic quality of her life. Bearing, caring, giving in and finally giving up. I long to know her and to tell her that I am her shadow sister who walks with her, and that I will keep her trust to my death. In the process of this almost surreal relationship, she and I have been knit together by a trust without any guarantees. Not faith or hope exactly, because no promise has been given, merely the amazement of two distant and unlikely fates inextricably intertwined through one little life. By association I try to imagine the lives of women all over the world who have been wrenched from their children by external forces that range from personal and familial, to political and cultural arrangements. I think of the children who live with loss and speculation around their origins. I am grateful to have entered this circle of grief and to define my life in light of this tragic knowledge.

Constructing Motherhood in the West

Nancy Chodorow, the feminist sociologist, advances the question as to how it is that women come to "mother" and considers the implications of this social arrangement for society. In an essay she wrote on "Gender Personality and the Reproduction of Mothering,"[3] she argues that the social dimensions of motherhood must be explained in terms of the surrounding social structure. That (most) women's capacities for gestation and lactation lie in the realm of biology, and that prehistoric conditions necessitated some form of sexual division of labor need not be debated. But these do not explain sufficiently the question of how women come to mother. Conventional explanations of gender socialization where boys and girls are taught and learn differently are inadequate. For Chodorow it takes more than individual abilities to explain the societal reproduction of physical human re-creation. There are other social, psychological factors at work. She combines psychoanalytic and sociological perspectives to suggest that in industrialized societies, early infant experiences with mostly female caregivers have exponential effects in multiple social spheres which then result in gendered social structures.

Chodorow suggests that a woman's act of mothering contains within itself the ability to re-create itself. This practice results in gendered parenting outcomes whereby women are equipped with specific psychological capacities and men are denied these abilities to execute their role as primary parents. Parenting experiences with women lead females to seek to mother more than males, that is, they are more likely to enter into the role of primary care for a child, to be satisfied in this relationship, and to express psychological, emotional and relational abilities to mother.

Mothers tend to treat their male children as opposites of themselves while male attachment to their mothers is suppressed, hence a naturalisation of women as mothers takes place while men by virtue of their incapacities are excluded from the role. Shared experiences of being cared for by a woman leads to the perception by both men and women that mothers naturally fix their energies and interests on the infant's well being. By extension it is expected that women supply care to children of all ages naturally and therefore these "natural" qualities can be expressed and expected in non-domestic spheres as well. Chodorow concludes that the naturalisation of women's child bearing and rearing potential leads to the structural association of women with the domestic sphere and their location within it. This contributes to the unequal social organization of gender and economic organization of production. One notes that these arrangements with women and children have precluded male participation in these contexts as caregivers, and therefore it is difficult to establish the thesis that "women are natural caregivers/mothers." Male capabilities and proficiencies have already been established in other traditionally "female" preserves such as cooking, tailoring, design and decoration, nursing and teaching.

One can only speculate then of the potentially revolutionary possibilities that can take place in the home under alternative societal arrangements that facilitate and welcome the presence and participation of men:

> Women's mothering also reproduces the family as it is constituted in male dominated society. The sexual and familial division of labor in which women mother creates a sexual division of psychic organization and orientation. It produces socially gendered women and men who enter into asymmetrical heterosexual relationships; it produces men who react to, fear, and act superior to women, and who put most of their energies into the nonfamilial work world and do not parent. Finally, it produces women who turn their energies toward nurturing and caring for children—in turn producing the sexual and familial division of labor in which women mother.[4]

Social theorists understand such women's work as "caring labor."[5] Other activities like nursing, kin work, teaching, elder care also fall under the rubric of "caring labor." What are the considerations given to the caring labor force in societies pervaded by contemporary global market capitalism? How do we tease out Nancy Chodorow's point that the mother's re-creation propagates the gendered labor structure that is fairly universal in our societies? This discussion is necessary for the translation of the preceding conceptual discussion of motherhood, and for the transformation of gendered societal structures. This is a complex and exhaustive undertaking; I shall attempt only a topical treatment of the question here.

One of the chief obstacles in the social validation of the caring labor force is the manner in which societies understand and value "work." Implicit in our consideration of "work" is the attachment of monetary worth to human production. Further, the selection of certain activities such as "work" has an instrumental dimension to it, i.e., the promotion of the goals of the controlling elites and the state. The overarching nature of patriarchal power dictates the automatic negation of women from the calculus of work and worth. Productive activity outside the home is considered "work," while work at home is not merely undervalued but is classified as "nonproductive" and placed instead on the hallowed mantle of love and care.

Philosopher Virginia Held laments that scholars including feminist women have

> moved so little distance beyond the mistaken view that the birthing and upbringing of children are essentially natural processes drenched in immanence, as distinct from the transcendence of the work performed in the polis, (and thus) deepens our awareness of how subservient vast stretches of our thinking are to these faulty conceptual assumptions....
>
> Not only has the dominant culture denigrated the giving of birth; it venerates intellectual and artistic creation, which it takes to be a form of giving birth, and it associates this kind of creation with the male. The capacity to "give birth to" wisdom, knowledge, and art has long been set beside the mere bodily capacity to give birth to infants. Such metaphors of creativity suggest that men too can give birth; and they may fix the association of the term "male" with the former and "higher" type of creativity and the term "female" with mere propagation of the species.[6]

Feminist and social science research show that while child bearing is a biological process that is specific to female persons, it is transformed into a political process by patriarchal relations that superimpose a woman's destiny by reason of her biological abilities. The institutions of family and marriage, legal and social institutions such as education, religion and the labor force are so structured that they serve to enforce child bearing and rearing as primarily a female vocation.[7] Yet, it is women through their biological and social investments in children who provide the ingredients and the tools for human culture. The "nature or nurture" discussants of human development tend to treat the subject of nature as an immutable given that is predetermined by biology and women are seen as preprogrammed players in this scheme. We now know that such an understanding of nature is a distortion in light of our social ecological realities. We can see that the entire body of nurture which comprises the institutions of education, industry, government and art are created by agents of so called "nature," i.e., specific persons who in turn engender the human species to be able to carry on the work of nurture. Clearly, in this cycle the task of creation lies with individual persons who have been birthed by and cultivated by mothering persons. It is grossly unjust then to endow massive social institutions of government and production with innovative powers while neglecting or discounting the work done in families, specifically by mothering women.

Adrienne Rich in a series of journal entries on Motherhood suggests that the idea of a "natural" mother is an unexamined assumption that deserves questioning:

> Motherhood—unmentioned in the histories of conquest and serfdom, wars and treaties, exploration and imperialism—has a history, it has an ideology, it is more fundamental than tribalism or nationalism. My individual, seemingly private pains as a mother, the individual, seemingly private pains of the mothers around me and before me, whatever our class or color, the regulation of women's reproductive power by men in every totalitarian system and every socialist revolution, the legal and technical control by men of contraception, fertility, abortion, obstetrics, gynecology, and extrauterine reproductive experiments—all are essential to the patriarchal system, as is the negative or suspect status of women who are not mothers.[8]

MOTHERHOOD BEYOND THE WEST

I shall suggest that the incidental and immanent treatment of women's biological (deeply connected to their sexual) contributions and subsequently the layers of social meaning imputed to women in the domestic and public sphere is what brings the women from the many cameos sat forth at the start of this essay together in our globalizing world. Domestics and nannies in Manhattan and Saudi Arabia, mail order brides in Germany, sex workers in Italy all stand under the big umbrella of "caring labor." Their contributions to society are overlooked or marginalized because they are seen as "female," "domestic," and therefore implicitly "unproductive." In all the instances laid out, the (woman's) act of caring has been appropriated by global capitalist patriarchy for the subjugation of women and women's bodies that are poor, dependent and frequently from the South and the East. The racialized other is superimposed on the female other for the defense and the maintenance of the present world order and indulgent lifestyles in Western societies. According to Adrienne Rich such domination and exploitation is "essential" to the patriarchal maintenance of society, and I would add that it is constitutive of the system.

In the logic of a hierarchical and layered system of social (nee patriarchal) use and value, class, race, gender, region and religion are significant variables in the build up of power and violence. The increasing economic gap within and between countries under industrialization and post-industrialization has meant that there has been a traffic in human beings across national borders. Women, children and people of color have been particularly affected by this development The vulnerability of women and children in political and economic exchange is historic and ongoing. Today, the system works with a new vehemence. While the last half of the twentieth century has witnessed a "brain drain"—the flight of highly trained professionals from their home countries to more promising opportunities and lifestyles in the West, Barbara Ehrenreich and Arlie Hochschild in their book *Global Woman* write of the "care drain" that is going on today when the migration of women who would otherwise have cared "for the young, the old, and the sick in their own poor countries (now) move to care for the young, the old, and the sick in rich countries, whether as maids and nannies or as day-care and nursing-home aides."[9] Likening the First World to that of an "old-fashioned male in the family" who is unable to fend for himself, and poor countries to that of a "traditional woman" who is patient and self-giving, Ehrenreich and Hochschild suggest that this was a division of labor that Western feminists decried when it was local and now it has gone global. Most of the female migrants into the US are in their twenties and most come from countries in South and South-East Asia. In these countries where the birth rates are high and women's primary identity is that of mother, these female migrants, due to visa restrictions and restrictive work environments, have to leave their children in the care of others and are separated from them for long periods of time. Many of these women report horrendous work conditions where they are physically, sexually and psychologically abused. Yet, they stay on under these dreadful conditions in order to provide for the children and families they have left behind in their home countries. Sex workers and imported brides perform similar functions of caregiving in the First world and are similarly implicated in the present global market economy.

While patriarchy is a game plan envisioned by males, and many men are trapped in its logic, Hochschild tells us that women are doubly trapped.

> But if the First World middle-class women are building careers that are molded according to the old male model, by putting in long hours at demanding jobs, their nannies and other domestic workers suffer a greatly exaggerated version of the same thing. Two women working for pay is not a bad idea. But two working mothers giving their all to work is a good idea gone haywire. In the end, both First and Third World women are small players in a larger economic game whose rules they have not written.[10]

Another related but more sensitive and therefore submerged subject which demands our attention in the present day is the phenomenon of what one might call the "global child." In our time, the supply of children from China, Korea and many Third World countries for adoption into families in the West also manifests many of the same dynamics present in the discussion of Third World women's migration as caregivers in the West. These children too are embroiled in the politics of "development" whereby their societies have placed a premium on their ability to thrive and they then are displaced into alien cultural and racial terrain, becoming key providers of love and affection for Western individuals. Indeed, the opening up of a home to a child can only be a good thing, but it ceases to be a benign and neutral decision in light of the forces of globalization and therefore must be subject to scrutiny. Under present conditions the deck is stacked systematically in one direction—from the Third world to the First into uncertain racial, cultural and familial circumstances for the child and her future.

INVISIBILITY OF MOTHER WORK

The ideology of motherhood is a powerful one and prone to define the entirety of many women. Relegating the work of women who are caregivers into the realm of the "natural" means that many women are forced to move into the public sphere to engage in work that is remunerative, including the professional "services" discussed above. In this situation, women are faced with the challenge of balancing the domestic and the public world in a way that their male partners are not. Patriarchal ideology leaves the brunt of a woman's career entirely in her hands while, simultaneously, expecting her to be responsible for child care. Thus, while women are entrusted with the responsibility of motherhood, they have little leverage in redefining the structural conditions which keep them from executing these responsibilities. Child care is one of the major barriers for women's participation in the public sector. While having a child is a single event, child care has a significant impact on the woman's contributions in the public sphere. The cost of child care is a formidable deterrent in women's freedom of choice to stay home or to leave it. Clearly, workplace arrangements where working conditions are inflexible—unequal wages, lack of health care benefits, inadequate leave provisions, partial treatment of part time employees—all discriminate against female employees.

Additionally, post World War II trends in employment show that the traffic between home and employment has been one-way, where women have joined the workforce in large numbers while men have not found their way back to share in child care and domestic responsibilities. Is it possible that shared parenting can contribute to a partial transformation of the presently gendered division of labor, where women are confined to the private sphere and men to the public? Perhaps the gendered perception of work itself according to which men's work is seen as a product of effort and monetarily valuable, while women's contributions are seen as "natural" and thus "nonproductive," will come to be altered if there is an interchange of the sexes in these hitherto separate spheres. Proponents of Mother's wages, parent's wages and children's allowances here and abroad have argued for a shift away from the perception that child bearing and child rearing are private familial functions. Rather, it is recognized that every child's birth is profoundly a societal function as it ensures social survival and continuity. Female and male efforts and energies invested in child rearing and socialization should be considered as fundamental components of the GDP.

Indeed, the unpleasant truth needs to be faced that unless society compensates mothers for their partly voluntary, partly forced withdrawal from the labor market and for the assumption of the complex tasks of childbearing and rearing, it is actually exploiting the biological role of women as a basis for the recruitment of "child care slave labor."[11]

In addition to just social policies towards women, it would be of great value to consider what co-parenting can do for the transformation of men, and for social change at large in light of Chodorow's thesis about how women who mother "reproduce" mothering in their daughters. The gender apartheid that modern patriarchy has created means that both men and women are forbidden from exercising their full humanity. When the epicene qualities in both sexes are prohibited or restricted from expression, a kind of dehumanization takes place and a stunting of the species is in process. Males are particularly vulnerable in this sense, due to the strict separation of the private and public spheres and their primary occupancies in the latter. Intimacy and the ability to care do not belong to female provenance uniquely. In light of the vast scientific literature on the subjects of gender and sexuality, we are aware that both sexes share many traits that were hitherto considered to be mutually exclusive. When gender roles and statuses are freely exchanged between men and women, they will each live out their potential more fully; then sons and daughters will experience a different socialization, and women can be decoupled from their expected roles as sole caregivers. Social anthropologists have noted these possibilities in other cultures, and we in the West also know this to be the case through anecdotal and episodic experiences in communities where men are turning to caregiving in their families. Social policies and social structures including economic and cultural institutions will have to be innovative about addressing these realities, and they can be key agents in moving towards peace and away from the war path we have been on for sometime.

Earlier, as a student of market economics and allied fields in the social sciences, I learned that human societies operate around rational exchange and contract bound relations. Much of Western social theory stands on these promises. While I have been reluctant to support the validity of these assumptions (in light of my observations of social relations in communities outside the West), it has been my experiences as a mother that have been revelatory in the disestablishment of these prevailing world views about human behavior. The virtues of market relations in the present climate of globalization are hailed as if they are sacrosanct and therefore any moral scrutiny of them is made difficult. The first hand information that mothers and mothering persons are receiving is that while the buyer-seller relational model may be functional in the market, it is hardly descriptive of daily relations in other social spheres, especially as it affects mother-child relations.

In an excellent discussion on mothering and markets, philosopher Virginia Held addresses the subject of social transformation through the lessons mothers and mothering persons offer up from their experiences.[12] Contrary to relations founded on competition, conflict independence, instrumentality and domination, mother-child relations show that public institutions can be founded on and transformed by social trust that is constituted by caring, attention, love and empathic imagination. It seems to me that the crux of maternal experience may prove elemental and essential for the transformation and restructuring of our public institutions. Those aspects of human nature tapped into by mothers and children who find themselves in the relationship more by chance and less by choice merits our attention, over against the standard market-reduction of human nature as essentially contractual where humans are rational calculators engaged in beneficial exchange. The extraordinary affection bestowed on severely disabled children by their mothers or others in their attendance is an instance worth reflecting on. The implications for the formulation of an alternative public morality as seen in the experience of mothering is singular and unique. Held goes on to suggest that the development of ethical theory grounded in family relations may actually help with relations in the wider world, "where the members of impoverished societies have not chosen their circumstances and where models of social contracts—or friendships—freely entered into seem to be of so little help in deciding what to do here and now."[13]

It is not that I want to privilege mother-child relations as being somehow paradigmatic for all other relations. We are all aware of how this relationship is fraught with violence and oppression in many instances. We need to understand how violence is a response to violent assault in situations where alternative nonviolent ways of protecting life and property are not available. Mothers know well their own tendencies to violence and thus an absence of ambivalence to the subject would be dishonest and puerile. "The history of existing social practices is overwhelmingly patriarchal and even human mothering, engaged in primarily by women, is suspect as an existing practice because of the extent to which it is embedded in male dominated cultures and societies."[14] Nevertheless, mothers have had palpable glimpses of peace through the exercise of self-restraint and self-knowledge that I alluded to earlier. Peace, on this side of human experience, is *processual* in nature, and, inasmuch as it is a process, the experiences of mothers and caregivers are invaluable input for the goal of peace.

While mothering persons have not been spared from the wide reaching tentacles of patriarchy, caregiving contains within itself a microcosm of humanhood which lies well outside patriarchy's reach. From a religious perspective, life in the family can have a sacramental quality to women who mother. Frequently, in acts of caring one experiences a release of one's full humanity. The objects and subjects of care are both enriched by the process. Under healthy circumstances, children and their caregivers are echoes of God's presence and love to one another. In a constructive maternal relationship, a child can facilitate an understanding of Divine Love as the mother contemplates the mode of her attentiveness and care for her child day by day. Mothers know the value of presence and availability for their children. They have some sense of the infinite worth of their attention to those in their care. Motherhood is also chastening, as one is called to silence and suffering, and to withhold or postpone one's egotism and negate one's self. The experience of mothering has been revelatory for me as I find myself caught painfully in the cross currents of two worlds, one, of my higher noble self (often ideal and hoped for), and the other, of my quotidian self (shouting, impatient, mean-spirited and without charity).

Mothers often have the sense that God is looking over and back at them. In her attempts to grant grace, peace, mercy and love to the child, the mother often has the sense of standing in for God or acting as God would unto her. In the laser-like appropriateness of children's perceptions, in the spirit of their forgiveness and forgetfulness, in the trust they mutually enjoy in each other, elements of the Divine are reflected back. The infinite and spiraling dynamic between forgiveness and love is both a humbling and exhilarating experience that mothers know in their own growth, and children potentially know by example. This dyad embodies the earthly signs of spiritual graces.

Adoptive relations have heightened these sensibilities for me. I have a keen sense of what it means to be a recipient of trust. In my circumstances, I am mindful that my daughter has been entrusted to me by one woman in particular, and by God at large. This awareness serves as a constant corrective in my intentions and for this I am deeply grateful. There are concentric effects to this consciousness of being a guardian of trust in terms of connections with other life forces in our world. Beginning with concerns for the plight of women and children as this essay has attempted to do, extending it to men and the ecological well being of the planet, an understanding of the self as a trustee is an essential ingredient for the pursuit of peace. For all the grief I know, there is no doubt that the world was worth coming into and life is a great gift. This conviction was the primary impetus for our adoption of our daughter. In the end, all life is worth living and the world offers us extraordinary opportunities to flourish. As a mother it is a special privilege to be able to introduce life and the world to a child and thus stand as a minuscule link in the gigantic cosmic chain.

How do mothers and caregivers find the space to articulate the riches of their experiences for public change? At a time when the u.s. military is one of the most venerated public institutions among the nation's young, at a time when superpower states see militarism as the most popular means of bringing democracy to the world and at a time when mass movements protesting these moves have gone unheeded it is only a distant hope that some of the observations made in this essay will be heeded by world leaders. Even so, the fact remains that mothers and mothering persons through the ages have called the bluff of social pundits and marketeers who assume that human beings are chronic calculators and will do little out of love and care. And as long as there are those who care, they will have the last word on human possibility, even if it is only spoken and heard indoors. Vive la Care!

NOTES

1. "Father" is also subject to similar treatment.

2. *Gender in Cross-Cultural Perspective*, eds. Caroline B. Brettell and Carolyn Sargent, Prentice Hall, 2001.

3. *Social Theory: The Multicultural and Classic Readings*, ed., Charles Lemert, Westview Press, 1999, pp. 406-409.

4. Ibid., p.409.

5. Ruddick, Sara, "Maternal Thinking as a Feminist Standpoint," *Feminist Philosophies*, eds., Janet A. Kourany, James P. Sterba and Rosemarie Tong, Pearson Professional Education, 1993, pp. 404-412.

6. Held, Virginia and Catherine Stimpson, *Feminist Morality: Transforming Culture, Society, and Politics*, University of Chicago Press, 1993, pp. 134-5.

7. *Capitalist Patriarchy and the Case for Socialist Feminism*, ed. Zillah R. Eisenstein, Monthly Review Press, 1979.

8. Rich, Adrienne, *Of Woman Born*, 10th anniversary edition, W.W. Norton and Co, 1986, p. 226.

9. Barbara Ehrenreich and Arlie Russell Hochschild, *Global Woman*, Metropolitan Books, 2003, p.17.

10. Ibid., p.20.
11. Gil, David G., *Unraveling Social Policy*, Schenkman Books, 1992, p. 308.
12. *Feminist Morality*, University of Chicago, 1993, pp. 70-73.
13. Ibid., p. 73.
14. Ibid., p. 79.

Harem

Leila Ahmed

THE ATMOSPHERE IN GRANDMOTHER'S receiving room was always wonderful. I do not remember a single occasion when it was not a pleasure to be there with the women. Relaxed, intimate, affectionate, rarely solemn, their conversations and exchanges were often extremely witty and sharp and funny. My aunt Aisha in particular, the youngest and the most irreverent, would reduce us all to helpless laughter. She and Fanda were particularly good at imitations and could do hilarious renderings—exaggeratedly grand, authoritarian, and pompous—of Grandfather.

The room was furnished with deep, wide sofas all the way round. Grandmother, always on her particular sofa, always in the same corner, would sit cross-legged or with her legs tucked up beside her under her black robe. On the carpeted floor beside her sat Umm Said, joining in the conversation when moved to do so or when invited to comment. Generally, though, she sat quietly listening, gently massaging Grandmother's feet and lower legs. This kind of massage, called *takbees,* was much valued in that part of the world. Umm Said, about the same age as Grandmother, had been with her since girlhood and had come with her to her new home when Grandmother married. Her own marriage had been arranged by Grandmother's family: her husband, once a worker on Grandmother's family estate and now a butcher, after a few years of marriage—and two sons by Umm Said—had taken another and younger wife. He had not divorced Umm Said and she did not press for divorce—although he sometimes came back and harassed her for money—because, ambivalent and at times deeply scornful of him though she often was, occasionally she would also wonder, somewhat wistfully, whether he might not yet see sense one day and come back to her. Being permitted to sit with the women, privy to their conversations and intimate revelations, was a privilege granted only, among the servants, to Umm Said. Other women working in the household came to bring in or take away, for instance, coffee cups, but they did not remain or share in the conversation.

The rest of the company sat, cross-legged or legs drawn up beside them, on the sofas all around. They would drink Turkish coffee, smoke (although not all of them, and never Grandmother), and munch on *lib* (a salted, roasted seed that has to be cracked open) as they talked. Grandmother's receiving room was the first room on the left at the top of the stairs as one came in at the front door; on the other side of the stairs, on the right, was Grandfather's "study" (although he never studied and was rarely there anyway), which smelled faintly and deliciously of cigars, the handsome empty boxes of which we children sporadically collected.

Sometimes Umm Said would read the women's coffee cups after the coffee dregs had been duly swirled and the cups overturned in the requisite manner, but she did not have the reputation of being a particularly gifted coffee-cup reader. Occasionally one, of the visitors who knew how to read cups would read them or someone visiting downstairs (a relative of one of the servants) who was thought to be gifted would come and read them, but it was not something that people took seriously. If, for example, the coffee-cup reader said, "I see you coming to a road that forks, and down one of the forks I see a stranger," someone would usually jump in with a bit of jocular speculation.

I used to love running in to Grandmother and, after greeting her, resting my head in her lap as she gently stroked my hair. Her eyes, a kind of green-gold that we call 'asali, honey-colored, looked down from under wide, unplucked eyebrows with love and without artifice. I was often told as a child that I looked like her and that I was in fact just like her, and so I would lie looking up at her, studying intently, upside down, the planes and curves of her face, searching it to see who I was and what exactly I was like.

But we children could only stay with them a short while. We were soon told to go out and play or, on the rare occasions when it was raining, to go down into the *badraun*. Obviously our presence would have inhibited the freedom with which they could talk.

Grandfather was only occasionally at Zatoun. He spent four or five days a week, sometimes longer, on his farm at al-Fayyum. His land was given over to the farming of fruit, grapes especially but also oranges, lemons, bananas, and tangerines. Sometimes, though less as I got older, we would visit al-Fayyum for a few days. He had a lovely house there, with orange and lemon trees planted all around, their blossoms scenting the air in the spring.

Grandfather was an astute and dedicated farmer who devoted much of his time to attending to the land. But he also had other pastimes at al-Fayyum as well, like playing cards with other landowners at a club on Lake Qarun near his farm.

When Grandfather returned to Zatoun from one of his sojourns at Fayyum, a message would somehow run through the household, a whisper like a breath of wind through wheat, that he had arrived: *"El-bey el-kebir! El-bey el-kebir geh!"* ("The senior master! The senior master is here!") or "Baba!" ("Father!") or "Grandpapa!" depending on who was speaking. Servants would scurry off to do whatever they were supposed to be doing, and everyone—my aunts and mother and whoever was there visiting with Grandmother—would rearrange how they sat, adjust themselves, stifle their laughter. Not that Grandfather ever entered Grandmother's receiving room. No man, not even Grandfather, ever set foot there, to my knowledge: his presence would have been a violation of the seclusion rights of any woman present who was not his wife or daughter or close relative. (My brothers and cousins, so long as they were mere boys, were of course a different matter.)

My aunts and mother and uncle were very formal and deferential in Grandfather's presence. If he came into a room where they were sitting, they would scramble to their feet, the very hurriedness of their motion probably being part of the appearance of respect that was due him. They would then present themselves to him and make to kiss his hand in greeting, whereupon at almost the same instant and before his hand touched their lips, he would draw them to him instead and plant a kiss on their heads. The sight of my mother, herself such an august figure, standing before Grandfather, head bowed, eyes lowered until he invited her to sit down, was always astonishing to me. We grandchildren were not obliged to observe this code, although we were required to troop in to greet Grandfather when he arrived. He would take the small ones on his knees and give them loud, smacking kisses, often on the lips, then put them down. Even the older grandchildren got those loud kisses. I remember still how big, and blubbery his lips seemed to me, and his nose and his entire face, and his domed, knobbly, clean-shaven head. He was very big and tall but also svelte, with a hawk nose and piercing blue eyes. An athlete once, he had regularly swum the length of the Alexandria coastline as a young man. He had a loud, resonant, and naturally booming voice. I never heard him shout at anyone, except (rarely) at his valet, who went everywhere with him. This man, Abdel Athim, held himself aloof from the rest of the servants, considering himself a rank apart. He dressed differently from the other servants, in particularly fine brocaded caftans, cummerbunds, and turbans.

Grandfather himself dressed, always very elegantly, in European-style suits; outdoors, he wore his red felt tarboosh. Grandmother invariably wore a long black robe and a black head veil that closely framed her face. On occasion, when she was at prayer, she might wear a softer-shaped white head veil. She never left the house, as far as I know, except to travel in the summer to Alexandria and, in her younger days, to Fayyum and, once that I remember, to attend a funeral. (I remember noticing her stern, handsome, budded black shoes—I was used to seeing Grandmother only in slippers and stockinged feet.) I don't believe that she ever even went to the cinema. On those rare occasions when she stepped outdoors, she traveled always in Grandfather's main car, its curtains drawn.

Observing this strict etiquette of deference, Grandfather's children nevertheless made him the butt of their humor in private. But they were also quite fond of him. My two surviving aunts, Aisha and Nazli, speak lovingly of Grandmother and of my mother and their other siblings and of how they look forward to meeting up with them soon. And they even look forward to seeing Grandfather again. When I visited recently, Nazli said, "I always mention him in my prayers, along with everyone else." "Me too," said Aisha. Then Aisha said that she had been wondering recently whether it was a sin to ask at the end of salat (formal prayer) for God to take one. "It's enough now," she said, "enough." Nazli thought it was a sin; it was up to God to decide when one's time was up. Aisha was depressed—things had been hard the last few years. Her husband, in his eighties, had been suffering for several years from what was probably Alzheimer's, and she alone had been looking after him, although someone came in two days a week to cook and clean. Then, the subject of death still on our minds, Aisha said that Amm Saleh, the Nubian head servant at Zatoun and Alexandria, whom everyone had been very fond of and who had retired to a small plot on Aisha's land, had been to see her a few days before he died and had told her that he knew for certain that he was going to die very soon, although he was in good health. "How do you know?" she had asked him, and Saleh had replied that for several nights in a row he had dreamed that Grandfather was calling out to him in his great booming voice, "Saleh! Saleh! Come here! Saleh, come here!"

"Are there going to be servants up in heaven, too?" I asked. "Is Saleh doomed forever to be a servant?"

"How do we know?" said Aisha. "I am just telling you what happened."

"Did Grandmother ever hit you when you were children?" I had been asking my aunts to tell me about their childhoods and I returned now to the subject.

"Never! Don't you remember her? How gentle and loving she was?"

"What about Grandfather, did he ever hit you?"

"Hit us! He had a doctorate in hitting! His brother Halim—do you remember him?—he was a gentle, sensitive man. He would call your grandfather whenever his children misbehaved and needed a beating."

"But," said Nazli, "we always deserved it—we were very mischievous children."

"What did you do?" I wanted to know. But I got no answer.

Only Grandmother was exempt from making the show of deference and obedience with which everyone treated Grandfather, at least to his face. The relationship between the two of them was extremely courteous and formal, but it was a relationship—at least in outward conduct and manners—of equals. If anything, it was Grandfather who deferred to Grandmother, treating her with a more humble courtesy than she him. Grandmother, for her part, although always utterly civil and courteous, held herself aloof. And he, in the way that he looked at her sometimes, seemed contrite, as if imploring her forgiveness.

As a child, I did not know the story behind this. I did not know that their son Fuad had committed suicide and that Grandmother believed, and in retrospect Grandfather perhaps concurred, that it had been Grandfather's stubborn hardness of heart that had driven his son to it. I was told that the young man had died of typhus when he was a student in Vienna. Grandmother had seen him in a dream, I was also told, the night of his death. He had come on a white horse to bid her adieu. The telegram bringing news of his death arrived the next day, and then his coffin was brought home.

I finally learned the truth sometime in my teenage years. Fuad, who was the next child after my mother, had been a student in Vienna and had fallen in love with an Austrian girl and wanted to marry her. Grandfather was adamantly set against the marriage and steadfastly refused to permit it.

It was this tragedy that lay behind the mysterious and terrifying Locked

Room of Zatoun. This was Fuad's room, kept exactly the way it was when he was alive. Grandmother kept the key with her always and entered it at regular intervals with Umm Said to dust. I never caught even a glimpse of the inside, and if I happened to pass the sealed white door, I would run by as fast as I could.

Grandmother was in perpetual mourning. That was why Mother and my aunts needed to spend so much time at Zatoun with her, because without them her grief would be unendurable. Although she had always been pious, Fuad's death had transformed her, they said, from a cheery person who had laughed easily to a quiet, often sad person, who performed many extra prayers besides the required five and always dressed in black. Her voice was soft now (in the old days she could be as sharp as anyone, they said) and her laughter, in the rare moments when she laughed outright, was also quiet and gentle.

No one seemed to think that Grandmother's unending mourning was strange. (I found myself thinking about this just the other day, watching a program on American television in which a woman was consulting a psychiatrist because her daughter had been dead six months and she was still grieving.) It seemed, on the contrary, to be accepted as a terrible but appropriate grief, a grief that did honor to the depths of her feelings as a mother. And it was dogma that nothing, no loss or suffering, equaled the suffering of a mother who had lost a child. I seem to remember that my father once or twice cautiously broached the idea that perhaps it was time that Grandmother put the past behind her just a little. My mother would agree that it was hard that she still suffered so much, but how could my father say such a thing? What did he know of a mother's heart?

Motherhood was mysterious. It was sacred, but it had little to do, apparently, with actually looking after or tending to one's children. It was, I suppose, about having one's children around one, under one's broad physical and moral guardianship and protection—even if, in the routines and practicalities of daily life, it was someone else who actually looked after them. And it connoted also some powerful, unseverable connection of the heart. Everything my mother did seemed to be an expression of this notion of motherhood, from her apparent lack of interest in the dailiness of our lives to the scenes she made at the quayside in Alexandria, waving her large white handkerchief in a tear-drenched goodbye as one or another of us and sometimes several of us left for England.

I remember now, recalling her there at the quayside, a song my mother sang. It was one of Asmahan's. "*Adi'ı habayib 'al gambein*," the song went. "With my loved ones all around me, what sweeter joy has heaven to offer?" My mother would croon it to herself on those increasingly rare occasions when all of us—all her children—were back in Egypt at the same time.

For my mother, these were some of the hidden, uncounted costs of colonialism: her children's growing up speaking a language she did not understand and going off in their teens to college in a faraway land and a culture that would eventually steal them away. Among other things, there were hard, practical consequences. The children would not be there in the way that children traditionally (and according to both the Bible and the Quran) were supposed to be there when parents grew old and frail....

It is easy to see now that our lives in the Alexandria house, and even at Zatoun, were lived in women's time, women's space. And in women's culture.

And the women had, too, I now believe, their own understanding of Islam, an understanding that was different from men's Islam, "official" Islam. For although in those days it was only Grandmother who performed all the regular formal prayers, for all the women of the house, religion was an essential part of how they made sense of and understood their own lives. It was through religion that one pondered the things that happened, why they had happened, and what one should make of them, how one should take them.

Islam, as I got it from them, was gentle, generous, pacifist, inclusive, somewhat mystical—just as they themselves were. Mother's pacifism was entirely of a piece with their sense of the religion. Being Muslim was about believing in a world in which life was meaningful and in which all events and happenings were permeated (although not always transparently to us) with meaning. Religion was above all about inner things. The outward signs of religiousness, such as prayer and fasting, might be signs of a true religiousness but equally well might not. They were certainly not what was important about being Muslim. What was important was how you conducted yourself and how you were in yourself and in your attitude toward others and in your heart.

What it was to be Muslim was passed on not, of course, wordlessly but without elaborate sets of injunctions or threats or decrees or dictates as to what we should do and be and believe. What was passed on, besides the very general basic beliefs and moral ethos of Islam, which are also those of its sister monotheisms, was a way of being in the world. A way of holding oneself in the world—in relation to God, to existence, to other human beings. This the women passed on to us most of all through how they were and by their being and presence, by the way *they* were in the world, conveying their beliefs, ways, thoughts, and how we should be in the world by a touch, a glance, a word—prohibiting, for instance, or approving. Their mere responses in this or that situation—a word, a shrug, even just their postures—passed on to us, in the way that women (and also men) have forever passed on to their young, how we should be. And all of these ways of passing on attitudes, morals, beliefs, knowledge—through touch and the body and in words spoken in the living moment—are by their very nature subtle and evanescent. They profoundly shape the next generation, but they do not leave a record in the way that someone writing a text about how to live or what to believe leaves a record. Nevertheless, they leave a far more important and, literally, more vital, living record. Beliefs, morals, attitudes passed on to and impressed on us through those fleeting words and gestures are written into our very lives, our bodies, our selves, even into our physical cells and into how we live out the script of our lives.

It was Grandmother who taught me the *fat-ha* (the opening verse of the Quran and the equivalent of the Christian Lord's Prayer) and who taught me two or three other short suras (Quranic verses). When she took me up onto the roof of the Alexandria house to watch for angels on the night of the twenty-seventh of Ramadan, she recited the sura about that special night, a sura that was also by implication about the miraculousness of night itself. Even now I remember its loveliness. It is still my favorite sura.

I remember receiving little other direct religious instruction, either from Grandmother or from anyone else. I have already described the most memorable exchange with my mother on the subject of religion—when, sitting in her room, the windows open behind her onto the garden, the curtain billowing, she quoted to me the verse in the Quran that she believed summed up the essence of Islam: "He who kills one being [*nafs*, self, from the root *nafas*, breath] kills all of humanity, and he who revives, or gives life to, one being revives all of humanity." It was a verse that she quoted often, that came up in any important conversation about God, religion, those sorts of things. It represented for her the essence of Islam.

～

I happened to be reading, when I was thinking about all this, the autobiography of Zeinab al-Ghazali, one of the most prominent Muslim women leaders of our day. Al-Ghazali founded a Muslim Women's Society that she eventually merged with the Muslim Brotherhood, the "fundamentalist" association that was particularly active in the forties and fifties. Throughout her life she openly espoused a belief in the legitimacy of using violence in the cause of Islam. In her memoir, she writes of how in her childhood her father told her stories of the heroic women of early Islam who had written poetry eulogizing Muslim warriors and who themselves had gone to war on the battlefields of Islam and gained renown as fearless fighters. Musing about all this and about the difference between al-Ghazali's Islam and my mother's pacifist understanding of it, I found myself falling into a meditation on the seemingly trivial detail that I, unlike al-Ghazali, had never heard as a child or a young girl stories about the women of early Islam, heroic or otherwise. And it was then that I suddenly realized the difference between al-Ghazali and my mother and between al-Ghazali's Islam and my mother's.

The reason I had not heard such stories as a child was quite simply that those sorts of stories (when I was young, anyway) were to be found only in the ancient classical texts of Islam, texts that only men who had studied the classical Islamic literary heritage could understand and decipher. The entire training at Islamic universities—the training, for example, that al-Ghazali's father, who had attended al-Azhar University, had received—consisted precisely, in studying those texts. Al-Ghazali had been initiated into Islam and had got her notions as to what a Muslim was from her father, whereas I had received my Islam from the mothers, as had my mother. So there are two quite different Islams, an Islam that is in some sense a women's Islam and an official, textual Islam, a "men's" Islam.

And indeed it is obvious that a far greater gulf must separate men's and women's ways of knowing, and the different ways in which men and women understand religion, in the segregated societies of the Middle East than in other societies—and we know that there are differences between women's and men's ways of knowing even in non-segregated societies such as America. For, beside the fact that women often could not read (or, if they were literate, could not decipher the Islamic texts, which require years of specialist training), women in Muslim societies did not attend mosques. Mosque going was not part of the tradition for women at any class level (that is, attending mosque for congregational prayers was not part of the tradition, as distinct from visiting mosques privately and informally to offer personal prayers, which women have always done). Women therefore did not hear the sermons that men heard. And they did not get the official (male, of course) orthodox interpretations of religion that men (or some men) got every Friday. They did not have a man trained in the orthodox (male) literary heritage of Islam telling them week by week and month by month what it meant to be a Muslim, what the correct interpretation of this or that was, and what was or was not the essential message of Islam.

Rather they figured these things out among themselves and in two ways. They figured them out as they tried to understand their own lives and how to behave and how to live, talking them over together among themselves, interacting with their men, and returning to talk them over in their communities of women. And they figured them out as they listened to the Quran and talked among themselves about what they heard. For this was a culture, at all levels of society and throughout most of the history of Islamic civilization, not of reading but of the common recitation of the Quran. It was recited by professional reciters, women as well as men, and listened to on all kinds of occasions—at funerals and births and celebratory events, in illness, and in ordinary life. There was merit in having the Quran chanted in your house and in listening to it being chanted wherever it was chanted, whereas for women there was no merit attached to attending mosque, an activity indeed prohibited to women for most of history. It was from these together, their own lives and from hearing the words of the Quran, that they formed their sense of the essence of Islam.

Nor did they feel, the women I knew, that they were missing anything by not hearing the exhortations of sheikhs, nor did they believe that the sheikhs had an understanding of Islam superior to theirs. On the contrary. They had little regard, the women I knew, for the reported views and opinions of most sheikhs. Although occasionally there might be a sheikh who was regarded as a man of genuine insight and wisdom, the women I knew ordinarily dismissed the views and opinions of the common run of sheikhs as mere superstition and bigotry. And these, I emphasize, were not Westernized women. Grandmother, who spoke only Arabic and Turkish, almost never set foot outside her home and never even listened to the radio. The dictum that "there is no priesthood in Islam"—meaning that there is no intermediary or interpreter, and no need for an intermediary or interpreter, between God and each individual Muslim and how that Muslim understands his or her religion—was something these women and many other Muslims took seriously and held on to as a declaration of their right to their own understanding of Islam.

No doubt particular backgrounds and subcultures give their own specific flavors and inflections and ways of seeing to their understanding of religion, and I expect that the Islam I received from the women among whom I lived was therefore part of their particular subculture. In this sense, then, there are not just two or three different kinds of Islam but many, many different ways of understanding and of being Muslim. But what is striking to me now is not how different or rare the Islam in which I was raised is but how ordinary and typical it seems to be in its base and fundamentals. Now, after a lifetime of meeting and talking with Muslims from all over the world, I find that this Islam is one of the common varieties—perhaps even *the* common or garden variety—of the religion. It is the Islam not only of women but of ordinary folk generally, as opposed to the Islam of sheikhs, ayatollahs, mullahs, and clerics. It is an Islam that may or may not place emphasis on ritual and formal religious practice but that certainly pays little or no attention to the utterances and exhortations of sheikhs or any sort of official figures. Rather it is an Islam that stresses moral conduct and emphasizes Islam as a broad ethos and ethical code and as a way of understanding and reflecting on the meaning of one's life and of human life more generally.

This variety of Islam (or, more exactly perhaps, these familial varieties of Islam, existing in a continuum across the Muslim world) consists above all of Islam as essentially an aural and oral heritage and a way of living and being— and not a textual, written heritage, not something studied in books or learned from men who studied books. This latter Islam, the Islam of the texts, is a quite different, quite other Islam: it is the Islam of the arcane, mostly medieval written heritage in which sheikhs are trained, and it is "men's" Islam. More specifically still, it is the Islam erected by that minority of men who over the centuries have created and passed on to one another this particular textual heritage: men who, although they have always been a minority in society as a whole, have always been those who made the laws and wielded (like the ayatollahs of Iran today) enormous power in their societies. The Islam they developed in this textual heritage is very like the medieval Latinate textual heritage of Christianity. It is as abstruse and obscure and as dominated by medieval and exclusively male views of the world as are those Latin texts. Imagine believing that those medieval texts on Christianity represent today the only true and acceptable interpretation of Christianity. But that is exactly what the sheikhs and ayatollahs propound and this is where things stand now in much of the Muslim world: most of the classic Islamic texts that still determine Muslim law in our day date from medieval times.

Aurally what remains when you listen to the Quran over a lifetime are its most recurring themes, ideas, words, and permeating spirit, reappearing now in this passage, now in that: mercy, justice, peace, compassion, humanity, fairness, kindness, truthfulness, charity, mercy, justice. And yet it is exactly these recurring themes and this permeating spirit that are for the most part left out of the medieval texts or smothered and buried under a welter of obscure and abstruse "learning." One would scarcely believe, reading or hearing the laws these texts have yielded, particularly when it comes to women, that the words "justice," "fairness," "compassion," "truth," ever even occur in the Quran. No wonder non-Muslims think Islam is such a backward and oppressive religion: what these men made of it *is* largely oppressive. Still—to speak less judgmentally and, in fact, more accurately—the men who wrote the foundational texts of official Islam were living in societies and eras rife with chauvinism, eras when men believed as a matter of categorical certainty that God created them superior to women and fully intended them to have complete dominion over women. And yet, despite such beliefs and prejudices, here and there in the texts they created, in the details of this or that law, they wrote in some provision or condition that, astonishingly, does give justice to women. So, even in those bleak days, the Quran's recurring themes filtered through. They did so, however, only now and then in a body of law otherwise overwhelmingly skewed in favor of men.

I am sure, then, that my foremothers' lack of respect for the authority of sheikhs was not coincidental. Rather, I believe that this way of seeing and understanding was quite common among ordinary Muslims and that it was an understanding passed on from mothers and grandmothers to daughters and granddaughters. Generations of astute, thoughtful women, listening to the Quran, understood perfectly well its essential themes and its faith. And looking around them, they understood perfectly well, too, what a travesty men had made of it. This ingrained low opinion that they had of sheikhs, clerics, and ayatollahs stemmed from a perfectly just and astute understanding of their world, an understanding that they passed on to their daughters and indeed their sons.

Leaving no written legacy, written only on the body and into the scripts of our lives, this oral and aural tradition of Islam no doubt stretches back through generations and is as ancient as any written tradition.

One could even argue that an emphasis on an oral and aural Islam is intrinsic to Islam and to the Quran itself, and intrinsic even to the Arabic language. Originally the Quran was an aural, and only an aural, text recited to the community by the Prophet Muhammad. And it remained throughout his life, and indeed for several years after his death, only an aural text. Moreover, a bias in favor of the heard word, the word given life and meaning by the human voice, the human breath (*nafas*) is there, one might say, in the very language itself. In Arabic (and also Hebrew) script, no vowels are set down, only consonants. A set of consonants can have several meanings and only acquires final, specific, fixed meaning when given vocalized or silent utterance (unlike words in European script, which have the appearance, anyway, of being fixed in meaning). Until life is literally breathed into them, Arabic and Hebrew words on the page have no particular meaning. Indeed, until then they are not words but only potential words, a chaotic babble and possibility of meanings. It is as if they hold within them the scripts of those languages, marshaling their sets of bare consonants across the page, vast spaces in which meanings exist in a condition of whirling potentiality until the very moment that one is singled out and uttered. And so by their very scripts these two languages seem to announce the primacy of the spoken, literally living word, and to announce that meaning can only be here and now. Here and now in this body, this breath (*nafas*) this self (*nafs*) encountering the word, giving it life. Word that, without that encounter, has no life, no meaning. Meaning always only here and now, in this body, for this person. Truth only here and now, for this body, this person. Not something transcendent, overarching, larger, bigger, more important than life—but here and now and in this body and in this small and ordinary life.

We seem to be living through an era of the progressive, seemingly inexorable erasure of the oral and ethical traditions of lived Islam and, simultaneously, of the ever-greater dissemination of written Islam, textual, "men's" Islam (an Islam essentially not of the Book but of the Texts, the medieval texts) as *the* authoritative Islam. Worse still, this seems to be an era of the unstoppable spread of fundamentalist Islam, textual Islam's more narrow and more poorly informed modem descendant. It is a more ill-informed version of old-style official Islam in that the practitioners of that older Islam usually studied many texts and thus at least knew that even in these medieval texts there were disagreements among scholars and many possible interpretations of this or that verse. But today's fundamentalists, literate but often having read just a single text, take it to be definitive and the one and only "truth."

Ironically, therefore, literacy has played a baneful part both in spreading a particular form of Islam and in working to erase oral and living forms of the religion. For one thing, we all automatically assume that those who write and who put their knowledge down in texts have something more valuable to offer than those who simply live their knowledge and use it to inform their lives. And we assume that those who write and interpret texts in writing—in the Muslim context, the sheikhs and ayatollahs, who are the guardians and perpetuators (perpetrators) of this written version of Islam—must have a better, truer, deeper understanding of Islam than the non-specially trained Muslim. Whereas the fact is that the only Islam that they have a deeper understanding of is their own gloomy, medieval version of it.

Even the Western academic world is contributing to the greater visibility and legitimacy of textual Islam and to the gradual silencing and erasure of alternative oral forms of lived Islam. For we too in the West, and particularly in universities, honor, and give pride of place to, texts. Academic studies of Islam commonly focus on its textual heritage or on visible, official institutions such as mosques. Consequently it is this Islam—the Islam of texts and of mosques—that becomes visible and that is presented as in some sense legitimate, whereas most of the Muslims whom I know personally, both in the Middle East and in Europe and America, would never go near a mosque or willingly associate themselves with any form of official Islam. Throughout history, official Islam has been our enemy and our oppressor. We have learned to live with it and to survive it and have developed dictums such as "There is no priesthood in Islam" to protect ourselves from it; we're not now suddenly and even in these new lands going to easily befriend it. It is also a particular and bitter irony to me that the very fashionableness of gender studies is serving to disseminate and promote medieval men's Islam as the "true" and "authentic" Islam. (It is "true" and "authentic" because it is based on old texts and represents what the Muslim male powers have considered to be true for centuries.) Professors, for example, including a number who have no sympathy whatever for feminism, are now jumping on the bandwagon of gender studies and directing a plethora of dissertations on this or that medieval text with titles like "Islam and Menstruation." But such dissertations should more aptly have titles along the lines of "A Study of Medieval Male Beliefs about Menstruation." For what, after all, do these men's beliefs, and the rules that they laid down on the basis of their beliefs, have to do with Islam? Just because they were powerful, privileged men in their societies and knew how to write, does this mean they have the right forever to tell us what Islam is and what the rules should be?

Still, these are merely word wars, wars of ideas that, for the present anyway, are of the most minor significance compared with the devastation unloosed on Muslim societies in our day by fundamentalism. What we are living through now seems to be not merely the erasure of the living oral, ethical, and humane traditions of Islam but the literal destruction and annihilation of the Muslims who are the bearers of those traditions. In Algeria, Iran, Afghanistan, and, alas, in Egypt, this narrow, violent variant of Islam is ravaging its way through the land.

~

If a day won't come
when the monuments of institutionalized religion are in ruin
...then, my beloved,
then we are really in trouble.

Rumi

It has not been only women and simple, unlearned folk who have believed, like the women who raised me, that the ethical heart of Islam is also its core and essential message. Throughout Muslim history, philosophers, visionaries, mystics, and some of the civilization's greatest luminaries have held a similar belief. But throughout history, too, when they have announced their beliefs publicly, they have generally been hounded, persecuted, executed. Or, when they have held fast to their vision but also managed to refrain from overtly challenging the powers that be and thus avoided violent reprisal, they have been at best tolerated and marginalized—accepted as eccentrics outside the tradition of "true" Islam. From almost the earliest days, the Islam that has held sway and that has been supported and enforced by sheikhs, ayatollahs, rulers, states, and armies, has been official, textual Islam. This variant of Islam has wielded absolute power and has not hesitated to eradicate—often with the same brutality as fundamentalism today—all dissent, all differing views, all opposition.

There has never been a time when Muslims, in any significant number, have lived in a land in which freedom of thought and religion were accepted norms. Never, that is, until today. Now, in the wake of the migrations that came with the ending of the European empires, tens of thousands of Muslims are growing up in Europe and America, where they take for granted their right to think and believe whatever they wish and take for granted, most particularly, their right to speak and write openly of their thoughts, beliefs, and unbeliefs.

For Muslims this is, quite simply, a historically unprecedented state of affairs. Whatever Islam will become in this new age, surely it will be something quite other than the religion that has been officially forced on us through all these centuries. [...]

Veiled Truth

Reading Djebar From The Outside

Elizabeth Morgan

IN A RECENT REVIEW OF Edward Said's *Reflections on Exile and Other Essays*, philosopher and development ethicist Martha Nussbaum paraphrased his definition of the role of the university as "basically Socratic: to unsettle and oppose, to test all orthodoxies, to offer routes by which young minds may travel from one culture to another and learn a valuable type of estrangement from their own." What a beautiful invitation to think across borders, including theological borders, encountering what is *out there* and questioning what is *in here*! It has been this writer's experience that reading the work of Algerian writer Assia Djebar is, in this sense, a "university" experience, particularly when it comes to her treatment of what has become one of the West's favorite "cases" against the East and Islamic fundamentalism—the veiling of women.

Veiling, in Algerian history, and in the work of Djebar, who interestingly enough, began her academic career as a historian, is like a palimpsest, a rich and complex "text" on which multiple messages are inscribed, overlaid, and intertwined. It is an issue whose encounter invites outsiders to overcome their estrangement from the other by recognizing estrangement from self, particularly as a study of veiling is a study of how persons are separated from *and* separate themselves from intimate exchange. Djebar's writing provides a provocative location of estrangement, a place where national history, personal history and aesthetic re-creation converge. It is, among many other things, a place where Christians of a variety of sorts are able, if not directly invited, to ponder anew the complex layering of revelation and tradition, the two consistent cornerstones of church in the West, particularly as they relate to the complexities of gender construction. These connections will be explored in this essay, not by way of familiarizing Djebar's texts, but of allowing them to defamiliarize those precepts and practices that we often accept without questioning them.

The Algerian Context

Algeria is a country that has been "covered" multiple times by multiple empires, all projecting their shadows over the land and culture. In 146 B.C., Rome destroyed Carthage and soon conquered coastal Algeria. By the end of the fifth century A.D., the Berbers and Vandals had descended into Algeria and eroded Roman control. In the early sixth century, the Byzantine Empire established a thin veneer of unity and order over North Africa. Then in the seventh and eighth centuries, Muslim Arabs conquered the Byzantines. In the fifteenth century, Spain removed the Muslims, not only from its own land but from the coastal cities of Algeria as well. With help from Turkish pirates and the Ottoman Empire, the Spaniards were then sent packing, and Algeria became part of yet another empire. The French entered in June, 1830, and had established almost total control by 1847. During WW II Algeria came under the Vichy government but later housed the Free French government of De Gaulle. After a long bloody struggle, the Algerians voted for independence in 1962 and entered a complex period of power struggles among Berbers, Francophone Algerians, Islamic fundamentalists, and socialist ideologues. Algeria's political and social struggles—the plight of the still disaffected Berber population, complaints by international human rights agencies and democracy activists about the government's ill treatment of Islamic militants—are in the news today, the country's cultural identity still a matter of layer upon layer of ethnic transcript.

The veiling of Algerian citizens is thus a complex physical and symbolic act. Women are the obviously veiled objects, but all citizens are veiled in so many ways. Psychiatrist Frantz Fanon, author of the stark, anti-colonial classic *The Wretched of the Earth,* but also of the lesser-known "Algeria Unveiled," now published as an appendix to *A Dying Colonialism,* does much to problematize the issue. As he argues, the function of veiling in Algerian society changed radically as the French strategized to unveil Algerian women *and* as Algerian women began to participate in the struggle against colonialism, thus complicating the very idea of "woman."

It was true at the time of the independence struggle, and is still true, that the West often sees the veiling of Muslim women as the ultimate sign of women's oppression under Islamic religious law. This plays into the West's tendency to see all Muslim societies as monolithic, totalitarian regimes needing Western enlightenment (meanwhile ignoring the history of female "covering" that permeates Jewish and Christian tradition). The French colonial powers counted on this unitary thinking and attempted to unveil Algerian women in an effort to impress the international community with their "civilizing" intentions and to drive a wedge between men and women seeking independence. Fanon represents the colonial mindset in this way: "If we want to destroy the structure of Algerian society, its capacity for resistance, we must first of all conquer the women; we must go and find them behind the veil where they hide themselves and in the houses where the men keep them out of sight" (38). What the French did not realize, however, is that any forced attempt to "see into" the Algerian woman's world by the outsider would be perceived by nationals as violent denuding and cultural rape. As Rita Faulkner describes Fanon's psychological concern, such unveiling "leads to Algerian/male dishonor due to colonial domination either of the land or of the nation" (847).

Fanon thus came to see the wearing of the veil as a symbol of solidarity with the colonial struggle, and, according to Faulkner, Djebar, and others, he seemed less concerned with the fact that this too was a form of unitary thinking that rendered the Algerian woman a battlefield. It was, indeed, a battle over women's bodies. If the French could control the way women thought about the veil, they could control their bodies, therefore, possess them, therefore bring shame to Algerian men and increase their ability to control them. "Women would be symbolically raped because they would be gaping open to a ravishing conqueror" (Faulkner 848), and Algerian fathers, husbands, brothers and sons would lose their cultural prerogative and be vulnerable to defeat. For Fanon, then, wearing the veil became a sign of an Algerian woman's patriotism, a sign of her "resistance to French cultural hegemony" (Faulkner 849).

In the face of this controversy, it becomes hard to assess the participation of women in the independence struggle. Did they enter battle on their own initiative or were they driven to participate to prove their loyalty and usefulness? At times women, particularly lower class women, were used as replacements for men who had become wounded or killed. At others they took on the courageous task of smuggling bombs under their amply obscuring veils. Paradoxically, when the French had discovered how "strategic" the veil could be, Algerian women, loyal to the independence struggle began to wear Western dress and carry bombs in their purses, reverting to the veil when this tactic too became suspect (Woodhull 20). More than signaling loyalty to nation and providing cover for bomb carriers, the veil became a symbol that Algerian women embraced their own culture, that they believed in the extended family, and that they accepted the sexual power of their own bodies. Wanting to validate this "marking" of commitment to non-Western cultural modesty, Fanon writes of the disorientation that he believes is part of the unveiling of the traditional woman. He claims that she would not have "the normal mobility before a limitless horizon of avenues, of unfolded sidewalks, of houses, of people dodged or bumped into" ("Algeria" 49); she would commit "errors of judgment as to the exact distance to be negotiated," not to mention feeling "improperly dressed" ("Algeria" 50).

Djebar, herself a participant in the struggle for Algerian independence and respectful of Fanon's anti-colonial stance, nonetheless argues that the return to the veil as a patriotic "necessity," both during and after the war, is a prison for women: "women have merely exchanged one autism for another" (qtd. in Faulkner 848). In all of her writing she argues this point, while readily admitting that there are *multiple* reasons for veiling and for feeling bereft of traditional female life if one does not veil. Algerian women do so as a matter of genuine piety, and of solidarity with other women. Veiling establishes continuity in a woman's life, with her tradition, with her roots. It can be simultaneously a public affirmation of modesty, of not being a sexual object, and a public declaration of disenchantment with the prevailing political order, or with the West. It is a way of keeping peace in the community and of resisting scrutiny. Women in Algeria veil for financial reasons—to secure their husband's economic support, even as they pursue jobs on their own; the veil allows women to circulate in public without recognition, reduces their husband's anxieties about such circulation, reduces clothing costs, and, at the same time allows them to assert class status (Woodhull 4-5). As Fadwa El Guindi points out in her recent study, *Veil: Modesty, Privacy and Resistance,* the word "veil" connotes at least four different kinds of covering: the material (clothing and ornament), the spatial (a screen dividing physical spaces), the communicative (language as concealment and silence as invisibility) and the religious (seclusion from the world and sexual intimacy) (6). All make their way into Djebar's analysis of why women veil and refuse to veil.

The issues surrounding motivations for veiling are similarly complex in Iran where the Ayatollah's crack down following the Revolution in 1979, setting Iranian human rights for women back a century, caused educated upper class women to declare solidarity with their lower class sisters by voluntarily wearing the veil, even as the new laws affronted religious women who charged that they changed "what had been a freely chosen expression of religious faith into a rote act imposed on them by the state" (Nafisi 10). Young girls in Iran have taken to using the veil as an instrument of protest, leaving part of their hair showing or giving glimpses of colorful clothing underneath. If a primary motive for veiling is avoiding inflammation of the male erotic imagination, these young women are giving the veil it's own seductive power.

Egyptian activist and writer Nawal el Saadawi emphasizes that the veiling of women in Egypt, a practice she has refused for herself and consistently critiques, is never far from issues of social class, although with many ironies. Here a woman hidden from the world within her home is perceived to be the wife of a well-off man and the envy of peasant women. She takes her enclosure out into the world with her in the form of heavy veils and male escort and suffers illness rather than allowing a doctor to see her body. Thus her advantage becomes her entrapment, and she may well, in turn, envy the laboring peasant woman. Meanwhile, Sherifa Zukur declares that as the conservative movement gains ground in contemporary Egypt, piety in dress has become, in part, a matter of privacy and control, crossing class lines as a woman's way of seeking personal sanctuary in an overcrowded and often intrusive society.

Ultimately, whatever regional complications prevail, the social power of the veil seems to hinge on the power of "looking." Who gets to see and who or what is seen? Djebar beautifully illustrates this in her comparison of the Delacroix and Picasso renderings of Algerian harem women painted during the colonial period. Delacroix, invited into the home of a wealthy man in 1832, painted his host's women in their apartment. Although he *never* would have been invited into their quarters before the French conquest of Algeria in 1830, he now joined the colonial venture by participating in the colonial right to gaze. Picasso's "Women of Algeria," however, opened the cloistered chambers to sunlight. It is this painting that most captured Djebar's attention as a young writer.

By way of revealing a parallel, it is interesting to note how contemporary American poet Julia Kasdorf, both interpreting and writing her way out of the confines of Christian Mennonite theology and culture, has chosen to use as the cover of her first book of poems, *Sleeping Preacher*, a painting that depicts a young girl (herself?) sleeping under a traditional quilt as a large, black-hatted Amish man looks down on her (from a window? a second painting on the wall?). As the author explains the irony of this jacket art in a subsequent book of essays, "Pull the quilt off the cover of *Sleeping Preacher*, and this painting is a pastiche of traditional nudes, such as Titian's *Venus*.... Pull the plain dress off of an Amish or Mennonite person, and there is only a human body; behind the veil of my ethnic identity articulated in *Sleeping Preacher* is only a woman" (*Body and Book* 51). In her second book of poems, *Eve's Striptease*, Kasdorf allows this "woman" to come into the dazzling light of a contemporary Eden and speak her stories.

DJEBAR'S "FRAGMENTED AUTOBIOGRAPHY"

Like Picasso and Kasdorf , Djebar's desire is for sunlight; she "turns to the past to vitalize the present, conceiving of a future where women are mobile and doors open to sunlight exteriors and not to darkened hallways" (Mortimer, "Reappropriating" 862). Descended from freedom fighters buried and burned in caves by the invading French, she retells their story in *Fantasia: An Algerian Cavalcade* in order to bring into the light the stories of Algerian women past and present.

Born into the middle class, Djebar was "privileged" to have a father who taught in the colonial educational system and who could unilaterally decide that his daughter would not be veiled, but, in fact, receive the same education as a son. Although Arabic was the "mother tongue" used in Assia Djebar's home, she was educated in a French boarding school. Because French was the language of business and public debate at the time of her pre-independence childhood, it was an unusual gesture for an Arab girl to be initiated into its world. While Djebar admits to a deep gratitude for her father's gesture of freedom and encouragement, she also admits to feeling alienated from the rich exchange that goes on among traditional women in gatherings of matrons referred to as "the harem," and to maintaining a love-hate relationship with the French language.

Taking an advanced degree in history, she began to publish both fiction and nonfiction until she was 30 and the muse deserted her. After ten dry years she broke silence with a film entitled *Nouba* (1979) and has been writing prolifically since that time, including completion of three of the four novels projected for her Algerian Quartet.

Although the basic facts of her life are known, Djebar gives biographical interviews sparingly, favoring a "fragmented autobiography," as Mortimer refers to it, available through fiction. As she admits at the end of *Fantasia*, through a persona to be sure, "My fiction is this attempt at autobiography, weighed down under the oppressive burden of my heritage" (218). Because of the burden of this heritage, she has taken a pseudonym that both protects her family from what she writes and veils herself from public scrutiny. Asking her fiancé to recite ritual modes of address, she chose *djebbar* for her name, a word indicating praise of Allah. Transcribing the Arab word into French script, however, resulted in *djebar*, meaning "healer," which has remained her added burden ever since.

Because of her education, Assia Djebar must cope with the stigma of being an Algerian Western Woman, an unveiled sexual object, a turn-coat among her own people. Such women are expected to think in terms of imported ideas and to desire to "transgress what is sacred and based in nature and culture" (Bouatta and Cherifati-Merabtine 195). For Djebar to tell her story in fragmented fictional form is to admit how fragmented her life has been; to read it is to admit how fragmented our own lives are and to agree for a few brief moments to raise the veil of self-enclosure for the sake of looking out and letting the light of her words in.

The Women of Algiers in their Apartments introduces themes key to her continual disclosure within obscurity. The city of Algiers is a place where women are kept in wraps, enclosed within their apartments and woolen veils. The only truly unveiled woman appears to be the city itself, "revealing herself without complexes, open to the world, an open port baring her orifices without shame in the light of day" (Faulkner 852). Even women of Algiers who *are* unveiled seem to be afraid of their freedom and anxious "to become entangled in other veils, invisible but very noticeable ones" (48). To suddenly walk free is to risk Fanon's projected malady of not being sure of where the edges of one's body are:

> The body moves forward out of the house and is, for the first time, felt as being "exposed" to every look: the gait becomes stiff, the step hasty, the facial expression tightens.

Colloquial Arabic describes the experience in a significant way: "I no longer go out *protected* (that is to say, veiled, covered up)" the woman who casts off her sheet will say, "I go out *undressed* or even *denuded*." The veil that shielded her from the looks of strangers is in fact experienced as a "piece of clothing in itself," and to no longer have it means to be totally exposed. (139)

Nevertheless, there is desire in such an act and all acts that open the self to scrutiny and danger. Djebar posits that for a certain kind of Arab woman, the only way out of shame and intimidation appears to be to talk, breaking the shrouded silence that so often is her lot, to talk without ceasing, to talk to one another in the traditional women's quarters, and in city housing projects as well (50). For Djebar, language—any language, even the colonial language—is the way out, a theme that she develops in all of her subsequent works. The speech may be colloquial, it may be Berber or Bengali, it may be muffled, but it must never be in another's stead (2), which is why the story of the water carrier in the women's steam bath is so poignant. She, the Excluded One, has finally begun to tell her life (37ff) and she may never stop. In spite of her own periods of silence, Djebar too has found her life in words. [...]

When we come to *A Sister to Scheherazade* (1987), a more focused fictional narrative, the centers of ambiguity shift to harem and hammam, to all that can take place in the cloistered world of traditional women, *and* to an eavesdropping Westernized woman who revels in her freedom while longing to step "inside" the experience she has left behind. In this double-narrative by Assia Djebar, a liberated woman not only tells her own story but imagines the life of the traditional second wife that has replaced her in the home of her ex-husband. The narrator, Isma, is the shadow behind the new marriage, the one struggling to understand her relationship to the second wife whom she has herself chosen.

Isma begins to weave her tale by imagining the thoughts and actions of Hajila. Using the intimacy of the second person pronoun—"This morning, Hajila, as you stand in the kitchen" (7)—Isma tells Hajila's life as if she is telling it *to* Hajila. Yet, Hajila does not yet know Isma, except as a vague projection of "Meriem's mother," a woman Hajila only thinks about with "passive curiosity" (10).

Isma is, like Djebar herself, the fortunate "unveiled" daughter of a progressive father, who has made sure that she is fluent in French and can make her way in the wider world outside Algeria. Falling in love with an

Algerian businessman who has international connections, she has taken up a life of travel, weaving European thought and experience with Arab/Muslim tradition. One of her "gifts," in addition to her freedom from the veil and language mobility, is that she has married for love, rather than custom or expediency, and experiences almost obsessive pleasure with her husband— "The Man." It is this all-encompassing intimacy that ultimately comes to frighten Isma and to make her feel that she is not as free as she at first thought she might be.

Eventually, Isma resists sexual intimacy with The Man altogether, part of that resistance stemming from an expanded understanding of the meaning of veiling and disclosure. Living without the veil has set her free, but it has also stripped her of the intimacy of the harem and the anonymity of complete disguise, without freeing her from the social masking that accompanies *any* attire and the psychological veiling that she has experienced in relationship to her husband:

> I was to jeer at him, "Are men ever really naked? You are never free of fetters, you are bound fast by fears of the tribe, swathed in all the anxieties handed down to you by frustrated mothers, shackled by all your obsessions with some ill-defined elsewhere! [...] Show me one really naked man on this earth, and I will leave you for that man!" (86).

While she strips herself naked in body and soul every time they make love, he remains shrouded, and so she leaves him, not for some mythically unshrouded man, but for what she believes to be the naked truth of *herself* (86).

First, however, she fulfills the role of the responsible first wife and arranges for her "second," a girl from a poor family whose widowed mother, grateful for such a wealthy and worldly wise son-in-law, is sure to be an accomplice in the arrangements. Then, she constructs lengthy scenarios in which Hajila sneaks out of the apartment, at first veiled and happy for this disguise of unbleached wool. Later, Isma imagines an encounter between Hajila and an unveiled woman with henna-ed hair (she could *not* then have been French) playing with her child out of doors, and she "watches" Hajila remove her veil in order to move about with dangerous freedom: "You tuck the *haik* under your arm; you walk on. You are surprised to find yourself walking so easily, at one fell swoop, out into the real world!" (31).

Eventually inspired by the empathetic accompaniment by which the sister to Scheherezade stayed the storyteller's execution, Isma desires a more permanent freedom for her sister (and alter ego) Hajila and so arranges to meet her in the hammam, the steam bath, the one place where Arab women can be freely naked and vulnerable. They wash one another's shoulders and backs, exchange a ritual kiss; then Isma presses an extra key to the apartment into Hajila's hand. Hajila is now as free as she can possibly afford to be, and it is a deft writer's hand that allows Hajila's final act—imagined or real? accident or chosen? desperate or bold?—to remain open to conjecture.

Isma returns to the village of her birth. Hajila sets out for...who can imagine? Their roles have crossed and crossed over in ways that will never be fully extricated, and we readers from outside, eavesdroppers all, are introduced to the power, not only of speech, but of watching and being watched. Isma watches Hajila's every move, even ones she has constructed for her. The veiled women stare at Hajila walking freely through the city. In an internal story entitled "The Outcast," a young wife's dreams are brutally destroyed by the surveillance of family and neighbors. Veiled, she cannot be seen, but is constantly watched.

In *So Vast a Prison* (1995), Djebar continues to explore the connections between the gaze and the veil. In this three-part narrative we meet a contemporary Algerian woman struggling with issues of passion and fidelity, hear stories of the early wars of conquest, and accompany the protagonist into her first attempts at filmmaking. Like the protagonist of *Fantasia* she admits that, as an unveiled adolescent, she assumed a psychological disguise whenever a man, stranger or friend alike, complimented her. Only later was she to realize the full power of being seen:

> Thus a man had watched me dance and I had been "seen."
> And even more than that, I was keenly, consciously, happily aware of myself (nothing to do with self-love, or narcissistic vanity, or laughable interest in one's appearance...) as being truly "visible" for this almost adolescent young man with the wounded gaze.
> Visible for him alone? My visibility for him made me visible to myself. (64)

It's a terrible power and an energizing one that she recognizes in herself, yet it does not protect her, at the point of "losing" this young man, from feeling every bit as psychologically quarantined as cloistered village wives, nor does it save her from recognizing how dis-empowering the male gaze can be for traditional women in these villages and everywhere.

Perhaps the most liberating scene in the entire work is the one where, in the process of filming, the protagonist realizes how much the triangular eye slot for the veiled woman is like a camera lens, with all of the complications pertaining thereto. Veiled women, covered so they cannot be seen (and thereby triggering erotic imaginings on the part of passing males: "they have learned to make out your hips" [179]), have the odd advantage of being able to observe anonymously (a power in itself: "they spy, they watch, they search, they snoop!" [179]). Tourists aim their cameras at these women; they find them picturesque. But when the camera is placed in their hands, when the camera is lifted to their triangular "eyes," their hidden power becomes real: "We are the ones finally who are looking, who are beginning" (180). Like Djebar, historian, novelist, filmmaker, this protagonist and her veiled sisters are looking, talking, writing, and those of us who have believed we were freer than they are learning valuable lessons.

READING FROM THE OUTSIDE

Addressing the Western obsession with veiling in African and Asian cultures, Sondra Hale speculates that our habits of binary thought ("honor/ shame, patron/client, public/private") have caused us to draw sharper gender distinctions for Middle Eastern and Muslim cultures than they often do for themselves. Exacerbating the problem are historical writings that depict Muslim women as "secluded, mysterious, and erotic." She references a book by Malek Alloula titled *The Colonial Harem* which reproduces a collection of photographs (some turned into postcards) of "over-eroticized/exoticised Algerian women," claiming that a common photo pose is that of a veiled but bare-breasted woman (3). Guindi terms this collection of studio portraits a "quest for the exotic inferior other," a quest that has lived well beyond French colonial fantasy (45), yet Hale points out that only approximately 16% of women in the Middle East are physically veiled. Thus, emphasis on material veiling may tell us more about the West than the East. It forces the other to remain visibly other, all of which calls us to examine the stereotypes we perpetuate and our reasons for holding them dear.

Saadawi tells a wonderful story of attending an international women's conference at which a French scholar held forth that the veil was linked exclusively to Islam (in spite of Jewish and Christian roots). To Saadawi's questions she responded, "'I am Christian but I am not veiled,'" at which point Saadawi noticed that the woman was wearing a thick coat of make-up.

"She was not aware that she herself was also wearing a veil" (170).

This may be why the writings of Assia Djebar are so valuable. Not only do they unmask and problematize the pain of seclusion for Algerian women, past and present, they invite the reader from outside to be honest about her own history. They invite her to think about the ways that young girls everywhere are silenced and made to feel ashamed. They allow her to unmask cultures where seven-year old girls diet and where many women become estranged from their bodies, judging them deficient by the ideal body fantasy. They cause her to assess the current craze in the West for tattoos and piercings, identity markers of multiple urban and suburban "tribes." They provoke her to think about the glances she receives on the street—whether they are truly compliments or invasions—and to recognize the internalized male gaze accompanying her everywhere, so that even when alone she judges her own body as an object.

Reading Djebar, women tired of perpetual competition with other women, long for a safe place like the hammam, where comfort in real bodies, "freely naked and vulnerable," might start a healing process which would allow them to be finally at home in theirs. Still, unmasking the Western beauty industry, with its prolific cosmetic surgery ads, skeletal models touting grapefruit breasts, and gyms full of lycra-clad bodies, is a start, the beginning of resistance. Now the reader can question whether the fact that men are increasingly the targets of beauty ads is a sign of equality or raw consumerism. And her own self-questioning can change from "How do I look?" to the deeper critical question: "How have I been taught to see myself?" To see the cultural strings pulling her would be a dawning, like the one experienced by Hajila and one described by writer Patricia Foster: "It has taken me years to understand how my own culture has constructed myths that have denied women power over and respect for our bodies and have repressed the urge to speak. For a long time I couldn't see this. I thought my failure was simply personal" (6).

The clear connection between body dis-ease and lack of voice rings true everywhere. In Western culture, according to philosopher Susan Bordo, the construction of femininity requires women to embody an impossible contradiction: on the one hand, to be a compliant, small and self-sacrificing woman, unobtrusive in every way; on the other hand, simultaneously to be confident, in control, and able to assert herself successfully in the public sphere. Western women reading Djebar can relate to Hajila's sense of shame

in unveiling, which leaves her speechless, and to her "obligation" to raise
or lower her eyes in the presence of perceived authority figures according
to complex unwritten codes. Women everywhere can empathize with her
inability to resist unwanted sexual experience because she cannot speak out.
They can understand the safety afforded by traditional ideas of femininity
and the rewards of remaining the "good" and "nice" girl.

The recognition that readers from the "outside" find in the writings of
Assia Djebar goes even further and deeper than cultural mores. Her words,
like Saadawi's, hold up a mirror to Western Christianity which all too often
castigates Islamic "barbarism" without seeing the made-up face and silencing
gaze of its own religious past and present. The prayer veil, while always an
act of piety in the Mennonite community, did not become an ordinance
until 1960, and, as Julia Kasdorf points out, has always marked women as
subordinate to men as well as differentiating Mennonites from the rest of
society. Another denomination is contemplating a return to the forced
wearing of hats by women to church. The ordination of women is still hotly
debated and resisted in Catholicism and some Protestant denominations, and
women in *all* denominations are silenced in age-old ways. From Augustine's
bidding that women be veiled because of their sex, to the glossing over of
women's stories in the Bible, to the current debate over inclusive language
for God, Christian women know a history of silencing, even if they cannot
articulate it. They are surprised to learn that traditional theology's definition
of sin as pride and willfulness may reflect the gender of the male theologians
who dominate the history of Christian thought, even as it simultaneously
masks what may hold truer for women: sin as passivity resulting from lack
of voice and agency, a redefinition suggested by current women theologians.
If having voice means: "having ability to express oneself and the right to be
heard [...] knowing one's mind and will and trusting that one can express
oneself in one's community" (Hess 69), then to speak on God's behalf in
communities of faith which maintain women's silence (blatantly, or subtly)
may be radical resistance to sin.

As Kasdorf admits and Djebar clearly points out, exposing one's thoughts,
one's words is a way of exposing one's body, one's material presence in the
world. The cultural shame brought on by such transgression can be paralyzing.
Kasdorf thus speculates, "Perhaps there is some connection between a sense
of modesty in dress, including my choice to wear the prayer veil as a young
woman and the feelings of shame and depression that I used to get after giving

public readings, especially those that seemed to have been successful" (*Body and Book* 72). What we all conceivably seek, then, is neither modesty nor prideful assertion, but rather a deeper experience of self-respect, something greater than any shame-based cultural marker can supply.

As is our habit in the Christian West, we often look to Scripture for illumination of complex moral issues, yet we first have to face the fact that our text is itself veiled truth. For Djebar, the colonial language of French is both liberating and violent; ultimately, however, we must realize that *all* language is violent, especially language for God, and one doesn't have to be in a post-colonial situation to feel its strictures. As philosopher John Caputo says, each concept of the divine that we verbalize "seizes God round about, measures the divine by humanly comprehensible standards, [...] and cuts off the infinite, incomprehensible depths of God" (132). But since we *must* talk about ultimate realities, theological and otherwise, the real feat is not to seek a non-violent, pure discourse, but to give into the discourse at hand generously, making it do unusual things, letting metaphors proliferate.

When one thinks about the biblical text, written over hundreds of years and in several languages, then translated over and over again, one realizes not only how many gaps exist between and within the narratives, but how many interpreters have entered those gaps. (Just read as many contemporary versions of a single biblical narrative in a major language as you can find to grasp the point.) To the innate veiling of linguistic markers is added the palimpsestic "cross texts" of human, albeit inspired, translators—liberating and obscuring, unmasking and reconfiguring the face of God all the while. If there is no unmediated divinity, then, if it all comes *through* the text, we had better prepare ourselves for the hard work and the often surprising joy of glimpsing, discerning, uncovering, recovering truths to live by, all the while conscious of our inevitable personal mis-readings and the necessity of participating in trusted interpretive communities.

This said, we find that the Qur'an and the Bible do not have strict laws about veiling–only random events to be deciphered. The creation myth in the Qur'an shows us a simultaneous creation of the sexes, such that there is no gender primacy. Both male and female participate in the fatal temptation, yet a biological difference emerges as central to Islamic views of modesty in that the womb is seen as a safe place—a sanctuary, if you will. Both men and women's dress is defined as an extension of this sacred privacy, yet, since it is women who actually possess wombs and shelter children there, their dress becomes the more pronounced marker of safety, "linking women as the guardians of family sanctuaries with the realm of the sacred in this world" (Guindi 96). The question asked by those pondering the present isolation of women in many Islamic cultures is when protection of the divine became a source of women's vulnerability and an imperative for total concealment, particularly as the Qur'an forbids men and women to be veiled during worship (112).

Going to Judeo-Christian Scripture we find a creation story already talking about male primacy in creation and gender strife as a result of sin.[1] Both Adam and Eve cover themselves out of shame, but veiling as a discrete motif enters the story later, and, at first, erratically. When Rebekah approaches Isaac in Genesis, she asks, "Who is that man in the field coming to meet us?" (24:65). And when the servant answers, "He is my master," she takes her veil and covers herself, only removing the veil after marriage. Later in Genesis, Tamar uses a veil to disguise herself toward the end of deceiving her father-in-law into sleeping with her (38:14,19). In the first book of the Bible, we see the veil used for women's modesty (reminiscent of Paul's New Testament admonitions about head coverings) *and* trickery.

When scripture gets into discussions of revelation, veiling becomes even more paradoxical and cross-gendered. Moses is veiled when he returns from speaking with God on Mt. Sinai (Exod. 34), which seems to suggest that, as temporal beings, seeing through a glass dimly, we cannot behold God face to face, nor even fully receive the experience of another. Matthew 10:26, however, no less than I Corinthians 13: 13-16, promises us that this will not always be the case: when we finally see God "face to face," "there is nothing concealed that will not be disclosed [unveiled]," and we will know or see God even as we are known or seen by God, knowing and seeing ourselves fully for the first time. Paradoxically, in 2 Corinthians 4 we are told that the gospel is only veiled to those who are perishing, suggesting that God has blinded the eyes of unbelievers. Are we to assume that there are layers of spiritual insight at play here, that none see absolutely, but some, by faith, far more than others? How might these "secondary veils" be removed?

In the gospels of Matthew (27:51) and Mark (15:38), the veil dividing the Holy of Holies splits from top to bottom at the death of Jesus, and in Luke (23:45) during the crucifixion. Hebrews 10:20 refers to this as the rending of the veil of Jesus' flesh, allowing for new life for the faithful. Is God thus unveiled? Is this the ultimate proof that God was revealing God's self through

Jesus: his person, his words, his deeds—all of them veiled references of sort but ultimately unmasked through the rending of the body itself? We are told that only Hagar, Sarah's slave girl and Abraham's concubine, the marginal woman, was allowed to see God face-to-face, to name the God she saw, and to live. (The likeness of Sarah and Hagar's relationship to that of Isma and Hajila, including the clarity that comes to the most obscure "sister" in the pair, is remarkable.) Did those who saw Jesus after the crucifixion, then, have their sight veiled for their own safety?

Such reflection leads to the most interesting question of all: does every significant unveiling (the crucifixion and resurrection of Jesus as prime examples) involve, of necessity, a further veiling? Isma leaves The Man for the truth of herself, but that truth is only revealed through the veil of her stories. Is there a truth here that cuts to the heart of *all* revelation? In personal correspondence, biblical scholar John Linton asks:

> Is the idea of revealing the truth a disclosure, an unveiling? Does every revelation involve a further veiling in the sense that God's subjectivity is never an objectivity? That is, God does not reveal predicates that apply to the noun God as much as events happen that compel some to trust God because a glimpse of God allows them to excitedly use predicates that are no substitute for the glimpse. Predicates don't reveal naked subjectivity.

This would seem to imply that when we speak of God, we give God a body, a moving, acting body that captures the limited amount of God's glory that we can hold in any one telling. We never see the fullness of God entire—our sight is veiled for our safety, lest we die—yet we desire to give what we *do* see, what we *do* know materiality, and we do so, at our best, with full awareness of the blessing and vulnerability which that action requires. In such a dynamic we may be both discovering and responding to a profound humility in the person of God, a reluctance of God to force God's self on creation, in lieu of an invitation to humanity to respond to pervasive clues that God is present and real—clues that are seen more clearly some days than others, by some persons more than others, but that speak both the glory and the sorrow of our world's sustainer and that can speak us into faith. Is it possible to say, then, that God assumes a veil toward the end of bringing God's creatures into the light, which might well mean bringing them from *behind* the cultural markers they construct both to keep each other in the dark *and* to hide from the threat of the other?

One thing is certain. When women *and* men have the biblical texts opened to them, they come to see that they can engage Scripture as subjects in conversation with it. They may even become empowered to question old interpretations, knowing that the God who accompanies them is always revealing God's self while remaining graciously veiled.

Djebar's works take us inside the world of the harem and the hammam where Algerian women seek this kind of intimate security. This is the gift she gives us at considerable risk to herself and her relatives. She asks in return that we become outsiders to our own cultural past and institutions, seeing them with similar scrutiny and puzzlement, allowing new messages to be inscribed over old assumptions. All truth is veiled; all cultural and religious histories are palimpsests. That is the kind of oblique world that we live in. However, where clues of the divine Other can be glimpsed and articulated in surprising and life-giving ways, where thinking and rituals can be creatively reconfigured to let in more light, to bring cultural ideas of modesty closer to radical humility, for male and female alike, we would be fools not to try.[2]

NOTES

1. My reflections here on Scripture are particularly indebted to John Linton.

2. This essay was conceived and developed within the context of the Women's Studies May Term of the Oregon Extension, where feminist theorist Nancy Linton, poet Julia Kasdorf, biblical scholar John Linton, and I engaged in long and lively conversations. Portions of this essay were previously published in my *Aeroplane Mirrors: Personal and Political Reflexivity in Post-Colonial Women's Novels*.

WORKS CITED

Bordo, Susan. *Unbearable Weight*. Berkeley: U of California P, 1993.

Boutta, Cherifa and Dorea Cherifati-Merabtine. "The Social Representation of Women in Algeria's Islamist Movement," *Identity Politics and Women: Cultural Reassertions and Feminisms in International Perspective*, edited by Valentine M. Moghadam. Boulder: Westview, 1994. 183-201

Caputo, John. "How to Avoid Speaking of God: The Violence of Natural Theology," *Prospects for Natural Theology*, edited by Eugene Long. Washington: Catholic U of America P, 1992. 128-50.

Djebar, Assia. *Fantasia: An Algerian Cavalcade*, translated by Dorothy S. Blair. Portsmouth, New Hampshire: Heinemann, 1993.

—. *A Sister to Scheherazade*, Trans. Dorothy Blair. Portsmouth, (NH): Heinemann, 1993.

—. *So Vast a Prison*, translated by Betsy Wing. New York: Seven Stories, 1999.

—. *The Women of Algiers in Their Apartments*, translated by Marjolin de Jager. Charlottesville: UP of Virginia, 1992.

Fanon, Frantz. "Algerian Unveiled," in *A Dying Colonialism*, translated by Haakon Chevalier. New York: Grove, 1965. 35-67.

—. *The Wretched of the Earth*. New York: Grove, 1986.

Faulkner, Rita A. "Assia Djebar, Frantz Fanon, Women, Veils, and Land," *World Literature Today* 70:4 (Autumn 1996): 847-855.

Foster, Patricia, ed. *Minding the Body: Women Writers on Body and Soul*. New York: Doubleday, 1994.

Guindi, Fadwa. *Veil: Modesty, Privacy and Resistance*. New York: Berg, 2000.

Hale, Sondra. "The West and Veiling," UCLA Forum "On Veiling and the Media," sponsored by UCLA G.S. von Grunebaum Center for Near Eastern Studies, New York University and Columbia University. 20 May 1998.

Hess, Carol Lakey. *Caretakers of Our Common House*. Nashville: Abingdon, 1997.

Kasdorf, Julia. *The Body and the Book: Writing from a Mennonite Life*. Baltimore: Johns Hopkins UP, 2001.

—. *Eve's Striptease*. Pittsburgh: U. of Pittsburgh P, 1998.

—. *Sleeping Preacher*. Pittsburgh: U. of Pittsburgh P, 1992.

Morgan, Elizabeth. *Aeroplane Mirrors: Personal and Political Reflexivity in Post-Colonial Women's Novels*. Portsmouth (NH): Heinemann, 2001.

Mortimer, Mildred. "Assia Djebar's Algerian Quartet: A Study in Fragmented Autobiography," *Research in African Literatures* 28:2 (Spring 1991): 102-17.

—. "Reappropriating the Gaze in Assia Djebar's Fiction and Film," *World Literature Today* 70:4 (Autumn 1996): 859-867.

Nafisi, Azar. "The Veiled Threat: The Iranian Theocracy's Fear of Females," *The New Republic* (February 22, 1999).

Nussbaum, Martha. "The End of Orthodoxy," *The New York Times Book Review* 15 Feb. 2001: 28.

El Saadawi, Nawal. "Women and Islam," *The Nawal El Saadawi Reader*. London: Zed, 1998. 73-92.

Woodhull, Winifred. *Transfigurations of the Magreb: Feminism, Decolonization, and Literatures*. Minneapolis: Uof Minneapolis P, 1993.

Zukur, Sherifa. *Revealing Reveiling: Islamist Gender Ideology in Contemporary Egypt*. Albany: State U of New York P, 1992.

The Christ for African Women

Elizabeth Amoah and Mercy Amba Oduyoye

Introduction: Christology and Women

"Christology" is a familiar word among Christian theologians and one that is quite able to stand by itself and be explicated as a theological issue and concept. The curiosity that arises—if any—will be in relation to the word "women" and the conjunction "and." The import of the conjunction is to my mind that of a question, which could be stated in various ways: What have women to do with the concept of Christology? What do women say about Christology? Is there such a thing as a women's Christology? Do the traditional statements of Christology take into account women's experience of life? What we shall do here is to share some thoughts on the Christ from the perspective of African women.

To do this, however, it is undoubtedly of use and interest to begin with what African men say about Christ, since they have dominated the field of written theology. This will necessitate taking a look at scriptures and church history, alongside African Christianity and traditional religions, before coming to what the women of Africa wish to say about Christ.

The Christ of Scriptures and Traditions

Most Christians refer to Scripture as meaning the Hebrew Bible and its Christian supplement, the New Testament, but we would like to start with a reference to the "unwritten Scriptures" of the Fante of Ghana, When the Fante were journeying to their present home in southern Ghana, they crossed vast tracts of waterless plains and they thirsted. Such was the agony of a people on the move, but their leader, Eku, the matriarch, did not despair. She spurred them on. They were to press forward until they came to a place where they could settle in peace and prosperity. Following her encouragement, they dragged their weakened legs along. They then came to a pool of water. Having suffered much treachery on their journey, none dared to salve the parched throat with the water now presented invitingly before them. It could have been poisoned by their enemies. Matriarch Eku took her life into her hands, drank from the pool, and gave to her dog to drink. The people waited. They peered at the woman and her dog with glazed eyes. Neither human nor animal had suffered from drinking the water of the pool. All fell to and drank their fill, shouting "Eku aso" (Eku has tasted). And so the place where this happened is to this day called Ekuaso. Eku has tasted on our behalf; we can now drink without fear of death.[1]

All human communities have their stories of persons whose individual acts have had lasting effects on the destiny and ethos of the whole group. Such are the people remembered in stories. Not all are Christ-figures; only those whose presence has led to more life and wholesome relations are commemorated as having been "God-sent." In the Hebrew story, the idea of the "God-sent" figure crystallized into that of the Messiah, the anointed of God. The Messiah was expected to be a male figure of power, as a ruler of God's people and a prophet called by God to guide the people. Much else accrued to the figure of the Messiah as the lot of the people passed through political changes. One such metamorphosis taken over by Christians is the Messiah as the Suffering Servant of God. But even cast in this lowly mold, the figure of the Messiah remains powerful and victorious and male. Messiah is a servant who suffers but one whose presence always tells the people how God's future for humanity stands inviolate in spite of all appearances. As Jesus of Nazareth and most all who fell into his way of life and thinking were Jews, they had been brought up on the various images of the messianic figure and had prayed for the timely arrival of the anointed one of God, who was being expected by the whole nation.

We are not aware of the concept of the expected one in African mythology. However, deliverers abound; some are memorialized in legends, but they are not always male. The folk etymology of the name of the village of Ekuaso illustrates this. There have also been instances of "innocent" persons, women as well as men, who were being sacrificed to bring peace and prosperity to communities. One such legend will suffice for illustration.

A feud arose between two Nigerian communities as a result of adultery. In those days, the offense was punished by the execution of the man involved. In the case under review, the man was from an ethnic group that did not execute adulterers. After long periods of struggle, a compromise was reached. A nameless woman was sacrificed to "atone" for the man's infringement of the adultery taboo.[2] Such an event cannot be reckoned as vicarious suffering, and contemporary African women must resist such a model.

There are also instances of persons who are made scapegoats and who suffer the fate of "the goat of Azazel" in the Hebrew atonement ceremonies. They are banished from their communities, carrying the sins of the whole people so that the community may live more fully in the coming years.[3] But the myth of a future utopia to be ushered in by "One Who Is to Come" is a rare one among Africans. African myths tell of a past of perfection in primeval times, not of a future of plenty and bliss. The individual, however, lives in hope, almost a certainty, that tomorrow will be better. The immediate morrow that those who are alive now may hope to see is the immediate concern of prayer in the traditional religion.

The Christian religion raised in Africa the hope of a future when all things would be righted and be "gathered up" in Christ. Classical Christologies that have been taught in Africa include that of the Christ enthroned in glory, who, as a magnanimous potentate, oversees all and orders all according to the will of God. The imagery is that of Luke's Jesus of Nazareth, whose central concern was the kingdom of God. The royal Christ fitted into the colonial ambiance of the propagation of Christianity as well as the missionary's self-image of a benevolent paternal figure who knows what is best for African converts. The need for a conqueror to overcome the evil forces that cross the way of the African was brushed aside as superstitious fear. The classical Western Christologies have been appropriated by the Western churches in Africa, which are faithfully carrying on the legacy of the Western missions. "Jesus is Lord" remains the keynote of this Christology—"Lord" in terms of a benevolent ruler.

Christ has also been preached in terms of the one who is sacrificed to wipe away inauspiciousness and free us for a new beginning. The eschatology that accompanies this Christology has, however, focused almost entirely on "the end of the age" and often on a supramundane realm where all is well. African Christians have had to support this Christ with spiritualities from their own traditions, which assure them of immediate well-being in the now and in the near future. The inadequacy of the received Christology with its emphasis on the end of the age is part of the reason for the rapid growth of the African charismatic churches that offer a Christus Victor.

The predominant myth of Christianity in Africa, however, remains the paradise to come: the messianic hope of a golden age has even begun to surface in political terms as "African unity." In the church, it is stated in terms of a single unified church. As these ideals retreat or, rather, tarry long, people either buy deeper into the apocalypticism of the "Coming One," and therefore of Christ the King who sits in judgment of his subjects to reward faithful Christians with bliss and unbelievers with torment, or they simply give up.[4] This Christology, we suggest, is not up to the task of empowering Christians for life in Africa today, with its material and spiritual demands. It masks the relevance of Christ in the business of living today and in the immediate future.

Africans require a holistic view of life. This demands a Christ who affects the whole of life and demonstrates that there is nothing that is not the business of God. The need to rewrap Christology in African leaves may be illustrated by questions that African students often raise concerning sacrifice. We read in the Old Testament that God does not approve of human sacrifice, so why does God use the cross as the means of salvation, they ask. If Jesus of Nazareth, the Christ-figure, represents "the right and good way of being human,"[5] what does that say to human suffering and especially voluntary acceptance of limiting conditions? What are the implications of the Christian affirmation that the anointed one of God, the Christ-figure, is anointed of God to bring victory over all the powers that seek to alienate us from this road to true humanity? Are there other Christ-figures apart from Jesus of Nazareth?

Johannine Christology has established a firm principle that there is no other name. If this is so, then the One Name ought to cope efficiently with the whole life of the whole people, all the "people that on earth do dwell," and therefore all of Africa and the life of all who live in Africa as Africans and not as bleached into anything else. The whole business of the whole of Africa is God's business and therefore demands a Christology that explicates how that business is Christ's business.

AFRICA'S BUSINESS

The devil is a reality in Africa; witches actually operate to release life-denying forces into the world. Individual people may be possessed and used by negative forces to prevent life-affirming and life-giving environments and activities. Evil is real, and evil is embodied in persons as well as unleashed on people by spiritual forces. Further, the spirit world is a powerful reality in Africa. God created not only the palpable world but living spirits whom we do not see but whose presence we certainly feel and who, we believe, definitely impinge on our lives for good. They are the servants of God, a sort of intricate administrative and executive service managing God's business in God's *oikos*. Such a cosmology calls for a Christology that consciously deals with the relation of Christ to God, the relation of Christ to the spirit world, and how the Christ, in the context of the belief in spirits, stands in relation to Africans in their dependence on God. Is the Christ the "chief executive," giving us confidence that, however precarious our circumstances, all is in fact under control?

The theology of the people sees the Christ in this role. At a recent performance by the Dwenesie Singers of Ghana, the lyricist, weaving her words from the event of "the stilling of the storm" produced a tapestry with a picture of the Christ as the one who brings under control all that would have brought us death. She gave a vivid description of a life in which nothing holds together! "When we try to hold onto poles, they break. When we try to hang onto ropes, they snap. You who speak to the tumultuous sea, still our world, control the elements, direct our ways, and aid our efforts." The Christ of the theology of the people is the Christ who breaks the power of evil and empowers us in our life's journey.

In Africa, where one's forebears retain an ongoing interest in one's affairs and continue to be involved long after they have departed to join their forebears; precedence has a strong hold on the regulation of ethical life. Is Jesus our ancestor, the quintessence of a life of faith? If so, then one begins to formulate Christology in terms of mediation and of participation in the divine-human axis that links humanity to divinity. In Jesus of Nazareth we see the return to earth of the Divine Spirit of God, the source of life, as an individual—just as in African tradition the ancestors return in the birth of new babies. This would, of course, imply that there can be many Christs as the spirit of a grandmother returns to grandchildren in perpetuity as long as such children are named after her, that is, called by her name.[6]

Does Christianity have room for the concept of many Christs, persons in whom the Spirit of God dwells in all its fullness? Has history seen many "Christs" and will such Christ-figures continue in perpetuity? These would be legitimate questions for a Christology that focuses on Jesus of Nazareth as our ancestor in religious obedience.

In Africa, where physical suffering seems endemic, where hunger and thirst are the continuous experience of millions, a suffering Christ becomes an attractive figure. However, Jesus of Nazareth is seen more as a comrade who did not accept deprivation as the destiny of humanity but, rather, demonstrated in his dealings with people that such suffering is not in the plan of God. You cannot be sad when Jesus is around; you cannot fast. Healing and eating and drinking were the experiences of those who were with him, and when they told their story they did not neglect to say so. In fact, they assigned large portions of their stories to the telling of these experiences. They were as impressed by these as by his death and resurrection. They did not report only what Jesus said, for they saw what he *taught* as made up of both what he did and what he said. His presence saved situations. This is another one of the reasons for the growth of African charismatic churches, whose prophets and healers are seen as mirroring the Christ. Jesus Christ in his life enhanced life where it had been overshadowed by death, even bringing life where physical death had arrived prematurely. Christ, the great Healer, is seen as the center of the Christology of these charismatic churches.[7]

The Christ who is on the side of life is seen as being on the side of God. He not only taught that laws which frustrate and stifle life are to be scrapped; he himself did that, healing on the Sabbath and defending his disciples against the scruples of religious legalism. Even his acceptance of death can be read as the outcome of love for life, since the will of God can only foster life, even if the path has to be through death. Africa's business has to be that of turning death into life.

WHAT AFRICAN MEN SAY ABOUT CHRIST

It is from this background that we turn to African men's writing. John S. Mbiti expresses clearly the fountainhead of African spirituality when he writes: "To live here and now is the most important concern of African religious activities and beliefs. There is little concern with distinctly *spiritual welfare of man* [sic] *apart from his physical.* No line is drawn between the spiritual and the physical....This is an important element in traditional religions, and one which will help us to understand the concentration of African religiosity."[8] Any Christology that aspires to meet such a spirituality must have a Christ that stands for spiritual-physical welfare. Disinterested religious zeal or one aimed at extraterrestrial well-being is not an indigenous African spirituality.

Spirituality in Africa is one of struggle that enables persons to live a good life here and now that they may die "a good death" and join the ancestors.

According to Emmanuel Milingo, Africa needs a Christus-Victor Christology, because "the people are ready to seek help from any source. Despair and disappointment drive people to all who claim to have the power to conquer evil." Milingo is not exaggerating when he adds that people "seek gifts of wealth and prosperity from the devil and make pacts with the devil." This is a clear demonstration that a Christus-Victor Christology is what Africa demands. Is this Victorious Christ, God? Victory over Satan, the embodiment of the forces of death, is what Africans pray for, and "Jesus precisely came to fight Satan and win us back from him. Jesus assures us that death, sin and Satan have been put down by him." Following Jesus' example and seeing the need for exorcism in Africa, Milingo felt called to a "ministry of deliverance."[9]

Milingo also deserves special mention among the African Christians who have offered the ancestor motif as a possible model for Christological construction, for it is he who says, "Jesus fits perfectly into the African understanding of ancestor." He describes Jesus as an ancestor in the community, intercessor between God and our human community, possessor of ethereal powers that enable him to commune with the world above and with the earth, being a citizen of both worlds. In this way Jesus is taken into the African cosmology in much the same way that Emperor Tiberius (A.D. 14-37) wanted to add him to the pantheon of the Greco-Roman world of the first century of the Christian era.[10] As a universal ancestor, Christ is made available to all who call the name of Jesus. Jesus, says Milingo, does not replace the ancestors of the individual family; he stands for all as the ancestor of the whole human family. In Milingo, Jesus replaces not only the ancestors but the gods and their priests, working only through those who cooperate in the quest for life and "neutralizing" the power of those who work for death. Milingo states categorically: "We are marrying Jesus with our ancestors... [not] merely making a comparison between the two and leave it at that." It is the *midzimu* or the *nananom*[11] who, together with Jesus, are the protectors and guardians of each and every family. There are several *nananom*, but one Christ.

Kwesi Dickson, in his *Theology in Africa*, devotes a chapter to the cross, and through a skillful discussion of the meaning and place of death in the African community he underlines the salvific nature of the cross, showing it to be a most potent symbol for Christology in Africa. Death, he says, is "an occasion for seeking more life."[12] The willingness to suffer that others might have more life is entirely consonant with the African communal ideology. This calls all baptized persons to Christ-like sacrifice.

The theology of sacrifice does have deep implications for Christology. Africans who first became Christians did so not for the reason that the blood of animals was "ineffective, but that the blood of Christ has much greater efficacy."[13]

Burgess Carr and Gabriel Setiloane join Kwesi Dickson in highlighting the cross. Carr associates it with "redemptive violence" that was necessary for the political freedom of much of black Africa and that continues to rage in apartheid South Africa where the forces of life and death have locked horns in what appears to be a last-ditch battle to settle the affirmation that there is only one human race.[14]

Setiloane's theology of the cross focuses on God's preferential option for the poor to the end that they may be led out of the captivity of dehumanizing conditions.[15] His poem "I Am an African" is now a well-known contribution to Christology in Africa.[16] For him the crucified Christ is the Christ of Africa, and the cross is the basis of hope in Africa. Carr reinforced this when he advocated support for the liberation movements of Africa "because they have helped the church to rediscover a new and radical appreciation of the Cross." Violence, when sanctified by God, becomes redemptive.

John Pobee has suggested the ruler-image,[17] Christ the King, a latecomer in Christological imagery, does pose problems. The human experience of this hierarchically organized system with its legalisms and usually patriarchal structures does not commend itself to the oppressed and marginalized of this world. Patriarchal/hierarchical structures have little room for the participation and inclusiveness that those whose humanity is being trampled upon yearn for. Christ for this situation is the prophetic figure of a Moses sent by God to stand up to the Pharaohs of our day. The reason for the royal imagery stems from the African system of rule in which the ruler is seen as the one who speaks the mind of the community and ensures its well-being. The traditional ruler in Africa is usually a constitutional monarch with limited powers, who is aware that power derives from the people. Pobee, however, reserves the ruler for God and makes Christ the *okyeame* (go-between) through whom the ruler speaks and through whom the people's voice reaches the ruler— often in more felicitous language than the original word of the people. The *okyeame* is not simply a mouthpiece, but also an interpreter. The *okyeame* is an ambassador and represents the ruler in "foreign courts and is treated as the ruler when holding the staff of office (*akyeampama*)."

WHAT AN AFRICAN WOMAN SAYS ABOUT CHRIST

Though most of the published studies on Christ in Africa are by male theologians, nonetheless there exist reflections by women, which are virtually unknown. Among these are the reflections, stories, and prayers of praise of Afua Kuma of Ghana.

Afua Kuma lives and works in the tropical forest of Ghana, a farmer and midwife from the Kwawu area. She belongs to the Church of the Pentecost. When in church, she is called Christiana Afua Gyane. She has had published prayers and praises to Jesus that capture vividly the language, culture, proverbs, folk tales, and court poetry of the Akan. Afua's theology and precisely her Christology—as most of her words refer to Jesus—is one that comes from the interplay of faith and life.

From Afua's words one gets some insight into what Christ means for the many in African churches to whom the word of God comes as a story, and who then make their own connections with Christ as they go about their daily routine, as well as in the high points of life. Some of Afua's "Praises" follow:

Yesu who has received the poor and makes us honorable, our exceedingly wise friend, we depend on you as the tongue depends on the jaw.

[You are] the rock. We hide under you, the great bush with cooling shades, the giant tree who enables the climbers to see the heavens.

Yesu, when you walk in the darkness you do not need a lamp. When you step out the sun goes before you and the lightning comes behind you.

He hangs out cloth on the sea to dry, and we are able to wear it. It dried.

Let us hear one wonderful story. There were bullets, and he used kapok to kill the elephant! When he was turning round, he stepped on a buffalo and it died.[18]

All one needs is a few gospel miracles to produce Jesus the wonder-worker among a people whose folktales, folklore, and legends are replete with the miraculous; where the elements are hostile and the forest full of animals that could become food if only they could be hunted with a minimum of danger. A Savior is one who can kill an elephant for the whole village to live on. Jesus, the enabler and friend, becomes a truly great and wise friend. "When we walk with him and meet war, we have no fear."

Afua uses much contemporary imagery as the rural and the urban are linked together when relations move to and fro. Her imagery of Jesus can be that of the ordinary folk, like teachers who influence the society for good. She even describes Yesu as the "Pensil" with which teachers teach knowledge to children. In the stanza following, Jesus is the enabler of a variety of people: he is the spokesperson for lawyers, the helper of the police, the one who gives victory to soldiers and food to prisoners. Because Jesus is all this, women praise him and Afua Kuma blesses people in the Holy Name of Jesus, promising them his gifts: "The kind one who gives to thousands, Yesu, has come. He has brought gifts for his people. This morning, what you are looking for your hands will touch." The needs of the people include food and shelter. She refers to Yesu as having a great hall that can accommodate all who come. Children, who usually occupy a large proportion of African prayers, appear only once, when she refers to Yesu as the one who makes the sterile give birth to twins. But she is preoccupied with the difficulties of clearing the forest and of meeting wicked people in the forest. In all this, one thing is clear: with Jesus, difficulties are bound to melt away. "We do not need guns and bullets, and the enemies disappear."

THE CHRIST FOR AFRICAN WOMEN

Much of what Afua Kuma has said about Christ sounds similar to what the male theologians of Africa who were quoted in the preceding pages have said. The Christological images of most Christian women in Africa will likewise have a familiar ring. This causes no small wonder, as the men and women of Africa share the same reality and tradition and learned their Christianity from the same Western, male-centered, clerically minded missionaries.

African women, however, have a different experience and interpretation of this common reality and of lived Christianity. For example, when Pobee suggests that Christ is the *okyeame* of God the ruler, to him the *okyeame* can be nothing else but male. Whereas in the Akan system of rule the *okyeame* can be either a man or a woman. Another example is the significance of the cross in the Christologies. In the Christological statements of the male African theologians, the cross, which looms so large in the theologies of

Western-trained academics and preachers, gets very scanty treatment in Afua's theological reflections. The cross, she says, has become the fishing net of Jesus. It is also the bridge from which Christians can jump into the pool of saving blood that leads to everlasting life. Here is a perception of the cross that demands not only that we admire what Jesus has done and allow ourselves to be caught in the net, but that we too stand ready to jump into the pool of blood through which we shall reach the life that is life indeed.

Though, in general, the women affirm the Christological position of the African men, at times they go beyond it or contradict it altogether. This can be gleaned not so much from the writings of African women as from the way they live and from their Christianity—their very spirituality, their witness to what Christ means for their lives.

The Christ whom African women worship, honor, and depend on is the victorious Christ, knowing that evil is a reality. Death and life-denying forces are the experience of women, and so Christ, who countered these forces and who gave back her child to the widow of Nain, is the African woman's Christ.

This Christ is the liberator from the burden of disease and the ostracism of a society riddled with blood-taboos and theories of inauspiciousness arising out of women's blood. Christ liberated women by being born of Mary, demanding that the woman bent double with gynecological disorders should stand up straight. The practice of making women become silent "beasts" of societies' burdens, bent double under racism, poverty, and lack of appreciation of what fullness of womanhood should be, has been annulled and countered by Christ. Christ transcends and transforms culture and has liberated us to do the same.

Jesus of Nazareth, by counter cultural relations he established with women, has become for us the Christ, the anointed one who liberates, the companion, friend, teacher, and true "Child of Women"—"Child of Women" truly because in Christ the fullness of all that we know of perfect womanhood is revealed. He is the caring, compassionate nurturer of all. Jesus nurtures not just by parables but by miracles of feeding. With his own hands he cooked that others might eat; he was known in the breaking of the bread. Jesus is Christ—truly woman (human) yet truly divine, for only God is the truly Compassionate One.

Christ for us is the Jesus of Nazareth, the Servant who washed the disciples' feet, the Good Shepherd who leads us only to "green pastures," to the kingdom of God, who in fact comes after us to draw us back to God. Christ seeks to save. Jesus Christ is "Lord" because Jesus of Nazareth was a servant, meeting the needs of humanity in obedience to the will of God even to the point of dying that we might be freed from the fear of physical death.

The Christ for us is the Jesus of Nazareth who agreed to be God's "Sacrificial Lamb," thus teaching that true and living sacrifice is that which is freely and consciously made; and who pointed to the example of the widow who gave all she had in response to God's love. Christ is the Jesus of Nazareth who approved of the costly sacrifice of the woman with the expensive oil, who anointed him (king, prophet, priest) in preparation for his burial, thereby also approving all that is noble, lovely, loving and motivated by love and gratitude.

Jesus of Nazareth, designated "the Christ," is the one who has broken down the barriers we have erected between God and us as well as among us. The Christ is the reconciler, calling us back to our true selves, to one another and to God, thereby saving us from isolation and alienation, which is the lack of community that is the real experience of death.

In Christ all things hold together. The integrity of the woman (a person) as born into a particular culture, and yet belonging to the community of Christ-believers, is ensured. The integrity of the woman (a person) as body/soul is ensured, recognized, and promoted by the way Jesus of Nazareth lived and interacted with women and with persons handicapped by death-dealing cultural demands and by physical and material needs. The Christ has held body/soul together by denouncing oppressive religious practices that ignored well-being. It is this Christ who has become for us, for African women and for Africa, the savior and liberator of the world. This Christ dominates the spiritual churches of Africa such as the one to which Afua Kuma belongs. The women give expression to a spirituality that enables them to face human struggles and problems. In fact, women have founded some of these churches and within them exercise their spiritual gifts of healing, solving marital problems, and so forth. God wears a human face in Christ. God in Christ suffers with women of Africa.

CONCLUSION

An African woman perceives and accepts Christ as a woman and as an African. The commitment that flows from this faith is commitment to full womanhood (humanity), to the survival of human communities, to the "birthing," nurturing, and maintenance of life, and to loving relations and life that is motivated by love.

Having accepted Christ as refugee and guest of Africa, the woman seeks to make Christ at home and to order life in such a way as to enable the whole household to feel at home with Christ. The woman sees the whole space of Africa as a realm to be ordered, as a place where Christ has truly "tabernacled." Fears are not swept under the beds and mats but are brought out to be dealt with by the presence of the Christ. Christ becomes truly friend and companion, liberating women from assumptions of patriarchal societies, and honoring, accepting, and sanctifying the single life as well as the married life, parenthood as well as the absence of progeny. The Christ of the women of Africa upholds not only motherhood, but all who, like Jesus of Nazareth, perform "mothering" roles of bringing out the best in all around them. This is the Christ, high priest, advocate, and just judge in whose kingdom we pray to be.

This has serious consequences, for Jesus of Nazareth has pointed out the Christ-figures among us. Whatever we do or do not do to the least of these figures, we are assured that we are relating to the Christ through our interaction with, or avoidance of, such people by the contribution we make to the oppression they live.

Finally, the only way we can convince Africa that Jesus of Nazareth is uniquely the Christ of God is to live the life we are expected to live as Christ-believers. Do not call "Lord, Lord" while ignoring the demands of God.

Christology down the ages, though derived from the experiences of the early companions of Jesus of Nazareth and those of their immediate associates, has been formulated in response to the actual historical realities of each age and place. Persons have contributed by the way each perceives and experiences Christ. "Christ" has been explained through imagery, cosmology, and historical events understood by both "speakers" and "listeners." This process continues in Africa. One thing is certain: whatever the age or place, the most articulate Christology is that silently performed in the drama of everyday living.

Notes

1. Narrated by Graecia Adwoa Asokomfo Tewiah, a specialist in children's education and a collector of Fante legends.

2. J.O. Awolalu, "Aiyelala, a Guardian of Social Morality," *Orita Ibadan*

Journal of Religious Studies 2 (Dec., 1968): 79-80.

3. See *The Carrier*, in Wole Soyinka, *Three Short Plays* (London: Oxford University Press, 1969), pp. 79-120.

4. J.S. Mbiti, *New Testament Eschatology* (London: Heinemann, SPCK, 1971), pp., 57-61.

5. Leonard Swidler, ed., *Consensus in Theology? A Dialogue with Hans Küng and Edward Schillebeeckx* (Philadelphia: Westminster Press, 1980), p. 19.

6. In the naming system of the Akan, my family name, Ewudziwa (and its masculine form, Ewudzi), returns several times among cousins, having been handed down by fathers who name their children after their own fathers. It is men who hand down these names; among the Akan, women do not name their progeny or anybody else, although their names may be "immortalized" as much as men's by their sons.—M.A.O.

7. Worship in the African charismatic churches is heavily punctuated with prayers that are a call for life. See A. Omoyajowo, "Prayer in African Indigenous Churches," in *The State of Christian Theology in Nigeria 1980-81*, ed. Mercy Amba Oduyoye (Ibadan: Daystar Press, 1986).

8. J.S. Mbiti, *African Religions and Philosophy* (London: Heinemann, 1969; New York: Doubleday, 1970).

9. Emmanuel Milingo, *The World in Between: Christian Healing and the Struggle for Spiritual Survival* (Maryknoll, N.Y.: Orbis Books; London: C. Hurst & Co., 1984), pp. 5, 31, 54.

10. Tertullian, *Apology* 5.

11. "Ancestor" in Akan is *nana* (pl.*nananom*). *Mudzimu* (spirit) is "ancestor: in Shona (quoted by Milingo, p. 83).

Attempts to explain the Christ in terms of African cosmology have at times cast him in the mold of the ancestral mediator. Since Harry Sawyerr's *God: Ancestor or Creator?* (London: Longman; 1971), and his *Creative Evangelism: Towards a New Christian Encounter with Africa* (London: Lutterworth, 1968), there have been several attempts by Africans to formulate theological statements that show an understanding of Africa's value system. See also J.S. Mbiti, *New Testament Eschatology in an African Background* (London: Oxford University Press, 1971), pp. 182-88. See also John S. Pobee, *Towards an African Theology* (Nashville: Abingdon, 1979), chap. 5.

12. Kwesi A. Dickson, *Theology in Africa* (Maryknoll, N.Y.: Orbis Books, 1984), pp. 185-99.

13. Milingo, *The World in Between*, p. 82.

14. Burgess Carr, "The Engagement of Lusaka," in *The Struggle Continues* (report of All Africa Conference of Churches Assembly, Lusaka; 1974); pp: 73-81. Carr's statement that "In accepting the violence of the cross, God, in Jesus Christ, sanctified violence into a redemptive instrument for bringing into being a fuller human life" raised much dust among the ecclesiastics who had gathered in Lusaka for the assembly and generated a lot of debate in the plenary discussion.

15. Edward H. Schroeder, "Lessons for Westerners from Setiloane's Christology," *Mission Studies: Journal of the International Association for Mission Studies 2*, no. 2 (1985).

16. See Setiloane's poem, "The God of My Fathers and My God," *South African Outlook*, October 1970.

17. John S. Pobee, *Towards an African Theology*, pp. 94-98.

18. The rendering here is by Mercy Amba Oduyoye. Only selected lines from stanzas are given here. The entire work is available in English translation under the title *Jesus of the Deep Forest*, transl. and ed. Peter Kwasi Ameyaw, Fr. Jon K'ubg, s.y.d., et al. (Accra: Asempa Publishers, n.d.).

Sarai, Hagar and Abram— Within Each of Us

Jennifer W. Davidson

IT IS ALWAYS DIFFICULT FOR ME to find my entry point to the familiar story of Hagar and Sarai in Genesis 16. The otherness of the whole story seems the most present thing to me. A woman, agonizing and desperate to bear children in order to secure her place in her world, offers a girl, a slave-girl, to her husband as a surrogate. And the husband, the head of the household, seems led around by the nose, rather dull-eyed and docile.

In some sense the story begins a few chapters earlier when Abram receives the promise from God that "I will make of you a great nation, and I will bless you, and make your name great, so that you will be a blessing" (Genesis 12:2). Yet despite this word, first Abram and then Sarai are swept in doubt and try to take things into their own hands.

Upon entering Egypt during a famine, and out of fear for his life, Abram gives Sarai to Pharaoh to be his wife. Though Pharaoh is afflicted with plagues because of this, Abram ends up prospering from the deal (12:10-20). Shortly after this in Genesis 15, we hear Abram questioning God's faithfulness regarding the promise: "O Lord God, what will you give me, for I continue childless, and the heir of my house is Eliezer of Damascus?" And again, as if God might not get the point, Abram urges, "You have given me no offspring, and so a slave born in my house is to be my heir." But God lavishly reassures him, "This man shall not be your heir; no one but your very own issue shall be your heir." Then God takes Abram outside and has him look up to the stars, "Look toward heaven and count the stars, if you are able to count them....So shall your descendents be" (15:2-6).

But Sarai never receives this word of assurance from God. Remaining childless, Sarai begins conceiving of how to provide her husband with an heir. She observes her Egyptian slave-girl, Hagar, and she sees her way out. And so, in Genesis 16 we find Sarai setting the wheels in motion to provide Abram (who seems to have utterly forgotten God's recent promise) with the children they both desire. She gives her slave-girl to Abram as a wife and she becomes pregnant.

Hagar, after she conceives, "looked with contempt upon her mistress" (16:4). Sarai clearly hadn't expected this and she writhes under the shift of power in the relationship. She approaches Abram who reminds her disinterestedly, "Your slave-girl is in your power; do to her as you please" (16:6). Sarai reasserts her power with vehemence; so much so that Hagar runs away into the wilderness.

It is in the wilderness by a spring of water that Hagar encounters God who nearly inexplicably instructs her to return to her mistress and "submit to her" (16: 9). Before sending her off, though, God suddenly confers the promise on Hagar, just as God had with Abram in the previous chapter, "I will so greatly multiply your offspring that they cannot be counted for multitude" (16:10). God then names Ishmael, meaning "God Hears," and gives him a dubious blessing. And Hagar responds by naming God: "So she named the Lord who spoke to her, 'You are El-Roi;' for she said, 'Have I really seen God and remained alive after seeing God'" (16:13)?

The power dynamics are thick. The hierarchy of players is clear—God at the top, then in descending order Abram, Sarai, and Hagar. But the way power is used in the story disrupts the hierarchy, unsettles easy assumptions. Sarai has the power to offer life to her husband—first by offering the life of the girl for his disposal, then by offering the child who will be conceived. Or so Sarai conceives of her power.

It is Hagar, the least in the hierarchy of players, who actually holds the power of life. Trapped in slavery, it's true she has no power over her own life. But it is the power in her body that will carry a baby to term, that will birth this first-born baby. It is this power that Sarai is attempting to commodify— but she ultimately will fail. Sarai believes she will be able to claim this child as her own—and legally she is right—but Ishmael will always remain a stranger to her.

Abram, the penultimate one in the hierarchy of players, moves with very little power, very little agency. It is Sarai who makes the proposal; it is Sarai who delivers the slave-girl "to her husband as a wife."

But the power dynamics and the hierarchy, the necessity for sons and the presence of slaves—it makes the story all the more slippery to me. Each time I try to come in close, to imagine what Hagar must have felt, to imagine what Sarai must have been thinking, to imagine what Abram thought he was doing—I find myself slipping off the surface of the story before I can get a grasp of it.

I turned for help to Ellen Frankel, a Jewish scholar who wrote *The Five Books of Miriam: A Woman's Commentary on the Torah*. Written in the Jewish tradition of Midrash, Frankel fleshes out the women in this story even more. Writing in Sarai's voice, "The Ancient One," Frankel reminds us that, "As a young beauty, I left my home, my family, my culture, and my faith and with my beloved Abram set off to follow the Voice-without-a-Face." Frankel also reminds us that Sarai herself was given away by Abram to be someone else's wife, not once but twice. She then asserts with a voice I imagine being heavy with bitterness: "I am wise because I have faced impossible choices and have nonetheless chosen. I am shrewd because I have learned to laugh at miracles and thereby to force God's hand."

Next, writing in Hagar's voice, "The Stranger," Frankel continues,

> I am the outsider, the alien, the rejected one. My name speaks my fate: *hajira*, the wanderer; *ha-gera*, the stranger; *ha-gerusha*, the one-who-has-been-driven-away. At my mistress Sarah's command, I lent my womb to Abraham to sire an heir; at her command, he banished me and my son from his camp. I am Israel's perpetual shadow—Egyptian, Canaanite, Arab. From outside my master's tent, I see his world quite differently. I have learned to see clearly in the desert's glare.

It was something in Frankel's description of these women that asked me to stop trying to enter this story, only to slip and lose my grasp on its surface; rather, to let the story enter me. The story is not for my working out, wringing out some message, some hope out of horror—rather, the story is for working within, the way memories do.

Two things happen to us when we read Scripture. First, we think, "This is the strangest, most alien thing I have ever read." Second, when we read Scripture we recognize ourselves. Our best readings of Scripture keep these two things in tension with each other, the utter strangeness and the visceral recognition. The feeling of strangeness keeps us from domesticating the revolutionary nature of God's word. We don't have to be able to make heads or tails out of it because God's word works *beyond* us. It has already done so for thousands of years before we set eyes on it. At the same time, the moment of recognition has the power to radically transform us. God's word also works *within* us.

So I invite you to let this story enter you; let it settle in and cast its own light and shadows in you. I invite you to let this story ask questions of you.

Consider these things.

Let us not constrict ourselves to one single person: Sarai or Hagar or Abram. Rather, look within and see all three—there within each of us.

Where is Sarai within you? The wise one, the one who has seen perhaps too much? What does she know? Look to see the one within, who works to your advantage. She sets things in order. Leads one to another. Commodifies and schemes. Look to see her fear. What is she afraid of? How is her security threatened? Now look on her with kindness. Can you forgive her?

Where is Hagar within you? The stranger, the alien, the one-who-has-been-driven-away. How is she unfamiliar—standing apart from the family? Look to see the one within, who looks for some way out. She disrupts things. Sometimes she's beaten down. But she's the one with the power of life within you. The power to name. Look to see her strength. Look on her with kindness. Can you free her?

Where is Abram within you? The distant one, the conspirator, the passive and dull one. Look to see the one within, who does not want to act. Who wants to just lie down, to take whatever is delivered, to listen to voices more strident than his. He watches life pass by. He tosses up his hands and walks away from conflict. Look to see his apathy. Now look on him with kindness. Can you call him to account?

There is a gift in finding these three within us. No longer a story held at arms length, I found when I drew the story within, that I was standing in need of God. When I was able to recognize that there is a part of me that bends patriarchy and consumerist culture in my favor when I am afraid of losing my footing—then Sarah, suddenly, did not seem so other. When I was able to recognize that there is a part of me that gets taken and used and beaten down by patriarchy and consumerist culture—then Hagar, suddenly, did not seem so other. When I was able to recognize that there is a part of me that wants to just let others deal with the problems that come up, so I can sleep comfortably in my own house built by patriarchy and consumerist culture—then Abram, suddenly, did not seem so other.

And, so, what about God—for whom I stand in need? When I return to the story I see that this God comes to the one who is in need—though not as we might desire. In our text, God tells Hagar to return to her mistress and submit. A jagged pill to swallow. But Elsa Tamez suggests,

> What God wants is that she and the child should be saved, and at the moment, the only way to accomplish that is not in the desert, but by returning to the house of Abraham. Ishmael has not been born . . . Hagar must wait a little longer, because Ishmael must be born in the house of Abraham to prove that he is the first-born and to enter into the household through the rite of circumcision. This will guarantee him participation in the history of salvation and will give him rights of inheritance in the house of Abraham.

I think we experience frustration—maybe even outrage—that God somehow chooses to work within the system that humans have set up. And I think God, at times, expresses this same frustration and outrage as well.

But as God does so often, God turns the tables on our expectations. There in the desert, with Hagar beaten, desperate, and pregnant, three remarkable things happen. God comes to Hagar—finds her there and speaks with her, face to face. Not even Moses, after fleeing Hagar's descendents (the Egyptians) and running into the desert himself, is afforded the privilege of seeing God face to face. Not even after all they've been through, Moses and God. No one sees the face of God and lives—but Hagar, the slave-girl.

A second remarkable thing is this: God gives the promise to Hagar, "I will so greatly multiply your offspring that they cannot be counted for multitude." It is an echo of God's promise to Abraham in Genesis 12 and 15. It is only ever repeated to men, the patriarchs, hereafter. But Hagar, the slave-girl, the one who was running away, is given the promise as well.

Finally, perhaps the most remarkable thing of all: Hagar names God. Ellen Frankel writes, in the voice of Hagar, the Stranger:

> An angel told me that the child I was carrying would be called *Ishmael*, for "God has paid heed (*shama*) to your suffering." Then I named the one who would later save my son from death: *El Ro'i*, the God-Who-Sees. In my Redeemer's name, I called the well that saved us both *Be'er-lahai-ro'i* "The well where I continued seeing after God saw me."

In naming God, Hagar preserves her experience of God in the canon of her captor's faith. Delores Williams points out, "My exposure to feminist studies has convinced me that women must claim their experience, which has for so long been submerged by an overlay of oppressive, patriarchal cultural forms. And *one way to claim experience is to name it*. Naming also establishes *permanence* and *visibility* for women's experience in history." Hagar's story is made visible and remains in Scripture perhaps precisely because she named her experience of God.

So Hagar returns to Abram and Sarai's household. Probably still shaken, visibly so. Certainly still the Stranger. And soon, only a few years down the road, she will become the one-who-was-driven-away. God will speak to her again in the wilderness—and this time God will not ask her to return but work toward her liberation. God will open her eyes to see the well that will save her son's life. Then God will go with her into the wilderness.

Our story will move on to other things. God still moving with and for the people that Hagar left behind. But we must remember that God went with the Stranger, too.

The eschatological vision is of the stranger being welcomed again into one household—no longer bound by patriarchy and alienation—providing for the well-being, the safety, the thriving of every life within it. The vision is birthed in the very promise itself when God declares to Abram, "In you all the families of the earth shall be blessed" (Gen. 12:3). It is echoed throughout both the Hebrew and Christian Scriptures—God has always been working for the reconciliation of the world, always working to overcome all that keeps us from full relationship with one another. It is this same vision that compelled the writer of Ephesians to announce: "So then you are no longer strangers and aliens, but you are citizens with the saints and also members of the household of God" (2:19). Can we hear these words, see this vision, as Hagar, and Sarai and Abram—as ourselves before God in need?

My Mother, Who Came from China, Where She Never Saw Snow

Laureen Mar

In the huge, rectangular room, the ceiling
a machinery of pipes and fluorescent lights,
ten rows of women hunch over machines,
their knees pressing against pedals
and hands pushing the shiny fabric thick as tongues
through metal and thread.
My mother bends her head to one of these machines.
Her hair is coarse and wiry, black as burnt scrub.
She wears glasses to shield her intense eyes.
A cone of orange thread spins. Around her,
talk flutters harshly in Toisan wah.
Chemical stings. She pushes cloth
through a pounding needle, under, around, and out,
breaks thread with a snap against fingerbone, tooth.
Sleeve after sleeve, sleeve.
It is easy. The same piece.
For eight or nine hours, sixteen bundles maybe,
250 sleeves to ski coats, all the same.
It is easy, only once she's run the needle
through her hand. She earns money
by each piece, on a good day,
thirty dollars. Twenty-four years.
It is frightening how fast she works.
She and the women who were taught sewing
terms in English as Second Language.
Dull thunder passes through their fingers.

I Search for Myself

Lisa Arensen

I search for
myself
in the pages of this
ancient book,
running beyond
the perpetual virgin, Our
Lady of Chastity, and
whirling Salome, seducer
of kings: I shake
their dust from my
feet. Where
is the woman
whose story I
know, where is elusive
hope? Many biblical
women are nameless, voiceless, suffering
violence: girl known
only as Jepthah's
daughter, woman called
merely the Levite's
concubine, Tamar, raped and
shamed, Others, the
silence roars in
my ear. I
gently tear

myself loose from their
clutching hands: sisters, I must go
onward. The solidarity of
Ruth and Naomi offers
light, but when they enter
her patriarchal heartland,
Naomi remembers
the ropes and marries Ruth off
to the kinsman redeemer; the story
degenerates into issues of
property. Jael shows courage
and resourcefulness, hammering
her way into the canon
with a tent peg, but
I do not resonate
with acts of
violence. Esther
inspires many women, but I
always see the hands of
her uncle Mordecai, urging her on
from beyond the women's
quarter, outside the palace
where he sees the
events of the city. Sarah,
given to Pharoah—called sister
by the man for whom she gave up an entire
life—lets her rage filter
down onto her Egyptian
maidservant. Hagar shows more
promise: she names
God and eventually finds
freedom in the desert, where her
son founds a great nation. Yet
she dies in exile, never making it back
home where she started
from. All christian women carry
Eve on our shoulders: original

temptress, scapegoat, centuries deep in
symbolism. First
woman, she spends her life
pregnant, trying to
reverse the curse. None of us
want to be
Eve, we know
the burden she
bears. And I
have not found myself: I
am neither dancer nor
blessed virgin mother; neither wife
nor concubine; I
have borne no children
yet; I bring no honor to any
man at a city
gate. I weave
tales, spin stories—is my
name nowhere to be
found? But I
speak too soon, here is Jesus
giving us God as the
woman with the lost
coin. She does not keep
herself hidden. She finds that
coin and runs to tell the
neighbors—no silence, no
shame—she celebrates, she shares her
sweeping tide of joy. I
also open my throat, lift my
voice: I too search for what has been
lost. In the image of
God I find
myself.

Anthology Biographies

Leila Ahmed, an Egyptian feminist Muslim, was the first Women's Studies Professor at Harvard Divinity School and is currently Victor S. Thomas Professor of Divinity. Her best known writings are *Women, Gender and Islam: Historical Roots of a Modern Debate* and *A Border Passage: From Cairo to America—A Woman's Journey*, what she calls her counter-book, where she weaves the lived experience of being Muslim with theological and academic understandings of its precepts.

Meena Alexander, poet, novelist and essayist, was born in Kerala, India, moved to Khartoum, Sudan, when she was five, and emigrated to the United States in her twenties. Her books include *The Shock of Arrival: Reflections on Postcolonial Experience, Manhattan Music,* and *Raw Silk.* Presently, she lives in Manhattan and teaches at the Graduate Center of the City University of New York.

Elizabeth Amoah is a Ghanaian Methodist who teaches in the Department for the Study of Religion at the University of Ghana. She is the editor of *Where God Reigns: Reflections on Women in God's World.*

Lisa Arensen, born in New York, grew up in Africa and Asia as the daughter of a missionary anthropologist. Receiving a BA in English from Houghton College, she moved to Cambodia to write, participate in rural economic development, and work with young women "rescued" from the sex trade. She studied at the Women's Studies May Term in 1996, and returned as associate faculty in 2000.

Marcia Bailey is an ordained American Baptist pastor serving at Central Baptist Church in Wayne, Pennsylvania. Her doctoral dissertation,

"Partnership: A Transformative Vision for Pastoral Leadership in the Web of Congregational Life" is being prepared for publication and articulates the vital basis for ministry at Central Baptist where she shares the pulpit in full partnership with Marcus Pomeroy. Bailey has been a visiting professor at The Women's studies May Term many times.

Rachel Bennett was a post-baccalaureate student the Women's Studies May Term in 2001. She currently works in social services and plans to return to school to become a midwife. As a practicing Sufi, she celebrates the spiritual life of the body in dance and in poetry.

Karen Bloomquist, an ordained Lutheran pastor, is on the faculty of Wartburg Seminary and is Director of Theology and Study at the Lutheran World Federation. Addressing the Wartburg community she recently offered this challenge: "We can challenge the global economy. We can address the illegitimacy of the debts which keep poor nations poor, and take seriously what it means to be in communion together." Her published works include *The Dream Betrayed: Religious Challenge of the Working Class.*

Rita Nakishima Brock directs the Bunting Fellowship Program at the Radcliffe Institute for Advanced Study and is an internationally acclaimed speaker on women's issues and feminist theology. She represented the National Council of Churches on a high-level delegation to support the peace process in El Salvador (1993) and was the first chair of the Common Global Ministries Board of the Disciples of Christ and United Church of Christ. She is the author of *Journey by Heart: A Chronology of Erotic Power* and coauthor of *Proverbs of Ashes: Violence Redemptive Suffering and the Search for What Saves Us.*

Katie Cannon is the Annie Scales Rogers Professor of Christian Ethics at Union Theological Seminary of New York. She boldly claims that her call to ministry entails "debunking, unmasking, and disentangling ideologies, theologies and systems of injustice, so as to embrace the well being of us all, in the name of our Creator and Sustainer." Her major works include *Black Womanist Ethics*, and *Katie's Canon: Womanism and the Soul of the Black Community.*

Jennifer Davidson is a doctoral student at the Graduate Theological Union in California, having graduated with a BA in English from Eastern University. She has written for and served as editor for *The Other Side* magazine and been both a student and faculty associate at the Women's Studies May Term.

Ada Maria Isasi-Diaz is professor of theology and ethics at The Theological School of Drew University. Born in Cuba, she became a political refugee in 1960, returning to the Latin world as a missionary to Peru in 1967. It was there that she "learned to respect and admire the religious understandings and practices of the poor and the oppressed and the importance of their everyday struggles, of *lo cotidiano*." Her books, including *En La Luclza/In the Struggle: Elaborating a Mujerista Theology* and *Mujerista Theology: A Theology for the Twenty-first Century*, embody that set of understandings.

Roxanne Dunbar-Ortiz is California State professor of ethnic and women's studies. A review of her book *Red dirt: growing up Okie* explains that, for her "growing up as 'poor white trash' in post-Depression Oklahoma is...as much a source of pride as it is a source of shame." Struggling to balance the academic with the personal in her analysis of rural Oklahoma, her work has become "infused with a hidden love for the very roots she disdains," and thus renders poverty a lived experience rather than merely a subject for study.

Toinette Eugene serves as director of the African American Catholic Pastoral Center for the Oakland Diocese. Concerned about the isolation experienced by Black Catholic teenagers, she has organized retreats for young girls, inviting them to talk about everything from "media images of black women to hairstyles to bulimia to sports to college." With James Newton Poling, she co-authored *Balm for Gilead: Pastoral Care for African American Families Experiencing Abuse*.

Ivy George, professor of sociology at Gordon College in Massachusetts, and associate faculty member at the Women's Studies May Term, was born in Kerala India, and came to the United States as a young woman. She is the author of *Child Labour and Child Work* and the co-author of *Uncommon Correspondence: An East-West Conversation on Friendship, Intimacy and Love*, a series of letters exchanged between George and her long time British friend Margaret Masson which measure traditional arranged marriage against Western notions of romance.

Carol Gilligan was a founding member of the Harvard Project on Women's Psychology and Girls' Development, a feminist research collaborative, and presently teaches at New York University. Much of her work stems from gender gaps she found in the distinguished work of Harvard colleagues

Erik Erikson and Lawrence Kohlberg. Thus, she has focused her career on listening carefully to women and girls, resulting in revisions of adolescent development theory for girls and boys. Her books include *In a Different Voice: Psychological Theory and Women's Development, Between Voice and Silence: Women and Girls, Race and Relationship,* and *The Birth of Pleasure.*

Carter Heyward, an ordained Episcopal priest, is Howard Chandler Robbins Professor of Theology at the Episcopal Divinity School in Cambridge, Massachusetts. She believes that love is hard work and requires both choice and commitment "a willingness to be present to others without pretense of guile." Her writings include *A Priest Forever: One Woman's Controversial Ordination in the Episcopal Church* and *God in the Balance: Christian Spirituality in Times of Terror.*

bell hooks (nee Gloria Watkins) is a writer, teacher and cultural critic, working out of the City College of New York in Manhattan. Unashamedly feminist, she nevertheless consistently argues that sexism be considered in the wider context of complex cultural oppressions. Her recent books include *killing rage: ending racism, reel to real: race, sex and class at the movies,* and *wounds of passion: a writing life.*

Julia Kasdorf is a poet and essayist who teaches writing at Penn State University and has been a consistent faculty member at the Women's Studies May Term in Oregon. Her books of poetry include *Sleeping Preacher* and *Eve's Striptease* and her prose includes a biography of Joseph W. Yoder entitled *Fixing Tradition.* Presently a practicing Episcopalian, Kasdorf remains grounded in her Mennonite roots and continues to explore their influence on her life and her writing.

Denise Levertov was born in Essex, England, in 1923. She served as a nurse in London during World War II and emigrated to America in 1948. She taught part-time at the University of Washington and was a full professor at Stanford, bringing a distinctive spirit to the English Department, especially to her students in the Creative Writing program. She died of complications due to lymphoma on in 1997. Levertov's radical politics are always articulated within the context of her sense of the holiness of all things: "Blessed / be the dust. From dust the world / utters itself We have no other / hope, no knowledge." Her books of poetry include *Selected Poems* and *Breathing the Water.* Her prose is gathered in *The Poet in the World* and *Light Up the Cave.*

John Linton is on the resident faculty of the Women's Studies May Term and is also professor of theology at the Oregon Extension. A biblical scholar of Hebrew and Greek, he loves the French feminists and is currently exploring Girardian themes in the biblical text. He has led many bible studies on texts that both trouble and intimidate women, helping them to engage the text differently. He is liberated thinker who well deserves to be included in these pages.

Nancy Linton teaches at the Oregon Extension and was co-founder of the Women's Studies May Term. In addition, she so-directs the summer program in contemplative practice for seminary students at the Oregon Extension. She has published in *The Other Side* magazine and *Perspectives* and both studies and practices spiritual direction.

Nancy Mairs is a poet, essayist and feminist convert to Catholicism who lives in Tucson, Arizona. A Research Associate with the Southwest Institute for Research on Women, she also serves on the boards of Kore Press, and the Coalition of Arizonans To Abolish the Death Penalty. Her books include *Ordinary Time: Cycles in Marriage, Faith, and Renewal,* and *Waist High in the World: A Life Among the Nondisabled,* where she records, with humor and grace, the indignities of being wheelchair bound.

Laureen Mar, a Chinese-American poet, studied creative writing at Columbia University, and has published in a number of journals and poetry magazines. She lives in Seattle, Washington.

Sallie McFague is retired from the Vanderbilt University Divinity School, where she served as the Carpenter Professor of Theology and as Dean in the late 1970s. She now teaches part-time at Vancouver School of Theology. Her interest in metaphor has taken her from literature to God-talk, and her ethical writings often involve an ecological model of the world as the body of God. Her books include *Speaking in Parables, Metaphorical Theology: Models of God,* and *Life Abundant: Rethinking Theology and Economy for a Planet in Peril.*

Elizabeth Morgan teaches literature and critical theory at Eastern University. Her writings include *Aeroplane Mirrors: Political and Personal Reflexivity in Post-Colonial Women's Novels.* With Laura Jackson, she has produced two public television documentaries following up on the work of the Fourth

World Conference for Women in Beijing, and a radio series entitled "The Power of Writing: Women's Voices from the Diaspora." She was co-founder of the Women's Studies May Term.

Martha Nussbaum is the Ernst Freund Distinguished Service Professor of Law and Ethics at the University of Chicago, with appointments that extend to the classics and philosophy departments, as well as the School of Theology. As a global ethicist, she worked along side economist Amartya Sen to define and apply the capabilities approach of economic development to the lives of Indian women. A Renaissance woman, to be sure, her published works include *Poetic Justice: The Literary Imagination and Public Life*, *Women and Human Development*, and *Upheavals of Thought: The Intelligence of Emotions.*

Mercy Oduyoye is a professor at Trinity Theological College in Accra, Ghana, and serves as an officer of the World Council of Churches in Geneva, Switzerland. Her writings include *Hearing and Knowing: A Theological Reflection on Christianity in Africa* and *Daughters of Anowa: African Women and Patriarchy.* She is a highly sought international speaker on issues of women, Africa and Christology.

Pat Parker was a poet, activist, and medical administrator who loved softball, women, and making trouble. She died in 1989 from breast cancer, leaving behind two daughters and the book *Movement in Black.* A contemporary of Audre Lorde, Adrienne Rich, and LeRoi Jones/Amiri Baraka, she has been called a "lead voice and caller" in the lesbian-feminist cultural scene.

Marge Piercy, poet, novelist, and essayist, is dedicated to exploring the multiple and, at times, mysterious connections between Marxist, feminist, and environmentalist ideas. "To name," she writes, "is not to possess what cannot / be owned or even known in the small words / and endless excuses of human speech." She has published fifteen books of poetry, including *Colors Passing Through Us*, and *The Art of Blessing the Day: Poems with a Jewish Theme.* She is the author of a collection of essays on poetry, *Parti-Colored Blocks for a Quilt*, and has published fifteen novels, including *Three Women*, and *Storm Tide.*

Jennifer Sanborn was a student at the Women's Studies May term in 1994 and came back as associate faculty in 1995 and again in 2003. She graduated from Eastern University with a BA in English, after dropping out for a semester to care for her dying mother. Obtaining a Masters in Student Development from Syracuse University, she now serves in the Multicultural Center at Wheaton College in Norton, Massachusetts.

Sally Smits attended the Women's Studies May Term when she was a sophomore at Hope College. After graduating, she participated for two years in Teach for America and is presently enrolled in and Masters of Fine Arts in Writing at the University of North Carolina at Wilmington.

Mary Stewart Van Leeuwen is professor of psychology and philosophy, and chair of the Gender Studies Department at Eastern University. Her published works include *Gender and Grace: Love, Work, and Parenting in a Changing World* and *After Eden: Facing the Challenge of Gender Reconciliation.* As the mother of two sons, she is as interested in male gender socialization as that of women, contrasting them in *My Brother's Keeper: What the Social Sciences Do (and Don't) Tell Us About Masculinity* and drawing helpful conclusions for parents trying to raise sons free of the "Boy's Code."

Acknowledgements

"Harem"
Copyright © 1999 from *A Border Passage: From Cairo to America—A Woman's Journey*, by Leila Ahmed. Reprinted by permission of Farrar, Straus and Giroux.

"Language and Shame"
Reprinted from *Fault Lines: A Memoir*, copyright © 2003 by Meena Alexander, by permission of the Feminist Press at the City University of New York, www.feministpress.org

"The Christ for African Women"
Copyright © 1988 from *With Passion and Compassion: Third World Women Doing Theology*, by Virginia Fabella and Mercy Amba Oduyoye. Reprinted by permission of Orbis Books.

"Blood"
By Lisa J. Arensen. Printed by permission of the author.

"I search for myself…"
Arenson, Lisa. *The Other Side* July/August 2000, p. 25. Reprinted by permission of *The Other Side*.

"Hope, Birthing, Healing"
By Marcia Bailey. Printed by permission of the author.

"Rafting"
By Rachel Bennett. Printed by permission of the author.